An Outdoor Guide
to Bartram's Travels

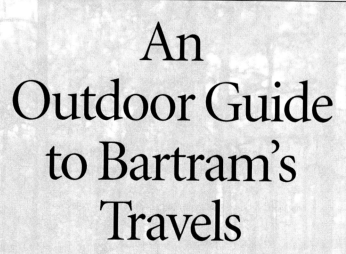

An
Outdoor Guide
to Bartram's
Travels

CHARLES D. SPORNICK

ALAN R. CATTIER

ROBERT J. GREENE

The University of Georgia Press   Athens and London

Publication of this book was supported in part by a grant from
Furthermore: a program of the J. M. Kaplan Fund

Set in Minion by Graphic Composition, Inc.
Printed digitally in the United States of America

Library of Congress Cataloging-in-Publication Data

Spornick, Charles D.
An outdoor guide to Bartram's travels / Charles D. Spornick,
Alan R. Cattier, Robert J. Greene.
xxii, 405 p. : ill., maps ; 24 cm.
Includes bibliographical references (p. 373–379) and index.
ISBN 0-8203-2437-X (hbk. : alk. paper)—
ISBN 0-8203-2438-8 (pbk. : alk. paper)
1. Bartram, William, 1739–1823. Travels through North & South
Carolina, Georgia, east & west Florida, the Cherokee country, the
extensive territories of the Muscogulges, or Creek Confederacy,
and the country of the Choctaws
2. Bartram, William, 1739–1823—Travel—Southern States.
3. Outdoor recreation—Southern States—Guidebooks.
4. Indians of North America—Southern States—History—
18th century. 5. Natural history—Southern States.
6. Southern States—Description and travel. 7. Southern States—
Tours. I. Cattier, Alan. II. Greene, Robert J. III. Title.
F216.2 .S65 2003
917.504'42—dc21   2002009183

Paperback ISBN-13: 978-0-8203-2438-8

British Library Cataloging-in-Publication Data available

This book is dedicated to our fathers,

who taught us the importance of the land

We shall not cease from exploration

And the end of all our exploring

Will be to arrive where we started

And know the place for the first time.

T. S. Eliot, "Little Gidding"

CONTENTS

ACKNOWLEDGMENTS

We thank the many rangers from the USDA Forest Service and the U.S. Army Corps of Engineers who offered their assistance: Jack Rodgers and Frank Findlay from the Nantahala National Forest; Hugh Cooper, Annette Cash, and Pepper Shields from the U.S. Army Corps of Engineers; James Poje from the U.S. Fish and Wildlife Service; and Allen Smith from the Chattahoochee National Forest. In particular we thank Jeff Owenby, from the Tallulah District, Chattahoochee National Forest, for his assistance and encouragement from the beginning of our project and for reading the trail sections for Georgia. Although the Georgia Bartram Trail Society is now defunct, Jeff filled much of the void with his recruitment of trail volunteers. Those volunteers included Boy Scouts and adult leaders from Scout Troop 100, Lilburn, in particular Jason Bach, Kevin Dunlop, Scott Houser, Jim Stallings, and Brian Hanley.

We also acknowledge the assistance of state park and historic site rangers from North Carolina to Louisiana: Howard Adams, Florida Department of Natural Resources, Paynes Prairie; Scott Alexander, Oconee Station State Park; Greg Potts, Port Hudson State Commemorative Area, who identified for us Browne's White Cliffs. Our thanks to Fred Benton, one of the original members of the Board of Managers of the Bartram Trail Conference, for his detailed information on the cliffs and for generously letting us print his photograph. We also acknowledge the assistance of Thomas Rice from Manatee Springs State Park, Ned Jenkins from Fort Toulouse–Fort Jackson, and Gail Whalen from LeConte Woodmanston Plantation. Tammy Forehand, from the South Carolina Institute of Archaeology and Anthropology, introduced us to George Galphin's Silver Bluff and allowed us to join her for one of her monthly archaeological outings at the site.

The library staff at a number of archives, academic libraries, and state historical societies were a great help to us, particularly Linda Matthews, Laura Micham, Elaine Wagner, and the interlibrary loan staff at Emory University; the Atlanta Historical Society; the University of Georgia; John Hardin at the Alabama Department of History and Archives; the American Philosophical Society; the Library of Congress; the West Volusia Historical Society; and the Georgia Historical Society. Librarians at public libraries throughout the Southeast were extremely helpful as well, in particular the staff at the Bladen County Public Library, the Rabun County Public Library, the Georgia Room at the Cobb County Public Library, and the Augusta–Richmond County Library. We also thank Karen Wallace, librarian at the Macon County Public Library, North Carolina; and Charlotte J. Cabaniss, director of the Bay Minette Public Library, Alabama. The assistance of Celeste Stover from the Bartram Trail Regional Library, Washington, Georgia, was particularly valuable.

We are especially indebted to Edward Cashin for reading our sections on Augusta and for directing us to so many Bartram enthusiasts, in particular Davida Hastie. We also thank Tom Hatley for reading our sections on Bartram's travels in Cherokee Country and Kathryn H. Braund for reading our sections on Bartram's travels in the Creek Nation. We are indebted to both for their support and encouragement. Thanks are also due Scott Ellis, Carole Meyers, and Bob McElroy for reading and proofreading many parts of our work.

Every guide springs from a vision, and we have been incredibly fortunate to have Barbara Ras, executive editor at the University of Georgia Press, there with us, helping us to see our way as we put this book together. Jennifer L. Reichlin and Sandra Hudson from the press walked hand in hand with us as we assembled the manuscript. Maps are critical to the success of any guide. Without the special contributions of Woody Hickcox from Emory University and Walton Harris from the University of Georgia Press we would surely have lost our way. We also acknowledge Walton's contribution to the narrative; he is the author of the trail guide for the Broad River. Finally, Mindy Conner, our copy editor, knew when we were moving off the beaten path. Her editing touch was always a signal in the right direction.

Our thanks to Joan Gotwals for supporting our project by providing Chuck Spornick with sabbatical time, and to our colleagues at Emory who endured countless tales of our adventures crisscrossing the South.

Finally, this work would not be possible without the unwavering support of our families, who gave up weekends and vacations in pursuit of Bartram's trail. Their interest and encouragement gave us the energy to pursue the *Travels* across seven states.

HOW TO USE THIS GUIDE

In the 1970s the Bartram Trail Conference sought to commemorate William Bartram's travels through the Southeast by establishing a Bartram Trail and asking the federal government to recognize it as either a national scenic trail or a national historic trail. Under the umbrella of the National Trails Act (1968) this status would legally protect and preserve many sites of considerable aesthetic, cultural, or recreational merit. The conference's goal was not to build a 2,400-mile continuous footpath, like the Appalachian Trail, cutting through the Southeast. Such a trail would be both impractical and undesirable. Bartram's route runs through mountain wilderness, but also along rivers, through farmlands and heavily developed areas like Myrtle Beach, and even through modern cities like Charleston and Savannah. Instead, the conference proposed a "broad interpretation" of a Bartram Trail so that users might have "Bartram-like" experiences seeing the southeastern landscape in its eighteenth-century context. The proposed Bartram Trail would also be "multimodal," allowing canoeing, biking, and horseback riding as well as hiking. The trail would be the recreational part of a Bartram Heritage Program identifying, recording, preserving, and interpreting important Bartram sites.

The conference did not succeed in establishing a Bartram Heritage Program or in obtaining national scenic (or historic) trail status for the trail. It did, however, leave an important legacy in the form of its *Bartram Heritage* report, the feasibility study submitted to the Department of the Interior in 1979 containing the blueprint for a heritage program. To meet the recreational and educational needs of the public the plan called for the creation of a series of Bartram memorials: trails, Bartram heritage sites, gardens, heritage centers, and heritage cities. Many of these memorials were established over the last thirty years of the twentieth century. Trail societies and garden clubs built and marked hundreds of miles of trails for hiking and canoeing. The conference identified more than fifty Bartram heritage sites in seven states, all inventoried state by state in the *Bartram Heritage* report. Garden club members and other dedicated citizens worked with the conference in marking many of these sites with the distinctive Bartram Trail historical marker. Bartram gardens and memorial parks were established in Florida, Alabama, and Mississippi.

It is the goal of this guide to bring all the parts of the trail together into a single unit and to complement the hiking trails and canoe paths with historic walking tours, driving tours, and bike trails.

STRUCTURE OF THE GUIDE

This guide is based on Bartram's five trips in the Southeast: his initial explorations, from the Georgia coast to Cherokee Corners; his explorations in East Florida; his "Journey to Cherokee Country"; his journey to Manchac through the Creek Nation; and finally, his return home to Philadelphia. Our goal is to capture the landscape that Bartram saw and recorded in the *Travels,* juxtaposing his experience with that of today's traveler. After a brief reconstruction of Bartram's route, we offer a series of four Bartram heritage sites, each featuring historic walking tours, driving tours, or short trails for hiking, biking, or canoeing.

The guide includes almost all of the Bartram heritage sites inventoried by the Bartram Trail Conference. Some of the important sites, notably Blue Springs on the Beaverdam Creek and Browne's White Cliffs on the Mississippi River, are on private land and can be seen only by canoe or with the owner's permission. Other Bartram sites, like Seneca and Keowee in northwestern South Carolina, now lie beneath modern reservoirs. Many of the sites are now part of state parks or historic areas, including Paynes Prairie and Blue Springs in Florida and Fort Toulouse–Fort Jackson State Park in Alabama. Other sites, such as Martin Creek Falls in the Chattahoochee National Forest, will soon be protected as scenic areas.

BARTRAM NATIONAL RECREATION TRAIL

We also include a detailed guide to the Bartram National Recreation Trail, found in four national forests: Sumter, Chattahoochee, Nantahala, and Tuskegee; and to the Bartram Trail along Clarks Hill Lake, north of Augusta. Taken all together there are more than 150 miles of foot and bike trails in three major segments. We have further divided these segments into sections designed to accommodate either day hiking or hiking with a car shuttle. Regrettably, each managing authority blazes the sections differently. The segments are:

Clarks Hill Lake: 26 miles in three sections for hiking. The Keg Creek Section is for both biking and hiking. The trail, where marked, is blazed with yellow paint. Managed by the U.S. Army Corps of Engineers.

Carolina and Georgia Mountains: 126 miles of hiking trail with one
section in South Carolina, four sections in Georgia, and seven
sections in North Carolina. The trail is blazed with yellow paint in
South Carolina, with yellow diamond-shaped plastic markers in
Georgia, and with yellow rectangular metal markers in North
Carolina. Managed by the Sumter, Chattahoochee, and Nantahala
National Forests.

Alabama: 9 miles for hiking and biking in one section within the
Tuskegee National Forest. The trail is blazed with white paint.

In North Carolina the seven sections are numbered 1–2 and 4–8; Section 3 has
not yet been built. Please note that our numbering and division of the sections differs from that of the North Carolina Bartram Trail Society. In this
guide, sections begin and end at roads for the convenience of hikers, and the
society's Section 6 is divided here into two parts.

RATINGS

We have assigned a "difficulty" rating to each of the trail sections and the
longer canoe or bike trails. The ratings are highly subjective and are intended
only as a planning aid. The actual difficulty will vary according to the weather
conditions, the season, the weight of the pack or canoe, and the stamina of
the hiker or cyclist.

1. Hiking trails
   Easy: mostly level, no steep climbs, good trail footing
   Moderate: some steep sections, for more experienced hikers
   Strenuous: not for beginners; includes steep sections (more than a
       500-foot increase in elevation within a mile) and a trail footing
       difficult for hiking
2. Canoe trails
   The canoe trails in Alabama, Georgia, Louisiana, and Florida are all
   on flat water. The chief hazards are submerged logs or debris and fast
   currents at times of high water levels. In North Carolina, the two trails
   on the Little Tennessee River do offer some whitewater, with class 2
   rapids. These rapids, depending on time of year and water levels, have
   clear channels and do not require scouting. They are well suited for
   the novice paddler. Access points for canoe trails are indicated on the
   maps using alphabetic designations.

SAFETY AND FIRST AID

We designed this guide to be used for day hikes and backpacking, and for short and long paddling trips. For extended hikes or paddling trips always bring adequate food, shelter, and clothing. First-aid materials are also a necessity, with training in their use desirable. The USDA Forest Service advises carrying ten items on any camping trip: map, compass, whistle (for signaling for help), flashlight, sharp knife, fire starter, waterproof matches, first-aid kit, extra food, and warm clothing.

Rain gear or clothing that stays warm when wet is essential on canoe trips or when hiking in the threat of rain or snow. The hiker or canoeist should also be aware of the signs of hypothermia, which occurs when the body's temperature drops because of exposure and exhaustion. Drowsiness, uncontrollable shivering, and stumbling are early indicators of this deadly condition. The victim needs to be quickly dried and warmed.

Never consume water from streams, ponds, or lakes unless it has been filtered, chemically treated, or boiled. No matter how pristine the appearance, most of the streams and ponds of the Southeast are infected with the parasite *Giardia*, which can cause prolonged and unpleasant intestinal distress.

Hiking alone is enjoyable but potentially dangerous. It is better to hike with a companion. Before leaving on any trip—hiking, canoeing, or biking—always inform others of your destination and your planned route.

GEAR AND INSTRUCTION: RECOMMENDATIONS

There are many excellent guides to hiking, canoeing, and biking. For the novice and the seasoned expert we recommend the four guides in the Trailside Guide series: *Hiking and Backpacking,* by Karen Berger; *Canoeing,* by Gordon Grant; *Kayaking: Whitewater and Touring Basics,* by Steven M. Krauzer; and *Bicycling: Touring and Mountain Bike Basics,* by Peter Oliver. Each guide provides a good overview of the gear needed (e.g., canoes, packs, tents, and clothing), techniques for each of the activities (e.g., paddling strokes, descending hills on a mountain bike), and instruction in many of the skills that will make for an enjoyable and safe outing (e.g., map and compass reading, fire starting, cooking, and how to set up a car shuttle). Each guide devotes a chapter to safety and first aid. All four have lengthy lists of sources and resources, including Web sites.

When it comes to canoeing, no guide can substitute for personal instruction. This is available in most areas through a canoe club or a paddling class.

INTRODUCTION
Traveling into the Past

A trail is a path between points, and a guide is a map of the path. A good guide informs the reader of what lies ahead without spoiling the sense of anticipation any explorer enjoys. For instance, it says where there is water but does not marvel about rainbows in mountain cataracts. It talks of steep, pitched ascents without overwriting the view that awaits the hiker. In short, the guide speaks to the body while seducing the imagination.

When William Bartram wrote *Travels through North and South Carolina, Georgia, East and West Florida* and published it in 1791, he knew that he was writing a guide to a landscape few had ever seen. Furthermore, he was describing flora, fauna, cultures, and terrains never before chronicled in a written text. Bartram's excitement at discovering plants and animals, peoples, and lands that heretofore knew reality only in the imagination pulsates through his book and engages the imagination of readers, energizing them with the desire to experience the same scenes.

William Bartram, our traveler, was born on April 9, 1739 (April 20 by the new calendar), the son of John Bartram, one of British America's leading "practical botanists." He grew up on the outskirts of Philadelphia in Kingsessing, Pennsylvania, where his father had established in the early eighteenth century a successful plant and seed trade. Bartram's youth was centered in Philadelphia, where he went to school and later had turned down on his behalf an apprenticeship with Benjamin Franklin.

His first travels with his father took him to New York, where in 1753 he went on his first plant-collecting expedition in the Catskill Mountains. The younger Bartram, raised around men who made their living studying and growing plants, was already using his considerable artistic talent to draw plants and animals. In 1765 John Bartram was appointed royal botanist for the North American colonies by King George III, and he invited his son William to join him on a plant- and seed-gathering expedition to Florida. The world the Bartrams experienced when they first set out from Philadelphia was a familiar one; they stopped in Charleston and Savannah, touring various gardens while visiting acquaintances. As they got nearer to Florida, however, they began to lose the sense of the familiar. The plants were obviously different from those known and grown in the Northeast, and the land was different as well—it was for the most part undeveloped and peopled by tribes of Native Americans.

When his father returned to Philadelphia in 1766, William chose to remain in this new and unfamiliar environment, founding a rice and indigo plantation in Florida. His attempt as a plantation owner, including his ownership of six slaves, was a dismal failure, and Bartram abandoned the plantation after only a few months. This strange new world had established a strong hold on William, however, and he would be unable to resist when it called him back. With the bad taste left by his failed enterprise still fresh in his mouth Bartram left Florida for the more comfortable climes of Philadelphia, where he executed drawings commissioned by various patrons, including a series on mollusks and turtles for Dr. John Fothergill. Bartram flirted with financial trouble and was truly safe only when his family settled his debts.

In 1772, financially strapped and unsure of his future, William contacted his former benefactor, Fothergill, with a proposal that he return to the South to collect plants and seeds and make drawings. Fothergill agreed to pay Bartram's travel expenses plus a modest salary. It was against this backdrop that William set out from Philadelphia on March 20, 1773, returning to Charleston and visiting points south for nearly four years of adventures that he chronicled in his narrative, *Travels through North and South Carolina, Georgia, East and West Florida.*

It is important to highlight three facts that frame the production of this work. First, the *Travels* is a chronicle of a landscape and culture far removed from the urbane world of Philadelphia where William Bartram was raised. Second, during the time between his trip with his father in 1765 and his own journey in 1773, the British American colonies moved inexorably toward political revolution, a subject on which William is remarkably silent in the *Travels* but which forms a distinct subnarrative. The energy of discovery found in this guide thus represents not only the energy derived from describing sights unseen, but also the energy derived from participating in a world undergoing radical change. Third, Bartram was raised within the Quaker tradition, one of whose most telling guidelines is an appreciation of divine order. The newness, wildness, and exoticness of the natural world of the American South upset his inculcated sense of the orderliness of nature. Indeed, the *Travels,* in particular Bartram's descriptions of Native American culture, manifest his need to provide examples of the balance in nature and the harmony attendant on it. Bartram thus wrestled with both a world in revolution and an environment that challenged his Quaker sense of order when he attempted to chronicle his journey through the South.

It is not particularly surprising that the *Travels* met with little attention and mixed success in the colonies, where people were preoccupied with the events surrounding the unfolding of their new nation. Published in Philadelphia in 1791, the work found few readers and was criticized for its florid prose. The British edition of the *Travels* published in 1792 met with a very different reception. Among its readers were English poets Samuel Taylor Coleridge and William Wordsworth, who found it a chronicle emblematic of the romantic imagination. Coleridge and Wordsworth saw in the *Travels* a metaphorical model for new and uncharted territory. It was, for them, the New World complete, a world marked by revolution inside and out, a world that defied reality and slipped into a new, evolving, unknowable, but imaginable landscape. That the English Romantics ended up securing William Bartram's place as America's first native-born naturalist is a curious piece of irony.

After his travels in the South, Bartram returned to Kingsessing and lived out his life amidst his father's celebrated gardens. He was appointed a professor of botany at the University of Pennsylvania, though there is no record of his ever teaching. Instead, he continued his work as an illustrator and gardener, and acted as the senior naturalist of the new nation. President Jefferson invited Bartram to serve as an adviser for an expedition up the Red River, but Bartram declined, citing his poor health. An undisclosed illness that struck Bartram in his journey along the gulf coast left him with weak eyes and poor vision. William Bartram died on July 22, 1823, at Kingsessing and was buried somewhere near there, though his final resting place was not recorded and remains unknown.

It should be clear from this narrative of Bartram's life and work that there is very little that is not unique in his history and his coming to prominence as America's firstborn naturalist. This guide attempts to trace both the places and the historical imprint that mark his celebrated journey as recorded in the *Travels*. As such, it is a guide to the land Bartram crossed in his journey, but it is also a guide to the history surrounding the *Travels* and a witness to the change that has occurred since the author's original text was written.

Most guides are content to tell the story of the path in one plane and in one time. One travels in the present, using the guide to supplement one's perceptions—one discovers without being immersed in the history of a place. That is not possible with this guide, which chronicles and reflects history. Snaking through the mountains of North Carolina, South Carolina, and Georgia; traversing the Piedmont on the way to the coast; moving on and off the barrier islands, in and out of coastal rivers to the great springs of central Florida and the Alachua Savanna; then along the gulf coast of Alabama, Louisiana, and

Mississippi, the travels of William Bartram, eighteenth-century naturalist and explorer, are irrefutably immersed in history. So, too, is this guide to his *Travels* and to the path that bears his name, the Bartram Trail, the preeminent long trail located entirely in the Southeast. Why is this guide different? From its opening pages, it recognizes the pull of place and time. We know there are names that play in our memories that at first glance seem unrecognizable, too distant to recover, and yet we long to find them. This guide is different specifically because it seeks to build a bridge from a book about the land to the land itself.

Bartram's book is no ordinary book, either. The *Travels* demands a lot from its reader. It requires knowledge to navigate the ongoing catalog of flora and fauna that the author registers on his journey. It requires focus to persevere through the denseness of the record, which a reader has to push through like an explorer moving through wild and uncharted land. The *Travels* is a literary landscape that continually connotes foreignness even though the physical land it speaks of is not geographically foreign to many of its readers. Its foreignness is rooted not in location but in the knowledge—or lack of knowledge—that the reader brings to the text. Readers unfamiliar with scientific names, for example, may bog down in their Latin coils. This guide attempts to bring the literary landscape of the *Travels* together with the land by providing the common names of many of the species inhabiting the regions that Bartram cataloged. It also attempts to map out the text against the land as we know it today, infusing a text of the past with the cartography of the present.

The land that Bartram traveled, the land that this guide attempts to map, is alive with the differences between his moment and ours. Bartram's living legacy is an invitation to see what has changed since his day and what is constant. Where are his metaphorical footsteps still visible? Where have they disappeared? This guide looks to the land for signs of Bartram's *Travels* to invite readers and travelers alike to experience his heritage.

A final difference is more difficult to describe but is essential to this guide. Apart from aspects of Bartram's *Travels* that are impossible to revisit because the landscape is so changed, there are aspects to Bartram's rendering of landscape that never existed anywhere but in the author's imagination. He writes, for instance, of traveling the land north of what is now Clayton, Georgia: "My winding path now leads me again over the green fields into the meadows, sometimes visiting the decorated banks of the river, as it meanders through the meadows, or boldly sweeps along the bases of the mountains, its surface receiving the images reflected from the flowery banks above" (T349–350). It is impossible to determine the location where he made that observation.

However, instead of treating this as a missed opportunity for a visitor to the area, this guide treats it as an invitation to experience Bartram's imagination acting upon the land. His sensibility, certainly romantic, shows a keen appreciation of the splendors of the natural world. This guide attempts to place its readers in close imaginative proximity to Bartram's *Travels* by placing them physically where they can re-create his path. This is not a mapping of nowhere; rather, it is an attempt to do justice to a landscape that flourishes in the pages of Bartram's book and still exists, as an opportunity, for the present-day reader and traveler. This guide seeks to offer these conjoined opportunities of past and present, historic and living, real and imagined, that are intrinsic to Bartram's encounter with the land. As such, it maps some unusual territory.

At its most general, this guide follows Bartram's route as he traveled the American South between 1773 and 1777; it divides many of his excursions into segments that offer different options for engaging Bartram's heritage. Some readers may prefer to visit points that coincide with Bartram's path by car, others by bicycle or canoe. There are also day hikes that lead into more remote locations where his imprint, though not visible, is available in his descriptions of place.

Finally, there is the Bartram Trail itself, a sprawling, multistate effort established in the late 1970s to re-create and preserve as much of the explorer's route as possible on the land that was available and near the original path. Today, more than 200 miles of foot, canoe, and horseback trails running in segments through four states comprise the Bartram Trail. It promises the adventurous traveler a challenging but rewarding opportunity to see some of the South's most spectacular natural sites. The trail is unique, too, in that it gives travelers the chance to experience the land in much the same manner as Bartram did, offering hiking, paddling, and horseback riding options as it winds through the landscape.

We heartily recommend two accompaniments to supplement this guide. First, Francis Harper's edition of Bartram's *Travels* is indispensable both for meeting William's original text and for seeing how one preeminent American scholar attempted his own reading of Bartram's journey. More than any other version, Harper's edition speaks of one man's passion for Bartram's work, a passion that inspired us when we first talked about writing this guide. The second accompaniment is topographical maps to supplement our regional maps for the Bartram Trail. The trail, particularly when one is on foot or horseback, goes through some extremely wild places where water and shelter are not always nearby. We have indicated the usgs topographical maps that should be associated with a section of trail on the more generalized maps, and we encourage those who follow in our footsteps, and Bartram's, to pay attention to these areas, which can be difficult to navigate.

Regardless of the mode of travel or the route pursued by its users, the mission of this guide is to be faithful to the practice and spirit of William Bartram's *Travels*. Our conjecture of the path he traveled in some places might not be historically exact, but it is in the spirit of the *Travels* to allow the imagination to color geography. As you follow Bartram, remember to look imaginatively when you look historically. The naturalist explorer will never be far away.

ABBREVIATIONS

JBC

Bartram, John. *The Travels of John Bartram 1734–1777.*
Edited by Edmund Berkeley and Dorothy Smith Berkeley.
Gainesville: University Press of Florida, 1992.

JBD

Bartram, John. "Diary of a Journey through the Carolinas, Georgia, and
Florida, from July 1, 1765, to April 10, 1766." Edited by Francis Harper.
Transactions of the American Philosophical Society, new series, vol. 33, pt. 1.
Philadelphia: American Philosophical Society, 1942.

O

Bartram, William. "Observations on the Creek and Cherokee Indians,"
in *William Bartram on the Southeastern Indians.* Edited and annotated by
Gregory A. Waselkov and Kathryn E. Holland Braund. Lincoln:
University of Nebraska Press, 1995.

R

Bartram, William. "Travels in Georgia and Florida, 1773–1774:
A Report to Dr. John Fothergill." Annotated by Francis Harper.
Transactions of the American Philosophical Society, new series, vol. 33, pt. 2.
Philadelphia: American Philosophical Society, 1942.

SHO

Bartram, William. "Some Hints and Observations concerning the
Civilization, of the Indians, or Aborigines of America," in *William Bartram
on the Southeastern Indians.* Edited and annotated by Gregory A. Waselkov
and Kathryn E. Holland Braund. Lincoln: University of Nebraska Press,
1995.

T

Bartram, William. *The Travels of William Bartram.* Naturalist edition.
Edited with commentary and an annotated index by Francis Harper.
New Haven: Yale University Press, 1958. Reprint, Athens:
University of Georgia Press, 1998.

Bartram's
Initial Travels

Coastal South Carolina

CHARLESTON

On March 20, 1773, William Bartram set sail from Philadelphia on the *Charleston Paquet* (R1:1, T1). After enduring a two-day storm at sea, the vessel arrived in Charleston Harbor on the last day of the month. Bartram's immediate destination was the "house of a very Antient and honourable Family" (R1:2). This was most likely the Lamboll family, who on at least four occasions were hosts to the Bartrams.

The Charleston that Bartram visited in the 1770s was the largest city south of Philadelphia and the fourth-largest city in the colonies, with a population of more than 12,000 (including slaves). It was also the commercial center of a planter society that had become rich from exporting rice and indigo. Nine out of ten of the wealthiest families in North America lived in Charleston; included in their number were several friends, associates, and benefactors of the Bartrams—Henry Laurens, Alexander Garden, Thomas and Elizabeth Lamboll, and John Stuart. These families were also leaders in Charleston's intellectual life, seeking to promote the port city as the cultural center of the colonies. They were patrons of the arts and the sciences, founders of the Library Society and a natural history museum. They were also committed horticulturists.

Like many other Charlestonians, they created and maintained elaborate flower and vegetable gardens. They also collected, identified, and exchanged botanical specimens. Often they sent specimens or seeds to botanists elsewhere in the colonies or in Europe. Their avocation won several of them recognition as botanists. The most notable was Alexander Garden, an "indefatigable collector of botanical specimens" who discovered and described a number of new genera and species.[1] He exchanged specimens and shared his observations with such renowned botanists of the day as Cadwallader Colden and John Bartram.

---

1. Berkeley and Berkeley, *Dr. Alexander Garden of Charleston*, 328.

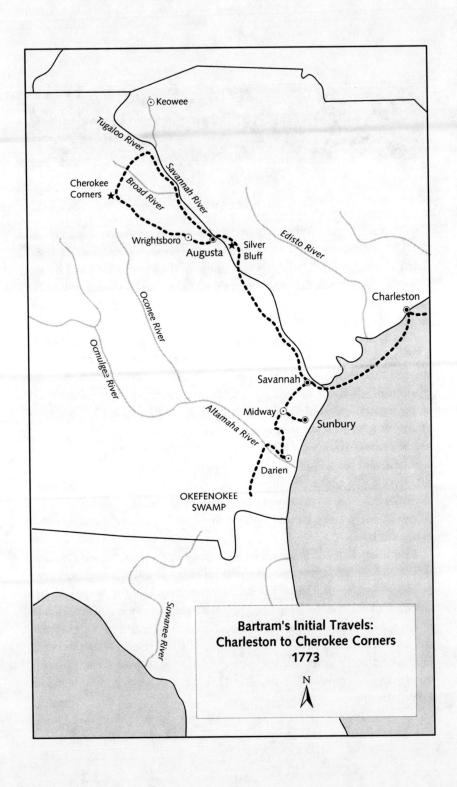

Keowee

Tugaloo River

Savannah River

Broad River

Cherokee
Corners

Wrightsboro
Augusta

Silver
Bluff

Edisto River

Charleston

Oconee River

Ocmulgee River

Savannah

Midway
Sunbury

Altamaha River

Darien

OKEFENOKEE
SWAMP

Suwanee River

**Bartram's Initial Travels:
Charleston to Cherokee Corners
1773**

N

When William Bartram arrived in Charleston he was thus in a city that had established itself as a colonial center of commerce and horticulture. He was also in a familiar setting, having already been introduced to many of the city's best families when he visited with his father in 1765. Surrounded by wealthy patrons and horticulturists in their formal, exquisitely planned gardens, William had a very civilized backdrop to his travels in the wilderness in 1773.

Walking Tour: Colonial Charleston

A tour of Charleston encompasses an architectural history of the South. South of Calhoun Street there are more than 100 structures built before 1775. Within three blocks on Tradd Street there are 22 surviving pre–Revolutionary War buildings. The focus of this 2-mile walking tour is limited to places associated with John and William Bartram.

The walking tour begins and ends at the **Old Exchange Building** at 122 East Bay. The building, constructed between 1767 and 1771, was commissioned by the colony's Assembly to be the "Exchange and Custom House" supporting Charleston's and Carolina's growing trade and commerce. The South Carolina signers of the Declaration of Independence, including Thomas Middleton, were elected here. The building's front is not on East Bay, but rather at the "rear" of the building. The Exchange's front faced the dock and harbor, which came right up to the building. One block toward the harbor is Waterfront Park, built upon a nineteenth-century landfill.

From the Old Exchange *walk to the south on East Bay. At Tradd Street, turn right.* On the left are the Lamboll Tenements, 8–10 Tradd Street. Immediately across the street is the **William Hopton House**, 13 Tradd Street, built by the wealthy merchant to replace the family's home after the fire of 1778. William's wife, Sarah, exchanged letters and plants with John Bartram. *Turn around and return to East Bay* and continue south. On the right is Rainbow Row, 79–107 East Bay, a series of residences and businesses for merchants. The ground floor of each building was used as the counting room and store, with the family living quarters above.

Turn right onto Stoll's Alley and walk for one block to Church Street. Directly across the street is the garden of Hugh and Mary **Dargan**, at 55 Church Street. This private formal garden was designed after the pattern common in eighteenth-century Charleston. Another re-created colonial garden, open to the public, is located at the **Heyward-Washington House**, a block north at 87 Church Street. Thomas Heyward, a rice planter and signer of the Declaration of Independence, and his son built the brick house as the family home in 1771.

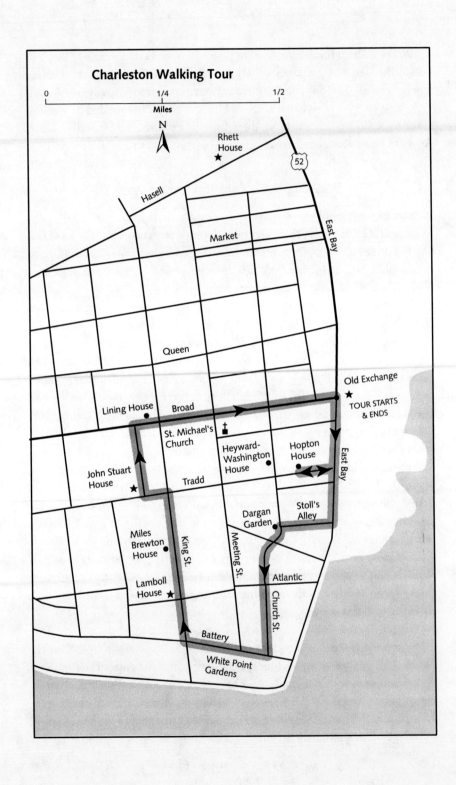

Charleston Walking Tour

0   1/4   1/2
Miles

N

Rhett House ★

52

Hasell

Market

East Bay

Queen

Old Exchange ★
TOUR STARTS
& ENDS

Lining House ●   Broad

St. Michael's
Church

Heyward-
Washington
House ●

Hopton
House ●

East Bay

John Stuart
House ★

Tradd

Stoll's
Alley

Miles
Brewton
House ●

King St.

Dargan
Garden ●

Meeting St.

Lamboll
House ★

Atlantic

Church St.

Battery

White Point
Gardens

Old Exchange Building, Charleston, South Carolina.

Heyward was one of the first "curators" of the newly established Charleston Museum, which featured a natural history collection of the "natural productions" of the province. In 1791 Heyward's home earned its double name, serving as George Washington's home for a week as he made his presidential tour through the southern states. By the middle of the nineteenth century the house

Garden at the Heyward-Washington House, Charleston, South Carolina.

had become a bakery with apartments on the second floor. The Charleston Museum purchased the house in 1929 and began its restoration, and it was opened in the 1950s as the city's first historic house museum. The interior of the house is furnished with Charleston-made pieces from the colonial period. Emma Richardson, the assistant director of the museum, re-created the garden using plans from other colonial Charleston gardens and plants typical of eighteenth-century gardens: crape myrtle, Cherokee rose, gardenia, and box. The garden is a long rectangle "incorporating a circular motif with concentric paths and brick-bordered beds."[2] The garden and the house, built in 1772, are open to the public for daily tours.

From either garden, *continue down Church Street* to the Battery. Across South Battery Street is the **White Point Gardens,** now a Charleston city park. *Turn right onto South Battery* and go two blocks. *At King Street turn right.* At 19 King Street is the **Thomas Lamboll House.** Constructed between 1735 and 1739, this was the residence of Bartram family friends Elizabeth and Thomas Lamboll. Here Mrs. Lamboll planted a "large and handsome flower and kitchen garden upon the European plan."[3] The garden originally extended

2. Cothran, *Gardens of Historic Charleston,* 96, 35.

3. Briggs, *Charleston Gardens,* 28.

Lamboll House, Charleston, South Carolina.

John Stuart House, Charleston, South Carolina.

beyond the house southward for two blocks to White Point Gardens. *Continue on King Street* past the **Miles Brewton House**, 27 King Street. This Georgian townhouse was constructed between 1765 and 1769. Behind the house lay one of Charleston's most notable gardens (see below). *At the intersection with Tradd Street turn left.*

On the right side of the street, at the corner with Orange Street, is the **John Stuart House**, 106 Tradd Street. The house was constructed between 1767 and 1772. Stuart fled the house in 1775 when the patriots seized control of the city. *Turn right onto Orange Street,* walking past the Elizabeth Petrie House, 3 Orange Street, built around 1768, and the Charles Pickney House, 7 Orange Street, constructed around 1769. *At Broad Steet, turn right.* After a short block, at the corner with King Street is the **John Lining House**, 106 Broad Street, which was constructed before 1715. This was the home of Lining, who conducted the first systematic weather observations in North America. In the 1780s it was the home of Andrew Turnbull, the founder of the failed Greek colony of New Smyrna in West Florida, which Bartram visited during his stay at St. Augustine. *Cross King Street.* On the left, at 98 Broad Street, was the residence of another Bartram friend and benefactor, Dr. Alexander Garden. The house was built in 1735 by one of Charleston's leading physicians, Dr. John Martino, who sold the house to Garden for his "in-town" residence. Otranto, 15 miles to the north, remained Garden's plantation residence. *Continue on Broad* to the intersection with Meeting Street. On the far corner is **St. Michael's Church**, 80 Meeting Street, which was constructed between 1752 and 1761 on the site of the old St. Philip's, the city's first parish church. Its steeple rises 186 feet, and it is still the tallest building in Charleston. William and John attended services here in the summer of 1765. *Continue down Broad Street*, returning to the Old Exchange.

Other Sites in Charleston

The approximate site of the garden of Mary Logan, a frequent correspondent with John Bartram, is located at the **Colonel William Rhett House**, at 56 Hasell Street, six blocks north of Broad Street. In 1730 the colonel's widow married Nicholas Trott and the property, outside the city's walls, was known as Trott's Point. Here she maintained extensive kitchen and flower gardens along an old Indian path leading to the city. John Bartram first met Mrs. Logan during his 1765 trip to Charleston. For the next fifteen years they regularly corresponded and exchanged plants and seeds. At the southeast corner of East Bay and Laurens Streets, approximately 1 mile north of the Old Exchange, is the site of the home of Henry Laurens, a friend of both Bartrams. The house was at the center of a 4-acre square that included the family's renowned garden. The square was subdivided in 1804, and the house was destroyed in 1916.

Charleston Museum

Founded in 1773, the museum offers exhibits on Carolina Indians, early trade and commerce, and plantation economy. The collection features natural history artifacts and specimens collected from the region.

The museum, located at 360 Meeting Street, is open daily, Monday–Saturday, 9 A.M.–5 P.M.; Sunday 1–5. Admission fee.

ACCESS

There is off-street parking just north of the Old Exchange, directly off East Bay. There is also street parking along East Bay and the streets around White Point Gardens.

St. Michael's Church, Charleston, South Carolina.

Horticultural Charleston

Town Gardens

The gardens of Charleston's famous horticulturists did not survive. Nevertheless, we can determine the outline and design of many of them, and we know with some certainty the flora they displayed, through eyewitness accounts, newspaper articles, and the correspondence of "practical botanists." Plans or drawings for a select few still survive. One of the most complete plans is that for the garden at the Miles Brewton House, 27 King Street, near the Lamboll House. It reveals a block-long garden divided into two sections. The first section, a pleasure garden, comprised a series of flowerbeds outlined by paths forming symmetrical designs. In the beds were a variety of flora, including vitex, mimosa, pink blossoms, and oleanders. In the other section, a vegetable garden, were plants used for either cooking or medicine. The twentieth-century owners of the house have restored both the house and the gardens, as much as is possible, to their late-eighteenth-century state. Garden plans have been used to restore or re-create a number of Charleston's gardens, including Samuel Adams's, Forian Mey's, and Colonel William Rhett's.

Middleton Place

In the middle of the eighteenth century, more than seventy plantations lined the Ashley and Cooper Rivers, and most had formal gardens. Only one garden survives today, at Middleton Place. In the 1750s the formal gardens of Middleton Place were famous in England and throughout the colonies. André Le Notre, the landscape architect of Versailles, designed the gardens for Henry Middleton. Although the original plantings are largely gone, the outline of Le Notre's design is still apparent. Immediately to the east of the house, on the high ground above the former rice fields, are a series of formal gardens occupying more than 40 acres. The gardens are shaped as squares or circles, with one octagon, which was once the site of a bowling green. The other gardens are bordered by a series of paths or alleys lined with camellias or shrubs.

The symmetry of Le Notre's design is established by the 90-degree triangle that he superimposed on the gardens. The top of the triangle intersects the centers of three of the gardens: Octagonal Garden; Sundial Garden, shaped like a great wheel; and the Mount. The main axis of the triangle bisects the Greensward at the back of the house, the house, and the Parterre at the front. Two Green Walks, cutting through beds of flowers, flank the Parterre. At the eastern edge of the Parterre are a series of steep terraces that lead down to the Butterfly Lakes. To the right is the Rice Mill Pond, to the left lie flooded rice

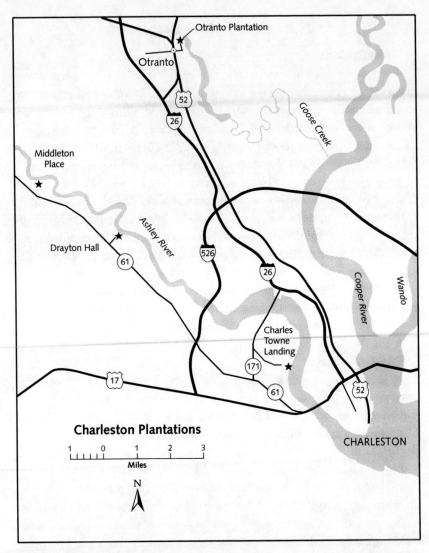

Otranto Plantation

Otranto

52
26

Middleton
Place

Goose Creek

Ashley River

Drayton Hall

61

526

26

Cooper River

Wando

Charles
Towne
Landing

171

17

61

52

Charleston Plantations

1 0 1 2 3
Miles

N

CHARLESTON

fields, and directly ahead is the Ashley River. The bottom of the edge of the triangle is a two-lane path on the eastern edge of the Reflection Pool.

To the east of the Reflection Pool in the garden west of the Sundial Garden is one of the few surviving original plants—the largest known specimen of crape myrtle, introduced to the garden by André Michaux. According to Middleton family tradition, the French botanist also donated to the family four camellias, the first planted in America. They are located on the North Green Walk, also known as the "Reine de Fleurs."

Otranto, the plantation house of Dr. Alexander Garden, Goose Creek, South Carolina.

Middleton Place is 14 miles northwest of downtown Charleston on S.C. 61—Ashley River Road. Open daily, 9 A.M.–5 P.M.

Drayton Hall

Drayton Hall is the only pre–Revolutionary War mansion on the Ashley River that survived the Civil War. John Drayton purchased land for the plantation in 1738, adjacent to his family's plantation, and followed the lead of other plantation owners on the Ashley in building a two-story brick house in the Georgian tradition. As seen from the rear, the facade is symmetrical, balanced on a central axis. The roof is hipped and the foundation is raised. The front of the house, facing the river, is one of the finest examples of Georgian-Palladian architecture in America with its inset two-story portico. The floor plan of Drayton Hall is that of an English manor, with the main entrance of the house leading into a parlor. The house is now owned by the National Trust for Historic Preservation and is open to the public for tours.

On the grounds are two walks, each less than a mile in length. The Marsh Walk circles the wetland to the southeast of the house. Two hundred years ago this marsh was the site of acres of rice plantation. The River Walk begins at the front of the house, facing the Ashley. As the footpath approaches the river, it passes by the foundation of the greenhouse. Here the Draytons grew both exotic and native plants, some of them donated by Thomas Jefferson and André Michaux.

Drayton Hall is 9 miles north of downtown Charleston on S.C. 61—Ashley River Road. Open daily to the public, with tours of the house on the hour.

Otranto

In 1771 Dr. Alexander Garden purchased land for a plantation on Goose Creek in Berkeley County. The present house is, according to Berkeley and Berkeley, "a replica of the one that Garden built." Otranto is located in the city of Hanahan, approximately 15 miles north of Charleston. The house is surrounded by a subdivision sharing the house's name, just east of U.S. 52 on Otranto Street.

Coastal Georgia

When William Bartram first arrived in Savannah in 1773 he was fresh from a visit to Charleston. In both cities he found much that recalled his past visit with his father, John, as well as the world in which he and his father lived. Bartram had been through coastal Georgia on his father's expedition eight years previously, and at that time they met and stayed with many of Georgia's major political and mercantile figures. On his return, William took advantage of these privileged associations to lodge and provision himself well as he made his way through coastal Georgia.

Yet Bartram also began making forays into a landscape that was less and less the plantation world of his father's friends and more and more uncharted territory, wilderness. In the description of his celebrated voyage up the Altamaha River, Bartram is clearly finding his way, not only as a naturalist, cataloging what he sees, but as the imaginative chronicler of the *Travels* as well. "Thus secure and tranquil," he writes, "and meditating on the marvelous scenes of primitive nature, as yet unmodified by the hand of man, I gently descended the peaceful stream, on whose polished surface were depicted the mutable shadows from its pensile banks; whilst myriads of finny inhabitants sported in its pellucid floods." Bartram's language labors to relate his enthusiasm for the prospect before him. A reader moving in Bartram's wake senses the naturalist's struggle to capture the difference between a known world with established descriptors and an unknown and as yet undefined world. As Bartram camps, "the sun now below the western horizon, the moon majestically rising in the east; again the tuneful birds become inspired; how melodious is the social mock-bird! The groves resound the unceasing cries of the whip-poor-will; the moon about an hour above the horizon; lo! a dark eclipse of her glorious brightness comes slowly on; at length, a silver thread alone encircles her temples: at this boding change, an universal silence prevails!" (T50–51). Bartram's Altamaha world becomes speechless.

Reading of Bartram's travels in coastal Georgia and visiting the places he described give a reader some understanding of how the features of a landscape (and the creatures, as well) can change while the relationship between types of landscapes remains constant. To move from present-day Savannah to the shores of the Altamaha is to undergo that same journey between a colonial city and the wilderness.

Wild coastal Georgia still offers a distinct contrast to the more established metropolitan areas that line the Atlantic. In particular, Sapelo Island and Cumberland Island, once plantation communities, have reverted to wilderness spaces that offer the wonder and power of a very distinctive southern landscape. On Sapelo, Bartram beheld "the great ocean, the foaming surf breaking on the sandy beach, the snowy breakers on the bar, the endless chain of islands, checkered sound and high continent all appearing before us" (T268). A visitor to Sapelo today slides by the old R. J. Reynolds home, now a cultural center, to explore the view below Raccoon Bluff where the waves break upon an undeveloped shore much as they have for millennia. To spend a day pedaling on rented bikes, visiting the shell ring that stands on the island's northeast shore, is to feel the freshness of a landscape that is awe-inspiring in its difference from the developed coast.

Cumberland Island stands in even starker contrast to its developed companions along the Atlantic seaboard. While a visitor can circumnavigate Sapelo on a bicycle, Cumberland is strictly a walk into the past—and from there into wilderness. Not ten minutes from the ferry landing, armadillos and wild horses are fellow pedestrians on the narrow, palmetto-lined paths. Farther along, in the federally defined wilderness area, deer, alligator, and snakes slip into the underbrush as hikers approach. Few places offer the luxury of a sunrise over the Atlantic, with dolphins skimming the surf, and a sunset over the coastal marshes, with white herons swimming through purple light. There are homes on Cumberland, and a passing pickup truck sometimes breaks the reverie, but overall the experience is one of total dislocation from the mainland. As Bartram discovered in the wilderness of coastal Georgia, there are few words to describe it.

Bartram visited the coast relatively early in his travels. As he explored, he uncovered difference—from his experiences traveling with his father and from the scenery he expected to see. That difference is his departure point into language that soars to encompass a landscape that seems to defy description. Fellow travelers following Bartram's route along the coast and onward into Florida face the same challenge. Sometimes, as Bartram suggests, it suffices to look and listen: "But yet, how awfully great and sublime is the majestic scene eastwards! the solemn sound of the beating surf strikes our ears; the dashing of yon liquid mountains, like mighty giants, in vain assail the skies; they are beaten back, and fall prostrate upon the shores of the trembling island" (T61).

From Charleston, Bartram sailed on a small schooner to the capital of Georgia. After three days in **Savannah** he set out on horseback to the south on the Old Post Road, traveling the route he and his father had ridden in 1765. After a little more than 20 miles he arrived at Midway and attended services at **Midway Church**, where he was "intraduced by some of my fellow Travilers being inhabitants of that part of the Country" (R1:4). From here, he traveled 9 miles to the east to visit the bustling port city of **Sunbury**. After a brief visit and an excursion to Colonels Island, he returned to the Midway district to visit the plantation of Benjamin Andrews, who had extended an offer of hospitality when they were introduced a few days earlier in Savannah. From Midway he extended his explorations farther south to **Darien** and the plantation of Lachlan McIntosh.

Bartram remained at the McIntosh plantation until the end of April. According to his report to Fothergill, a more reliable travel narrative than the *Travels,* he made a short trip to the newly established colonial port of Brunswick. Traveling to the northwest, he crossed the Altamaha River at **Fort Barrington** and then "kept a Path through the Pine Forests generally in sight of the low lands of the river" (R1:10). En route he visited one of the Georgia plantations of Henry Laurens of South Carolina. After reaching the site of Georgia's newest city, he retraced his route to the McIntosh plantation. The narrative of the *Travels* substitutes the trip to the St. Marys River via the Post Road from Fort Barrington for the trip to Brunswick. Given the greater reliability of the narrative in the "Report to Dr. John Fothergill," and considering that he stayed at McIntosh's plantation less than a week, it is likely that the trip to the Satilla River took place either in the fall of 1773 or in 1776 (T338).

Walking Tour: Colonial Savannah

Gen. James Oglethorpe founded Savannah in 1733. His plan for the city included a series of wards, each with a public square at its center. This 1.5-mile tour begins in downtown Savannah in Reynolds Square and passes through seven of the city's oldest squares, including three of those laid out by Oglethorpe. The tour route passes the only two buildings built before the Revolution that survived Savannah's devastating fire of 1796 as well as a number of other structures built shortly after the fire. The sites of public buildings, the town cemetery, the remnants of the city wall, and the Trustees Garden can also be seen.

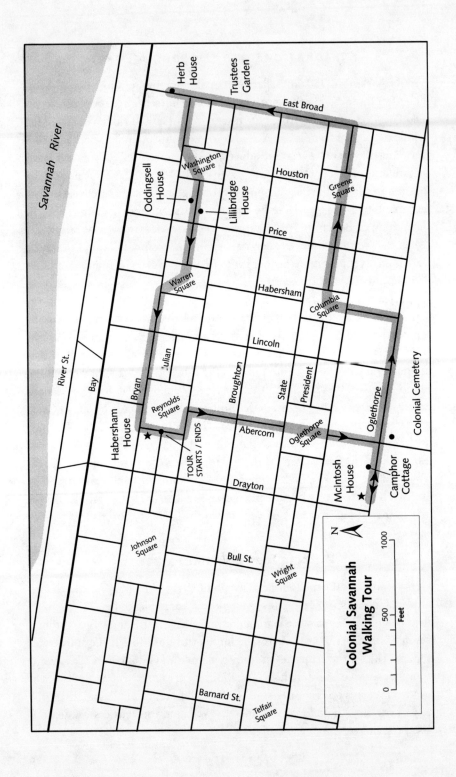

Savannah River

River St.

Bay

Herb
House

Trustees
Garden

East Broad

Oddingsell
House

Washington
Square

Houston

Greene
Square

Lillibridge
House

Price

Warren
Square

Habersham

Columbia
Square

Julian

Lincoln

Broughton

State

President

Oglethorpe

Colonial Cemetery

Bryan

Habersham
House

Reynolds
Square

Abercorn

Oglethorpe
Square

McIntosh
House

Camphor
Cottage

TOUR
STARTS / ENDS

Drayton

Johnson
Square

Bull St.

Wright
Square

N

1000

Colonial Savannah
Walking Tour

500

Feet

0

Barnard St.

Telfair
Square

At the time of Bartram's visit in 1773, Savannah was the second-largest city in the colonies south of Philadelphia; only Charleston was larger. The population was approximately 3,500, in comparison with Charleston's 12,000 or so. Savannah's citizens lived in more than 500 homes in the city and its three suburbs, Ewensburgh, Yamacraw, and Trustees Garden. The city was still centered on the six public squares laid out by its designer and founder, General Oglethorpe, in the winter of 1733. Each square was the center of a ward. Immediately surrounding the open square were public buildings, which were in turn surrounded by a series of tithes—groups of ten private residences. With its growing population and the quality of its harbor at Cockspur Island, Savannah emerged as the colonies' trade center. By the early 1770s the port would clear more than 200 vessels a year. The city was also a retail center with a bustling market located at Ellis Square and was home to three churches, three libraries, and a small theater. Almost all of these colonial structures were destroyed in the citywide fire of 1796.

The walking tour begins at **Reynolds Square**, at the corner of Abercorn and Julian Streets. Oglethorpe laid out this square in 1734 as the first new ward to be added to the original four, which are immediately to the west. Across the street from the square, between Bryan and Julian Streets, is the **Habersham House**, 23 Abercorn Street. This two-story Georgian structure was built in 1789 for James Habersham Jr., who made his fortune as an exporter and rice planter. The house is brick with pink stucco, thus its name the "Pink House." The square was also the site of the old Silk Filature. Abandoned for its intended purpose in the late 1760s, the building has just been renovated for concerts, balls, and other public events.

Continue south on Abercorn Street for four blocks to Oglethorpe Square. This square, laid out in 1742, was the sixth and last square designed by Oglethorpe. *Exiting the square, continue on Abercorn* to the intersection with Oglethorpe Avenue. *Turn right.* On this side of the street are the only two buildings built before the Revolution that survive today. The first structure is the **Christian Camphor Cottage** at 122 East Oglethorpe Avenue, a clapboard frame house built in 1760. In 1870 it was raised on top of a brick foundation as the second story of the rebuilt house. Just beyond it, at 110 East Oglethorpe, is the **McIntosh House**, which was built as a two-story house sometime before 1782. From 1782 to 1806 it served as the home of Bartram's dear friend Gen. Lachlan McIntosh. George Washington stayed here as a guest on his visit to Savannah in 1791. *Return to Abercorn Street.*

Cross to the other side of Abercorn Street and then *cross (to the right) Oglethorpe Avenue.* At the southeast corner of the intersection is the entrance to

*James Habersham House, Savannah, Georgia. Its pink stucco gives
the house its more commonly known name, the "Pink House."*

the **Colonial Cemetery**, the burial site for the Habershams and other notable
Savannah families. *Walk along Oglethorpe Street* to the intersection with Habersham Street. *Turn left*, and in two short blocks you will enter **Columbia Square**,
laid out in 1799 on the site of the old Bethesda Gate. In the late 1760s colonial
Governor Ellis commissioned the construction of city walls around the royal
capital with Bethesda Gate as one of the six land entrances into the city. *Exit
the square on the right onto President Street*, renamed after the Revolution from
King's Avenue. On President Street walk past Price Street and the Williams
House, 503 East President. This two-story Federal-style house was built between 1799 and 1808. The street soon enters **Greene Square**, laid out after the
Revolution to honor one of the war's principal heroes, Nathaniel Greene.

Walk along President Street to the intersection with East Broad Street. *Turn
left* and follow Broad toward the river. Just beyond the intersection with
Bryan Street is the **Herb House**, at 26 East Broad.[1] This was the location of the

---

1. Toledano reports that "some insist that the little Herb Garden house is part of
the original Trustee Garden, and it is claimed to be the oldest building in Georgia";
see *National Trust Guide to Savannah*, 86. Morrison's *Historic Savannah* (52) assigns
a date to the house of 1853.

Christian Camphor Cottage, Savannah, Georgia.

western border of the Trustees Garden, a 10-acre plot that was laid out for the settlers within months of their arrival in 1734. The garden was abandoned after four years. In the early 1760s the land was the site of a colonial fort. *Return to Bryan Street, turn right,* and walk to the west to **Washington Square**, also laid out after the Revolution. *Veer to the left through the square and exit on Julian Street.* In the first block past the square, to the right, is the **Charles Oddingsell House**, 510 East Julian. This one-story gabled house was built in 1797

McIntosh House, Savannah, Georgia.

as the home of a wealthy Skidaway Island planter. Across the street, at 507 East Julian, is the **Hampton Lillibridge House**. This wood frame two-and-one-half-story house was built about 1796. It was originally located at 310 East Bryan Street, but was moved to its new location and restored in 1962.

Continue on Julian Street to Warren Square. As Julian approaches the square, the street is flanked by two postcolonial homes. On the right, 22 Habersham Street, is the Spencer House, built between 1790 and 1804. On the left, 24 Habersham, is the house built for John David Mongin in 1797. In the square, *follow the path angling to the right to Bryan Street. Then follow Bryan Street to the west* to Abercorn Street, returning to Reynolds Square. To visit one of the four original squares laid out by Oglethorpe in 1733 continue east on Bryan for two additional blocks to **Johnson Square**, named for Governor Robert Johnson, one of the benefactors of the settlement. The stake in the center of the square is the burial place of Nathaniel Greene. Off the square, at 28 Bull Street, was the site of Georgia's first church, Christ Church.

ACCESS

Public parking is available at a city parking deck off Reynolds Square at the corner of Abercorn and Bryan; the entrance to the deck is on Abercorn. Metered public parking is available at the Factor's Walk on the Savannah River, just two blocks from Reynolds Square, and on most downtown streets.

Wormsloe

Ten miles southeast of Savannah is the site of the plantation of one of Georgia's earliest settlers, Noble Jones, who accompanied Oglethorpe when he established the colony in 1733. William Bartram first visited the Jones plantation in the company of his father on their journey to St. Augustine. After visiting Bethesda, according to John Bartram's diary, they "rode to A gentleman's house which was delightfully situated on A large tide salt creek where ye oisters is as thich as they can be within a stone cast of his house" (JBD30).

Although the entry for September 25, 1765, does not explicitly name Jones's plantation, Wormsloe, the house John Bartram described was in all likelihood Noble Jones's. By the 1760s Jones was well known for his experiments with plants, making Wormsloe a likely destination for the newly appointed royal botanist. John Bartram refers specifically to the "great improvements in fruites" such as oranges, figs, pomegranates, and nectarines (JBD30).

In 1765 Wormsloe plantation comprised 500 acres. The first fortified house, a mud-and-daub structure, was built on the site in 1739. On the plantation Jones planted mulberry trees for silk farming, but he also devoted land to

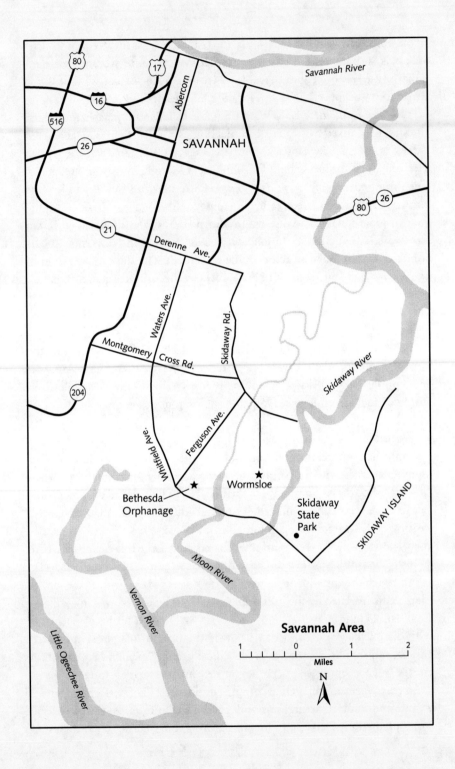

Savannah Area

1   0   1   2
Miles

N

*Wormsloe ruins, the remains of Noble Jones's tabby house
at Wormsloe State Historic Site, Savannah, Georgia.*

raising rice, cotton, and cattle. On the Narrows, Jones built a one-and-a-half-story fortified tabby house, one of the most imposing structures in the Savannah area. The house was constructed between 1739 and 1744, with a possible addition added after 1750. At the time of Bartram's visit the house had five rooms and more than one floor. The first floor was surrounded on all four sides by a large porch. Located on the main southern channel to the Savannah River, the house also served as a fort guarding Savannah against an attack by Indians or the Spanish. Jones commanded a company of marines, usually numbering ten, who patrolled the waterway and lived on the grounds in huts made of mud and wattle.

Today, only the foundations of the tabby house survive. The house and a family cemetery have been preserved as the Wormsloe State Historic Site. The site offers a "Colonial Life Area" with living history demonstrations and an interpretive trail with wildlife prints by Mark Catesby.

ACCESS

Wormsloe is 10 miles southeast of downtown Savannah, at 7601 Skidaway Road. Open 9 A.M.–5 P.M., Tuesday–Saturday, and Sunday afternoons.

Driving Tour: Midway District

This tour begins southwest of Savannah at the junction of U.S. 17 and I-95. The tour follows Ocean Highway south along the route of the Old Post Road to Midway, the home of the **Midway Church**, where Bartram attended services, and the cemetery where many of Georgia's Revolutionary era leaders are buried. From Midway the tour turns eastward for 9 miles to the site of the colonial port of Sunbury. To the east of the town is Fort Morris, authorized by the Continental Congress as part of the city's defenses. Returning to Ocean Highway, the tour continues southward on the Post Road, which is still a sand road as it traverses the northern reaches of McIntosh County. En route, the tour passes the LeConte-Woodmanston Plantation and then turns eastward again toward the shore, ending at U.S. 17 near South Newport.

At the junction of U.S. 17 and I-95, Exit 87, take U.S. 17 South. From downtown Savannah to Midway, U.S. 17 closely follows the track of the Old Post Road—the major north–south artery in the colony. Continue south on U.S. 17, entering Liberty County. From the county line it is 6 miles to Midway and the junction with the Old Sunbury Road **(mile 10.8)**.

Midway

In the early 1750s a group from Dorchester, South Carolina, settled here—"mid-way" between the Savannah and Altamaha Rivers. These Carolinians were direct descendants of the Puritans of Dorchester, Massachusetts. In this area, from Colonels Island 15 miles to the east to Riceboro, they continued the livelihood that they and their slaves had pursued in South Carolina: rice farming. By 1771 the area immediately surrounding Midway had a population of more than 350 white settlers and 1,500 slaves. Nearly half of the white settlers were members of the congregation, which held its worship services at the Midway Meeting Hall, built in 1756 at the junction of the Post Road and the road to Sunbury. With the emergence of Sunbury as the main city and trading center for the region, Midway continued to function as the spiritual center for St. John's parish.

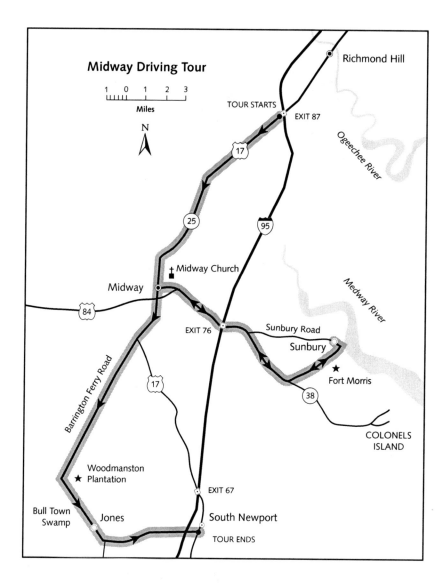

Midway Driving Tour

```
  1   0   1   2   3
  └┴┴┴┘
      Miles
```

N

Richmond Hill

TOUR STARTS

EXIT 87

17

25

95

Ogeechee River

✝ Midway Church

Midway

84

Medway River

EXIT 76

Sunbury Road

Sunbury

★ Fort Morris

Barrington Ferry Road

17

38

COLONELS ISLAND

Woodmanston
★ Plantation

EXIT 67

Bull Town
Swamp

Jones

South Newport

TOUR ENDS

Bartram attended Sunday services at the Midway Meeting Hall in 1773 and heard a sermon given by "Mr Percey" (William Percey was in charge of the Bethesda Orphanage). Bartram found the Midway congregation "respectable and genteel. The Religious and Pious Spirit throughout the whole Audience reflects a shining light on the Character of the inhabitants [of] Midway and Newport"(R5). The white wood-frame church was built in the New England style with a U-shaped gallery, a gabled roof at the front, and a square tower. The gallery was reserved for slaves, with a seating arrangement that placed

Midway Church, Midway, Georgia.

them completely out of view of the congregation below, save for the minister in the high pulpit. During the Revolution, the British burned the church to the ground as part of their campaign to seize Sunbury. After the war the congregation rebuilt the church on the plan of the original. Completed in 1792, that is the building standing today. Immediately south of the church is the cemetery, where members of many of the leading families of the colony—including James Screven and Daniel Stewart, generals of the Revolutionary army—are buried.

One-tenth of a mile south of the church, turn left onto Martin Road (part of the Old Sunbury Road). *Continue east for a little more than 1 mile* to the junction with U.S. 84. *Turn left* and follow U.S. 84 east, past the interchange with I-95 **(mile 14.3)** to the intersection with the Old Sunbury Road **(mile 15.3)**. This single-track sand road was the main road connecting Sunbury with Midway and the Post Road. Here Bartram observed bald cypress, tulip poplars, catalpa, and southern magnolias as well as trumpet-creeper and coral honeysuckle. The road is passable only by vehicles with high clearance. *Most vehicles should continue east* on the paved highway, now Ga. 38, and in 3 miles **(mile 18.3)** *turn left onto Trade Hill Road.* In less than 1 mile the road ends at Fort Morris Road. At the junction, turn left and follow Fort Morris Road to the entrance to the **Fort Morris Historic Site (mile 21)**.

From the entrance to Fort Morris continue north on Morris Road. In 0.75 mile the road intersects the Old Sunbury Road. *Turn left* at the intersection and follow the Old Sunbury Road for 0.1 mile to Dutchman's Cove. *Turn right onto Dutchman's Cove* and in less than 0.25 mile the cemetery appears directly ahead **(mile 22)**. The cemetery was at the southeast corner of the Sunbury Church Square. Thirty-four grave markers survive; most were destroyed before 1870. This is all that remains of Georgia's third largest city in the eighteenth century. **Sunbury** was burned to the ground after the British captured it in January 1779. Although it was rebuilt, the town never recovered its prominence. By 1885 fewer than eight families lived here. By the end of the nineteenth century, Sunbury was identified as one of Georgia's dead towns.

Sunbury

Founded in 1758, Sunbury became the urban center for the settlers of the Midway region. The concentration of plantations in the area from the delta of the Medway River to present-day Riceboro was second only to that between the Savannah and Ogeechee Rivers. As rice became the colonists' "staple of commerce," the settlers of Midway abandoned the Post Road for transporting their crop to Savannah and looked to Sunbury as a port for trans-

FORT MORRIS

This fort was built in 1776, authorized by the Continental Congress to protect the port city of Sunbury, immediately to the west of the fort. The fort was located at the site of a log fort built in 1760 to protect colonists from Indian attacks. The British laid siege to the fort in November 1778, but patriot forces under the command of John McIntosh withstood the attack. When the British commander, L. V. Fuser, demanded the fort's surrender, Colonel McIntosh replied with a terse and now famous response: "Come and take it." Fuser and the British declined and withdrew to Florida. Sunbury and Fort Morris did not fare as well in January 1779. British army troops led by General Prevost captured the fort and city en route to occupy Savannah. Fort Morris was renamed for George III and became a military prison until 1782, when the British evacuated it.

The fort was star shaped with bastions at each corner, and was constructed entirely of wood and dirt. Surrounding the fort was a moat lined with palisades. Today only remnants of the walls survive. Thirty years after Fort Morris was abandoned, the U.S. government built a new fortification, Fort Defiance, within the walls of the old fort to protect the Georgia coast from a British invasion during the War of 1812. Both forts are protected and interpreted as the Fort Morris State Historic Site. A brief walking tour takes the visitor through the walls of Fort Morris over the eroded walls of Defiance to the Medway River and the first town lot of Sunbury.

At the parking area, near the entrance, is a visitors' center that offers exhibits and a video on the history of Sunbury and the Midway region.

---

porting rice by sea. Its growth was rapid, and Sunbury soon rivaled Savannah as a trading center. Bartram visited Sunbury for the first time in 1773 and described it in his report to Dr. Fothergill: "This pretty town is situated on the sound apposite St. Catherin Island, and commands an agreeable prospect of the Inlet 4 or 5 Miles from the Barr. There are about 100 houses in the Town neatly built of wood framed, having pleasand Piasas round them" (R1:5). In 1773 the city's population was nearly 1,000. The 100 houses Bartram referred to were built on lots laid out on a grid centered on three large public squares: Kings, Church, and Meeting. Many of the houses had long porches on two sides, the "pleasand Piasas" referred to by Bartram. That evening he "supped and spent the evening of genteel and polite ladies and gentlemen" (T5).

From Sunbury, return to Midway via Fort Morris Road, Ga. 38, U.S. 84, and the Old Sunbury Road to U.S. 17 **(mile 33.2)**. At Midway, Bartram was the guest of one of the area's leading citizens, Benjamin Andrews.

From Midway, take U.S. 17 South. At the junction with Barrington Road, turn right **(mile 35.8)**. In less than 2 miles the pavement stops and the road be-

Sunbury Cemetery, Sunbury, Georgia.

comes sand; it is passable by conventional automobiles. In another 3 miles, on the left, is the entrance to the **Woodmanston Plantation (mile 40.8).**

John Eatton LeConte Sr. of New Jersey began purchasing land on the north side of Bull Town Swamp in 1760. By 1774 the plantation had grown to more than 3,300 acres, making it the largest in the area. LeConte continued to live in the North for most of the year, taking up residence at his plantation only in the winter months. Although neither the *Travels* nor Bartram's report to Fothergill mentions Bartram meeting LeConte, it is likely that the two men's paths crossed at either the plantation or at Midway Church.[2] LeConte had two sons, Louis and John Eatton Jr., who did make Bartram's acquaintance in later years in Philadelphia. Louis inherited the plantation in 1810 and made it his permanent home. He built a garden there that was renowned for its splendor. It was, notes Claude A. Black, "celebrated all over Europe and the United States, and botanists from the north and from Europe came to visit it."[3]

Save for a lone camellia, crape myrtles, and a sabal palmetto, the garden has vanished. The Georgia Department of Natural Resources (DNR) and the

2. Bartram, "Report to Dr. Fothergill." Harper says that "Bartram may very likely have met the senior LeConte at Midway Meeting House, if not at the plantation" (173).

3. Black, "The Botanical Heritage of LeConte-Woodmanston," 24.

After an evening at Sunbury, Bartram was "desirous of visiting the islands." His destination was Colonels Island, not Catherines Island, which is farther to the east. Harper notes that Bartram reached the island by fording a "narrow shoal"; such a ford is not possible for Catherines, even during the lowest of tides. On the island Bartram excavated a shell midden. Among the conical mounds he observed "fragments of earthen vessels, and of other utensils, the manu- facture of the ancients," including the rim of a pot (τ6). On the island's ridges he observed southern magnolia, live oak, cabbage palm, and eastern red cedar.

To visit the island, turn left at the intersection of Colonels Island Road and Fort Morris Road. For 6 miles the road bisects the high ground of the "island" ending at Yellow Bluff, overlooking the salt marshes between the mainland and St. Catherines Island.

Garden Club of Georgia now own and manage the site as part of the LeConte-Woodmanston project and are restoring the formal gardens that were located near the plantation house. To the south of the gardens is the northern edge of the **Bull Town Swamp** and one of the plantation's many rice fields.

Slaves cleared the land for the rice fields, building a dam around the perimeter of the field. The inside of the field was divided into a series of squares, each crisscrossed by smaller dikes and ditches to allow flooding and drainage of the rice field as needed. Each square was about 200 feet long and 75 feet wide. Four of the squares have been cleared of trees to create a rice-growing demonstration area. This area can be seen on the 1-mile nature trail that circuits the rice field on the perimeter dam. Past the demonstration area, only the outlines of the squares can be seen; the swamp has reclaimed most of the field. More than twenty-five species of trees have been identified and marked on the trail, including wax myrtle, bald cypress, and water tupelo. The trailhead for the loop trail is at the bridge crossing the canal to the rice fields.

From **Woodmanston** return to Barrington Road. *Turn left and continue to the south.* After crossing the South Newport River, the road becomes Jones Road. To the left and right are views of the Bull Town Swamp, where Bartram lost his way in the spring of 1773. After 4 miles **(mile 44.8)** leave the sand road and *turn left onto Townsend Road.* In 3 miles the road will pass through the small town of Jones. Continue on the paved highway, formerly Ga. 131, for a little more than 5 miles to U.S. 17, Ocean Highway **(mile 49.8)**.

To return to Savannah, turn left onto U.S. 17 and follow it through South Newport. In 1 mile U.S. 17 will intersect I-95, Exit 67. To visit Sapelo Island,

Benjamin Andrews owned one of Midway's largest plantations, with more than 100 slaves and annual rice production of 1,600 barrels (R1:6–7). He made a number of improvements in rice agriculture, including the use of water-powered machines to shell the grain and clean the rice (T11). One of Andrews's neighbors invited Bartram to stay as his guest, and he was "hospitably entertain'd" there for several days while he "serch[ed] out the Natural productions of the Country" (R1:7). On one of the day excursions he accompanied Andrews and some friends on a small fishing party "in a shaded retreat, in a beautiful grove of magnolias, myrtles, and sweet bay trees" on the bank of a creek that wound through the plantation (T11–12).

---

turn right and take the highway 8 miles south through Eulonia to the junction with Ga. 99. Turn left and take Ga. 99 to the visitors' center for Sapelo Island.

SAPELO ISLAND

Bartram visited this coastal island in either late 1773 or 1776; the date cannot be established from either his *Travels* or his report to Fothergill. According to his account in the *Travels* he "with a few friends" descended the Altamaha River to "make a party of amusement at fishing and fowling on Sapelo." They crossed the sound and "landed on the North end of the island, near the inlet, fixing our encampment at a pleasant situation, under the shade of a grove of Live Oaks and Laurels, on the high banks of creek which we ascended" (T268). Perhaps Bartram and his party ascended Blackbeard Creek and camped on the bluffs on its western bank. It is not certain that this was the site of their encampment, but one can stand today on Raccoon Bluff and look out over the "foaming surf breaking on the sandy beach, the snowy breakers on the bar."

Sapelo Today

Sapelo Island, 10 miles long and 3 miles wide, is Georgia's fourth-largest barrier island. It is located between the mouths of the Sapelo and Altamaha Rivers. The entire island except for the 400 acres comprising the community of Hog Hammock is part of the R. J. Reynolds State Wildlife Refuge. To the east is an extensive salt marsh, also protected as part of the Sapelo Island National Estuarine Research Reserve, which encompasses approximately 6,000

Dike for rice plantation, Woodmanston Plantation, south of Midway, Georgia.

acres between the island and the mainland. Blackbeard Island, immediately to the northeast, is part of the Blackbeard National Wildlife Area. The beach on the ocean side of Sapelo features primary and secondary dunes. The primary dunes are younger, made up of a Holocene strand nearly 17,000 years old. Inland, often separated by streams or marshes, are the older sand ridges, such as Raccoon Bluff. These ridges are the remains of Pleistocene beach ridges that have now been eroded. On the high land are meadows, ponds, and freshwater marshes.

Sapelo's History

With the notable exception of the African American community at Hog Hammock, Sapelo is now largely depopulated, much as it was in the seventeenth century, although the island was inhabited for much of the last 6,000 years. Its first inhabitants were Native Americans of the Late Archaic period (4000–700 B.C.). As the sea level rose at the end of the last Ice Age, the advancing waters surrounded the sand ridges, creating an island. A ring of marshland offering a rich variety of seafood in turn surrounded the island's high ground, the site of the first settlements. The oldest is at the northwestern corner of the island, near the Mud River. Its only monuments are shell middens and a massive shell ring. The Sapelo Shell Ring dates to 1800 B.C. It is approximately 250 feet in diameter with walls 5–10 feet in height and more than 30 feet thick, making it the largest shell ring in the eastern United States. The walls are made of shells from oysters, conchs, clams, and mussels. The use or purpose of the ring is unknown. Surrounding the ring are numerous shell middens that are most likely refuse piles from the vanished settlement.

South of the Sapelo Shell Ring on the western shore of the island is Kenan field.[4] In the 1970s archaeologists excavated a large section of a Savannah-phase village (ca. A.D. 1300) here. They uncovered the foundations for two large structures separated by a plaza. The foundation of each structure revealed a series of "post-holes" that once held supports for a wooden roof. Structure 1 was a platform, 120 by 100 feet, constructed on a low earthen mound. Structure 2, 180 by 100 feet, was located at the north end of the plaza. A large earthen mound immediately to the east was also a part of the complex. Archaeologists believe that the structures were for some type of community use, although one of the buildings—Structure 1—may have been a residence as well.

4. Simpkins and McMichael, "Sapelo Island: A Preliminary Report."

Europeans "discovered" Sapelo in the early 1520s. At the point of contact, Spanish colonists and explorers encountered Guale Indians, a Muskogean-speaking people who inhabited the coast from the Satilla River northward to the North Edisto River. Occupying numerous permanent settlements on the coastal islands and the mainland, they, like their Mississippian ancestors, hunted, gathered, and fished while growing sufficient maize to maintain surpluses. Politically they were divided into three chiefdoms, each headed by a chief, or *mico*. Sapelo belonged to the southernmost chiefdom, Asao-Talaxe. By the 1560s the northern chiefdoms had become subject to Spanish rule. The Spanish established their first garrison on St. Catherines Island north of Sapelo. The soldiers were soon followed by Jesuit missionaries and then Franciscans who built missions and set to work converting the Indians to Christianity. In the 1660s invading Indians from the Carolinas attacked the Guale settlements. In 1689, in the face of these attacks and the threat of British attacks as well, the Spanish abandoned the Atlantic coast from Cumberland Island northward.

For the next fifty years the Sea Islands were largely uninhabited. Oglethorpe entered into a treaty with the Creeks, winning for the British the coastal islands between the Altamaha and the Savannah. The island's first planter was Andrew Mackay. After his death in 1769, William McIntosh and his brother Lachlan continued planting on Sapelo. After the Revolution the island was purchased by a group of French investors, whose infighting assured the failure of their plan for a plantation. One of the French investors, the marquis de Montalet, moved from the mainland to the island to live in "Le Chatelet." Remains of the structure survive today, along with the name as rendered by the island slaves, "Chocolate." In 1802 Thomas Spalding, the son of trader James Spalding of St. Simons and a friend of Bartram, purchased 4,000 acres on the south end of the island. Over the course of the next fifty years he enjoyed remarkable success managing his plantations for sugarcane and rice. The end of the Civil War brought the end of plantation society on Sapelo.

After the war, the Spaldings abandoned the island. In 1912 the automobile magnate Howard Coffin purchased the island and restored the house at the south end as a vacation home. Soon he expanded and remodeled the mansion, making it the Coffins' permanent home. Roads and bridges were built, and fields were cleared for farming. Shortly after Coffin's death, the family sold the mansion and the island to Richard J. Reynolds, the tobacco magnate. Like Coffin, Reynolds raised cattle and farmed on the island. He also designated uncultivated areas of the island as bird blinds and wildlife areas for hunting. After his death, Reynolds's widow sold the northern portion of the island to the state of Georgia. This area, administered by the Department of Natural Resources, is now the R. J. Reynolds State Wildlife Management Area.

The only public access to the island is by the ferry that operates daily between the dock at Meridian and the island. Today's visitor can see the island either on a guided tour or by foot or bicycle. The DNR offers guided tours on Wednesdays and Saturdays year-round, with an extra tour on Fridays during the summer months. Tours take visitors to Chocolate, Hog Hammock, Cabretta Island, and the southern end of the island with its newly restored lighthouse and the Reynolds mansion. The tour on the last Saturday of the month visits the Sapelo Shell Ring and Raccoon Bluff on the northern part of the island. Camping is permitted on the island, but only at the primitive group camp at Cabretta Island. The DNR provides a shuttle service from the ferry to the camp. Reservations are required, and group size is restricted to twenty-five people. Private accommodations are available at Hog Hammock, with shuttle service to and from the dock. The island roads and trails can be hiked or biked, although the bicycles must be rented on the island.

The Sapelo Visitors' Center has exhibits on the history and ecology of the island. It is also the parking area for the ferry and the site where tickets for guided tours are sold. The center is located on Ga. 99, 8 miles north of Darien.

Driving Tour: Darien to Brunswick

This 35-mile tour begins in the coastal city of Darien. To the east is the site of Fort King George; to the west is a spur tour to Fort Barrington following the path of the colonial road through Cox to the site of the ferry crossing over the Altamaha River. From Darien, the main tour heads to the south through the remnants of the many plantations that flourished along the Altamaha's four channels. At Brunswick, the tour crosses over the Intracoastal Waterway to St. Simons Island, with both driving and biking tours to Fort Frederica and Bloody Marsh battlefield. The route continues southward through the colonial city of Brunswick. To the south of Brunswick is Jekyll Island, offering beach access and biking trails.

Darien

Bartram's destination on his first trip to the coast was Darien. Today the city is located on U.S. 17, 7 miles east of I-95 on Ga. 251. Like Savannah, Darien was established by General Oglethorpe. In 1735 Oglethorpe commissioned Hugh Mackay and George Dunbar to recruit Scottish Highlanders to settle

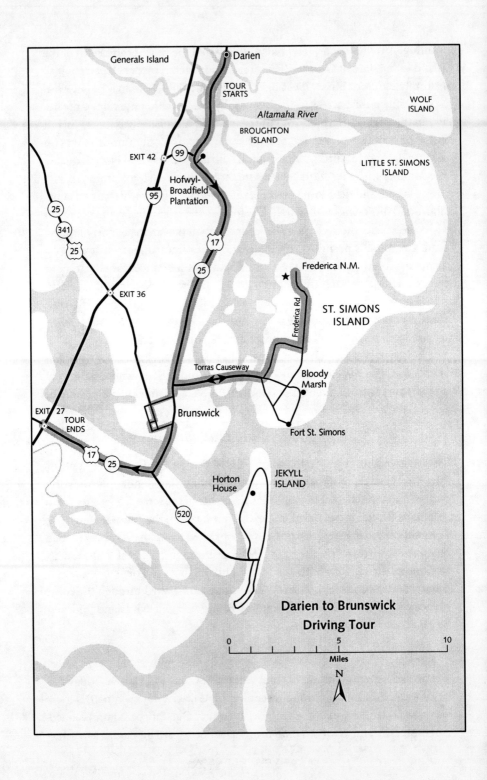

Darien to Brunswick
Driving Tour

0   5   10
            Miles

N

on the north bank of the Altamaha. In 1736, 166 Highlanders arrived at the high bluff east of the abandoned Fort King George. There, following a plan designed by Oglethorpe, the settlers constructed a fort, a chapel, and several huts. By 1739 the town's population had grown to more than forty families. When the war with Spain broke out, these families left to seek safety in outlying areas and the town was nearly deserted. By the late 1760s Darien had rebounded, although it remained little more than a village. In the report of his 1773 journey Bartram comments that "Darien Bluff is a fine situation for a Town" with water to the south "deep enough on the Barr, for large Vessells" (R432). The report also recounts a visit to "some ruins of the old town of Darien." Shortly after the Revolution, Darien flourished, emerging as both the center of commerce for the many river plantations that surrounded it and a major coastal shipping center. The site of Fort Darien is at the intersection of Broad Street and the bridge, although neither the fort nor any other colonial building survived the many fires that devastated the city in the nineteenth century.

Bartram visited Darien on four occasions, always as the guest of Lachlan McIntosh. McIntosh emigrated from Scotland in 1735 and first settled at the mouth of the Altamaha. He left Georgia to work in the countinghouse of Henry Laurens, then returned to become a land surveyor. During the Revolution he led patriot troops into battle in Georgia and Virginia. Lachlan McIntosh's plantation was probably on today's Generals Island—directly across from Darien on the north channel of the Altamaha. Mr. McIntosh not only offered Bartram his hospitality and friendship, he recommended his nephew John as a traveling companion (the *Travels* mistakenly refers to John as McIntosh's son). John McIntosh accompanied Bartram on his journey to Augusta and Cherokee Corners.

In the 1770s Darien was flanked by two abandoned British forts: Fort Barrington, 20 miles upstream; and Fort King George, less than a mile downstream. To visit Fort King George, which is now a state historic site, take Broad Street east from the north end of the U.S. 17 bridge in the center of town. Soon the road changes its name to Fort King George Drive.

Fort King George

The Carolina Assembly of 1720 suggested the construction of forts at Savannah Town and at the mouth of the Altamaha River to form a protective screen against Spanish incursions from the south and French advances from the west. These outposts would also serve as centers for trade between the colonists and the Indians. The British government approved the construction of only one fort—near the mouth of the Altamaha. The British built the fort in 1721 on the site of an abandoned Spanish mission, over the protests of the Spanish government. Triangular in shape, the fort was surrounded by a moat on two sides and bordered on the third by the Altamaha River. Its location offered a commanding view of the river upstream and the sound out to sea. Within its walls was a three-story wooden blockhouse with barracks, a house for officers, and a hospital/guardhouse. The fort was destroyed in a fire in 1725. Although partially rebuilt, the British withdrew the regiment bivouacked there to Port Royal in 1727. Five years later the fort was abandoned altogether.

Bartram visited the abandoned fort on one of his many journeys to Darien and reported that "about a mile below the Town on a Bluff of the River, remains part of one of the Angles of the Fort" (R432). There was no trace of the blockhouse or any other of the fort's buildings. By the 1770s the river had "encrouched upon the bluff" and carried with it the fort's foundation. Today, parts of the moat and parapet—a 6-foot-tall earthen embankment—have been restored. The blockhouse was reconstructed according to eighteenth-century plans in the 1980s and can be toured. Outside the current fort is the cemetery that was uncovered in the 1960s, with markers for the British soldiers who served and died at the fort. Also outside the fort is the site of a Guale Indian village—with the remains of fifteen houses constructed of wattle and daub. The Guale tribe inhabited the coastal region, from the Altamaha to Cumberland Island, until the middle of the eighteenth century. Attacked by a tribe to the north, the Guale abandoned the village for Sapelo Island.

The state historic site also offers a museum with exhibits and a film on the Guale; the Spanish mission, Santo Domingo de Talaje; and the history of the first British fort in Georgia. To continue the tour, return to Darien.

Fort Barrington

In the spring of 1773 Bartram left Darien for a trip to Brunswick. He traveled to the northwest 15 miles to Fort Barrington, following a route through present-day Cox. Both the paved road, Ga. 251, and the sand road between Cox and the fort closely approximate the road Bartram followed on that trip. Less than 2 miles from Cox is the site of the bog where Bartram and his father discovered *Franklinia*. That same day he reached the fort, which, although abandoned, was still standing. The British built the fortress in 1760 as a part of the colony's defense system against Indians and the French to the west. In the aftermath of the British victory in the Seven Years' War the fort no longer

Fort King George near Darien, Georgia. This structure at Fort King George State Historic Site is a replica of the British fortress.

had any strategic value. It did continue, well into the nineteenth century, as the site of the public ferry for the "high road," later the Old Post Road, connecting Savannah to the southern coastal settlements. Here Bartram crossed the river and continued his journey to Darien.

No trace of the ancient fortification survives today. The site is now a McIntosh County park with a campground. From Darien *take U.S. 17 North to the junction with Ga. 251. Turn left* and take Ga. 251 past I-95 **(mile 2.4)** to Cox **(mile 11.0)**. Just beyond Cox, *turn left onto Barrington Road*. Take the sand road for 4 miles; at its end is the park **(mile 15.0)**.

Across the river is the Sansavilla Wildlife Management Area. Here the Georgia DNR is developing a Bartram Trail—a loop more than 4 miles long with spur trails to the right bank of the river. The trail will be developed for both hiking and biking.

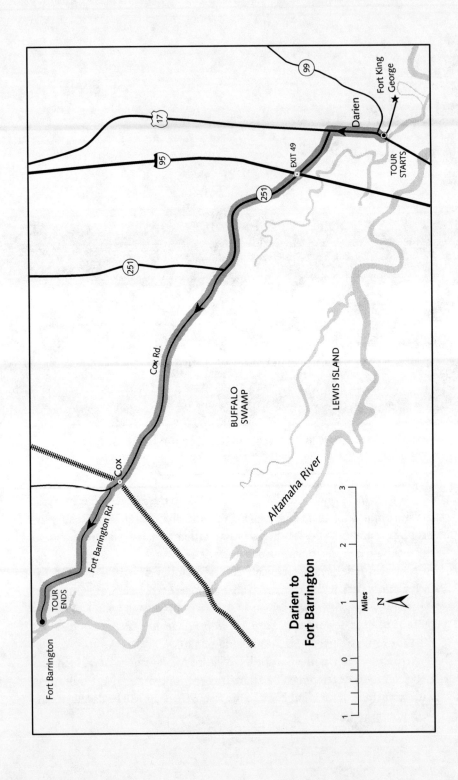

Darien to
Fort Barrington

N

Miles

0   1   2   3

99

Fort King
George

Darien

17

95

EXIT 49

251

TOUR
STARTS

251

Cox Rd.

BUFFALO
SWAMP

LEWIS ISLAND

Altamaha River

Cox

Fort Barrington Rd.

TOUR
ENDS

Fort Barrington

Fort Barrington, Georgia.

To begin the main tour to the south, *take U.S. 17 South from Darien.* Over the next 4 miles Ocean Highway crosses the four main channels of the Altamaha River. Immediately across the first channel is Generals Island, the likely home of Lachlan McIntosh's plantation, although no trace of either the plantation or McIntosh's home survives. Continue south over the next two channels of the river. After the third channel crossing, immediately to the left is Broughton Island—the site of the Laurens plantation Bartram visited in his journey to East Florida in early 1774. No trace of the plantation remains. To the south of Darien, Bartram visited the site of another ancient fort: "On the west banks of the south channel, ten or twelve miles above its mouth, and nearly opposite Darien, are to be seen the remains of an ancient fort, or for-

This plantation, not in existence during Bartram's expeditions, does provide the traveler of today with some sense of the many river plantations that were once found along the Altamaha. William Brailsford of Charleston settled this plantation around 1807, following in the footsteps of many Carolina planters who moved to Georgia in the late 1770s and early 1800s to establish rice plantations along the rich river delta. With slave labor, legal in the colony since 1749, planters were able to carve thousands of acres from the cypress swamps. By the Civil War, the plantation had grown to a size of 7,300 acres, with more than 300 slaves. The plantation slowly fell victim to the war and the lack of labor. In 1973 the Dent family willed it to the state of Georgia.

The Main House does include furnishings from the 1790s. On the grounds near the house are two live oaks that are 400–500 years old. On the way to the visitors' center is a 1-mile nature trail that skirts the marsh to the north and passes remnants of the old rice fields. There are two overlooks and an observation deck in the marsh.

---

tification. It is supposed to have been the work of the French or Spaniards" (T53). The site of this fort has not been located.

South of the last channel, marked "Altamaha River" **(mile 4.0)**, *continue south past Ga. 99.* One-tenth of a mile past the junction is the entrance for the **Hofwyl-Broadfield Plantation (mile 5.0)**.

Exit the historic site, returning to U.S. 17 South. Follow the highway south for more than 10 miles past the Brunswick city limits to the junction with the Torras Causeway **(mile 16.0)**. *Turn left, and follow the causeway over the Intracoastal Waterway* to St. Simons Island. To the right are views of the marshes of Glynn, set into poetry by Sidney Lanier. On the island, *turn left at Sea Island Road* **(mile 20.0)**. Follow the road for approximately 2 miles to Frederica Road. Turn left; in 3 miles the entrance for Fort Frederica will appear on the left **(mile 25)**.

Fort Frederica

On January 26, 1734, sailing from Savannah, Oglethorpe landed at the bluff that was to be the site of Fort Frederica. The bluff was strategically located at the middle of two right-angle bends in the Inland Passageway that would force any hostile vessel to slow down and turn right at the base of the fort, exposing it to Frederica's cannons before it was able to turn and fire its own guns. Immediately to the east was a clearing of more than 30 acres that

Fort Frederica, Fort Frederica National Monument, Georgia.

would serve as the land for the town supporting the fortress. By the spring of 1736 more than 100 men, women, and children, all recruited by Oglethorpe to settle his new colony, populated Frederica. That same year a garrison of British regulars, with their families, was ordered to the newly completed fort.

Bartram visited St. Simons and Frederica in the spring of 1774. As he landed at the fort, he noted that it "was regular and beautiful, constructed chiefly with brick, and was the largest, most regular, and perhaps most costly, of any in North America, of British construction" (T62). Frederica was the largest fort in Oglethorpe's defense system and one of the most expensive fortresses built by the British in the colonies. Its purpose was to protect the newly settled lands south of the Savannah River from Spanish incursions.

The defense system included three other fortresses: one on the southern shore of St. Simons and two on Cumberland Island. On St. Simons, Ogle-

Old Military Road near Fort Frederica at St. Simons Island, Georgia.

thorpe ordered the construction of a road connecting the island's two forts. The road, appropriately named the Military Road, was built in one day by the garrisons of the two forts. Bartram took this 9-mile road to the southern end of the island. In addition to the fortresses with garrisons there were a number of small forts on St. Simons and the mainland manned by rangers who scouted for Spanish and Indian intruders.[5]

Fort Frederica was built in the form of a star; a palisade and moat separated it from the town. At the fort's center was a magazine, part of whose tabby walls survive. Flanking the magazine were two storehouses whose foundations were excavated in the 1950s.

Town of Frederica

By 1740 the town had grown to more than 1,000 residents. Shortly after the battle at Bloody Marsh in 1742, Frederica suffered the same fate met by many of Oglethorpe's other settlements, depopulation. With the defeat of the Spanish and the Treaty of Aix-la-Chapelle in 1748 ending the war between Spain and Britain, the Frederica Regiment was disbanded. As the soldiers left, so did their families, soon followed by other settlers and tradesmen. Frederica's citizens either left for new lands or returned to England. Sealing Frederica's fate was the removal of the seat of government to the new colonial capital, Savannah. In 1758 most of Frederica's buildings were destroyed in a fire. What Bartram saw when he visited the fort in 1774 is similar to what the traveler of today sees: "The ruins also of the town only remain; peach trees, figs, pomegranates, and other shrubs, grow out of the ruinous walls of former spacious and expensive buildings" (T62). The town was not completely abandoned then, however; the fort was still occupied by a small garrison. Bartram noted "a few neat houses in good repair, and inhabited" remaining. He attributed the small recovery to the mercantile efforts of the island's president, James Spalding. The Spalding house, like the other Frederica houses, did not survive, although its foundation was excavated in the early 1950s. Bartram stayed at the house, where he received both hospitality and assistance for his forthcoming trip to East Florida. Spalding provided Bartram with letters to his agents on the St. Johns River "ordering them to furnish [Bartram] with horses, guides, and every other convenient assistance" (T58).

5. Ivers, "Rangers, Scouts, and Tythingmen," 158–159. Ivers notes that "by 1732 each southern colony had experimented with and adopted when necessary the system of ranging horsemen as the most convenient and reliable early warning system for frontier defense" (157).

Spalding House, Fort Frederica National Monument, St. Simons Island, Georgia.

From Frederica, continue the driving tour via the Torras Causeway to U.S. 17 **(mile 34)**. At the junction, *take U.S. 17 South*. To view the site of colonial Brunswick, *turn right onto Gloucester Street* **(mile 34.6)**.

Brunswick

Take Gloucester to the intersection with Newcastle. Turn left and follow New-castle for three and one-half blocks to Hanover Square. Like Savannah, Brunswick was planned as a grid centered on six large squares and four minor squares. Hanover Square, laid out in 1771, is one of the town's six original squares and the only one that survives in its original size. No colonial building, and only two antebellum structures, survived the Civil War. *From the square, continue on Newcastle to 1st Avenue. Turn left onto 1st and follow it to U.S. 17 and the end of the tour at the junction with I-95.*

Bicycle Tour: St. Simons Island

St. Simons Island has a system of paved bike paths from **Frederica** to the southern end of the island and from the Torras Causeway to the ocean.

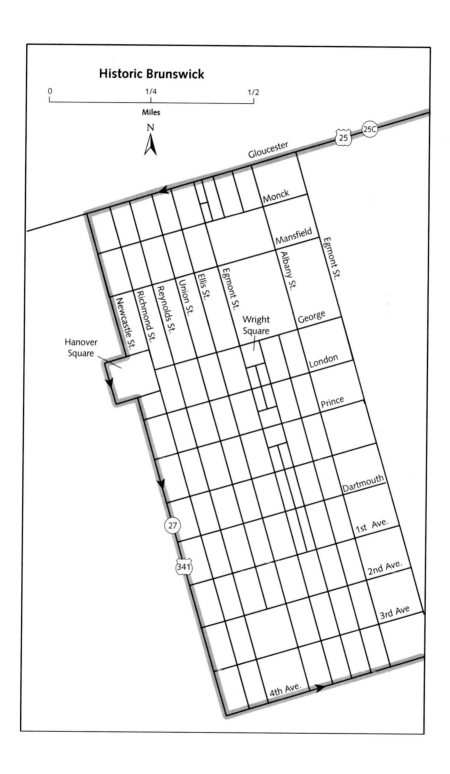

Historic Brunswick

0   1/4   1/2

Miles

N

25   25C

Gloucester

Monck

Mansfield

Albany St.

Egmont St.

George

Wright Square

London

Prince

Dartmouth

1st Ave.

2nd Ave.

3rd Ave

4th Ave.

Newcastle St.

Richmond St.

Reynolds St.

Union St.

Ellis St.

Egmont St.

Hanover Square

27

341

After crossing the Sidney Lanier Bridge, U.S. 17 South intersects the Jekyll Island Causeway on the left. *Take the causeway and follow it 6 miles to the island.* Jekyll Island is ringed by two roads: Beachview Drive on the east and Riverview on the west. Adjacent to these roads are more than 20 miles of bike trails.

Near the northern tip of the island is the site of the Horton House. Constructed around 1740, this two-story tabby house was the home of one of Oglethorpe's most trusted officers, William Horton. The tabby walls survive and are maintained as part of the Jekyll Island Historic District.

This tour is approximately 16 miles round-trip, beginning and ending at the fort.

From Frederica, *turn right onto the bike path parallel to Frederica road. Take the path south, past Sea Island Road, to Demere Road* **(mile 5.0)**. *Turn left and follow the path on the left to the east.* At the bend is the site of the **Battle of Bloody Marsh (mile 5.6)**, where the defensive network designed by Oglethorpe faced its expected challenge in the summer of 1742. In retaliation for the attempted British invasion of St. Augustine in 1740, the Spanish tried to destroy the center of the colonies' defense, Frederica, with an invasion force of fifty-two vessels. In early July men from the ships landed on the southern and western shores of St. Simons. On July 7, 1742, as they marched northward to Frederica, they were met on the Military Road at the edge of the marsh by British troops. The British routed the Spanish and forced them to retreat to the shore.

Continue on Demere Road to the East Beach Causeway. Turn left and follow the bike path for a little more than 0.5 mile to the junction with Ocean Boulevard **(mile 6.8)**. To the north are views of Bloody Marsh. From the junction, Massengale Park, with restrooms and beach access, is straight ahead. *At the junction, turn right and follow the path on Ocean Drive, past Arnold Drive* **(mile 7.1)**, to the intersection with 10th Street—10th Street is a continuation of Demere Road to the south. *Turn left onto 10th Street* and in two blocks the road turns to the right, becoming Beachview Drive as it enters St. Simons Village. Continue on Beachview Drive to 14th Street, with Neptune Park **(mile 8.0)** on the left. The park is named for Neptune Small, a former slave of the King family of Retreat Plantation who returned to the island after the Civil War and was given the land in recompense for his past service to the family. The park offers parking for both autos and bikes. At the eastern end of the

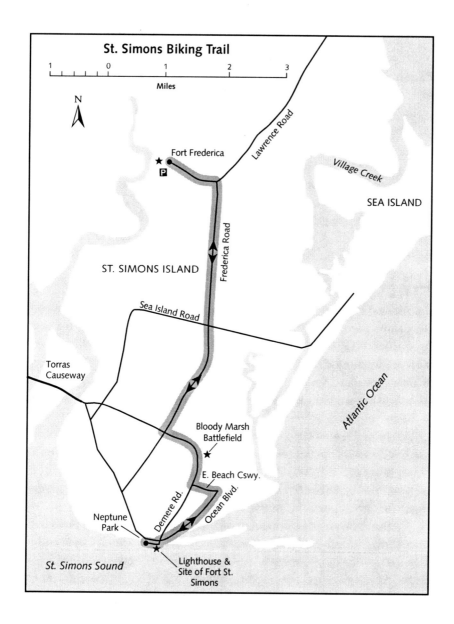

St. Simons Biking Trail

Miles

N

Fort Frederica

P

Lawrence Road

Village Creek

SEA ISLAND

Frederica Road

ST. SIMONS ISLAND

Sea Island Road

Torras Causeway

Atlantic Ocean

Bloody Marsh Battlefield

E. Beach Cswy.

Demere Rd.

Ocean Blvd.

Neptune Park

St. Simons Sound

Lighthouse & Site of Fort St. Simons

park is the St. Simons lighthouse. To the east was the site of **Fort St. Simons,** which was washed away by the ocean.

Return to the fort by backtracking on Beachview Drive and Ocean Drive, or more directly by staying on Beachview until it becomes Demere Road. *At the junction with Frederica Road, turn right* and return to the fort.

Parking is available at Fort Frederica, Neptune Park, and East Beach.

Bartram's description of the Okefenokee Swamp in the *Travels* is probably the most famous of the early accounts of the swamp.[6] He called this vast marsh by its Indian name, Ouaquaphenogaw, which means "trembling earth"—a reference to the movement of the ubiquitous peat islands. Although they look solid, they are floating islands that move or "tremble." Bartram understood the marsh to be immense, estimating its circumference at 300 miles. He also recognized its seasonal variation: "This vast accumulation of waters, in the wet season, appears as a lake, and contains some large islands or knolls, of rich high land" (T25–26).

Bartram's description includes two legends about the early inhabitants of the swamp. The first, also recorded by the British surveyor William de Brahm, claims that a "peculiar race of Indians" with "incomparably beautiful" women lived on one of the large islands in the swamp, referred to by the Creeks as the "most blissful spot on earth."[7] The women rescued lost hunters. The rescues were short-lived, however, for the women's husbands were strong and were known for their cruelty to strangers. Hunters who escaped told of these settlements and the kindness of the "daughters of the sun." The young men of the region, Bartram noted, "were inflamed with an irresistible desire to invade, and make a conquest of, so charming a country; but all their attempts hitherto have proved abortive."

The second legend has the swamp inhabited by "a fugitive remnant of the ancient Yamasess." In 1715 the Yamasees, joined by the Creeks and many other tribes, attacked the colonists in South Carolina. After a bloody conflict they were repelled by the British and forced southward into Florida—or, according to this legend, into the inner reaches of the swamp.

The beautiful and mysterious Okefenokee Swamp certainly captured Bartram's imagination. More than 400,000 acres in size—25 miles wide and 35 miles long—the swamp is one of the largest freshwater wetlands in the United States. Although called a swamp, it is actually a peat bog that formed 7,000 years ago on a shelf that might once have held a shallow marine lagoon.[8] As the sea level declined, the Trail Ridge—a 50-mile-long ridge of sand and clay that was a remnant of an ancient sea island—trapped water on the terrace.

6. W. Bartram, *Travels*, Harper's commentary, 339.

7. Coulter, "The Okefenokee Swamp," 174.

8. Wharton, *The Natural Environments of Georgia*, 87; *National Water Summary on Wetland Resources*, 164.

The trapped water supported a rich plant life, which decomposed after dying to create the peat swamp. Today an average of 2 feet of water stands on top of as many as 8–10 feet of peat created by plant matter that has decayed over the course of 7,000 years. Although small streams to the north and west supply some of the swamp's water, most of the Okefenokee's water comes from rainfall. Given peat's capacity for water retention, there is no direct correspondence between the swamp's water level, or stream flow, and rainfall. The highest levels of rainfall are during the summer months, whereas the highest levels of stream flow are in the late winter and spring. Every 30–40 years a dry period occurs, exposing large areas of peat to the atmosphere. Exposed peat and lightning strikes combine to produce wildfires. Every 100–200 years the swamp is subject to a severe drought resulting in extensive damage. During the last such drought, in 1954–55, more than 80 percent of the swamp burned. Without these fires the swamp would follow the natural course of succession and the wetland would be replaced by a mixed forest.

The swamp's flora is remarkably diverse. Cypress forests make up approximately one-fourth of it. Most of these are mixed with a subcanopy of dahoon holly, loblolly bay, and black gum. One-third of Okefenokee is "shrub swamp" dominated by fetterbush, titi, and dahoon. Prairies make up another quarter of the swamp. These treeless wetlands are of two types: grass-sedge prairies, with grasses that give the appearance of prairies from the Great Plains; and aquatic prairies, with water lilies, pickerel weed, and bladderwort. The swamp's seventy or so islands occupy more than 10 percent of its area. Finally, there are a number of lakes and ponds that vary in size and depth. As is true of most of the water near the coast, Okefenokee water is nearly black because of its high acid and tannin content.

Okefenokee History

Creek Indians inhabited the swamp until the early 1840s, when they were driven out by white settlers. In the late nineteenth century most of the swamp, then held by the state of Georgia, was sold to the Suwannee Canal Company, which planned to construct a canal between the St. Marys River and the Suwannee River to aid shipping from the Atlantic to the Gulf. The company also planned to drain the swamp and harvest the valuable cypress timber. More than 18 miles of canal was dredged, but at the end of the 1890s the company fell into bankruptcy. The swamp was sold in 1901 to Charles Hebard of Philadelphia. He and his brother established the Hebard Lumber Company, which successfully harvested the cypress timber. Unlike their predecessors, the Hebards did not attempt to drain the swamp. The loggers camped at Billy's Island and navigated through the swamp via hundreds of miles of tram railways. By the late 1920s they had harvested the most profitable timber, including cypress trees more than 900 years old. In 1927 the Hebards discontinued their logging operations, although they leased land to smaller mills on the swamp's eastern edge. In the early 1930s Francis Harper and many local residents tried to preserve the swamp when the state of Georgia revived interest in constructing a shipping canal from the Suwannee River to the St. Marys. Jean Harper, Francis Harper's wife, petitioned the president to save the swamp from destruction. Her petition was successful; on March 30, 1937, President Franklin Roosevelt signed an executive order making the greater part of the swamp a national wildlife refuge. Today, more than 90 percent of the swamp is administered by the U.S. Fish and Wildlife Service, making it the largest wilderness area in the eastern United States.

There are three entrances into the swamp: East, West, and Kingfisher. The Suwannee Canal Recreation Area at the East Entrance and Stephen C. Foster State Park at the West Entrance offer recreational opportunities. At the Suwannee Canal there are a variety of ways for the day visitor to experience the swamp—on foot, by bike or car, or by boat or canoe. Stephen C. Foster State Park offers the same opportunities along with camping and rental cottages. The best way to experience the swamp is by traveling its 120 miles of waterways, in particular the trails set aside for wilderness canoeing.

Okefenokee Swamp Canoe Trails

Each canoe trail is limited to one party daily; the size of a party can range from two to twenty. Six areas in the swamp are designated for wilderness camping: five are on wooden platforms, and one is on Floyd's Island. The Red, Green, Blue, and Orange Trails are described below.

Red Trail

Section: Kingfisher Landing to Stephen C. Foster State Park
Distance: 31 miles
Hazards: narrow passages; snags
Highlights: Floyd's Prairie

The trail winds for 12 miles through shrub swamp, small prairies, and five small lakes. As the trail approaches Maul Hammock Lake, it enters Sapling Prairie. Beyond the shelter, the trail continues through the prairie to Dinner Pond. From the pond to Big Water Lake the trail passes through a number of

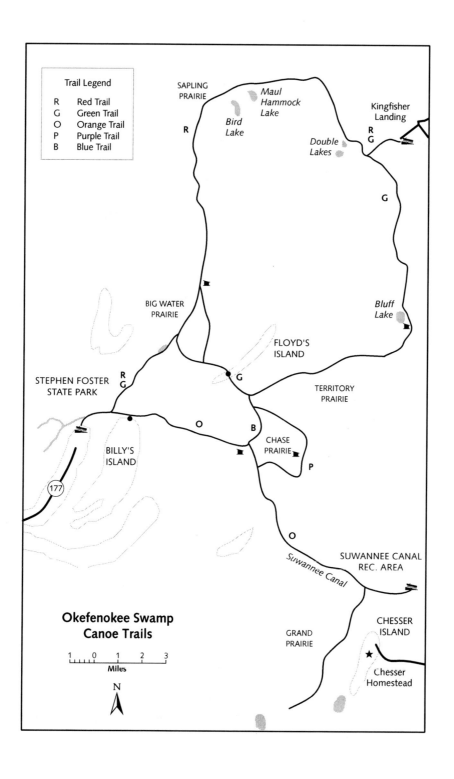

Trail Legend

R   Red Trail
G   Green Trail
O   Orange Trail
P   Purple Trail
B   Blue Trail

SAPLING PRAIRIE

Maul Hammock Lake

Bird Lake

Double Lakes

Kingfisher Landing

R

R
G

G

BIG WATER PRAIRIE

FLOYD'S ISLAND

Bluff Lake

STEPHEN FOSTER STATE PARK

R
G

G

TERRITORY PRAIRIE

O

B

CHASE PRAIRIE

P

BILLY'S ISLAND

177

O

Suwannee Canal

SUWANNEE CANAL REC. AREA

CHESSER ISLAND

GRAND PRAIRIE

★ Chesser Homestead

**Okefenokee Swamp
Canoe Trails**

1   0   1   2   3
Miles

N

narrow channels lined by cypress forests and scrub swamp. The trail crosses Big Water Lake, which is nearly 2 miles long—the second-largest lake in the swamp. Exiting the lake, the channel remains wide as it approaches the northern edge of Floyd's Prairie and the Big Water Shelter **(mile 22)**.

At the shelter is a spur trail to the east leading to Floyd's Prairie. The Red Trail continues to the south on the main channel, along the western edge of Floyd's Prairie. Soon the trail is joined from the left by the Green Trail, which leads in a little more than a mile to Floyd's Island. From the junction south, the Green and Red Trails share the same route. Less than 2 miles from the junction both trails enter Minnies Lake. To the east is a platform for those who want to take a break or have a picnic lunch. The trails continue to work to the south, entering an extensive cypress swamp as they leave the lake. The swamp ends, and the channel widens as the trails approach Billy's Lake **(mile 29—Red Trail)**. The trail turns to the right and crosses the wide lake, heading to the west. Here the Orange Trail joins with the Red and Green Trails. In less than 2 miles all the trails reach Stephen C. Foster State Park, after turning to the south to enter the canal to the boat dock.

Green Trail

Section:	Kingfisher Landing to Stephen C. Foster State Park
Distance:	26 miles
Hazards:	narrow passages; cypress knees; may be impassible in low water
Highlights:	Bluff Lake, Chase Prairie, Floyd's Island

The trail winds for a mile through shrub swamp. For the next 7 miles, to the Bluff Lake Shelter, the trail follows the course of a channel originally cut for peat mining. The channel winds through four small lakes and small prairies that feature floating iris and pitcher plants. South of the shelter **(mile 8)**, the trail winds through a number of hammocks, with channels both narrow and shallow, then widens as it enters two small lakes **(mile 10)**. Soon the channel widens as the trail enters Territory Prairie, then narrows again **(mile 14)** as the trail leaves the prairie. To the west, the trail enters Chase Prairie. Here, in May 1998, a black bear crossed (or rather swam across) the trail 100 yards ahead of our canoe. Soon the trail intersects the Blue and Purple Trails to the left. To continue on the Green Trail, make a sharp right at the junction.

As the Green Trail approaches **(mile 16)** Floyd's Island, it enters a cypress swamp. After a little more than a mile the trail reaches the island. There is a

*Cypress trees lining the Red–Green Canoe Trail near Billy's Lake,
Okefenokee Swamp, Georgia.*

0.5-mile portage across the island. The foot trail passes the Hebard family's hunting cabin, which is open for campers. Surrounding the cabin are many suitable areas for camping. On the west side of the island the canoe trail continues, following the southern boundary of Floyd's Prairie—the largest in the swamp. From the island the path heads to the northwest for nearly 2 miles, intersecting the Red Spur Trail. Continue on the Green Trail to the left. In a little more than a mile the trail intersects the main channel of the Red Trail **(mile 19.6)**. From the junction the trail turns to the southwest and the two trails follow the same route to Billy's Lake and Stephen C. Foster State Park. See the earlier description of the Red Trail for the remainder of the route.

Blue Trail

Section: Green Trail to Orange Trail
Distance: 3 miles
Hazards: none
Highlights: views of Territory Prairie

This trail connects the Green and Orange Trails. The Blue Trail works to the southeast through Territory Prairie and ends at the Orange Trail after a little more than 3 miles.

Orange Trail

Section: Suwannee Canal to Stephen C. Foster State Park
Distance: 17 miles
Hazards: narrow passages; cypress knees west of canal
Highlights: Billy's Island

The first 9 miles of this trail follow the canal built by the Suwannee Canal Company between 1891 and 1894. The canal soon intersects **(mile 2.0)** the day-use trails leading to Grand Prairie and Gannett Lake to the south. To the north is a short trail into the southern portion of Mizell Prairie. The trail continues upstream, intersecting the southern trailhead for the Purple Trail **(mile 7.0)**. In 2 miles the canal reaches the junction with the Blue Trail **(mile 9.0)** leading to the Green Trail and Floyd's Island. At the junction is a rest area with boat dock, picnic tables, and latrine. A mile beyond the junction, on the canal berm, is the Canal Run Shelter for overnight camping **(mile 10.0)**. Past the shelter the narrow trail winds for 5 miles, ending at the northern end of Billy's Island **(mile 15.0)**. The last 2 miles pass through the wide and deep lake, ending at Stephen C. Foster State Park.

Suwannee Canal Recreation Area

This recreation area offers a number of different ways to experience the swamp. Thirty miles of day-use trails for canoes and motorboats with engines less than 10 horsepower afford the opportunity to visit three of the Okefenokee Swamp's largest prairies: Chesser, Grand, and Mizell. In addition, there are guided trips on pontoon boats, approximately 2 hours in length. Near the boat and canoe dock is a visitors' center with exhibits on the flora and fauna of the swamp.

Swamp Island Drive

The visitors' center is also the trailhead for Swamp Island Drive—an 8-mile loop for driving or bicycling that leads to one of the swamp's largest islands,

Chesser Island. En route to the island the drive passes two short hiking trails, the Canal Diggers Trail and the Peckerwood; a small pond usually affording views of alligators; and an exhibit on the value of prescribed burns. On the northern edge of the island is the Chesser family's homestead **(mile 0.0)**, built in 1927; it has been restored for tourists. Near the homestead is one of the swamp's many Indian mounds, evidence of the culture that occupied this area nearly 4,000 years ago. At the western end of the island is a 4,000-foot boardwalk into the swamp that is connected to the homestead site by both the Deerstand Trail, for hiking only, and the paved Swamp Island Drive. The distance for both routes is just over 0.5 mile. The boardwalk ends at the northern edge of Sea-grove Lake, where an observation tower offers outstanding views of Chesser Prairie. On the boardwalk are two side boardwalks leading to photo blinds.

Stephen C. Foster State Park

This 80-acre park is totally within the boundaries of the wildlife refuge. Located on Jones Island, it serves as the western entrance to the Okefenokee Swamp, although it lies 6.5 miles east of the swamp's western edge. Aside from the scenic drive into the refuge, the park offers a short hiking trail and access to day-use waterways in the swamp. The Trembling Earth Nature Trail is a little more than 1 mile in length. Its trailhead is at the park office and trading post. The loop begins to the right and in a little more than 0.25 mile reaches the boardwalk. This elevated path leaves the island and heads for more than 0.5 mile into the swamp. Returning to the loop, the trail leads back to the trading post.

The use of the 25 miles of day-use waterways is coordinated at the trading post. The day-use routes follow sections of the refuge's Red, Green, Brown, and Orange Trails. The most commonly canoed section of the Red Trail is the 10-mile round-trip to Minnies Lake. On the western side of the narrow lake is a day-use shelter. The day-use section of the Red Trail does extend as far north as Big Water Lake, another 7 miles north of Minnies Lake. The round-trip distance of 24 miles is better suited for a motorboat. The day-use section of the Orange Trail leads, to the east, to Billy's Island. This 4-mile trail (round-trip) passes through Billy's Lake, the longest and largest of the Okefenokee Swamp's lakes. Just south of the dock on the island is the trailhead for a short hiking trail (ca. 0.3 mile) that passes by a shallow Indian mound and the site of the logging community. In the 1920s and 1930s this was a bustling town with a population of more than 600 people. To the west are two day-use trails: the Brown, approximately 10 miles round-trip, passes through the western end of Billy's Lake and leads to the Suwannee River Sill at the river's head. Along the sill is another day-use trail, 4.6 miles long from the Suwannee River

Sill boat ramp on The Pocket to Pine Island. At **mile 1.5** the sill trail intersects the Brown Trail coming from the east.

The museum offers interpretations of the park's history and ecosystem. The park has a developed campground, cottages, and concessions including motorboat, johnboat, canoe, and bicycle rentals. Also offered are guided boat tours, three times a day.

CUMBERLAND ISLAND

Bartram visited Cumberland Island in the spring of 1774 en route to Florida. He departed Frederica on a trading vessel bound for Spalding's Lower Store on the St. Johns River. The vessel sailed "betwixt a chain of sea-coast islands, and the main," following the same safe passage that is today's Intracoastal Waterway (T63). As they progressed southward through Cumberland Sound they encountered a trading schooner heading north with bad news: Indians had plundered Spalding's Upper Store, "and the traders escaped, only with their lives" (T63). The Lower Store, 40 miles downstream from the Upper Store, also anticipated an attack and most of the store's goods had been hidden on an island 5 miles to the south. This stash included Bartram's chest, forwarded earlier from Savannah. After hearing this news the captain of Bartram's vessel decided to return to Frederica for instructions. Bartram was resolved to continue his southward journey, anxious to recover his valuable books and papers, which he "could not do well without" (T64). The captain put Bartram and another passenger who did not want to return to Frederica down on the western shore of Cumberland. It is not clear where they landed, although the *Travels* indicates that they were anticipating a walk of a "few miles to a fort, at the south end of the island" (T64).

The fort was Fort William, built in 1740 as a part of General Oglethorpe's defense against Spanish aggression. By 1774 it had ceased to be a military outpost and was instead home to the St. Marys River pilot, who guided ocean ships into the sound or the river (R158). When they reached the fort, Bartram and his co-traveler asked the pilot to ferry them across the river to Amelia Island, which he did the following day.

Cumberland Today

Cumberland, 17 miles long and 3 miles wide at the north end, is the largest of Georgia's twelve barrier islands. The island comprises more than 15,000 acres

Cumberland Island, Georgia; view of the Atlantic from the North Cut on the north side of the island.

of high land and 8,000 acres of saltwater marsh, with an ocean beach as wide as 300 feet at low tide bounding the eastern side. Inland from the sandy shore are first the primary dunes, some as high as 50 feet, and then the secondary dunes, often buffered by dune meadow with wax myrtle and willow, and in drier areas by saw palmetto and yucca. Much of the interior of the island is either mixed oak-hardwood forest or oak-pine forest. The former, which dominates in freshwater lowlands, has a canopy of live oak, laurel oak, bay, cabbage palm, and southern magnolia with staggerbush and wax myrtle lower to the ground. The latter is a mixture of oaks and pine, with pine dominating in some areas. Near the sound and the saltwater marshes are maritime strands of live oaks draped with Spanish moss joined by cabbage palm, shadowing thickets of yaupon, and saw palmetto.

Cumberland's History

The National Park Service brochure for Cumberland suggests that part of the island's attraction is its relatively unspoiled environment. People have lived on the island for thousands of years, but never, the brochure says, "in such numbers as to permanently alter the character of the landscape."[9] Many areas of the island do appear pristine, but this appearance is deceiving. As John Ehrenhard notes in the Southeast Archaeological Center's (SEAC) survey of Cumberland's archaeological and historical resources, "the history of Cumberland is one of intensive and sometimes drastic modification" of the island's physical geography.[10]

Seventeen thousand years ago Georgia's Atlantic shoreline was nearly 200 feet below today's level. For the next 12,000 years the sea level rose, reaching today's levels around 2500 B.C. As barrier islands formed, aboriginal peoples ventured out to exploit the abundant food resources of the emerging marshes. Small shell middens or ridges near their old villages and camps bear witness to that abundance. On Cumberland there are nineteen prehistoric sites, all but one along the marsh fall line. Four of the sites date back to 2000 B.C.: two near Plum Orchard, one near Hush Your Mouth Island, and the largest at Dungeness. These sites are distinguished by Orange-culture ceramics contemporary with the St. Simons culture on other parts of the Georgia coast. Both cultures constructed either shell middens or ridges and crafted pottery by adding fiber to raw clay. This culture was followed by the Deptford (A.D. 500–750), with prominent sites at Stafford and Table Point, and then the Wilmington (750–1000), with sites at Dungeness and the Raccoon Keys.[11]

Of the nineteen prehistoric sites inventoried by the SEAC, most have been damaged either by natural forces such as wave action or by vandalism or mining. Traces of the cultures that inhabited these areas do remain for today's visitors to inspect.

At the time of European contact a tribe called the Timucua inhabited Cumberland. The Timucuans controlled northeastern Florida from Lake George

9. National Park Service, *Cumberland Island National Seashore, Georgia: Official Map and Guide.*

10. Ehrenhard, "Cumberland Island National Seashore," 37.

11. Milanich, *The Timucua,* 21–23.

to the mouth of the St. Johns River and occupied the Georgia coast from Cumberland Island to the Altamaha River. These coastal lands were part of Tacatacuru's chiefdom, which was forged by the Spanish in the middle of the sixteenth century into the Mocama district. The leading town for the Mocama district was San Pedro, located near today's Dungeness Wharf. Mission work to convert the Timucuans to Christianity had begun as early as 1585. By 1602 Franciscan missionaries had constructed a sizable mission at San Pedro and claimed more than 300 converts. There was another mission at San Antonio and a second major mission at the northern end of the island, San Pablo de Puturiba—located at today's Brick Hill Bluff. By 1685 the missions and towns had been deserted as the result of brutal attacks by other tribes and pirate raids. The island's inhabitants migrated south, closer to St. Augustine on Amelia Island.

The early eighteenth century saw the demise of the Timucuans and signaled the end of Spanish rule on the Georgia coast. During the Yamasee War of 1715, the Creeks, Choctaws, and Yamasees rebelled against the Carolina settlers. The Carolinians retaliated with a massive offensive, routing their attackers. The Yamasees fled into Spanish Florida, doubling the native population of St. Augustine, and the Timucuans became a minority in their own land. For fifty years their numbers declined. When Florida was surrendered to the British in 1763, the surviving Timucuans accompanied the Spanish refugees to Cuba.

Britain's determination to defend Carolina from both Indian aggression and the Spanish was bolstered with the creation of the buffer colony of Georgia. As part of the colony's defense, General Oglethorpe commissioned two forts on Cumberland. Fort St. Andrew was built in the late 1730s near the northern end of Cumberland. Fort William was built at South Point. These fortresses lost their strategic value after the defeat of the Spanish at Bloody Marsh in 1742. According to the journal of Isaac Levy, visiting Cumberland in 1753, Fort St. Andrew was in ruins and a corporal and six men occupied Fort William. Not one of the twenty families who once held plantations in the Dungeness area remained. The plantations were deserted, and, aside from the men in the southern fort, "there was not a single inhabitant on the island."[12]

Cumberland was not deserted for long. In 1759 the Quaker "secessionist" Edmund Gray and 200 of his followers moved to the island. The settlement did not succeed, although an undetermined number of Gray's followers con-

12. Bullard, "Cumberland Island's Dungeness," 74.

tinued to live on the island into the 1760s and 1770s. By 1765 the British crown had decided to issue land grants for Cumberland, and that same year Jonathan Bryan acquired 800 acres at Dungeness. By 1770 he owned a substantial portion of the entire island. He in turn sold the land to two South Carolinians: Alexander Rose and Thomas Lynch.

After the Revolution the Lynch properties were passed along to family heirs. The Rose lands passed through a number of owners until Gen. Nathaniel Greene, the Revolutionary War hero, purchased them, hoping to build a mansion and plantation at Dungeness. After his untimely death in 1786, Greene's widow, Catherine, went ahead with his plans to build the home. Completed in 1802, it was called Dungeness, and it was the heart of a thriving cotton plantation until the Civil War. Two other large-scale cotton plantations and a number of smaller yeoman farms joined it, but the Civil War ended all farming activities on Cumberland Island. In 1866 Dungeness burned to the ground. In 1884 Thomas M. Carnegie, who now owned the plantation, replaced the mansion with his own brick mansion. It too was destroyed by fire, in 1959. In the mid-1950s the National Park Service completed feasibility studies for a national recreation area on Cumberland. Seeking to stop development of the island, the Carnegies sold their holdings to the National Park Service in 1971; a year later Congress established Cumberland Island National Park.

The National Park Service administers approximately 85 percent of the island and leases extensive plots of land to the original landowners and their descendants. To maintain the island's ecology, the Park Service limits the number of visitors to the island to 300 a day. The park has more than 50 miles of hiking trails, and the seashore offers visitors four camping areas: three in the backcountry and one developed campground: Sea Camp. Sea kayakers traveling the Intracoastal Waterway can use the backcounty campsite at Brickhill Bluff. From April to November there are daily passenger ferries. Reservations are required for visitation and camping. No vehicles or bicycles are allowed save for those belonging to permanent residents and their guests. The Carnegie family's icehouse at Dungeness dock has been converted into a small museum. The National Park Service opened the Mainland Museum in the city of St. Marys in early 2000.

ACCESS

St. Marys is 8 miles east of I-95 on Ga. 40, a little more than 30 miles north of Jacksonville, Florida. The visitors' center provides parking for both day visitors and campers. The boat dock for the passenger ferry is located at the visitors' center. Web site: www.nps.gov/cuis/

Cumberland Island Hiking Trails

Dungeness Trail

Section: loop from Sea Camp dock
Distance: 3.9 miles
Hazards: none
Highlights: Sea Camp (on the ocean); Dungeness

From the Sea Camp dock, take the trail marked for the Sea Camp camping area. Heading to the east, the footpath intersects the Main Road in a little more than 0.5 mile. Cross the sand road and continue on the path. From the dock to the campground the trail passes through a stand of oak-palmetto forest. Spanish moss drapes the canopy of live and laurel oaks, and the ground is covered with palmetto grass. Just as the trail approaches the dunes it enters the campground **(mile 0.5)**. To the right is a shelter with a restroom and purified water. Continue straight ahead and the path reaches a long wooden boardwalk that crosses the primary dunes. The boardwalk ends and the path reaches the beach-crossing post **(mile 0.6)**.

From the beach post turn right and walk down the beach to the south. In just over 1.25 miles the Dungeness beach post appears to the right. Turn to the right, toward the post **(mile 1.9)**. Follow the path cutting across the wide, tall primary dunes and then the secondary dunes. The trail levels into an open area known as Beach Field, then briefly enters a hardwood forest with a mature stand of live oaks. To the left is a short spur trail leading to the south end cemetery **(mile 2.4)**. As the path approaches an intersection, the carriage house and servants' quarters are on the left. The Carnegie family employed as many as 200 servants to maintain Dungeness and three other mansions. The path soon becomes a road, still in use, leading to the **Dungeness** mansion.

The ruins are all that remains of the mansion built by Thomas and Lucy Carnegie in the late 1880s and destroyed by fire in 1959. They stand on the site of the original Dungeness, built by the Widow Greene and her second husband. Both mansions were built on a terrace constructed from the leveled remains of a shell mound that once rose above Cumberland's southern marsh. Follow the road to the right, to the front of the mansion. At the front, turn right and take the main drive through the Dungeness gates.

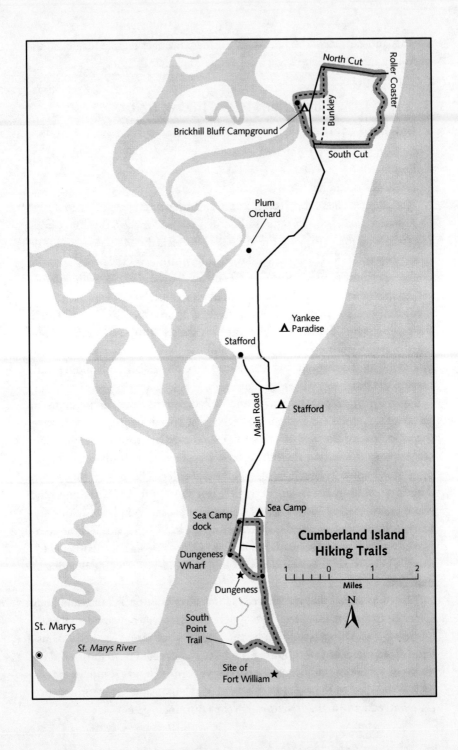

North Cut

Roller Coaster

Bunkley

Brickhill Bluff Campground

South Cut

Plum Orchard

Yankee Paradise

Stafford

Stafford

Main Road

Sea Camp

Sea Camp dock

Cumberland Island Hiking Trails

Dungeness Wharf

Dungeness

South Point Trail

1   0   1   2
Miles

N

St. Marys

St. Marys River

Site of Fort William

Turn left, leaving the Main Road, at the first crossroads **(mile 2.9)**. After 0.25 mile the road reaches the Dungeness dock **(mile 3.1)**. Just before the dock, turn right and walk past the Ice House Museum, which has exhibits on the history of the island. From there follow the River Trail northward. The path follows the channel to the west for 0.25 mile, then returns to the maritime forest. After approximately 0.75 mile the trail reaches the Sea Camp dock **(mile 3.9)**.

Roller Coaster Loop

Section: loop trail from Brickhill Bluff
Distance: 6.4 miles
Hazards: hiking across dunes
Highlights: sand dunes near Whitney Lake; ocean views

This loop comprises all or part of five trails at the northern end of the park's wilderness area. The loop starts and ends at the northernmost campground, Brickhill Bluff. Two outstanding features on the trail are the secondary dunes north of the lake and the shallow bluffs overlooking Cumberland Sound (or river). Unlike the forest near the Sea Camp dock, much of the vegetation here is very young, with thick (and impassable) ground cover and a canopy of scattered scrub pines. The trail also skirts one of the island's largest lakes, Lake Whitney, which is surrounded by extensive wetlands.

From the campsite continue northward on the Brickhill Bluff Trail. The path stays close to the shore of the river for less than 0.2 mile, then turns sharply to the right and the east. In a little more than 0.25 mile the trail intersects the Main Road **(mile 0.5)**. Continue across the road. In less than another 0.5 mile the trail intersects the Bunkley Trail. The area surrounding this intersection has just recovered from the extensive logging that went on until the late 1960s.

Turn left onto the Bunkley Trail, which ends at the North Cut Road **(mile 1.6)**. *Turn right and take the road to the east.* To the left and right are areas of newly restored forest and marshland. As the road reaches the secondary dunes, the trailhead for the Roller Coaster Trail is on the right **(mile 2.9)**. *Turn right and follow the trail, on the bed of an old road, to the southwest.*

After a few hundred feet the road enters the vast secondary dunes—white sand dunes up to 40 feet tall with a few palms and palmettos interspersed. The trail leaves the road **(mile 3.6)** at the northern edge of Lake Whitney, turning to the left. For the next 0.3 mile the path rolls up and down over a series of dunes, making for difficult hiking, then descends toward the lake on

*Roller Coaster Trail, looking out over Whitney Lake,
Cumberland Island National Seashore, Georgia.*

the back side of the dunes. Returning to a maritime forest, the footpath continues southward for more than 0.5 mile until it reaches the junction with the **South Cut Trail (mile 4.6)**.

This trail is one of the series of east–west roads that cross the island providing its year-round residents with access to the beach. To reach the beach, turn left and follow the trail for approximately 0.2 mile. To complete the loop and return to Brickhill Bluff, *turn right and follow the South Cut Trail to the west*. This trail is a sand road, still in use. In 1.25 miles the road ends at the Main Road **(mile 5.9)**. *Turn right*. The southern trailhead for the Bunkley Trail is 0.2 mile on the right. Continue on the road to the junction with the Brickhill Bluff Trail (on the left) and the Killman Field Trail (on the right) **(mile 6.3)**. *Turn left* and follow the trail a little more than 0.1 mile to the campsite.

ALTAMAHA RIVER

*How gently flow thy peaceful floods, O Alatamaha! How sublimely
rise to view, on thy elevated shores, yon Magnolian groves, from whose tops
the surrounding expanse is perfumed, by clouds of incense. (T 48)*

The occasion for Bartram's ode to Georgia's most majestic river was his 50-mile canoe trip in 1776. By then the Altamaha was already a familiar sight to him. In 1765 he and his father had explored the area surrounding Fort Barrington, west of today's Cox, where they discovered a rare flowering tree that they named *Franklinia altamaha,* for Benjamin Franklin and the Georgia river. William returned to the Altamaha in April 1773 and stayed at the McIntosh plantation on Generals Island in the river's wide delta. Later that month he returned to Barrington, ferrying across the river to visit Brunswick. On a later trip to St. Marys via the Post Road he returned to the ferry and the river. Finally, after his return from a visit to the Creek Nation in 1776 Bartram revisited "several districts in Georgia and the East borders of Florida" (T 467).

In the summer of 1776 Bartram "ascended this beautiful river, on whose fruitful banks the generous and true sons of liberty dwell, fifty miles beyond the last white settlement."[13] Along the Altamaha's four main channels were a series of rice plantations sustained by the river's gentle floods. The plantation owners included some of Bartram's friends and benefactors, notably Lachlan McIntosh and Henry Laurens, who were indeed "sons of liberty" in their support of the Revolutionary cause. Fifty miles beyond the last plantation would have brought our traveler just beyond Jesup, Georgia, perhaps as far upriver as Beard's Bluff.

13. W. Bartram, *Travels,* Harper's commentary, 346. The narrative suggests the canoe trip was in the spring of 1773. Harper places the trip three years later, in 1776, for two reasons. First, Bartram witnessed a lunar eclipse. No eclipse occurred in 1773 or 1774, but a partial lunar eclipse occurred on July 31, 1776. Second, Bartram reports viewing the *Franklinia* in "perfect bloom." A fall trip up the river would have been far past the tree's flowering season.

Bartram made his journey alone, traveling in a light cypress canoe provided by Henry Laurens. For the first 15 miles the river was tidal, so he could have floated upstream with the tide. For the remainder of the journey, upstream of today's Altamaha River Park, Bartram paddled hard against "the mighty floods of the river" (T49). As he traveled upstream he observed the bluffs "in nearly flat horizontal masses" made of "sandy lime-stone." After a few days, Bartram returned downstream to Broughton Island.

Today the Altamaha remains a "large majestic river, flowing with gentle windings through a vast plain forest" (T53). In terms of volume it is Georgia's largest, draining more than a third of the state. It is formed by the confluence of the Oconee and Ocmulgee Rivers approximately 100 miles from the coast. Bartram believed that the Altamaha extended northward into the mountains in Cherokee country (T51). Although that is not true, the headwaters of the Oconee and Ocmulgee Rivers do reach far into the Piedmont, as far as the South and Yellow Rivers in suburban Atlanta. The Altamaha is also one of Georgia's widest rivers, averaging a width of 500 feet for most of its last 50 miles, and approaching 1,000 feet before it divides into a series of channels before reaching Darien Sound. It is the only large river on the eastern shore that has never been dammed or channelized. Its course cuts through wide marshes, forming a complex series of side streams interrupted by small islands.

It is still possible to experience this majestic river with its "marvelous scenes of primitive nature, as yet unmodified by the hand of man" (T49) on the Bartram Canoe Trail from Doctortown to Darien. A traveler can enjoy the bluffs at Joyner Island, the deep forests and distant hills that still flank the river, and the sight and sound of sandhill cranes. The forests remain, but with one exception the virgin stands of enormous cypress and other hardwood trees Bartram described were the victims of two centuries of lumbering. In their place are second-growth forests, most of them in state wildlife management areas, protecting habitats for birds and other animals. Spared the lumber mill are the old-growth stands of hardwoods on Lewis Island, 5 miles upstream from Darien. The Georgia Nature Conservancy calls this 8-mile-long island "a unique remnant of the great hardwood forests that once cloaked Georgia's river floodplains."[14] One of the largest and oldest stands of tidewater cypress and tupelo gum trees in Georgia grows here. One tree is thought to be 1,300 years old; many others have diameters of 6 or 7 feet. This remote area is accessible only by boat.

14. Burger, *Georgia Wildlands*.

Bartram Canoe Trail: Altamaha River

This 50-mile trail follows the course of the Altamaha River from Doctortown, near Jesup, to Darien. For the first 30 miles the trail winds through the Penholoway Swamp, passing islands and high bluffs. This section is remote, with the only emergency access at private docks. The river widens from 200 feet to an average of 400 feet as it approaches Fort Barrington. South of the fort, the river becomes tidal and wider. As the Altamaha approaches the Darien River, two channels appear on the left. These connect with Lewis Creek, providing paddlers with an alternate route to the wide river. Both Lewis Creek and the river to the south pass Lewis Island. The trail ends, taking Rifle Cut to Darien and the dock at the U.S. 17 bridge.

Doctortown to Fort Barrington

Section: Doctortown to the landing at Fort Barrington
Distance: 30 miles
Hazards: 26-mile section with no access; motorboats
Highlights: river bluffs; sandbars; wildlife

From the put-in at Doctortown it is 3 miles downstream to Doe Eddy. The first reliable camping (except in times of low water) is another 7 miles farther, at Big Water Oak Round **(mile 10)**. From there it is 6 miles by river to Bug Bluff. The bluffs to the east are part of Joyner Island; to the west they are part of Boyles Island. These bluffs, ranging from 30 to 50 feet high, are the edges of high plateaus. Continuing downstream, it is another 3 miles to Sturgeon Hole, with the river averaging 200 feet in width along the way. In the next 7 miles it widens to 300–400 feet at Upper Sansavilla, the first public boating access south of Doctortown **(mile 26)**. It is another 1.5 river miles to Lower Sansavilla, which has a boating ramp with easier access. In a little more than 3 miles there is a channel on the left leading to **Fort Barrington**.

ACCESS POINTS

Doctortown: Located immediately to the east of U.S. 25 in Jesup, Georgia. The public put-in is just to the east of the Rayonier plant, on the south side of the river.

Lower Sansavilla: The put-in is on the southeast side of the river, in the Sansavilla Wildlife Management Area. Access to the put-in is off Sansavilla Road, north of Mount Pleasant. Mount Pleasant is on U.S. 25 north of Brunswick.

Fort Barrington: From Darien, take U.S. 17 North to the junction with Ga.

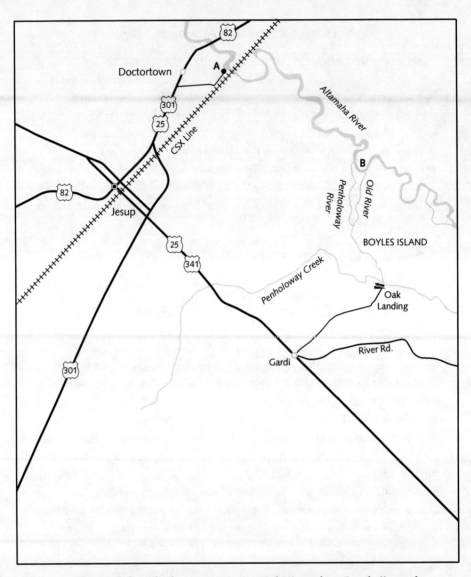

251. Turn left and take Ga. 251 past I-95 **(mile 2.4)** to Cox **(mile 11.0)**.
Just beyond Cox, turn left onto Barrington Road. Take the sand road
for 4 miles; at its end is the park **(mile 15.0)**. Near the landing are
restrooms and a public campground.

Fort Barrington to Darien

Section: Fort Barrington Landing to Darien
Distance: 19 miles

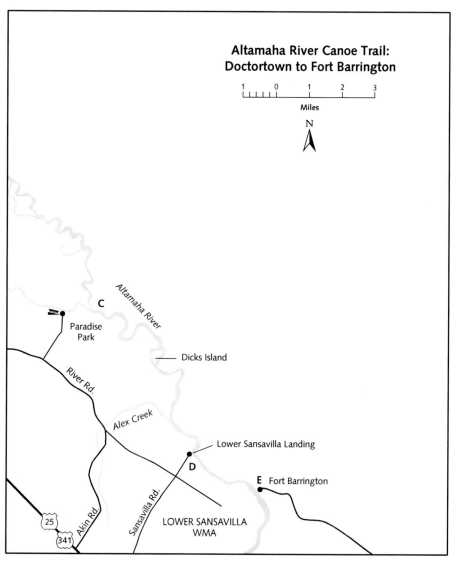

**Altamaha River Canoe Trail:
Doctortown to Fort Barrington**

1 0 1 2 3
Miles

N

C
Paradise
Park

Altamaha River

Dicks Island

River Rd.

Alex Creek

Lower Sansavilla Landing

D

E Fort Barrington

Sansavilla Rd.

25

341

Akin Rd.

LOWER SANSAVILLA
WMA

Hazards: tidal river; crosswinds; motorboats
Highlights: Lewis Island

The river grows increasingly wider as it continues toward the coast. Three miles south of Barrington is the tidal barrier. From here progress on the river is determined by the ebb and flow of the tide. Five miles from Barrington is the Altamaha River Camp, which has a boat dock and campground. Five miles south of the camp, on the north side of the river, is the mouth of Stud Horse Creek. *For a more intimate canoeing experience, turn left into the creek.*

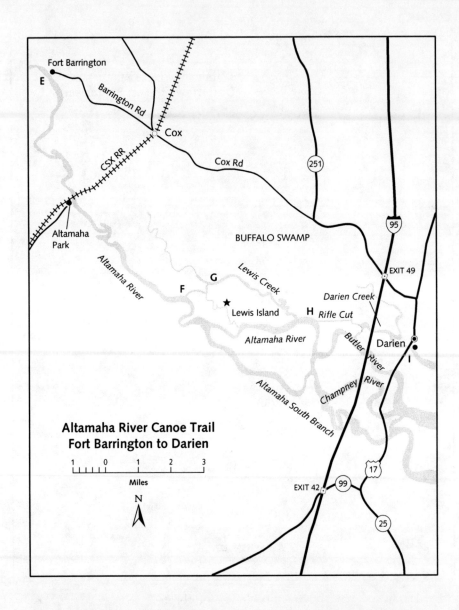

**Altamaha River Canoe Trail
Fort Barrington to Darien**

In a mile it ends at the larger Lewis Creek, passing from left to right. *Turn downstream into Lewis Creek.* In 0.75 mile there is a primitive camping area on the right-hand bank. In a little more than 2.5 miles Lewis Creek empties into the main channel of the Altamaha.

From the Lewis Island campsite continue the detour down the creek, which soon returns to the Altamaha. At this point the river is more than 700 feet

Rifle Cut, formerly a logging channel, connects the Altamaha River and the Darien River.

The best way to view the cypress stand on Lewis Island is from the primitive campsite on Lewis Creek. Paddle upstream to the mouth of Stud Horse Creek. Backtrack on Stud Horse to the sharp bend (now to the right). From here, continue straight ahead onto Pico Creek. In 0.25 mile, Big Buzzard Creek appears on the left. Take this winding creek for more than a mile into the island's interior (1.5 miles from Stud Horse). On the left are two logging channels. The first old channel, usually marked, leads to the trees. From here it is a 1,000-foot hike north to the trees, usually through muck and mud. There is no trail, so either follow the marked trees or orient with a compass.

wide. Leave the main channel in less than 0.5 mile at Rifle Cut, a logging channel that remains open to small craft. The cut ends at Darien Creek, which empties into the Darien River. Follow the Darien River downstream, underneath I-95, to the Darien dock on your left.

ACCESS POINTS

Fort Barrington: From Darien, take U.S. 17 North to the junction with Ga. 251. Turn left and take Ga. 251 past I-95 **(mile 2.4)** to Cox **(mile 11.0)**. Just beyond Cox, turn left onto Barrington Road. Take the sand road for 4 miles; at its end is the park **(mile 15.0)**.

Darien: The Darien dock, off the Darien River, is just below the U.S. 17 North bridge.

Journey to Cherokee Corners

The Road to Augusta

After traveling the Georgia coast, Bartram turned to the interior. He had previously learned of a "Congress to be held at Augusta between the Creek Indians and the White People" and decided to attend, accompanied by John McIntosh, Lachlan's nephew. On May 1, 1773, the two men set out on horseback. The trip to Savannah took two days. When they reached the intersection with the Augusta Road, they turned to the northwest. This road was familiar to Bartram, who had traveled it with his father on their trip to Augusta in 1765. On the first night outside Savannah, Bartram and McIntosh stayed at a "publik house" near the abandoned settlement of Abercorn; most likely they lodged at Dacres Tavern. On the second night they passed through **Ebenezer**, the German colonial settlement.

Farther to the north, between Black Creek and Buck Creek in today's Screven County, the road forked. Bartram and McIntosh followed the western branch, farther away from the Savannah River. They crossed Beaverdam Creek at the site of today's Jacksonboro Bridge. Less than a mile downstream was the site of Bartram's "Blue Springs," first visited by William and his father in 1765. The route continued northward through today's Hilltonia and Sardis, coinciding with today's Ga. 24. As the road approached Bean Creek, William and young John took a spur to the northeast to Shell Bluff, a 150-foot bluff overlooking the river that contains huge oyster fossils. After crossing the Savannah, they traveled northward on the Carolina side to **Silver Bluff**, the home of George Galphin. Bartram and McIntosh continued northward to the site of an abandoned British fortress, Fort Moore, where they crossed at the sandbar. They took the old Indian trail on the last leg into Augusta.

Colonial Augusta

In 1736, two years after founding the colony of Georgia, James Oglethorpe made plans to build a town just below the falls on the Savannah that marked

*Old Augusta Road at New Ebenezer. This is a portion of
the main road between Augusta and Savannah.*

*Jerusalem Church was built in 1769 at the center of the
Salzburger settlement, Ebenezer (New Ebenezer).*

the end of the river's navigation—the cataracts can still be seen today. The
Georgia Trustees authorized the building of a fort and town there for the
stated purpose of providing for the security of the new colony "by way of an
Out-guard against Invasion by land."[1] Their true motive was not security,
however; both Oglethorpe and the Trustees sought to control the lucrative
fur trade with the Creeks and Cherokees, diverting it from South Carolina
to Georgia. This new Georgia settlement would capture trade intended for
Fort Moore, 3 miles to the south on the Carolina side. Land was cleared in
the summer of 1737, and workmen from Savannah joined by Chickasaw Indians built the new town. Within a year the new settlement, named Augusta
in honor of Princess Augusta, the wife of Fredrick, Prince of Wales, was full
of storehouses and traders.

Bartram visited Augusta three times during the 1770s. His first and longest
visit was May–June 1773, to witness the Indian Congress at which merchants

1. Robertson and Robertson, "The Town and Fort of Augusta," 59–60. See also
Cashin, *The Story of Augusta*, 10.

and traders, with the full support of the royal governor, negotiated with Creeks and Cherokees the resolution of outstanding debts owed by the Indians. The *Travels* provides a detailed description of the first day of the meeting, which was attended by 300 Creeks and 100 Cherokees. The meeting nearly ended on that day as well when the Creeks learned that the Cherokees had sold land near the Tugaloo River to the Georgia colonists. One of the Creek chiefs stood up and asked the Cherokee chiefs "what right they had to give away their lands, calling them old women" (T486). The Cherokees did not reply, and the meeting continued. The negotiations lasted through the end of June, when the Creeks and Cherokees ceded more than 2 million acres to the colony to cancel out their debts. This land constitutes what is now most of northeastern Georgia.

Bartram returned to Augusta in July of that year, after touring the newly ceded land with the royal surveyors, and did not return again until 1775, when he was en route to Cherokee country. His final visit was in January 1776, as he returned from West Florida and the Creek Nation.

Augusta Walking Tour

This walking tour, also suitable for biking, is a 3.5-mile loop through downtown Augusta that approximates the historical trail marked by the Georgia Bartram Trail Society for the U.S. Bicentennial. A few signs for the trail are still standing. Our tour visits the sites of Fort Augusta, Meadow Garden, and the Old Springfield Church. It begins and ends at the Cotton Exchange Visitors' Center at the corner of 8th Street and Reynolds.

The Cotton Exchange, founded in 1872, was the commercial center of an industry that made Augusta the second-largest inland cotton market in the world. Today it houses the city's Welcome Center and Museum, with displays on the history of Augusta and the surrounding area. The center also offers maps of the area, including a self-guided walking tour of the city's many post-colonial historical sites.

From the Exchange take Reynolds Street to the east for two blocks. Immediately before the railroad tracks to the left is **St. Paul's Episcopal Church**, 605 Reynolds Street **(mile 0.2)**. A church has been located at this site since 1749; the current building, constructed in 1919, is the fourth. It replaced a similar building from 1820 that burned in the great fire of 1916, which destroyed much of Augusta, including many of its historic buildings. At the rear of the churchyard is a Celtic cross indicating the site of Fort Augusta. The original

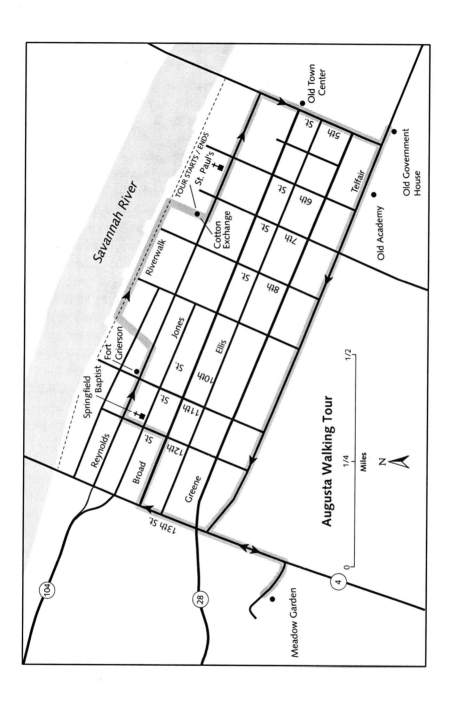

Savannah River

TOUR STARTS / ENDS

St. Paul's

Cotton
Exchange

Riverwalk

Fort
Grierson

Springfield
Baptist

Reynolds

Broad St.

13th St.

Greene

12th St.

11th St.

10th St.

Jones St.

Ellis

8th St.

7th St.

6th St.

5th St.

Old Town
Center

Old Government
House

Telfair

Old Academy

Meadow Garden

104

28

4

Augusta Walking Tour

N

Miles

0   1/4   1/2

St. Paul's Church, built in 1749, stood immediately to the left of the fort. Both fort and church were located on "The Bay"—the riverfront—at the northwest corner of the settlement. William Few, one of Georgia's delegates to the Constitutional Convention, is buried in the church cemetery.

Fort Augusta, completed in April 1738, was the first structure built in Augusta. Although the original plan for the fort has not survived, archaeologists Heard Robertson and Thomas H. Robertson have been able to reconstruct its size and shape. It was a wooden stockade, 110 feet square, with a sentry box at each bastion. A 9-foot-high wooden fence connected the bastions. At the base of the fence, spanning its length, was an interior walkway 2 feet above the ground. Five buildings stood inside the fence: the rangers' barracks, officers' barracks, kitchen, stable, and a magazine and storeroom. The fort's wooden construction required frequent repair and restoration. It was completely rebuilt in 1759 and again in 1767. By 1773 it was again in a state of disrepair, but this time it was not replaced. The recent cession of lands at the Indian Congress required a royal fort farther to the north, and Fort James was built at the mouth of the Broad River on the Savannah near the proposed town of Dartmouth. During the Revolution, the British constructed a new fort on the site of Fort Augusta, Fort Cornwallis, to protect the city from patriot attacks.

Continue walking down Reynolds Street, past the Augusta–Richmond County Museum. The museum houses exhibits on southeastern Indians and the history of Augusta from the colonial period to the present day. *At 5th Street, turn right* **(mile 0.4)** and proceed to the intersection with Broad Street. This corner, today's 5th Street and Broad (in the eighteenth and nineteenth centuries, Center Street and Broad), was the center of the **Old Town**. Oglethorpe's grid design was similar to those he used at Savannah, Ebenezer, and Frederica. He specified four blocks on each side of Broad Street, each block divided into five 1-acre lots. By the middle of the 1770s Augusta had grown from the original 40 lots to more than 100. The growth was orderly, as it continued to follow the grid designed by Oglethorpe and surveyed by Noble Jones. The city's buildings also extended up the Savannah River for nearly 2 miles to the cataracts "formed by the first set of rocky hills" (T32). These rapids are located just upstream from today's municipal water works.

From the corner of Broad and 5th Streets, continue walking to the south on 5th Street. In two blocks 5th Street reaches the intersection with Telfair Street. *Turn left onto Telfair.* On the right is the **Old Government House**, 432 Telfair **(mile 0.8)**. This brick with stucco building, constructed in 1801 as the Richmond County Courthouse, is the oldest remaining public building in Au-

This Celtic cross at the rear of St. Paul's Church indicates the site of Fort Augusta.

gusta. In 1822 it was converted to a private residence, which it remained until the 1950s. The city of Augusta restored the building in 1988, and it is now used as a reception center. On the grounds are several old trees, including a gingko tree said to date to the eighteenth century. *Return to 5th Street on Telfair. Cross 5th Street and continue walking west on Telfair.* Halfway down the block on the left is the **Old Academy of Richmond County**, 540 Telfair. This brick with stucco building was also built in 1801. It was extensively remodeled in the 1850s, when Gothic Revival features were added. The academy was chartered in 1783 and is still in operation, making it the oldest chartered school south of Virginia.

Continue waking on Telfair Street to the intersection with 13th Street **(mile 1.9)**. *Turn left and follow 13th Street* over the Augusta Canal to Independence Drive. *Turn right on Independence Drive.* On the left is the home of George Walton, the **Meadow Garden (mile 2.3)**, 1320 Independence Drive. George Walton, also one of the signers of the Declaration of Independence, was the state's governor in 1779 and in 1788. The two-story "raised cottage" was built in two stages. The original building, with two stories and two rooms on each floor, is the southern part of the current structure—the left section of the house. It was constructed on this site by its previous owner in the 1780s. By 1792 George Walton and his family had taken possession of the house. In the early nineteenth century the right-side structure was added, more than doubling the size of the house. The addition is apparent in the two front doors and the two sets of front steps. Before the house was renovated in the twentieth century, Meadow Garden also had two rooflines. The Daughters of the American Revolution (DAR) purchased the house in 1900, saving Augusta's oldest documented house from destruction. The Georgia Chapter of the DAR now operates it as a house museum. *Return to 13th Street on the Canal Trail and turn left.* Follow 13th Street to the intersection with Broad Street. *Turn right onto Broad Street for one block and then left onto 12th Street.*

On the right as 12th Street approaches the intersection with Reynolds is **Springfield Baptist Church (mile 3.0)**, 114 12th Street. The older structure visible at the rear of the church was built in 1801. Originally a meetinghouse for the St. John's Methodist congregation on Greene Street, it was acquired by Springfield in 1844. The Baptist church was organized in Augusta in 1787 but had its origins in 1774 at George Galphin's Silver Bluff plantation, where Galphin permitted David George, a freed slave, to preach to his slaves. The preaching resulted in a religious revival that led to the formation of a congregation at the plantation. After the Revolutionary War the congregation moved to Augusta, became Springfield church, and continued to exist as the

Meadow Garden in Augusta, Georgia, was the home of George Walton, one of the signers of the Declaration of Independence and the state's governor during the Revolution. Courtesy of the Georgia DAR.

oldest African American church of any denomination in the colonies.[2] *Continue down Reynolds Street to 11th Street.* This corner is the site of **Fort Grierson (mile 3.1)**, built by the British in 1780 when they occupied the city during the Revolutionary War. The British fort held until June 1781, when the British were routed by forces led by Elijah Clarke and Andrew Pickens in their campaign to free Augusta. Continue down Reynolds Street to 10th Street. *Turn left and follow 10th Street to the Riverwalk* **(mile 3.2)**.

Riverwalk

This 0.5-mile plaza along the south bank of the Savannah River was built by the city in the late 1980s. Near the river's edge, several paths wind through gardens and recreation areas. On the levee is a brick-lined path for biking and walking with signs and plaques interpreting the history of Augusta. One of these plaques features Bartram's reflections on the setting and stature of the city: "Augusta thus seated at the head of navigation, and just below the conflux of several of its most considerable branches, and without a competitor,

2. Cashin, *Old Springfield*, 14.

Springfield Baptist Church, Augusta, Georgia.

commands the trade and commerce of vast fruitful regions above it, and from every side to a great distance; and I do not hesitate to pronounce in my own opinion, will very soon become the metropolis of Georgia" (T317). On the river trail is a Bartram Trail historical marker noting the naturalist's many trips to the river city. There are three entrances to the Riverwalk: 10th Street, the main entrance at 8th Street, and 6th Street at Oglethorpe Park. Take the Riverwalk, either on the levee or the riverside, to the Cotton Exchange **(mile 3.5)** or to its end at Oglethorpe Park, at the rear of St. Paul's Church.

Ezekiel Harris House

Located 1.5 miles from downtown, the Ezekiel Harris House, 1822 Broad Street, was the plantation home of a successful Augusta tobacco merchant and trader. The house was built in 1797 and stood on an estate of more than 300 acres on the outskirts of the town. This two-story house is a beautiful example of postcolonial architecture with its vaulted hallway, tiered piazzas, and gambrel roof covering the front and rear porches. In the early 1960s the Georgia DNR restored the building to its original form. Currently, the house is owned by the city of Augusta and is operated as a public museum. For many years it was known as either the Mackey House or the "White House." It is open daily to the public.

Ezekiel Harris House, Augusta, Georgia.

ACCESS AND PARKING

Public parking is available at the Cotton Exchange Visitors' Center and at St. Paul's Church. Street parking, although limited, is available at most of the sites described above. Parking is available at the rear of the Ezekiel Harris House.

Bartram Trail: Augusta Canal Trail

Section: Augusta Canal Locks to Riverwalk (downtown Augusta)
Distance: 8.5 miles (5 miles not paved)
Hazards: city traffic downtown
Highlights: Bull Sluice; The Clearing

This trail spans 8.5 miles from the Augusta Canal Locks to the Riverwalk in downtown Augusta. It is wide and level, suitable for both biking and hiking. It closely follows the route of the "Wilderness" section of the Bartram Trail mapped and built by the Augusta Bartram Bicentennial Committee and the Georgia Bartram Trail Society in the mid-1970s. By 1990 much of this trail had become obscured or inaccessible. In the early 1990s the city of Augusta and the newly formed Augusta Canal Authority began to restore it. Renamed the Augusta Canal Trail, it is the centerpiece of the recently established na-

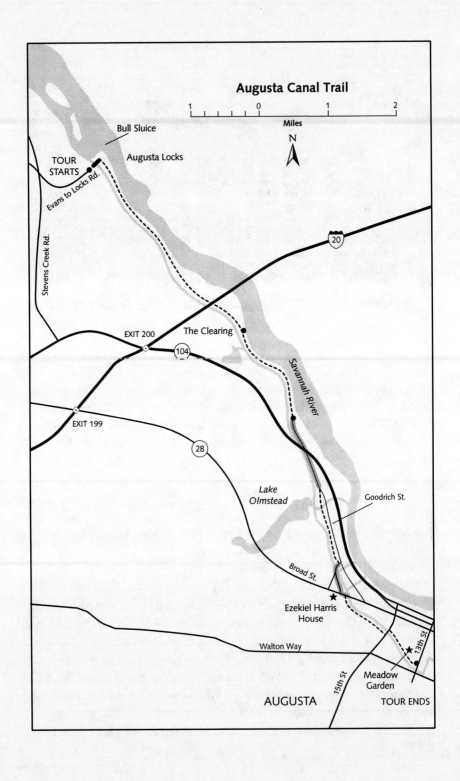

Augusta Canal Trail

tional heritage area. The trail is described from the northern trailhead at the locks to the Riverwalk.

The northern trailhead is at the headgates and locks for the canal. The canal was constructed in 1846 to divert shipping around the river's rapids and to provide power for industries. The canal was 7 miles long, 5 feet deep, and 40 feet wide at the surface—wide enough for narrow "Petersburg" boats carrying cotton from the backcountry to Augusta. From the parking lot, walk down to the canal and then cross over on the metal walkway to the towpath. For the next 7 miles the trail is built on the bed of the towpath along which mules towed the barges up and down the canal. At the river's edge, to the left, is one of the Savannah's deepest and most turbulent rapids, Bull Sluice **(mile 0.1)**. This is the beginning of the first series of cataracts that Bartram described on his first visit to Augusta as being "rapid and broken" (T 33).

Follow the trail downstream on the narrow strip of land between the river and the canal. On the right **(mile 0.2)** is a view of the mouth of Reed Creek entering the canal. The narrow creek winding over large boulders is reminiscent of mountain streams in north Georgia. A few hundred feet ahead on the left is a second set of rapids on the Savannah River. Just beyond the rapids, on the right side of the trail, is the state champion loblolly pine, with a girth exceeding 15 feet. As the trail continues, the river passes out of view. To the left are stands of sweetgum and sycamore trees, with cypress in the adjoining wetland, which continues on the other side of the I-20 underpass **(mile 2.0)**. Cattail, arrowhead, and trumpet-creeper vine—all plants described by Bartram in his travels along the river—are also found here.

As the trail continues toward Augusta, it approaches the Savannah again at The Clearing **(mile 2.8)**. Ten thousand years ago this spot was a Paleo-Indian campsite. More than 3,000 years ago Archaic Indians camped and fished here along the banks of the river. Today The Clearing is a popular picnic area and canoe landing. Below the landing are rapids that continue for nearly a mile and interfere with navigation. From The Clearing, the trail continues downstream, with the Savannah in view for much of the next mile. Soon the trail approaches, on the left, the Augusta Water Works Pumping Station **(mile 3.5)**. Across the railroad tracks and behind the fence is a parking area. Just before the tracks is the trailhead for two mountain-biking trails. Both are loop trails, in difficulty easy to moderate. One path is blazed in red, the other in white.

From the water works the trail setting takes on a more urban character. Paralleling the trail on the left is Goodrich Street. To the right is the River Watch Parkway, a four-lane limited-access highway. Soon the highway crosses over the canal and the Riverwalk, from the right to the left. In a little more than 0.3 mile the trail approaches Lake Olmstead on the right **(mile 4.6)**. The lake empties into a long spillway, passing overflow water from the canal into the old bed of Rae's Creek. As the trail approaches the narrow metal passageway that crosses the spillway, it descends to Goodrich Street. Follow the signs and cross the spillway on the street. Walkers can cross the spillway on the narrow walkway, which is equipped with handrails. On the other side of the spillway the trail rejoins the towpath. In less than 0.25 mile the trail crosses Rae's Creek, which empties into the Savannah.

South of Rae's Creek the trail continues to parallel Goodrich Street to the left. Soon the river levee appears on the left **(mile 5.2)**. Built in the early twentieth century to protect the city from the Savannah's floods, it continues for 7 miles to the south. The towpath loses its elevation, descending to street level near the corner of Goodrich and Eve Streets. Immediately to the left is the 168-foot-tall chimney of the Confederate States Powder Works, all that remains of the Confederacy's only arsenal. At the corner the trail turns to the right, crossing over the canal on the Eve Street Bridge **(mile 5.4)**. At the end of the bridge the trail turns to the left onto Pearl Street. To the left, on the bank of the canal, is Chaffee Park. At the intersection with Broad Street, turn left. To the right, one block to the west, is the **Ezekiel Harris House**. To continue on the trail into downtown Augusta, cross Broad Street and descend the concrete stairs to the towpath. From Broad Street to 13th Street the trail follows the bed of the towpath. At 15th Street the trail turns left, crossing over the canal on the Butt Memorial Bridge. On the other side of the bridge, the trail crosses 15th Street and follows the northern bank of the canal.

The trail passes underneath the Calhoun Expressway. On the left is **Meadow Garden**, the home of George Walton. The trail continues downstream to the gates for the first level of the canal **(mile 7.0)**, which maintained the proper level of the canal upstream, sending overflow into the second level. The trail reaches 13th Street and intersects the Historic Augusta Trail—which can be taken in either direction to the Riverwalk. From 13th Street the Augusta Canal Trail continues for another 1.5 miles on downtown streets to the Riverwalk. This section is routed over Fenwick, 12th Street, Greene Street, and 8th Street, ending at the Cotton Exchange Visitors' Center.

ACCESS POINTS

Savannah Rapids Pavilion: From downtown Augusta, take River Watch Parkway to the north. At the junction with Stevens Creek Road, turn right. Follow the road for just over 3 miles. At the junction with Evans to Locks Road, turn right. In a mile the road ends at the park. At the pavilion there is an overlook over the rapids. The trail begins at the bottom of the lower parking lot.

Water works: From downtown Augusta, take Broad Street to the west. At the junction with Eve Street, turn right. Take Eve over the canal and intersect Goodrich Street. Turn left on Goodrich and follow it upstream for 3.5 miles to the water works.

13th Street: This parking area, consisting of street parking on Independence Drive, is located directly across from Walton's Meadow Garden. The house and parking are adjacent to the Walton Rehabilitation Hospital near the intersection of 13th Street and Independence Drive.

George Galphin's Silver Bluff

En route to Cherokee country in the spring of 1775, Bartram left the "high road" between Savannah and Augusta to cross the Savannah River. His destination was Silver Bluff, the home and business place of George Galphin. The bluff, according to Bartram, sat "a considerable height upon the Carolina shore of the Savanna River, perhaps thirty feet higher than the low lands on the opposite shore" (T314). He first visited the bluff in September 1765 in the company of his father as they set out to visit Augusta. William returned to visit Galphin in 1773, this time with John McIntosh of Darien. There they waited "a day or two at this Place where were Numbers of People waiting the Congress to held at Augusta" (R1:20). Bartram returned again in 1775 and finally in January 1776 as he returned from his travels in West Florida and the Creek Nation.

Galphin had lived at Silver Bluff since the 1740s. A native of Ireland, he immigrated to South Carolina in 1737. At Silver Bluff he entered the Indian trade working as an associate for the leading trading firm of Brown, Rae, and Company. Over the course of the next decade Galphin established himself as the principal trader to the Lower Creeks.

For nearly thirty years Silver Bluff was a major trading center. In the early 1760s Galphin turned the operation of his warehouses and stores over to his sons. After he "retired from the forests" he augmented the family fortune with a series of land acquisitions.[3] From 1760 to 1770 Galphin more than tripled the size of his estate at Silver Bluff, bringing it close to 7,000 acres. Here he established a plantation for the large-scale growing of indigo and corn, and grazing land for a large herd of cattle. To profit from the bluff's

3. Cashin, *King's Ranger*, 46.

dense hardwood forests, he constructed two sawmills. Plantation agriculture required slave labor; by 1775 Galphin owned more than 100 slaves.

Silver Bluff was a trading center, a major plantation, and also a center for Indian diplomacy where Galphin kept an "open house" for his Creek and Cherokee friends. In 1775 Galphin gave Bartram letters of introduction to his trading representatives in the Creek Nation. As Kathryn Braund notes, these letters would have carried as much weight as those from the British superintendent for Indian affairs, John Stuart. When the Revolution started, the Continental Congress appointed Galphin "commissioner of Indian affairs." He was charged with countering the influence of John Stuart and Thomas Brown, and with keeping the Creeks neutral through the conflict. He succeeded in this policy until January 1779, when Augusta fell to the British army. In June 1780 Thomas Brown and the Florida Rangers seized Silver Bluff and charged Galphin with treason against the crown. He died that December, before action could be taken against him.

After the war, Galphin's heirs lost the family estate. In the nineteenth century the Galphin plantation house was dismantled, and after the Civil War the plantation was abandoned. For most of the twentieth century the land lay dormant and unoccupied. After it was proposed for an industrial site, the owners sold the property to the National Audubon Society to be managed as a bird and wildlife refuge.

Silver Bluff Sanctuary

Today, more than 3,000 acres of the original plantation are administered as the Silver Bluff Sanctuary. The Audubon Society, working with the South Carolina Institute of Archaeology and Anthropology (SCIAA), surveyed the land to identify the site of Galphin's house, his plantation, and the storehouses used in his trading business. The Savannah River Archaeological Research Program (SRARP), led by Tammy Forehand, has been conducting research at the Silver Bluff Trading Post (Site 38AK7) since January 1999. In 1980 SCIAA researchers surveyed the probable site of George Galphin's trading post.[4] At the time, researchers were unsure whether Galphin's trade warehouses had been eroded into the Savannah River or were merely buried. The results of excavations conducted in 1996 indicate that the warehouses may be intact underground. Ground-penetrating radar surveys identified potential sites for buildings associated with the post.

4. Hamer, "Indian Traders, Land and Power."

*Silver Bluff, South Carolina, the site of George Galphin's
plantation and business. There is a South Carolina Institute of
Archaeology and Anthropology field excavation on the site.*

The National Audubon Society also manages more than 3,000 surrounding acres, including extensive uplands and lowlands. Many acres are managed for timber sales, with great care devoted in the timber harvesting to wildlife habitat, aesthetics, and ecological impact. The plantation site is located on the bluff to the south of the road leading to the boat ramp. The Audubon Society and the SCIAA plan for public interpretation near the site. Tours of the sanctuary can be arranged through the sanctuary manager.

Silver Bluff is 14 miles southeast of Augusta, south of Beech Island, South Carolina. Address: 4542 Silver Bluff Road, Jackson, SC; phone: 803-827-0781.

Driving Tour: Augusta to Cherokee Corners

This 70-mile tour begins near Thomson, Georgia, 35 miles west of Augusta, on the old Quaker Road that ran between Augusta and the Quaker settlement of Wrightsborough. From Wrightsborough the tour roughly follows an old Cherokee path that led west-northwest to Cherokee Corners, just outside the city limits of modern-day Athens. This was the route Bartram took in June

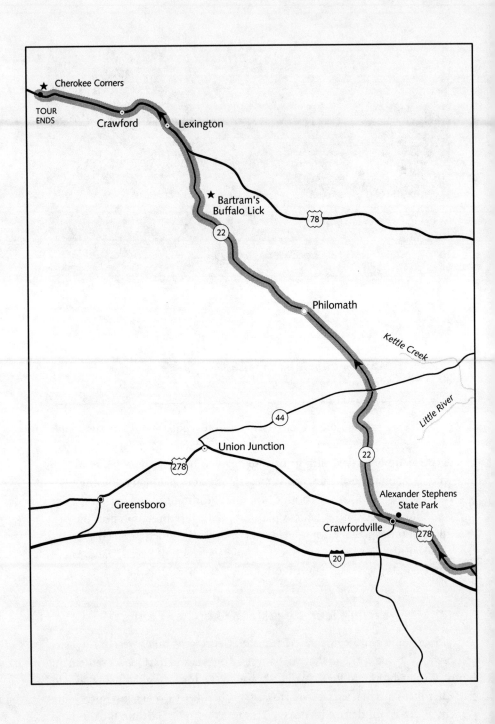

Cherokee Corners

TOUR
ENDS

Crawford

Lexington

Bartram's
Buffalo Lick

78

22

Philomath

Kettle Creek

Little River

44

Union Junction

278

22

Greensboro

Alexander Stephens
State Park

Crawfordville

278

20

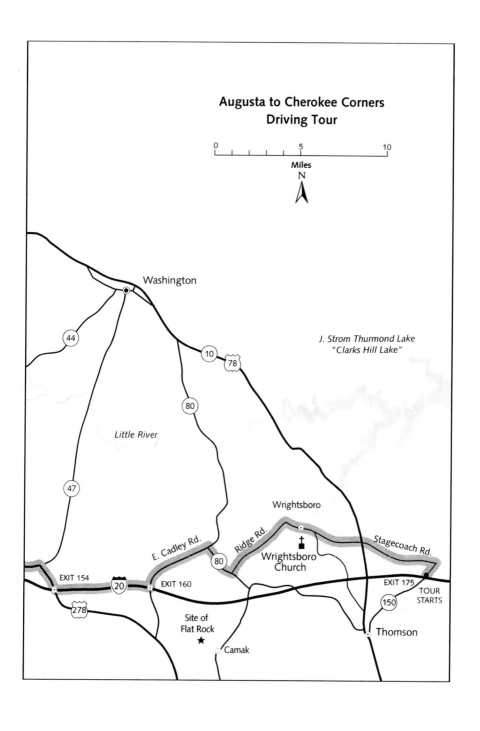

Augusta to Cherokee Corners
Driving Tour

0   5   10

Miles

N

Washington

44

10   78

80

Little River

J. Strom Thurmond Lake
"Clarks Hill Lake"

47

Wrightsboro

E. Cadley Rd.

Ridge Rd.

Stagecoach Rd.

80

Wrightsboro
Church

EXIT 154

20

EXIT 160

EXIT 175

TOUR
STARTS

278

150

Site of
Flat Rock

★

Camak

Thomson

1773 when he accompanied Edward Barnard on a survey of the lands recently ceded by the Creeks and Cherokees at the Indian Congress. On reaching the northwestern boundary of the new territory, or Cherokee Corners, Barnard, Bartram, and a small party turned to the northeast, heading for the mouth of the Tugaloo River on the Savannah River. From there they traveled southeast and returned to Augusta.

This driving tour begins at the junction of I-20 and Ga. 150, at Exit 175. *Go north on Ga. 150* for about a mile to Stones Crossing. When the highway meets **Stagecoach Road**, *turn left* **(mile 1.1)**. This road follows the bed of the colonial road built in 1768 linking Augusta to the newly established Quaker settlement at Wrightsborough. Bartram took this route on his first visit to Wrightsborough as he waited for the Indian Congress to begin. *Continue west on Stagecoach Road* past the intersection with Ga. 10 and U.S. 78 **(mile 5.7)**. In a few miles, just beyond Pleasant Grove Church, Stagecoach Road ends at **Wrightsboro Road (mile 8.3)**, another colonial road that ran from Wrightsborough to Augusta through present-day Thomson. This was the route taken in June 1773 by Barnard and his caravan of "surveyors, astronomers, artisans, chain-carriers, markers, guides and hunters, besides a very respectable number of gentlemen . . . together with ten or twelve Indians, altogether to the number of eighty to ninety men" on their surveying trip (T35).

From the junction of these roads, *continue west* to the Quaker settlement. Soon the **Wrightsboro Church** appears on the left **(mile 9.7)**.

Wrightsborough

Wrightsboro Methodist Church, built in 1810, stands on the site of the Friends Meeting House, the former center of a large eighteenth-century Quaker settlement. In February 1768 Governor Wright set aside 12,000 acres south of the Little River as a reserve for Quakers from North Carolina. By the end of the year, Joseph Maddock had led more than seventy families from Hillsborough, North Carolina, to Georgia. The settlement, located where a previous Quaker settlement had failed, was named Wrightsborough in honor of the governor. By 1775 the population of this southernmost colonial Quaker settlement exceeded 600, with 124 male Quakers holding grants to more than 30,000 acres. During the Revolutionary War the majority of the residents remained loyal to the crown, making them and their property targets for frequent attacks by patriots. Wrightsborough did not recover from the violence when the war ended. The recent hostilities and the emphasis on slave labor in the region's economy caused an exodus of the Quakers into new settlements in central Indiana and Ohio. The town continued to fall further into decline and by 1840 was listed as one of Georgia's "dead towns."[5]

The Quaker meetinghouse no longer exists. Surrounding the site, and the present-day Methodist church, is a burial ground containing the graves of some of the early Quaker settlers, distinguished from the other graves as rows of unmarked stones. Across the road from the church and cemetery are two wooden buildings built in the 1970s to represent the commonplace buildings found in typical eighteenth-century Quaker settlements. Tours can be arranged by appointment through the McDuffie County Chamber of Commerce. The restoration site has a small parking area and public restrooms.

From the site, *continue west on Wrightsboro Road.* At the intersection with Ridge Road **(mile 10.3)**, *turn left.* Take Ridge Road southwest to its ending at Ga. 80 **(mile 14.4)**. *Turn right and follow Ga. 80 to the north.* At the intersection with East Cadley Road **(mile 20.6)** *turn left. Follow East Cadley to the west* through the small town of Cadley. At the interchange with the interstate, **(mile 24.6)** *take I-20 west.* In a little more than 5 miles, *exit at the interchange for U.S. 278 (Exit 154). Follow U.S. 278 West* for 7 miles to Crawfordville. In the center of town, in front of the Taliaferro County Courthouse, is a historical marker **(mile 32.1)** for the "Common Road"—the Hightower Trail that led to the Etowah River. The marker mistakenly indicates that Bartram traveled this way en route to Cherokee Corners. As Harper notes, Bartram used a route farther north—a Cherokee trail on the ridge just south of the Little River (T343). This trail is less than 5 miles north of **Alexander H. Stephens State Park**.

Half a mile from the town square, U.S. 278 crosses Ga. 22 **(mile 32.8)**. *Turn right, and take Hwy. 22 East* to the north. This road crosses the South Fork of the Little River **(mile 37.5)** and then enters the small town of Lyneville. In this area the modern highway closely follows the old Cherokee trail, passing through the present-day Edgewood Crossroad, to **Philomath**. At the headwaters of the Little River, Bartram encountered a stately stand of black oaks. "To keep within the bounds of truth and reality in describing the magnitude and grandeur of these trees," he writes, "would, I fear, fail of credibility; yet, I think I can assert, that many of the black oaks measured eight, nine, ten and eleven feet diameter five feet above the ground, as we measured several that were above thirty feet girth" (T37).

Scattered among the black oaks were large tulip poplars and beech trees.

5. Hitz, "The Wrightsborough Quaker Town and Township in Georgia," 10–11, 16–17.

Wrightsboro Methodist Church. This church, built in 1810, stands on the site of the Wrightsborough Friends Meeting House.

Regrettably, there is no trace of this forest today. Barnard and the caravan continued northward on the trail to their immediate destination—the **Great Buffalo Lick**. Continue on Ga. 22 past the North Fork of the Little River to the junction with Ga. 44 **(mile 40.7)**. In 5 miles the road reaches "historic Philomath" **(mile 46.2)**.

Philomath

This small town was named for a nineteenth-century boys' boarding school. For a brief period in the 1970s it was the home of the Georgia Bartram Trail Society Library, which no longer exists. As the highway enters Philomath, there is a sign for the Great Buffalo Lick to the left. Recent research by Louis De Vorsey, however, has established that the lick was located not in Philomath but rather several miles to the north, off Ga. 22 near Buffalo Creek. As described by Bartram, "this extraordinary piece of ground" occupied 3–4 acres. The whitish clay soil had a "delicious vein" that appealed to the tastes of deer and buffalo. The lick was located on the "Great Ridge" dividing the watersheds of the Savannah and Altamaha Rivers.[6] It was a noted landmark

6. De Vorsey, "Bartram's Buffalo Lick."

The garden, which includes more than 300 acres, is a preserve set aside by the University of Georgia in 1968 for the study and enjoyment of plants. The garden comprises a number of theme gardens, including the Native Flora Garden, with species native to Georgia; the Shade Garden, with native plants from each of the seven Garden Club districts in the state; the Rhododendron Garden; and the Dahlia Garden. There are 5 miles of trails through natural areas; the longest is the White Trail along sections of the Middle Oconee River. Adjacent to the visitors' center is the International Garden, with eleven separate collections devoted to the interrelationship between plants and people. The garden also features a separate Bartram collection that includes many of the species described by father and son on their botanical expeditions. The International Garden offers an American South section as well as an herb garden and a physic garden. A visitor meandering through the various paths and collections of the State Botanical Garden can see most of the 358 plants described by William Bartram.

There is no admission fee for the garden, which is open daily from 8 A.M. to sunset; the visitors' center is open 9–4:30 on Tuesday–Saturday and 11:30–4:30 on Sunday. Located at 2450 South Milledge Avenue, Athens, 3 miles south of the University of Georgia campus. For more information. call 706-542-1244. Web address: http://www.uga.edu/botgarden/

for the Cherokee. There Barnard's party divided into three groups, each charged with surveying different parts of the newly ceded lands. Bartram stayed with the colonel's party as they continued to the northwest, by way of Buffalo Creek, to Cherokee Corners.

Continuing the tour, *stay on Ga. 22 from Philomath to the junction with U.S. 78* **(mile 58)**. *Turn left onto U.S. 78* toward Athens. Continue on U.S. 78 through Lexington and Crawfordville, reaching **Cherokee Corners** just before entering the city limits of Athens **(mile 68)**.

Cherokee Corners

Cherokee Corners marks the spot where Colonel Barnard and his party drew the boundary of the new territory ceded by the Cherokees. At the site today is a historical marker noting Bartram's visit. Near it is small picnic area bisected by Moss Creek. Near the creek is a boulder field of composite rocks. There is a parking area near U.S. 78. The U.S. 78/Ga. 10 Bypass around the southern end of Athens is 7.5 miles to the west. To return to Thomson, the most direct route is via U.S. 78 East.

State Botanical Garden of Georgia, Athens. The Bartram Garden is in the foreground.

Other Points of Interest

Alexander H. Stevens Memorial State Park

This state park is located in Crawfordville, the home of "Little Aleck"—Alexander Stephens, the orator and politician who served as U.S. senator, governor of Georgia, and vice president of the Confederacy. Stephens's home, Liberty Hall, has been restored to its mid-nineteenth-century condition. At the park is the Museum of the Confederacy. The park has a campground and two nature trails, Buncomb Lake and Sunset Drive. Taken together these trails form a system of approximately 4 miles for hiking or biking. The park, within the city limits of Crawfordville, is approximately 5 miles south of the trail followed by Barnard and Bartram in 1773.

Washington, Georgia

A little more than 20 miles north of Thomson on U.S. 78 is the city of Washington. The town, situated on land ceded by the Creeks to the colony, was chartered in 1780 and named in honor of the military leader of the ongoing Revolution. Six structures still standing date to the eighteenth century. Near the business district is the Neeson-Norman-Hodgson House, on Jefferson Street, built around the 1790s. East of the business district, at the corner of Court and Alexander, is the Women's Club, the former home of Col. John Griffin, built around 1780. Also to the east is the Toombs House, 216 East Robert Toombs Avenue. The original part of this clapboard house was constructed in 1797. In the eighteenth century it became the home of Robert Toombs, Confederate general and statesman. Southwest of the center of town, on Liberty Street, is the Liberty Inn, built around 1793. On the north side of town, near the new U.S. 78, are two notable homes. The first is Peacewood, 120 Tignall Road, a wooden clapboard home built around 1790. The second is the Wingfield-Blackmon House, on Alexander Avenue south of U.S. 78, built in 1784.

Washington is also the home of the Bartram Trail Regional Library, the public library for Wilkes County. The library has material on Bartram and the Georgia Bartram Trail Society.

Keg Creek Battlefield

The battlefield is located 8 miles southwest of Washington. On the morning of February 14, 1779, colonial patriots commanded by Andrew Pickens, John Dooly, and Elijah Clark ambushed a British encampment at Keg Creek. The British, led by Colonel Boyd, mounted a counterattack but were routed by Clark's men. Every February 14, Revolutionary War enactors re-create the famous battle.

Watson Mill Bridge State Park

This state park, 3 miles southeast of Comer, Georgia, is on the South Fork River, a tributary of the Broad River. Its namesake was the Watson Mill, which opened as a gristmill in 1798 and continued in operation until the nineteenth century. The mill disappeared early in the twentieth century. The park offers hiking and horse trails along the river and into the park's backcountry. Bartram would have traveled very close to the park on his route from Cherokee Corners to the Tugaloo River. The park offers camping and boating on the millpond and the river.

Bartram Recreation Trail
Clarks Hill Lake / J. Strom Thurmond Lake

In the 1970s the Georgia Bartram Trail Society, working with the U.S. Army Corps of Engineers, built more than 40 miles of foot trails along the shore of Clarks Hill Lake, also known as Thurmond Lake. The trail existed in two sections. Section 1 spanned the area from Thurmond Dam westward, winding in and out of a series of fingers along the southern shore of the lake to Keg Creek. Section 2 began at the Ridge Road Campground and worked westward to the Little River Bridge, also on Ga. 104. By the early 1990s most of the second section was overgrown, and long segments in the middle of the trail had vanished altogether. Many parts of the Section 1 trail were in dire need of work as well.

In the last five years the path of the original Section 1 trail has been restored. Scout groups, bicycle clubs, and the Bartram Trail Conference are working with the U.S. Army Corps of Engineers to improve the trail as a suitable path for both hiking and biking. This guide divides the original trail into three sections, from the dam westward to the trail around the headwaters of Keg Creek. The Corps of Engineers plans to fully restore the trail and also to complete new sections in Wildwood Park and west of Keg Creek.

Section 1

Section: West Dam to Petersburg
Distance: 6.2 miles from U.S. 221 to Petersburg Road
Difficulty: easy; mostly flat
Hazards: steep draws crossing streams
Highlights: Lake Spring Creek; greenway (site of the old airfield)

The eastern trailhead for this section begins in the U.S. Army Corps of Engineers West Dam Recreation Area. The trail begins a few hundred feet from U.S. 221 on the paved loop immediately in front of the entrance station. Facing the station, the trail begins to the left, heading west. In approximately 200 feet the trail intersects another footpath. The Bartram Trail continues to the

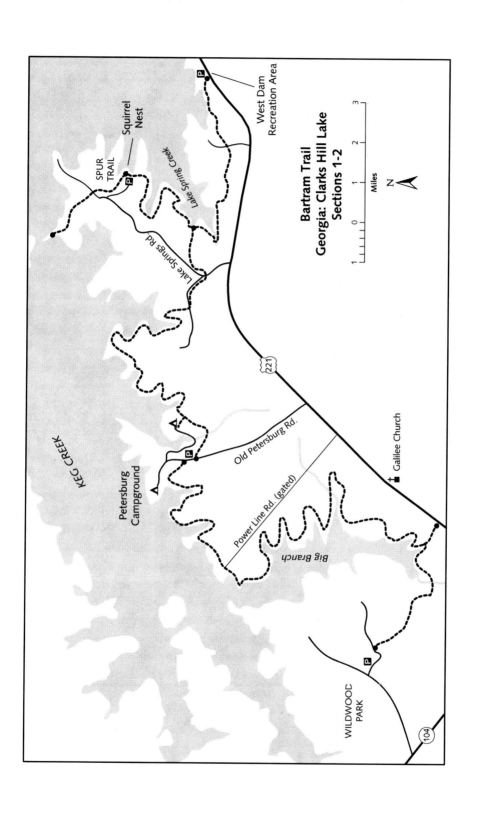

Bartram Trail
Georgia: Clarks Hill Lake
Sections 1-2

West Dam
Recreation Area

Squirrel
Nest

SPUR
TRAIL

Lake Spring Creek

Lake Springs Rd.

KEG CREEK

Petersburg
Campground

Old Petersburg Rd.

Power Line Rd. (gated)

Big Branch

Galilee Church

WILDWOOD
PARK

221

104

N

Miles

1   0   1   2   3

left, climbing a ridge, then descends and turns sharply to the right, heading toward the docks at the Augusta Yacht Club. The path then turns to the left and climbs another shallow ridge. After turning to the right **(mile 0.3)** the trail rolls up and down for the next 0.2 mile along the north face of a ridge. In this area the forest is mixed evergreen and hardwood, with sweetgum trees and loblolly pines.

The path crosses an old road **(mile 0.6)** as it continues to work in a westerly direction. In a little more than 0.1 mile it angles to the north, intersecting Yacht Club Road **(mile 0.8)**—leading to the left to U.S. 221. The path resumes its westerly direction until it crosses another old road, when it turns sharply to the right. For the next 0.4 mile the trail tracks to the northwest through a wide cove opening to the northwest. After crossing a steep draw **(mile 1.25)** the trail approaches the shore of the lake, then turns to the west to the mouth of Lake Spring Creek. From here the trail follows the creek upstream for 0.1 mile and then crosses it on a wooden footbridge **(mile 1.4)**. Here the trail turns sharply to the right and then proceeds down the left bank of the stream, crossing two draws **(mile 1.6)** that feed into the creek. After a few hundred feet the trail leaves the creek and turns left, to the north. Climbing a ridge, the path crosses the bed of an old road before it begins a descent into a wetland. Soon the trail intersects, to the right, the Lake Springs Spur Trail **(mile 1.9)**.

The trail continues to the left as it climbs to the west-northwest. Soon it approaches Lake Springs Road **(mile 2.2)**. The path levels and continues to the southwest. In 0.1 mile the Bartram Trail turns sharply to the right and then climbs for 200 feet to intersect Lake Springs Road **(mile 2.4)**, crosses it, and angles to the left on the other side. Just after the crossing is a wooden sign indicating, incorrectly, 5.7 miles to Petersburg.

Working down the ridge, the trail runs roughly parallel to the gravel road to its right. The descent ends as the trail enters a wetland **(mile 2.6)**. After a short climb, the trail turns to the north and crosses the gravel road (to the right, the road returns to Lake Springs Road). Passing some homes on the right, the trail works to the northwest to a narrow finger of the lake. It crosses two draws that drain into the finger, the second with a wooden footbridge over an unnamed stream **(mile 2.8)**. For the next 0.5 mile the trail turns more to the north, working along the western shore of the finger and going in and out of nubs along the lake. From here to the Petersburg Campground the trail is well out of the sight of roads, recreation areas, and homes. Patches of mistletoe grow high up in some of the loblolly and shortleaf pines.

At **mile 3.5** the trail reaches the northeast corner of the peninsula and then turns sharply to the left and the west. For the next 0.2 mile it follows the northern shore of this peninsula until reaching the greenway (mile 3.7). This was the site of the old Corps of Engineers airfield. In the greenway, follow, to the left, the posts with yellow blazes. In little more than 0.25 mile the trail reenters the forest (mile 4.0).

From the greenway the trail turns to the northwest, heading toward the point directly across from the old landing strip. From here it curls inland toward the base of the shallow cove (mile 4.3), then works its way out to the main body of Keg Creek, following the western shore of the cove. The forest throughout this area is predominantly pine, with several flat areas suitable for camping. At the end of the point the path turns to the southwest, following the shoreline along a nub into the lake. To the northwest are views of Petersburg Campground on the opposite side of the large cove. Crossing a shallow ridge via a short switchback, the path passes a second nub as the trail turns to the south and eventually to the southeast. At the base of a small inlet it crosses the stream that empties into the lake (mile 4.9). The trail then forms another arc, curling to the west and to the south, approaching the base of another cove. Crossing the unnamed stream (mile 5.1) on a wooden footbridge, the path turns to the northwest toward the campground. As it approaches the established campsite, which is well within view, the Bartram Trail turns sharply to the left, intersecting a path that leads to campsite 1. The trail continues to the left. In a few hundred feet the path intersects an old road to the right (mile 5.4). This road is the preferred access trail to the campground.

To continue on Section 1, turn left and follow the old road. In a few hundred feet the trail reaches a gully, crossing it without the benefit of a bridge. After a level section the path approaches another steep draw (mile 5.6). From here the trail follows the boundary of Corps of Engineers property, then parallels it to the right at a distance of no more than 100 feet. To the right there are views of Petersburg Campground; straight ahead is the pond that is dammed by the campground road. The trail works southward, with the pond on the right. In a few hundred feet it crosses the stream that feeds into the pond (mile 5.8). Shortly after the crossing, the path enters a soggy area as it approaches a second stream crossing. From here the Bartram Trail joins an old roadbed (mile 6.0) as it climbs to higher ground. For the next 0.2 mile the path winds to the west en route to the main road into the campground. It intersects the road just inside the campground gate (mile 6.2). The trail continues on the paved road past the entrance station, then leaves the road after a few hundred feet, turning sharply to the left, to the eastern trailhead for Section 2.

West Dam: From the junction of U.S. 221 and Ga. 104 in Pollards Corner, take U.S. 221 North. At the West Dam Recreation Area **(mile 4.6)**, turn left. Immediately outside the gate is a small parking area that holds only two vehicles. This area is intended for hikers only. Additional parking is available on the other side of U.S. 221, on the road leading to the Savannah River, or inside the recreation area for a daily use fee.

Lake Springs Road: From the junction of U.S. 221 and Ga. 104 in Pollards Corner, take U.S. 221 North. In 2.1 miles U.S. 221 intersects Petersburg Road. In a little more than 1 mile **(mile 3.4)** the highway intersects Lake Springs Road. Turn left onto the paved road. From the West Dam Recreation Area it is 1.3 miles to Lake Springs Road via U.S. 221 South. In 0.4 mile the road intersects the Bartram Trail. There are pull-offs on both sides of the road for day hikers.

Petersburg Road: From the junction of U.S. 221 and Ga. 104 in Pollards Corner, take U.S. 221 North. In 2.1 miles, U.S. 221 intersects Petersburg Road. Turn left onto the paved road. After 1.5 miles the road enters the Petersburg Campground. From the West Dam Recreation Area, it is 2.5 miles to Petersburg Road via U.S. 221 South.

Section 2

Section:	Petersburg to Big Branch
Distance:	6.4 miles from Petersburg Road to U.S. 221
Difficulty:	easy
Hazards:	trail difficult to find in sections
Highlights:	wetland west of the campground

This section begins in the Petersburg Campground, on the west side of Petersburg Road, approximately 300 feet north of the registration station. For several hundred feet the footpath meanders in a northerly direction in sight of the campground road. The forest it passes through is second growth; 90 percent of the trees are pines, 10 percent are hardwoods. As the trail turns away from the road, it approaches the western section of the campground. As the path nears campsite 75 **(mile 0.2)**, the trail makes an abrupt left turn, bypassing the campground.

In approximately 200 feet the trail crosses a small stream. Then, in 500 feet, the path crosses the first of five wooden footbridges. After the first crossing **(mile 0.3)**, the trail comes within 50 feet of the lake. Turning to the southwest, the path remains close to the lakeshore for more than 0.1 mile as it works down the eastern shore of the lake's finger. The trail then veers away from the shoreline, passing a small boulder field to the left. In a little more than 100 feet the Bartram Trail crosses the second wooden footbridge, and then, about 100 feet farther on, crosses the third over another unnamed creek **(mile 0.5)**. Just beyond the bridge is a faint trail leading to the lakeshore. As the trail approaches the end of the lake's finger, it crosses another footbridge, reaching the fifth bridge at the finger's end **(mile 0.6)**.

From the last bridge, the trail makes a slight ascent as it curls northwest. As the trail works up the west side of the finger, it passes a small peninsula to the right. From here the path continues northward, toward the main body of Clarks Hill Lake, cutting through a grove of flowering shrubs **(mile 0.9)**. In less than 0.1 mile the trail reaches the point of the peninsula. Directly across the small bay is the boat ramp for Petersburg Campground. From the point, the trail heads in a westerly direction for more than 0.25 mile, approaching the eastern shore of another of Clarks Hill Lake's fingers. The path reaches a small, pointed peninsula **(mile 1.2)** jutting into the main body of the lake. From here it continues to work to the southwest to the end of the lake's finger. As the path approaches the end, it crosses a stream and then cuts through a small wetland for approximately 0.1 mile **(mile 1.4)**.

Exiting the wetland, the Bartram Trail climbs a shallow ridge. The trail reaches an old roadbed in less than 500 feet **(mile 1.5)**, and then crosses a second stream in less than 0.1 mile. From here, the trail turns to the north to follow the western shore of this finger. As the path works its way northward, it comes within 50 feet of the lake **(mile 1.75)**. In approximately 100 feet the trail makes an abrupt left turn, climbing another shallow ridge and leaving the shore to cut across the peninsula through a young pine forest. The trail becomes faint in this section. On the other side of the peninsula the trail works its way to the northwest. The path crosses a stream and then heads directly for the shoreline **(mile 2.2)**. The Keg Creek section of the lake and some small circular islands just offshore are visible from here. Curling to the southwest, the Bartram Trail reaches the Power Line Road in a little more than 0.1 mile **(mile 2.4)**.

The trail resumes on the other side of the road, heading in a westerly direction. As the trail descends, it curls to the southeast toward Big Branch **(mile 2.6)**. In 0.1 mile the trail crosses over a shallow ridge as it nears the lakeshore, then curves to the left as it works up the bay formed by the impounding of Big Branch Creek. For the next 2 miles the trail will work in and out along a series of five fingers on the eastern shore of Big Branch.

The Bartram Trail continues to the southwest, following the contour of the peninsula, at first to the southwest and then turning to the southeast. It reaches the first finger **(mile 3.0)** as the path turns sharply to the left. After heading in a northerly direction for a few hundred feet, it crosses a steep draw. The path continues to the east, running parallel to a draw with exposed boulders. Shortly it crosses the second draw **(mile 3.2)** and then turns to the west to return to Big Branch. The trail works to the west and then turns to the south. In a short distance it heads southeast as it begins to follow the outline of the second finger. Heading to the east, it crosses two steep draws within 200 feet **(mile 3.6)**.

After the second crossing the trail turns to the west and then to the south, continuing down the eastern shore of Big Branch to the third finger. For a few hundred feet the path turns to the east, working up the short finger, and then crosses a draw **(mile 4.2)**, returning to the southwest. In a few hundred feet the trail reaches the next finger and begins to turn inland again. It crosses a small stream **(mile 4.4)** and turns to the southeast for about 0.1 mile, then turns sharply to the southwest, working down the narrow peninsula that separates the fourth and fifth fingers. As it approaches the point, the path angles to the south and then the southeast **(mile 4.8)** along the north shore of the fifth finger. To avoid the wetland and steep draw crossings the trail heads due east for nearly 0.2 mile. Here the trail turns to the southeast and crosses a small creek **(mile 5.3)**. In the next 0.1 mile it crosses two additional draws that drain into the finger.

The trail works back to Big Branch and then angles to the southwest along the bay. As it approaches a nub in the lake the footpath bends inland and then returns to its original track. At **mile 6.4** the trail turns to the west. For the next 0.5 mile it works in and out of two fingers on the southern shore of the bay. Crossing the draw that drains into the first finger, the trail turns sharply to the northwest. It climbs a shallow ridge and then descends to the eastern bank of the second finger and to an unnamed stream **(mile 6.7)**.

Continue on the Bartram Trail by crossing the stream and turning to the right. After a short climb the trail levels as it heads west. On reaching the boundary marker for the Corps of Engineers land, the trail continues west to Big Branch Creek **(mile 7.1)**. The Corps plans to build a bridge over the creek. Unless the lake level is low, it is impossible to cross the creek on a bicycle. In 0.2 mile the trail crosses a draw **(mile 7.3)** and then turns to the north, crossing the first of several small streams that drain into Big Branch.

The trail has now entered Wildwood Park, leased by the Corps to Columbia County. As it heads north, it climbs the base of a hill before turning to the

From the creek crossing, follow the faint trail on the right bank of the stream upstream. The trail stays close to the stream for nearly 0.2 mile. As you approach the fence, turn left and follow the trail to its end at the highway.

northwest and working down the ridge. The trail crosses two branches and then begins to climb to the northwest to its junction with the Wildwood Bike Trail. Turn left and follow the orange-blazed trail, as the two trails share the same path until they end at the road **(mile 8.3)**.

ACCESS POINTS

Petersburg Road (eastern trailhead): From the junction of U.S. 221 and Ga. 104 in Pollards Corner, take U.S. 221 North. In 2.1 miles U.S. 221 intersects Petersburg Road. Turn left onto the paved road. In 1.5 miles the road enters the Petersburg Campground. From the West Dam Recreation Area it is 2.5 miles to Petersburg Road via U.S. 221 South.

U.S. 221 (western trailhead): From the junction of U.S. 221 and Ga. 104 in Pollards Corner, take U.S. 221 North. In 1.1 miles there is a pullover on the left side of the road. This parking area is for the short access trail to the Bartram Trail. From the east, this pullover is 1 mile west of Petersburg Road and 0.1 mile west of Cana-in-Galilee Baptist Church.

Wildwood Park (western trailhead): From the junction of U.S. 221 and Ga. 104 in Pollards Corner, take Ga. 104 to the north. The entrance to the park is a little more than 2 miles on the right. Turn right and follow the road to the entrance station. Past the station, turn right on the paved road. The trailhead for the Bartram Trail is 0.5 mile on the right.

Lake Springs Spur Trail

Section: spur trail off Section 1
Distance: 2.4 miles
Difficulty: easy
Hazards: none
Highlights: Piedmont flora; 1 mile of the trail is paved and handicapped accessible

The southern trailhead for this section is at the junction with Section 1, north of Lake Springs Road. From the junction, turn to the right (coming from the east) and cross the stream at the head of the inlet. The footpath winds toward a small nub into the lake, then continues to work northward on the western side of Lake Spring Creek inlet. The path curls to the east **(mile 0.35)** and then to the southeast on a point that extends to the south. In 500 feet it turns again to the north, offering views of the main body of the lake. On reaching the northernmost point of the peninsula **(mile 0.6)** the trail turns to the west. For the next 0.5 mile it follows the outline of Bream Cove, from the southern shore to the northern one. Working to the west, the trail crosses a stream on a wooden footbridge **(mile 0.9)**, turning to the north around the eastern end of the cove. In just a few hundred feet the path turns to the east. Just to the left, in approximately 25 feet, is the access road from Lake Springs Road. After intersecting the walkway to the fishing dock, it enters a parking lot **(mile 1.1)** and angles toward the boat ramp. The footpath resumes near the comfort station as it continues to head east on Deer Run. The path angles toward the northern shore of Deer Run and turns back to the west. To the right are the first of many picnic areas that line the lakeshore. The path curls to the north and then the east into the parking area at Deer Run **(mile 1.4)**.

Cross the road to continue the trail (near the comfort station). This section, formerly known as the Lake Springs All Points Interpretive Trail, is paved and can be either biked or walked, and is wheelchair accessible. It has markers for the surrounding trees, plants, and land features. As the trail is restored, these markers will be replaced with interpretive displays on the area's flora and fauna, and on Bartram and his travels. The trail passes through a wetland on a boardwalk and crosses two streams, both on wooden bridges (the second at **mile 1.7**). Through this section grow many of the trees, shrubs, and flowers that Bartram described and inventoried on his visit to nearby Wrightsborough and the Little River, including red oak, white oak, silver bell, red cedar, and sweetgum.

At **mile 2.3** the trail exits the woods into another paved parking lot. To the right, the road leads to Mallard Point. The trail continues along the side of the parking area, then turns to the left following the road to the north. In the next parking lot the trail angles to the left and leaves the road to become a footpath again. The path ends in less than 300 feet **(mile 1.0)** at the boardwalk leading to the observation tower. The tower, located on a small island north of Mallard Point, offers panoramic views of the lake and its southern shore.

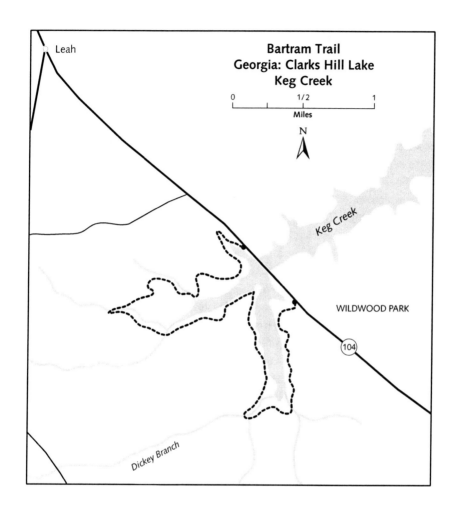

Bartram Trail
Georgia: Clarks Hill Lake
Keg Creek

Leah

0   1/2   1
Miles

N

Keg Creek

WILDWOOD PARK

104

Dickey Branch

Section 3

Section: Keg Creek
Distance: 7.3-mile loop
Difficulty: easy with several moderate ascents
Hazards: for bikers, steep draws crossing creeks, blowdowns, and
               riding on Ga. 104
Highlights: Keg Creek

This section of the Bartram Trail is not contiguous with Section 2. The path forms a 7.3-mile loop around two large fingers of Clarks Hill Lake. The loop is not complete; the northern and southern trailheads are 0.5 mile apart. The trail, blazed in yellow, works its way through gentle Piedmont hills and crosses a number of small streams, notably Keg Creek and Dickey Branch, and their associated wetlands. The trail is open to mountain bikes.

The trail begins at the paved parking lot, just north of the Ga. 104 bridge over Keg Creek. From here the trail dips to the lake, quickly rises, and then descends for a second time. In less than 0.1 mile the path crosses a small stream on a wooden footbridge. In a few hundred more feet there is a second footbridge as the Bartram Trail works up the side of the lake. The trail now parallels a small stream, moving away from the main body of the lake. There is a small boulder field, and then the trail turns to the left to cross the unnamed stream **(mile 0.25)**. The path then follows the steam toward the lake. Crossing another footbridge, it enters a mixed hardwood-pine forest. As the path approaches the main body of the lake it turns to the right **(mile 0.5)**. The forest in this area is predominantly evergreens dominated by loblolly pines.

Crossing another footbridge, the trail enters a grove of wax myrtles. Soon it intersects an old road, the bed of the Old Washington Road, or Old Petersburg Road, from Petersburg to Augusta **(mile 0.7)**. The trail works down to the main body of the lake, where it intersects an old jeep road **(mile 1.0)**. The Bartram Trail continues to the left, at first due north and then turning toward the west. After crossing a ridge, the footpath angles back to the lake, passing through a stand of beech, swamp maple, and loblolly pines. Near the lakeshore the trail enters the Keg Creek Wildlife Management Area **(mile 1.2)**. Angling to the north, the path crosses a stream after a little more than 0.1 mile. It then climbs a small ridge, skirting a canebrake. Finishing the arc, the path skirts the main body of the lake. In the floodplain of Keg Creek, the path continues in a westerly direction, then approaches an unnamed branch from the northwest **(mile 1.7)**. The trail turns and follows the branch upstream. In less than 0.25 mile there is a large oak near the stream branch with a circumference of more than 15 feet. More boulders appear in the stream, and the path crosses the stream near a large boulder **(mile 2.0)**.

On the west bank, the trail curls to the right and continues for more than 0.1 mile upstream. It then veers to the left to begin a steady climb up a ridge. Here the path is heading southwest, away from the creek. The climb continues via a gentle switchback as the top of the ridge comes into view. The trail then dips slightly near the boundary maker for the Corps of Engineers property **(mile 2.3)**. The short descent ends, and the climb resumes as the footpath becomes much more serpentine. The trail soon reaches the top of the ridge on a wide saddle. In a few hundred feet the path begins to descend in a southwesterly direction, past American holly and wax myrtle. There is an abrupt turn to the south-southwest as the trail enters the Keg Creek floodplain. Soon the trail reaches the creek **(mile 2.8)**, which is lined with boulders that make suitable picnic rocks; 150 feet upstream is the Corps of Engineers boundary marker.

The trail begins to follow the creek downstream, heading northeast. In a little more than 0.25 mile it crosses a small stream branch and then dips down into a steep draw **(mile 3.3)**. After making a sharp right turn, the path veers to the left, crossing another small branch. Soon the Highway 104 bridge comes into view to the east **(mile 3.6)**. The path at first curls to the right and then to the left (to the east) as it begins to work in an easterly direction on the southern shore of Keg Creek. The trail crosses an unnamed branch on a wooden footbridge as it continues eastward **(mile 3.8)**. Approaching the point of the peninsula, the path meets another section of Washington Road **(mile 4.1)**.

The trail then turns to the right and begins to head down the western shore of Dickey Branch, soon crossing another section of the old sunken road. To the south there is a view of the branch as the path enters another large wax myrtle grove. The trail then intersects an old road that heads into a nub into the lake. In a little more than 0.1 mile the path crosses a small branch, turns to the left to climb a shallow ridge **(mile 5.25)**, and then quickly descends to the right. To the left is a wetland. In this section the path continues to head in a southeasterly direction, rejoining the main body of Dickey Branch. In a few hundred feet the trail crosses Dickey Branch on a wooden footbridge **(mile 5.7)**.

The trail turns to the left and follows the branch downstream. In a few hundred feet it crosses over a second branch. Turning away from the branch, the path climbs a ridge. After leveling off it continues down the other side, veering away from the lake **(mile 6.0)**. The trail enters the wide floodplain of an unnamed stream, crosses the stream, and turns to the left to join an old roadbed. Now heading toward the lake, the footpath crosses another small stream **(mile 6.3)** and again turns away from the lake as it continues to work in and out of shallow coves.

The trail enters an open field with stands for duck hunting **(mile 6.9)**. The path crosses a small stream on a footbridge, with a second crossing in a few hundred feet. Soon the path intersects another section of the Old Washington Road **(mile 7.2)** and turns, heading south on the western side of a cove. After crossing another wooden footbridge, the path is now parallel to the sunken road. The trail descends, via steps, to a footbridge. After crossing the stream, it regains the elevation via another series of steps **(mile 7.3)**. Ga. 104 is now within sight as the path descends to another bridge and climbs up again. In a few hundred feet the trail reaches the road and the southern trailhead.

ACCESS POINTS

Both trailheads are located on Ga. 104, north of Pollards Corner. The **northern trailhead** is immediately north of the highway bridge over Keg Creek. Parking and access to the trail are on the west side of the road. The **southern trailhead** is 0.5 mile to the south. A tenth of a mile north of the trailhead there is a small parking area off the state highway.

Bartram Canoe Trail
Broad River

In June 1775 Bartram visited the Broad River on a botanical excursion with the desire "to collect some curiosities" (T375). It is easy to understand why a botanist would be entertained in the Broad River watershed. The variety and proliferation of the flora there continue to inspire and amaze those who see it. Bartram first visited the Broad in the summer of 1773 in the company of the surveying party sent out from the Indian Congress held in Augusta. He crossed the river en route from Cherokee Corners to the Tugaloo River. The party encamped on a "considerable branch" of the Broad and spent a day taking "the course distance, and observations on Broad River, and from thence down to its confluence with the Savanna" (T41). Bartram busied himself with "some very curious and new shrubs and plants, particularly the Physic-nut, or Indian Olive."

His description of the upper river is still accurate today: "This branch of the Broad River is about twelve yards wide, and has two, three, and four feet depth of water, and winds through a fertile vale, almost overshadowed on one side by a ridge of high hills, well timbered with Oak, Hiccory, . . . and on their rocky summits . . . Rhododendron ferruginium" (T44).

Later, on his way back to Augusta, Bartram noted that, "the surveyors having completed their observations, . . . we crossed the Broad River, at a newly settled plantation, near its confluence with the Savanna" (T46). This most likely was at the site of Petersburg, at one time among the most prosperous towns in early Georgia but today beneath the waters of Clarks Hill Lake.

Canoeing down the Broad

The northern tributaries of the Broad River tumble out of Stephens and Franklin Counties as the North and West Forks of the Broad River and out of Banks County as the Hudson River. They come together near Franklin Springs and are known thereafter as the Broad. From that point the river flows 50 miles through rock outcrops, pastoral countryside, and lush woodland to Clarks Hill Reservoir and on to the Savannah River.

The Broad is one of the last undammed rivers in the Piedmont. Along its course there are numerous sandbars, bluffs, branches, oxbows, and small islands. Basking turtles, flashing kingfishers, herons, and ducks are abundant. Large catfish hide under the banks, and otter and beaver are often seen swimming at dusk. The upper stretches of the river are flanked by high granite outcrops covered with mountain laurel and wild azalea. The languid flow of the lower stretches takes the river traveler quietly to Anthony Shoals. Here the river is wide and rocky with a picturesque vista. It drops down through the shoals for 0.5 mile into Clarks Hill Lake.

Section 1:   U.S. 29 to Ga. 72

Distance: 21.5 miles

Hazards: rocky shoals; waterfall; strainers

Highlights: rock outcrops; Indian fish weir; shoals; sandbars; wildlife

From U.S. 29 one can put in at either the Hudson River bridge or the Broad River bridge. The Hudson is a small, intimate, playful tributary of the Broad River. It flows into the Broad less than 0.5 mile from the Highway 29 bridge. Traveling down the Broad, one enters a river corridor with lush overhanging vegetation and rippling shoals. A mile or so downstream from the Hudson-Broad confluence is the remnant of an ancient Indian fish weir, easily identified in low water as stacked stones assembled in an inverted V across the width of the river. For another 5 miles the river passes through occasional granite outcrops and eventually reaches the Ga. 281 crossing. Just below the Ga. 281 bridge on the right side of the river is the Broad River Outpost, a longtime river outfitter where visitors can get oriented to the river's features, resupply, or arrange for excursions and shuttles.

On the 5.5-mile stretch of the river between Ga. 281 and Ga. 172 there are numerous class 1 and class 2 rapids, making for quite lively paddling. Below Ga. 172 the river passes through a few last sets of rapids and then settles down to a leisurely pace, winding past sandbars and merging creeks. Six miles below Ga. 172 Holly Creek enters the river. Opposite the entry point is a large sandbar and the last remote campsite before the Ga. 72 bridge, 3 miles farther downriver. The Highway 72 bridge, with its graceful cast concrete arches, has a rain gauge on its downstream side.

Section 2:   Ga. 72 to Clarks Hill Lake

Distance: 29 miles

Hazards: powerboats on Clarks Hill Lake

Highlights: river bluffs; shoals; sandbars; wildlife

From Ga. 72 the Broad flows steadily on in twists and turns, southeast at first and then gradually straightening out and heading east. About 2 miles

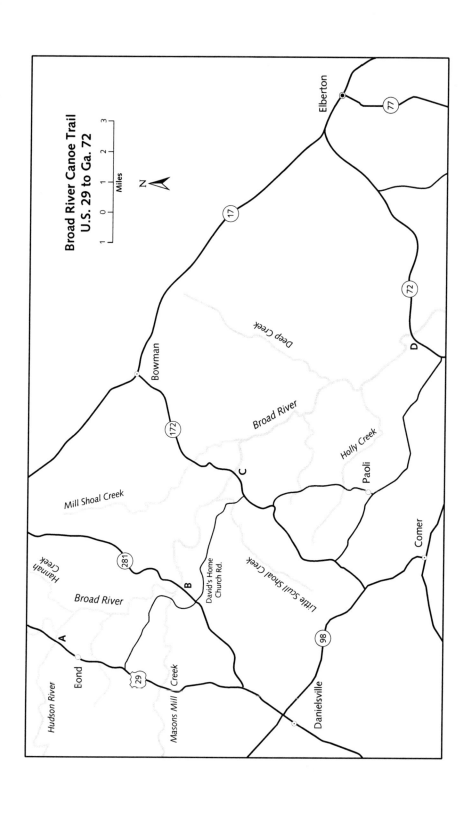

Broad River Canoe Trail
U.S. 29 to Ga. 72

N

Miles

1 0 1 2 3

Hudson River

Eond

A

Masons Mill Creek

29

Broad River

Hannah Creek

281

B

David's Home Church Rd.

Mill Shoal Creek

172

C

Bowman

Broad River

Deep Creek

17

Elberton

77

72

D

Holly Creek

Paoli

Little Scull Shoal Creek

98

Danielsville

Comer

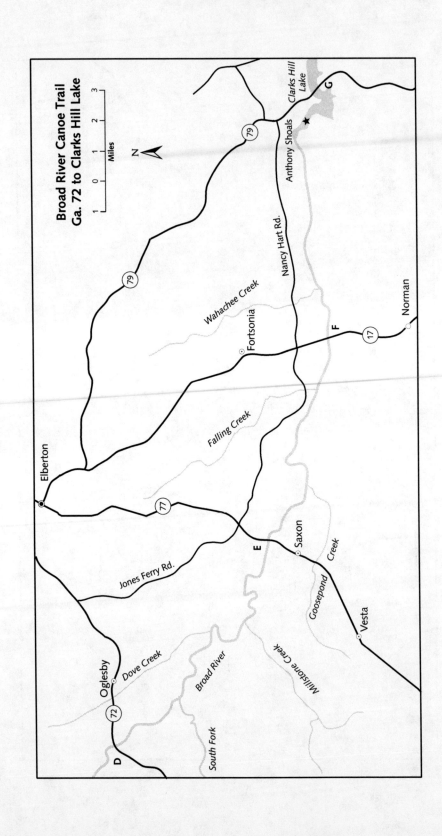

Broad River Canoe Trail
Ga. 72 to Clarks Hill Lake

N

Miles
1 0 1 2 3

Clarks Hill Lake
G
Anthony Shoals
79
Nancy Hart Rd.
Wahachee Creek
Fortsonia
79
Elberton
Falling Creek
77
F
17
Norman
Jones Ferry Rd.
Saxon
E
Goosepond Creek
Vesta
Oglesby
Dove Creek
Broad River
Millstone Creek
72
D
South Fork

from the Ga. 72 bridge is a large island with a few potential campsites. A mile downstream from there, the South Fork of the Broad River flows in on the right. Three miles or so below the South Fork, just after Dove Creek enters the Broad on the left, another large island has formed in a sharp bend of the river. Several camping opportunities offer themselves here: usually there is a big sandbar on the bend, and a high, remote sand bluff rises from there. The back side of the island also has several small, secluded nooks in the low forest cover. Five miles downstream is the Ga. 77 bridge.

From the Ga. 77 bridge it is an 8.5-mile paddle to Ga. 17 and then another 7 miles to **Anthony Shoals**. This stretch of the Broad River valley is a very relaxed, pastoral float. At Anthony Shoals the river widens and drops into Clarks Hill Lake. In late spring Anthony Shoals is the perfect place to take a "little botanical excursion." Magnificent stands of shoal spider lilies bloom among the rocky islets. From the bottom of the shoals, Clarks Hill Lake backs up into the river and it is a 2-mile paddle across the lake to Bobby Brown State Park.

Voyage to
East Florida

Lower St. Johns River

After his journey to Cherokee Corners Bartram returned to Savannah, where he "was alarmed by an express from Augusta that the Indians were for war" (R1:58). Bartram's alarm was justified. The Creeks were unhappy about the loss of the "New Purchase" lands ceded to Georgia under the Treaty of Augusta. Indian–settler relations were further strained when white colonists brutally murdered two young Cherokees in July. Although the murders were avenged by the subsequent killing of two whites, tensions continued to run high. On Christmas Day 1773 Creek Indians massacred Georgians at Wrightsborough and for the next three weeks terrorized white settlers in the countryside north and west of Augusta. Bartram had intended to travel into Creek and Cherokee country, but hostilities "put a stop to that scheme" (JBC769).

Bartram instead remained at the Georgia coast during the fall and winter of 1773 as a guest of the McIntosh family. He turned his attention southward and planned a trip to the familiar territory of East Florida, hoping to re-create the expedition he had made with his father in 1765. On that trip, made two years after the territory became part of Britain's New World empire, father and son had sought out the region's "curious and most valuable vegetable and mineral productions" and also looked for "the sources of great River St. Juan." Following the publication of John Bartram's journal in 1767, the first published report on Florida's flora, and of William's *Travels* in 1791, a string of naturalists pursued the track of father and son along the St. Johns; among their number were André Michaux, Thomas Say, George Ord, and John Eatton Le Conte (JBD6–8).

All were drawn by Florida's exotic landscape. Florida was unique in the British colonies, as it is today in the United States, in bridging the temperate and semitropical zones. The warm seas that surround the peninsula and the plentiful rainfall nurture a diverse flora that exceeds 3,000 species, more than any other state east of the Mississippi, making Florida a haven for eighteenth-century—and twenty-first-century—naturalists.

Bartram made four excursions in Florida. Two were on the St. Johns River, from Spalding's Upper Store upstream (i.e., south, because the St. Johns flows

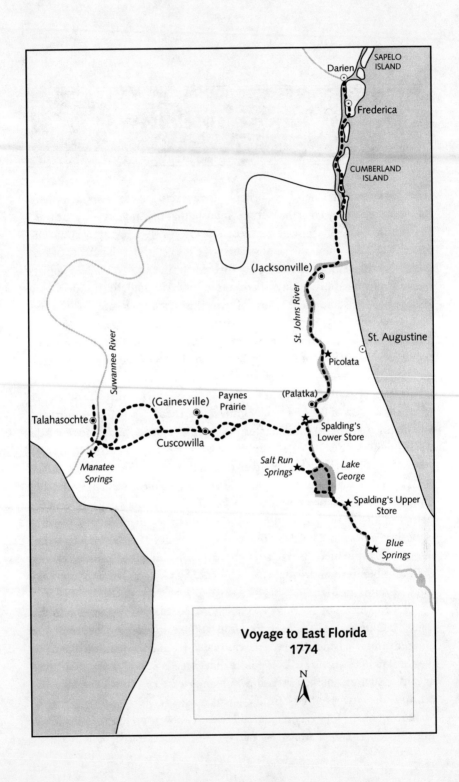

SAPELO
ISLAND

Darien

Frederica

CUMBERLAND
ISLAND

(Jacksonville)

St. Johns River

St. Augustine

Picolata

Suwannee River

(Gainesville)   Paynes
               Prairie   (Palatka)

Talahasochte   Spalding's
                                                Lower Store
              Cuscowilla

*Manatee   *Salt Run   *Lake
Springs*   Springs*   George

                                                Spalding's Upper
                                                Store

                                             *Blue
                                             Springs*

**Voyage to East Florida
1774**

N

north), as far as Blue Springs. His accounts of Salt Springs, the alligators at Battle Lagoon, and the Alachua Savanna continue to impress modern readers, just as they did the Romantic poets of the nineteenth century. East Florida also provided Bartram with another opportunity to meet the native inhabitants of the new land—this time the third major division of the Creeks, the Seminoles. Bartram made two journeys into Florida's Indian country, regarded then as the lands west of the St. Johns River, joining traders' caravans on two journeys to the leading Seminole town, Cuscowilla, near today's Micanopy. On the first trip he toured the Alachua Savanna, which led to one of Bartram's most celebrated passages in the *Travels* (T368). Bartram's second trip into Indian country took him farther west to the Suwannee River, the Seminole settlements along its banks, and Manatee Springs.

The landscape that John and William Bartram saw in 1765 was much altered when William returned nine short years later. The right bank of the St. Johns had been cleared for agriculture, and moss-draped oaks had been replaced by plantations. The most dramatic changes in the region have taken place more recently, of course, in the last 100 years. At the beginning of the twentieth century, more than 90 percent of the state's pine flatwoods remained uncultivated and 99 percent of the coastal strand retained its natural vegetation. Most of the swamp forests described by the Bartrams were intact.

Mere fractions of these ecosystems exist today. Through the twentieth century, in particular after World War II, commercial and residential development replaced them. Agriculture, flood control, and "ditch-and-drain" land management also exacted a toll. Three-quarters of the marshland around the St. Johns River between Orlando and Sanford was drained during the twentieth century for development and flood control. The pristine wetlands Bartram saw on his travels no longer exist.

Vigorous conservation efforts over the course of the last thirty years in Florida have managed to save some of the remaining wetlands. Part of that work is evident at Paynes Prairie in Alachua County, in the preservation of wetlands along the St. Johns River by the St. Johns River Water Management Authority, and in the preservation of the sand-hills scrub in the Ocala National Forest.

Gone, too, are the Indian cultures Bartram sought to visit; only a few traces and an occasional historical marker remain. The Indians cannot be brought back, but state archaeologists and historians are working to preserve what is known about their culture and to establish archaeological sites as points of public interpretation so that residents and tourists can learn more about Florida's former residents.

The huge difference between the natural landscape of East Florida described in the *Travels* and the physical landscape one sees in retracing Bartram's path is a stark reminder of how drastically American culture has affected the landscape in a relatively short period. In offering Bartram's terrain within this guidebook, the authors invite you to relish the land and its natural wonders, but also to witness the impact humans have had on it in just over 200 years. As befits Bartram's text, we predict astonishment, though not necessarily always awe.

To Spalding's Lower Store

Bartram planned to visit East Florida during the fall of 1773. Before the end of September he shipped his baggage to Spalding's Lower Store on the St. Johns River before he set off on horseback for the Altamaha River (R1:58). En route to Darien he fell seriously ill with a fever and was forced to delay his journey for more than two months. He recuperated as the guest of the McIntosh family. When he was well, Bartram set out for Florida but once again had to postpone the trip, "turned back again by expresses from Et Florida that the Indians were up in Arms against us in that Province having killed & captivated several white People" (JBC768–769). He remained in Georgia "waiting for a favorable turn," spending his time collecting "many valuable and new Vegitables."

Bartram set out once more for Florida in March 1774. He traveled down the Altamaha to St. Simons Island and **Frederica**, and visited the home of James Spalding, where he requested letters of introduction to Spalding's agent for his Florida stores. Then, letters in hand, Bartram left for Florida on one of Spalding's vessels. As the ship sailed down the channel east of **Cumberland Island**, the passengers received news from a northbound vessel that Spalding's Upper Store had been attacked by Indians. Once again the trip to Florida was in jeopardy. The captain of Bartram's vessel decided to return to Frederica rather than proceed, but Bartram was anxious to recover his chest with its valuable books and papers (T64). The captain agreed to put Bartram off on Cumberland Island to make his own way south.

From Cumberland Island Bartram was ferried to the northern shore of Amelia Island, where he and a young passenger who had decided to accompany him into East Florida headed south by land. They crossed Egan's Creek into the "New Settlement"—today's Old Town Fernandina. John Percival's indigo plantation occupied much of the northern end of the island, now part of Fort Clinch State Park. Bartram was the guest of the plantation's agent, Mr. Egan, who had extended an offer of hospitality. Bartram and his young companion spent several days at the plantation. As part of their tour they visited the "Ogeeche mounts"—a series of shell mounds in today's Fernandina Beach. Remnants of one of the mounds survived until 1940, but today all traces of them have vanished. Most of the mounds were used for road-building material. After their tour Egan, Bartram, and his co-traveler set out for Cow-Ford on the St. Johns River, the site of today's Jacksonville.

The three men set sail for the St. Johns in a "handsome pleasure boat" manned by four slaves "to row in case of necessity" (T70). Their route took them down Kingsley Creek (today's Intracoastal Waterway), which separated Amelia from the mainland. At the mouth of the creek they crossed over Nassau Sound. That evening they camped, most likely at the northern end of Talbot Island. Continuing to the south, they sailed down Sister Creek between Talbot Island and Black Hammock Island to the St. Johns. At the mouth of Sister Creek they turned west and sailed upstream on the St. Johns to Cow-Ford.

At Cow-Ford Mr. Egan procured a small sailing craft for Bartram for three guineas, and the three men parted ways. Egan headed by land to St. Augustine, the young co-traveler went out on his own, and Bartram proceeded south on the river to Picolata. He camped the first night on the west side of the river near Ortega, then crossed the wide river and was a guest at the **Fatio Plantation** at New Switzerland Point. He continued farther upstream to **Fort Picolata**. From here he crossed the river twice, camping at Clark Creek on the west bank and just below Tocoi Creek on the east bank. He returned to the west bank at Racy Point, where the river juts to the east. After sailing past Ninemile Point, he doubled around one of the river's most prominent bends—Forester's Point. As the river straightened he arrived at an unnamed Indian village near present-day **Palatka**.

Continuing upstream, Bartram visited the site of the failed colony of Charlotia, or Rollestown, founded in 1764 as the headquarters of a 40,000-acre colony to be populated by the dispossessed of England. Over the course of the decade, its founder, a man named Rolle, brought 100 or so families from England who were supposed to turn "the wild overgrown land along the St. Johns into a profitable plantation." Rolle chose his colonists unwisely, and the attempt was a resounding failure. "Those of them who escaped the constant contagious fevers, fled the dreaded place, betaking themselves for subsistence, to the more fruitful and populous regions of Georgia and Carolina" (T95). The town was still inhabited by a handful of colonists in 1774, but of the original buildings, only Rolle's mansion was still standing. No trace of either Rolle's settlement or the Indian village that preceded it survives. Today there is an electric power plant on the site.

At Rollestown, Bartram learned that his treasured chest had been secured on an island 7 miles upstream when the Indians threatened the Lower Store. Now that peace had been restored, the traders were in the midst of returning the goods to their principal store. Bartram sailed right by the island and would have missed the landing had sentinels not hailed him. Bartram recovered his chest, its contents still in good order, and continued upstream. He arrived later that day at **Spalding's Lower Store**, near today's Stokes Landing, one of the few tracts of dry ground extending out into the river in this marshy area. This was the largest of three trading houses operated by Spalding and Kelsall.

Driving Tour: William Bartram Scenic Highway

This 37-mile tour follows the entire course of the William Bartram Scenic Highway designated by the Florida Legislature in 1980. The road, Fla. 13, parallels the St. Johns River upstream from suburban Jacksonville southward, ending southwest of St. Augustine. The highway passes the site of the Fatio Plantation, Fort Picolata, and the site of William's failed rice plantation. Many sections of the road offer scenic views of the St. Johns.

The scenic highway begins at the Highway 13 bridge over Julington Creek, 5 miles south of the junction with I-295. The bridge offers views of the St. Johns River to the west. Bartram sailed from Cow-Ford down the far side of the river. From the bridge, the scenic highway is a four-lane road for its first 2 miles as it works southward out of suburban Jacksonville. A little more than 1 mile south of the bridge the road intersects Race Track Road **(mile 1.1)**; 1 mile farther on it becomes two lanes. Continuing to the south, Fla. 13 enters the Switzerland community **(mile 5.2)**, with the Switzerland Community Church on the left and the Switzerland Cemetery on the right. In a little more than 1 mile the road reaches New Switzerland Point **(mile 6.8)**. This was the heart of the large Fatio indigo plantation, which Bartram visited as he crossed over to the east side of the river. Fatio, a native of Switzerland, had extensive holdings on the St. Johns between today's New Switzerland Point and Mill Cove. Bartram was duly impressed by the size of the plantation and also by its garden, which contained a "greater variety than any other in the Colony" (R1:62). Fatio told Bartram about the recent congress held at St. Augustine between the British and the Seminoles to address the recent hostilities that had forced the evacuation of both of Spalding's stores on the St. Johns. Fatio reported that the meeting was amicable and that both parties left it satisfied. The traders were to be indemnified for any loss and were assured by the Creeks that they would be safe "in person and property" in Indian territory. Fatio's report

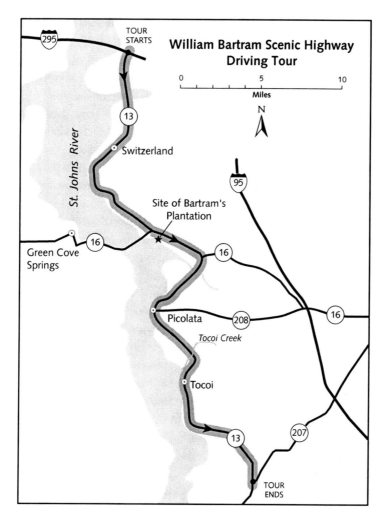

William Bartram Scenic Highway Driving Tour

convinced Bartram that he could continue his ascent of the river "without apprehensions"(T79).

A little more than 1 mile south of the point, the river comes into view again. The highway, set back from the river, works southward to the intersection with Fla. 16A **(mile 12.2)**. If you turn right onto Fla. 16A, in less than 0.5 mile the road crosses the wide river on the Shaunds Bridge, providing impressive views both upstream and downstream. Turning sharply to the left, to the southeast, is a view of Florence Cove, the site of William Bartram's failed plantation.

On the scenic highway, continue south from the junction with Fla. 16A. In 0.75 mile **(mile 12.9)** turn right onto Florence Cove Road to visit the approximate site of Bartram's plantation, where William and six slaves cleared swampland to grow rice. This road forms the southern boundary of Bartram's 500-acre plantation, which extended to the north to present-day Fla. 13 and Fla. 16. Near the terminus of the road, off the bank to the northeast, is the site of his home. Henry Laurens visited the plantation in the spring of 1766 and reported to John Bartram on William's condition. The land, Laurens said, was "the least agreeable of all the places [he] had seen—on a low sheet of sandy pine barren, verging on the swamp, which before his door is very narrow, in a bight or cove of the river, so shoal and covered with umbrellas, that the common current is lost and the water almost stagnated." Laurens's discouraging report continued with a description of William's plantation home, "or rather hovel," and the barely perceptible progress William and his slaves had made in clearing the land. Most troubling to John Bartram was Laurens's account of William's state of mind. William "had felt the pressure of his solitary and hopeless condition so heavily, as almost to drive him to despondency."[1] By October of that year William had abandoned his plantation and slaves and was living in St. Augustine. On his 1775 trek on the St. Johns, William sailed up the east bank past Florence and Little Florence Cove. His silence on passing his plantation is one of the strangest omissions in the *Travels*.

A little more than a mile from the cove, the highway crosses Trout Creek before coming to the entrance to Trout Creek Park at the intersection with Collier Road **(mile 14.5)**. The park offers picnic areas and a public boat ramp for Trout Creek that is less than 0.25 mile from the creek's junction with the St. Johns. By canoe it is less than 2 miles to Florence Cove.

The river is again out of sight as the road approaches the junction with Fla. 16 East **(mile 16.2)**. After crossing Sixmile Creek, the highway passes through Colee Cove and Bass Haven before entering Picolata. The site of the old Spanish fort is immediately west of the historical marker **(mile 20.2)**. In 1774 Bartram described the abandoned fort: "It is a square tower, thirty feet high, invested with a high wall, without bastions. . . . The upper story is open on each side, with battlements, supporting a cupola or roof" (T80). The Spanish originally established a garrison on the trail from St. Augustine to St. Marks, near the gulf coast, in the late 1600s. By 1735 they had constructed a fort on the site, **Fort Picolata**. When the British took control of East Florida in 1763, they con-

1. Laurens, *Papers*, August 9, 1766. Laurens suggested to John Bartram that William, "though a worthy, ingenious man, may not have resolution, or not that sort of resolution, that is necessary to encounter the difficulties incident to, and unavoidable in his present state of life." See Schafer, "The Forlorn State of Poor Billy Bartram," 7–10.

tinued to maintain the fort as a military outpost, but by 1769 it was no longer in use. Bartram first visited the fort in November 1765 to witness the "Piccolata Congress" between the newly established colonial government of East Florida and the Creeks. Here both sides pledged themselves to "sincere and perpetual peace." The agreement established the boundary of East Florida at the St. Johns River, with the British getting all the land east of the river. The site of the fort is approximately 650 feet west of the river's east bank near the present-day town of Picolata.

South of Picolata the highway intersects C.R. 214 **(mile 27.1).** In 1.5 miles the highway enters Riverdale; to the west is Riverdale Park **(mile 28.7)** with picnic areas and a public boat ramp. As the road continues southward, Racy Point is on the right, where the river juts to the east. As Bartram worked upstream, he camped at a "good harbour on the East shore" between Tocoi and the point (T85). The previous night he had camped on the western shore, most likely at the mouth of Clark Creek. The highway continues southward, moving away from the river, and intersects C.R. 305 **(mile 33.4)** and Fla. 13A **(mile 34.6)**. The highway ends at the junction with Fla. 201 **(mile 37.3)**, 5 miles north of Palatka.

Bartram continued upstream, sailing past Ninemile Point and doubling around Forester's Point. As the river straightened, he arrived at an unnamed Indian village near present-day Palatka. "It was a fine situation," Bartram noted, "the bank rising gradually from the water. There were eight to ten habitations, in a row, or street, fronting the water, and about fifty yards distance from it" (T92). At the upper end of the village was an orange grove, where "the trees were large, carefully pruned, and the ground under them clean, open and airy." Surrounding the village were acres of cleared land where the villagers grew corn, beans, squash, melons, and tobacco. This unnamed village was Bartram's first encounter with Seminole culture. No trace of the village survives.

St. Augustine

Bartram first visited St. Augustine in the company of his father on their travels through East Florida in 1765. Only two years earlier, after nearly three centuries of Spanish rule, the city had come into the hands of the British, who made it the capital of their new colony in East Florida. The city remained in British hands until 1783, when it was restored to Spain. The period of Spanish rule finally ended in 1823, when East Florida and St. Augustine became part of the United States.

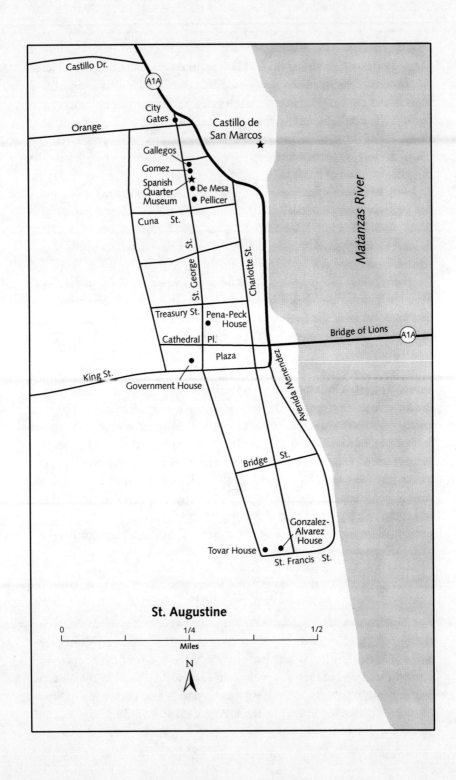

Castillo Dr.

A1A

City
Gates

Orange

Castillo de
San Marcos

Gallegos

Gomez

Spanish
Quarter
Museum

De Mesa

Pellicer

Cuna   St.

Matanzas River

St. George   St.

Charlotte St.

Treasury St.

Pena-Peck
House

Cathedral   Pl.

Bridge of Lions   A1A

Plaza

King St.

Government House

Avenida Menendez

Bridge   St.

Gonzalez-
Alvarez
House

Tovar House

St. Francis   St.

St. Augustine

0   1/4   1/2

Miles

N

Pellicer House, in St. Augustine's Spanish Quarter.

In 1766, after abandoning his plantation, William returned to St. Augustine and took a job working for William De Brahm as a surveyor on the East Florida coast. He was shipwrecked on the Mosquito Coast near New Symrna (see the map of East Florida in the *Travels*), returned to St. Augustine, and remained there until 1767, when he returned home to Philadelphia.

St. Augustine today boasts more than thirty colonial-era buildings. In the restored Spanish quarter, immediately south of the City Gates, there are a number of reconstructed buildings that date back to the Spanish colony, including the **Martin Gallegos House**, 21 St. George Street; and the **Gomez House**, 25 St. George Street, representative of mid-eighteenth-century wood-frame structures. Farther south on St. George is the **De Mesa–Sanchez House**, 43 St. George Street, dating to the 1740s. On the same block is the **Pellicer House**, 55 St. George Street, a wooden one-story British double house built around 1785. A block south of the Spanish quarter is the **Pena-Peck House**, at 105 St. George Street. The coquina first floor dates to the 1740s; the wood second story was added in 1838. The house was home to the Spanish royal treasurer; the British lieutenant governor, John Moultrie; and the last British governor, Tonyn, who oversaw the evacuation of the town in 1784.

Two blocks south of the quarter is the central **Plaza,** laid out in the early

"Oldest House," St. Augustine, Florida.

1600s. Surrounding the park were the church and government buildings, none of which survives. In the 1930s the city reconstructed the **Government House**, the British governor's house built on the site of the headquarters for the Spanish colonial government. Located on the plaza at St. George Street, it served as the city's post office; now it is the home of the St. Augustine Museum. Five blocks south of the plaza is the **Gonzalez-Alvarez House**, at 14 St. Francis Street, the "oldest house" in the United States. The first floor of this two-story building was built soon after 1715.

Castillo de San Marcos

To the east of the city gates and the Spanish quarter is the Castillo de San Marcos. The large stone fort, built by the Spanish, protected the city (and served as a refuge) during its conflicts with the British in 1683, 1702, 1728, and 1740. During the siege of 1740, more than 2,000 townspeople lived in the fortress while the British bombarded St. Augustine for thirty-eight days. It is the oldest building in the city: construction began in 1672 and lasted for twenty-four years. The fortress is now protected as a part of the Castillo de San Marcos National Monument. Open to the public daily.

Castillo de San Marcos, St. Augustine, Florida.

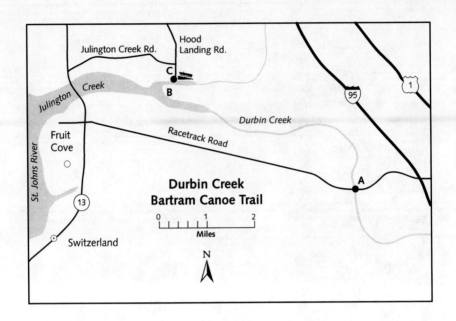

Bartram Canoe Trail: Durbin Creek

Section: Durbin Creek to Julington Creek
Distance: 8.5 miles
Difficulty: 1–2; flat water
Hazards: motorboats on Julington Creek
Highlights: Durbin Creek

The Bartram Canoe Trail begins in a wetland on Durbin Creek west of I-95. For the first 3 miles the trail is narrow and runs beneath a canopy of cypress trees. After passing under Racetrack Road the creek widens, although this section is still well suited for intimate canoeing and for observing wildlife such as waterbirds and alligators. At **mile 3.5** the creek is joined from the right by Corklan Creek. From here the trail turns to the west to the St. Johns. The intimate canoeing ends for the last 0.5 mile on Durbin Creek as it empties into Julington Creek. The creek quickly widens from 150 feet to more than 800 feet at the mouth. Stay to the right (the north side of the creek) on this section. At the mouth, double back on the north side of the peninsula, into Julington Creek. Slightly upstream and on the north side of Julington Creek is Clark's Boat Ramp, located on Hood Landing Road.

The put-in for the trail is west of I-95, south of Racetrack Road.

For more information on the trail and creek conditions, contact Outdoor Adventures in Jacksonville, Florida; phone: 904-393-9030.

Alachua Savanna

JOURNEYS TO CUSCOWILLA

Spalding's Lower Store at Stokes Landing served as the base for Bartram's four Florida expeditions. The first trip was to Cuscowilla and the Alachua Savanna. Bartram accompanied some traders hoping to meet with the chief Seminole mico, Cowkeeper, and other Seminole leaders so that they might reestablish trade with Alachua following the recent unrest (T170). Bartram, the traders, and a man referred to as the "old trader" from the Upper Store (most likely Job Wiggins) set off on the trading path to the southwest. At the site of present-day Rodman, the party turned west. They traveled over the sandhills to a spot just north of today's Kenwood before turning northwest and heading for modern-day Johnson. Just to the west was Bartram's "Halfway pond," Cowpen Lake. After camping at the south end of the lake, they rode the next day to present-day Hawthorne. From there the trail turned to the southwest, skirting the northern end of Watson Prairie and heading toward the northeastern corner of Orange Lake.

After crossing the River of Styx near the northern end of Lake Orange, the party continued west-southwest to Cuscowilla (T183), where they met with Cowkeeper. Bartram and a number of the traders then traveled 12 miles north to the southern edge of the great "Alachua Savanna" and began a three-day journey around the southern, western, and northwestern edges of the prairie. Ending their journey just east of the Alachua Sink, they retraced their route to the trading store on the southern rim. From there they worked their way back to the Lower Store.

Soon after making his first journey up the St. Johns, Bartram set off for his second and last trip to the Alachua Savanna. His ultimate destination was not Cuscowilla this time, but the Creek village on the Suwannee called Talahasochte. Again he traveled in a traders' convoy from the Lower Store. They followed the same familiar route to Cuscowilla, where they met again with Cowkeeper, then continued farther west along the southern edge of Paynes Prairie to the northwestern corner of Kanapaha Prairie. From the sink, Bar-

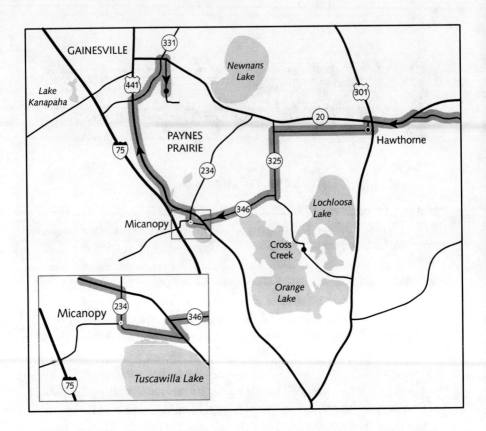

tram traveled southwestward through today's Archer on a path that coincides with Fla. 24 to Bronson. From there the trail continued westward to Long Pond, 2 miles south of today's Chiefland (T371). Farther to the west, on the east bank of the Suwannee River, they reached their destination: Tala-hasochte, within the boundaries of today's Manatee Springs State Park.

Driving Tour: Palatka to the Alachua Savanna — Paynes Prairie

This 58-mile driving tour approximates Bartram's route from the Lower Store on the St. Johns to the Alachua Savanna. Beginning in Palatka, the tour works westward past Cowpen Lake, goes through the Lochloosa Wildlife Conservation Area, and ends in Gainesville after cutting through Paynes Prairie.

The driving tour begins at the junction of U.S. 17 and Fla. 20 in Palatka, immediately to the west of the highway bridge over the St. Johns and east of the city's center. In Bartram's day, a Creek settlement stood on the riverbank

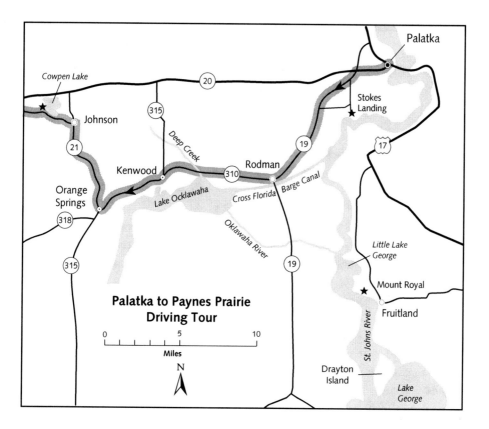

Palatka

Cowpen Lake

20

Stokes
Landing

315

Johnson

Deep Creek

19

17

21

Kenwood

Rodman

310

Orange
Springs

Lake Ocklawaha

Cross Florida Barge Canal

318

Oklawaha River

Little Lake
George

315

19

Mount Royal

Fruitland

**Palatka to Paynes Prairie
Driving Tour**

0   5   10

Miles

N

St. Johns River

Drayton
Island

Lake
George

to the east. *From the junction, take 9th Street (Fla. 20) to the south.* Within a few blocks the road turns to the right to become Crill Avenue. Just beyond the turn is a sign for Ravine State Gardens, six blocks to the south. Traveling to the west, Fla. 20 intersects Fla. 19 **(mile 2.6)**, a western bypass of the town. At the junction *turn left and follow Fla. 19 to the south,* past Peniel Road leading to **Stokes Landing**, the site of Spalding's Lower Store **(mile 6.0)**. In a little more than 5 miles the highway reaches the very small settlement of Rodman **(mile 11.4)**.

At Rodman, turn right onto Putnam C.R. 310, which forms the northern boundary of the Caravelle Ranch Wildlife Management Area. This 13,000-acre preserve extends south to the Ocklawaha River and east to the St. Johns. The area offers hiking, mountain biking, and horseback trails on old logging roads. Parallel to the county road, a little more than a mile to the south, is the Cross-Florida Greenway, a linear park constructed on the sides of the main channel of the abandoned Cross Florida Barge Canal. Construction on the

Peniel Road **(mile 6.0)** leads, via Stokes Landing Road, to the site of Spalding's Lower Store. In 0.5 mile Peniel Road reaches Stokes Landing Road. Turn right (to the south) and in 2.5 miles Stokes Landing Road ends near the west bank of the river. Stokes Island is visible from the turn-around. There is no public access to the St. Johns from the road. The public boat ramp is now closed. To return to Fla. 19, turn around. In a mile, at the junction with Marion Road, turn left. In another mile Marion Road ends at the state route.

---

controversial canal was halted in the early 1970s, and the route became the cornerstone of a greenway that runs from Rodman west to the Gulf of Mexico. A few miles farther south on Fla. 19 is a canoe put-in for one of Florida's most popular floats, the Ocklawaha. From the highway it is 4 miles downstream to the river's confluence with the St. Johns. Trailheads for the land trails are also on Fla. 19, between Rodman and the Ocklawaha. Putnam County and the state of Florida plan to construct a multimodal trail on the bed of the abandoned railroad line from Palatka to the northern shore of Lake Ocklawaha. Its route closely parallels the old trading path to the south of Fla. 19 and C.R. 310.

In Rodman, bear to the west on C.R. 310 and leave Fla. 19. Within a few miles the road crosses a shallow bay of Lake Ocklawaha **(mile 16.8)** that was created by a dam built downstream in the 1960s. From the lake the road begins the steady climb of the Florida sandhills: "The Pine groves passed, we immediately find ourselves on the entrance of the expansive airy Pine forests, on parallel chains of low swelling mounds, called the Sand Hills" (T173). Continue west to the junction with C.R. 315 **(mile 19.3)**. C.R. 310 ends at the intersection with C.R. 315 in Kenwood. *Turn left on C.R. 315* and in less than 1 mile is the access road for the Kenwood Recreation Area **(mile 20.2)**. The area, also a part of the Cross-Florida Greenway, offers camping and a public boat dock with access to Lake Ocklawaha. From Kenwood the trail followed by the traders and Creeks turned to the northwest, following a more direct course to present-day Johnson. No modern road parallels this route. The driving tour continues to the west and then to the southwest on C.R. 315 to Orange Springs. In this small settlement the road ends at Fla. 21 **(mile 25.4)**. At the junction, turn right and *take Fla. 21 to the north* for approximately 5 miles. *At the junction with Fla. 20A in Johnson **(mile 31)**, turn left.*

The road skirts the southern shore of **Cowpen Lake**, although the lake is not visible. This was the "Halfway pond" where Bartram and the traders camped on their journey to Cuscowilla in April 1774. He saw spotted gar, mudfish, catfish, and various types of bream in the pond, as well as softshell turtles, which are described at some length in the *Travels* (T176–177). To view the lake, continue westbound on Fla. 20A to Race Street **(mile 28.1)**. Turn right onto the gravel road that bends to the east. The road dead-ends at the western shore of the lake. Continuing the tour, take Fla. 20A westbound for a little more than a mile, where it ends at Fla. 20 **(mile 29.2)**.

Turn left onto Fla. 20. In a little more than 3 miles the highway nears the junction with U.S. 301 (see map 29). At the viaduct over the highway **(mile 33)**, *take the ramp to the right for Hawthorne. At the signal, turn left* and then immediately to the right onto Johnson Street entering the small town of Hawthorne. Continue south on Johnson Street for a little more than 0.5 mile to the junction with C.R. 2082. *Turn right* and take the county road to the west. After a bit more than 4 miles the pavement ends, although the road is passable by conventional cars. *At the junction with C.R. 325* **(mile 39.7)**, *turn left.* This road bisects, north to south, the **Lochloosa Wildlife Conservation Area**, more than 27,000 acres managed by the St. Johns River Management Authority that encircles Lochloosa Lake and reaches as far west as Paynes Prairie. Continue south on C.R. 325 until the junction with C.R. 346 **(mile 44)**. *Turn right and follow C.R. 346* to the junction with U.S. 441 **(mile 49)**. This highway crosses over the River of Styx near the "point or branch of the marshes" at the northern end of the lake (T183). Bartram and the traders traveled 3 miles on the route followed by today's C.R. 346 before reaching the "great and beautiful lake of Cuscowilla," today's Lake Tuscawilla (T366–367).

Cuscowilla

At the junction with U.S. 441, turn left. Take the divided highway south for approximately 0.25 mile, and then *turn right onto Ocala Road, C.R. 25A.* In less than 0.75 mile the road passes near the northwestern corner of Lake Tuscawilla. This area, approximately 0.25 mile from Micanopy, is the site of **Cuscowilla** (R184). Archaeologists have identified the site of the mound, but it is located on private land. "The Town of Cuscowela," Bartram reported to Dr. Fothergill, "consists of about 40 houses; placed pretty near to one another, sorounding a large open square, in the Center of which stands their Counsel House" (R1:72). With a population of several hundred persons, this was the largest Seminole settlement in Florida in the 1770s. Each of the town's homes had its own vegetable garden where families raised corn, beans, and squash. North of the town, the Seminoles raised cattle on common fields.

As the traders entered the town they were escorted by "young men and maidens to the chief's house," which stood on a high point and was "distinguished from the rest by its superior magnitude, a large flag being hoisted on a high staff at one corner" (T184). There they met Cowkeeper, the chief mico of Alachua. The chief welcomed them into his reception area, a 12-foot-high loft with a deerskin floor. The chief and his guests shared both the pipe and "thin drink"—a cracked hominy drink that was a Creek and Cherokee hospitality food.[1] After the reception the chief trader informed Cowkeeper, "in the presence of his council or attendants," of the reason for their visit. It was decided that the business of reopening trade between Kelsall and Spalding and the Creeks would be taken up in a council the next day.

The chief trader also informed the mico of Bartram's errand. In reply, the chief gave Bartram "unlimited permission to travel over the country for the purpose of collecting flowers, medicinal plants, etc." Along with this license the chief gave our traveler the name "Puc Puggy"—the "flower hunter." Bartram also met with the tribe's battle chief, Long Warrior, whom he had met with his father in 1765. The majority of the traders continued westward to Talahasochte. Several of Cowkeeper's men accompanied Job Wiggins and Bartram when they continued to the north to visit the Alachua Savanna, today's Paynes Prairie.

Continue on C.R. 25A for 0.25 mile into Micanopy. *Turn right onto C.R. 234 and return to the north to U.S. 441. Turn left* onto the divided highway. A mile on the right is the entrance for **Paynes Prairie State Recreation Area (mile 52)**. Continue north on the divided highway, which quickly descends into the prairie. For more than 5 miles the road bisects the savanna. The road has come at a great cost to the area's native inhabitants. This section of U.S. 441 is known as "Florida's deadliest highway" for the wildlife killed by automobiles. The Florida Department of Natural Resources is in the process of building animal paths under the roadway in an effort to stop the carnage. In the middle of the prairie is an overlook with a small parking area marked with a Bartram Trail sign commemorating his travels here. The highway climbs out of the prairie and continues north into Gainesville.

At the junction with Fla. 331 *turn right onto Williston Road* **(mile 57)**. Half a mile on the left is **Bivens Arm Park**. The entrance to the park is off Main

1. Hudson, *Southeastern Indians*, 305.

Street on the left. Continue the tour on Williston Road, which changes its name to North 11th Street as it turns to the north. *At the junction with Southeast 4th Street, turn right.* In a few blocks the road ends at Southeast 18th Street. *Turn right onto 18th Street,* Boulware Springs Park is less than 1 mile on the right. This park is the trailhead for the Hawthorne–Gainesville Trail and for hiking paths on the north side of Paynes Prairie, including the trail down to the Alachua Sink.

Other Sites of Interest

Bivens Arm Park

This Gainesville city park features a quarter-mile boardwalk into the marsh on the southeastern edge of Bivens Lake. At the pavilion are picnic tables and an exhibit on Bivens Arm. Open daily, 9 A.M.–5 P.M.

Florida Museum of Natural History

The museum has more than 19 million specimens and artifacts, making it the largest natural history museum in the Southeast. In 1998 the museum opened a new exhibition center, Powell Hall, where visitors see permanent exhibits on the waterways and wildlife of northwest Florida, the people and environments of South Florida, and Florida fossils, along with a variety of changing exhibits.

Powell Hall is located on the University of Florida campus at Hull Road and Southwest 34th Street. The museum is open Monday–Saturday, 10–5, and Sundays and holidays, 1–5. Web address: www.flmnh.ufl.edu

Lake Kanapaha

Bartram camped near this lake, now a part of the Kanapaha Botanical Gardens, southwest of Gainesville. Near the lake is a Bartram Trail marker for the site where Bartram camped on his second trip to the savanna. Francis Harper and Charlotte Porter locate the camping spot on the southern shore of Lake Kanapaha.[2]

At the southern shore of the lake, east of the water lily pond, are a number of live oaks that would have been standing during Bartram's visit in the area. There are more than a dozen gardens, including the state's largest herb gar-

2. Porter, *William Bartram's Florida*, 17.

den and bamboo garden. The garden is open Friday–Wednesday. There is an admission fee. Located 1 mile southwest of I-75 on Fla. 24, Archer Road.

PAYNES PRAIRIE

How is the mind agitated and bewildered, at being thus, as it were,
placed on the borders of a new world! On the first view of such an amazing
display of the wisdom and power of the supreme author of nature, the mind
for a moment seems suspended, and impressed with awe. (T189)

The *Travels* describes many locations that captured Bartram's fancy, but most readers agree that his description of the Alachua Savanna is unique. There is energy in Bartram's writing about this place, a wondering quality, as if his eyes were beholding the full splendor of the New World. He writes of a world of abundance: "herds of sprightly deer, squadrons of the beautiful, fleet Simi-nole horses, flocks of turkey" whose peaceful existence is interrupted only by the "painted, fearless, uncontrolled and free Siminole" (T188). It is a world bathed in light and life, and Bartram's awe is evident on every page.

A casual visitor to Paynes Prairie today will wonder about the source of Bartram's astonishment. The road to Paynes Prairie from Gainesville zips through the outlying areas of the city and suddenly places the driver squarely in the middle of an open, and apparently empty, expanse. There are few trees visible on the horizon, and no deer, horses, or turkeys meet the eye. The land looks dull and lifeless.

Only by moving off the road and approaching the savanna on foot can one get a sense of what Bartram must have experienced as he approached this open plain. Overhead, the shadowing boughs of giant oaks shade and darken the trail leading to the savanna. Magnolias and palms dot the canopy, and the visitor is bathed in the greenness of the surrounding vegetation. Bartram ex-perienced this leafy world for weeks on end as he made his way through the interior of Florida, and then, suddenly, burst into the sunlight when he ar-rived at the edge of the savanna. Where before there had been no vista, only thick vegetation, there were now thousands of acres of open land. Life teemed both on and above the scene before him. He was transported.

A modern visitor to Paynes Prairie can easily seize on what has been lost, on what one does *not* see when looking out over the savanna. But those who stop, pause, and wander a little off the beaten path may find the spectacle of Bartram's vision waiting. Walk out onto the dikes that cross the prairie and hear the far-off cry of the sandhill crane. Go to the Alachua Sink, perched on

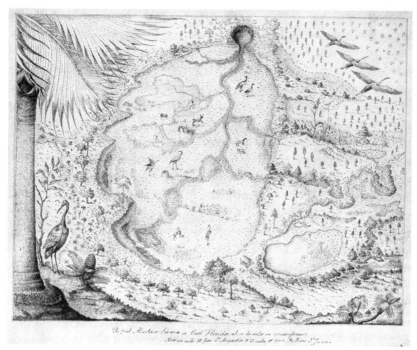

*Bartram's drawing of the Alachua Savanna. Courtesy of
the American Philosophical Society, Philadelphia.*

the northeast corner of the prairie, which literally teems with life. At dusk,
hundreds of alligators course through clear running water, hunting their dinner as the sun dips slowly in the sky. Bald eagles soar overhead while egrets lit
pink and gold by the flaming Florida sunset fly in to roost in the trees.

There are places where the world of Bartram's *Travels* seems an irretriev-
able part of distant history, but Paynes Prairie, the great Alachua Savanna,
still opens a window into the past, showing that there are sites that can sing
to the imagination today just as they did more than 200 years ago. One needs
only to walk and listen.

Bartram at the Alachua Savannah

As Bartram and the traders traveled north from Cuscowilla to the "Great Savanna" in 1774, they "entered a level grassy plain" interspersed with pine trees
and large patches of low shrubs. Then, after 2 miles, they ascended through a
dark grove of magnolia, live oak, and mulberry. According to our traveler:

"This continues near a mile; when at once opens to view the most sudden transition from darkness to light, that can possibly be exhibited in a natural landscape" (T187). The modern traveler can experience the same transition on the trail from the visitors' center to the observation tower, passing from the dark oak hammock to the rim of the open marsh. From the rim, Bartram looked out at the Alachua Savanna and recorded what he saw: "The extensive Alachua savanna is a level, green plain, above fifteen miles over, fifty in circumference, and scarcely a tree or bush of any kind to be seen on it. It is encircled with high, sloping hills, covered with waving forests and fragrant Orange groves, rising from an exuberantly fertile soil. The towering Magnolia grandiflora and the transcendent Palm, stand conspicuous amongst them" (T187–188). The prairie today is still bare of trees and shrubs; the small lakes, which were drained in the early twentieth century, have returned. The orange groves maintained by Cuscowilla's people have been replaced—either by new forest or by development. Both horses and bison can be seen today as they were in the 1770s. The sandhill cranes and bears have also returned.

Bartram, Wiggins, and the other traders camped their first night on a knoll near a trader's store to the west of Chacala Pond, near today's Jackson's Gap. The next day they rode 12 miles to the southwestern end of the prairie, passing through "ancient Indian fields, now grown over with forests of stately trees" (T198). Wiggins told Bartram that this was the site of the old settlement of Alachua. In the 1760s Cowkeeper had brought his band of Oconee Indians from the Oconee River in central Georgia to the prairie. Their settlement was short-lived, however, as he soon moved their chief town south to Cuscowilla. Bartram and the traders camped at the site, surrounded by the "remains and traces of ancient human habitation and cultivation." They next day they split into two groups: one group traveled directly across the prairie to the northern end; the second group, Wiggins and Bartram, continued to ride along the rim around the western end of the prairie.

Bartram and Wiggins rode another 12 miles to a "long projected point of the coast"—today's Bivens Arm on the north rim—where they were joined by their companions. Then all rode together to the east, crossing a "brook of clear water, rolling over gravel and white sand"—today's Sweetwater Branch. Afterward they climbed the "collection of eminences, covered with dark groves" that partly encircles the Alachua Sink. Forty feet above the sink they "came up to a long projecting point of the high forests, beyond which opened to view an extensive grassy cove of the savanna." This vista exists as an overlook on the Gainesville–Hawthorne Trail described below.

As they descended the bluff to the Alachua Sink, Bartram was struck by the extraordinary beauty of the rock formations that make up the sink. "These rocks are perforated by wells or tubes, four, five and six feet in diameter . . . forming a great ragged orifice" that drains the prairie's water into "hidden subterranean Passages no one knows where" (R1:80). In the waters surrounding the sink Bartram saw "incredible numbers of crocodiles, some of which are of an enormous size"; one could "walk over any part of the basin and the river upon their heads" (T205). When Francis Harper visited the sink in the 1940s, the alligators were gone and the sink was nearly obscured by water hyacinths. The hyacinths are gone now, and the alligators have returned. During our visit in the spring of 2000 we easily counted more than sixty alligators from one vantage point.

Paynes Prairie State Preserve

Bartram's savanna is a 15,000-acre highland marsh surrounded by uplands that create a dramatic backdrop for those entering the basin. Over the course of thousands of years, the groundwater below the surface of the marsh has dissolved the limestone and dolomite bedrock, creating a karst topography—a landscape marked by sinkholes with a noticeable absence of rivers.[3] The water level of the marsh is determined by rainfall, drainage, and the fluctuations of the Florida aquifer, and it can change dramatically. In the 1870s the prairie's main sink, Alachua Sink, became plugged. For the next twenty years much of the prairie became a lake deep enough to support steamboat operations. In 1891 the lake level began to drop, and by 1893 the marsh had returned. In 1998 the prairie's water level was the highest in the twentieth century, with numerous large lakes and ponds. By spring of 2000 the water level had dropped to record lows, with most of the marsh becoming mud and muck.

Paynes Prairie is a mosaic of different marshes: water lily, sawgrass, and maidencane flag. White water lily, yellow water lily, and bladderwort dominate the water lily marsh found in the prairie's ponds, ditches, and canals. Sawgrass marsh occupies the middle ground. The higher ground, crossed by Cone's Dike and Bolen Bluff Trails, is dominated by maidencane, southern cutgrass, and rushes. These marshes are the home of a wide variety of amphibians and reptiles. Hundreds of species of birds depend on the prairie as well, including the American bittern, white ibis, and great egret. From the

3. Brown et al., "Soils," 37–39.

Bolen Bluff Trail and at the Alachua Sink the visitor can see abundant red-tailed hawks, bald eagles, black turkey vultures, and other raptors. Each fall more than 1,500 sandhill cranes migrate from Wisconsin and Michigan to winter and mate at the prairie. At the beginning of each March they leave for their return trip north.

In 1972 the state of Florida established the Environmentally Endangered Lands Program to purchase endangered lands for conservation and recreation, and through it acquired most of Paynes Prairie. The state established the Paynes Prairie State Preserve and placed it under the management of the Florida Department of Environmental Protection's Division of State Parks. The goal of the state's management plans is to restore "as nearly as possible, the conditions that existed on and around the basin during Bartram's visit."[4] Park managers dismantled the dike system built to drain the marsh, conducted controlled burns, and removed exotic plants. More than fifty years ago Francis Harper lamented the disappearance of deer and sandhill crane. Both have returned, as have the bison, reintroduced in the late 1970s. The prairie is once again a paradise for birdwatchers.

On the north rim of the basin is the Gainesville–Hawthorne State Trail. Four miles of this "rails to trail" are in the preserve, with numerous vistas of the prairie. The north rim is also the trailhead for the La Chua Trail descending to the Alachua Sink. The south rim boasts more than 20 miles of hiking and biking trails, including a 1-mile nature trail. Also here is the Alachua Savanna Visitors' Center with exhibits on the formation of the prairie, its ecology, and the history of the humans who have lived here over the past 10,000 years. The exhibits include a number of quotations from Bartram's *Travels*.

The park offers a developed campground as well as a small area for tent camping. Canoeing and boating are permitted in Lake Wauberg, near the campground. Backpacking is not allowed in the preserve, except on ranger-led trips. On the first full weekend of each month from November through April, rangers lead a group on a backpacking trip from the Alachua Sink to Persimmon Point, the southernmost point of the north rim. The hike, 6.5 miles long, passes through pine flatwoods, hardwood hammocks, and marsh. Space is limited and reservations are required.

Contact: Paynes Prairie State Preserve Visitors' Center; phone: 352-466-4100.

4. Kushlan, "Freshwater Marshes," 357.

Paynes Prairie Trails

Chacala Trail

Distance:	6.5 miles for both loops
Difficulty:	easy; mild ascents
Hazards:	none
Highlights:	shady hammocks; Chacala Pond
Use:	horse, bike, and foot traffic

This trail is a series of three loops for hiking, horseback riding, and mountain biking. The bottom and middle loops, totaling 2.8 miles, pass through shady hammocks, pine flatwoods, and old fields. The northern loop, 2.75 miles long, passes through pine shrub and hardwood forests to the east of Chacala Pond. There is a 0.3-mile spur trail from the loop to the eastern shore of the pond.

The main trailhead for the trail is at the junction of Savannah Boulevard and the road to the campground.

Lake Trail

Distance:	0.85 mile
Difficulty:	easy
Hazards:	none
Highlights:	Lake Wauberg
Use:	foot and bike traffic

This short trail follows the bed of an old road from the Lake Wauberg parking area to Savannah Boulevard, ending a mile south of the visitors' center. The trail passes through open fields and is for hiking and biking.

Cone's Dike Trail

Distance:	8 miles (round-trip)
Difficulty:	easy
Hazards:	unshaded
Highlights:	trail winds through the prairie
Use:	foot and bike traffic

Paynes Prairie was divided by a series of dikes in the nineteenth and early twentieth centuries as part of efforts to drain the wetlands for farming. The dikes, fortunately, never succeeded. After acquiring the land for a state preserve, the state of Florida dismantled the locks and dams but could not afford to remove the dikes. Three of the park's trails—La Chua, Bolen Bluff, and Cone's Dike—follow old dikes into the wet prairie.

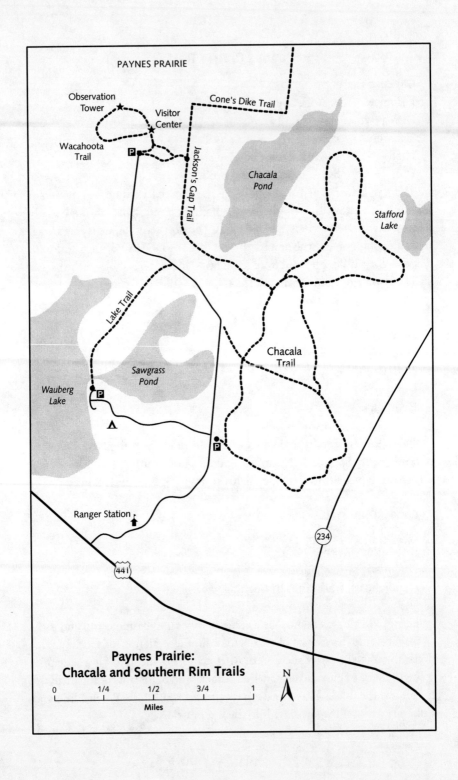

PAYNES PRAIRIE

Observation Tower

Visitor Center

Cone's Dike Trail

Wacahoota Trail

Chacala Pond

Jackson's Gap Trail

Stafford Lake

Lake Trail

Chacala Trail

Sawgrass Pond

Wauberg Lake

Ranger Station

234

441

**Paynes Prairie:
Chacala and Southern Rim Trails**

N

0   1/4   1/2   3/4   1
Miles

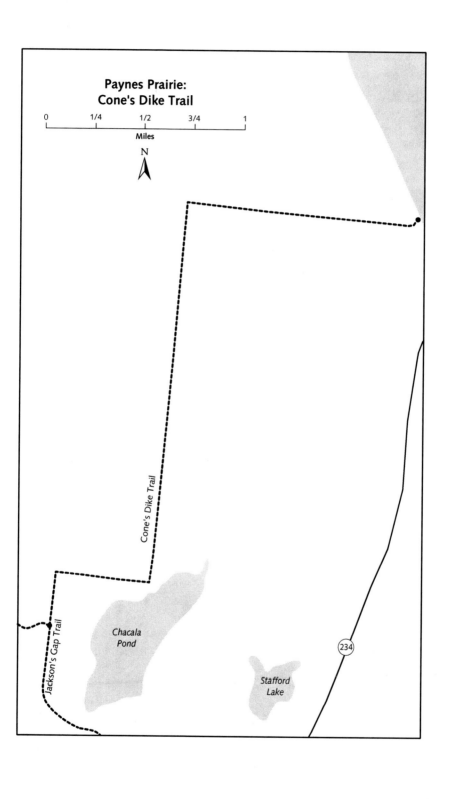

Paynes Prairie:
Cone's Dike Trail

0   1/4   1/2   3/4   1

Miles

N

Cone's Dike Trail

Jackson's Gap Trail

Chacala
Pond

Stafford
Lake

234

Cone's Dike Trail is 4 miles long from Jackson's Gap to an unnamed lake. Save for a few hundred feet near the gap, the entire trail cuts through the prairie. The trail's straight track, with three 90-degree turns, makes it a better biking trail than hiking trail.

Bolen Bluff Trail

Distance: 3.0 miles (round-trip)
Difficulty: easy
Hazards: none
Highlights: observation tower in the prairie
Use: foot and bike traffic

This loop trail begins on Bolen Bluff overlooking the prairie, then works through an upland hardwood forest before exiting into the prairie. Through the marsh the trail follows a dike to a two-story observation tower. During the winter the overlook provides a vantage point for viewing sandhill cranes and northern harriers.

The trailhead is off U.S. 441, 4 miles north of Savannah Boulevard, the main entrance to the southern part of the park.

Jackson's Gap Trail

Distance: 1.2 miles
Difficulty: easy
Hazards: none
Highlights: hammock and pine flatwoods
Use: foot and bike traffic

This short trail connects Cone's Dike Trail with the Chacala Trail system to the south. The trail follows the bed of an old road near the western shore of Chacala Pond.

Wacahoota Trail

Distance: 0.25 mile (round-trip)
Difficulty: easy
Hazards: none
Highlights: observation tower; hammock
Use: foot traffic only

This trail, for hikers only, goes from the visitors' center to the observation tower. The trail loops through a hammock with live oak, laurel oak, and magnolia and ends at the tower overlooking the southern rim of the prairie.

La Chua Trail — North Rim

Distance: 3.0 miles (round-trip)
Difficulty: easy
Hazards: alligators
Highlights: Alachua Sink, wet prairie, and marsh
Use: foot traffic only

From the North Rim Interpretive Center this footpath descends to the Alachua Sink. For nearly 0.25 mile it works along the southern edge of the sink, then veers to the south along a dike into the prairie. At **mile 1.5** the trail ends at an observation tower at Alachua Lake.

Gainesville–Hawthorne State Trail

Section: Boulware Springs to Hawthorne Trailhead
Distance: 16 miles (one-way); all paved
Difficulty: easy
Hazards: none
Highlights: overlooks Paynes Prairie, Lochloosa Wildlife Conservation Area

This 16-mile "rails to trail" follows the track bed of the old Atlantic Coast Railway. The path is paved, 10 feet wide, and level. Much of the route is scenic, passing through three large preserves: the Lochloosa Wildlife Conservation Area, the Prairie Creek State Preserve, and finally the northern section of Paynes Prairie State Preserve. The trail is marked (west to east) for mileage and has four trailheads with parking.

Traveling west to east, there are three overlooks of **Paynes Prairie** within the first 2 miles, all easily accessible by walking or biking from either Boulware Springs or the La Chua Trail. Less than 0.5 mile from Boulware Springs is the first overlook, of Sweetwater Branch, with views to the west where the small stream empties into the prairie. At **mile 1.5** is the **La Chua Trail** trailhead, with an interpretive center and a parking area (accessible from Southeast 15th Street). The La Chua Trail is a 1.5-mile spur into the prairie (see above). Continuing eastward on the Gainesville–Hawthorne Trail, in less than 0.25 mile is the paved spur trail to the **Alachua Lake Overlook**. This 0.25-mile trail leads to one of the most magnificent views of the prairie.

Farther east on the trail is an overlook over Red Wolf Pond **(mile 3.9)**. In a little more than 0.5 mile the trail crosses over Prairie Creek. This small waterway is an important connector between Newnans Lake to the north and

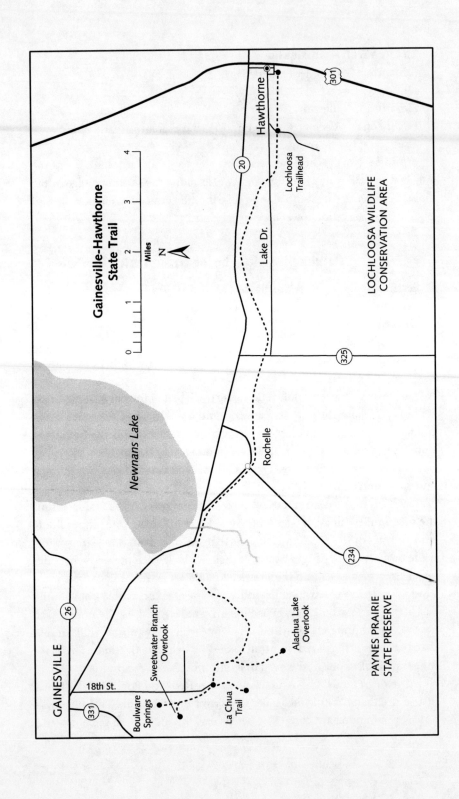

Gainesville-Hawthorne
State Trail

N

Miles

0 1 2 3 4

GAINESVILLE

26

331

18th St.

Boulware
Springs

Sweetwater Branch
Overlook

La Chua
Trail

Alachua Lake
Overlook

Newnans Lake

Rochelle

234

PAYNES PRAIRIE
STATE PRESERVE

325

20

Lake Dr.

Lochloosa
Trailhead

Hawthorne

301

LOCHLOOSA WILDLIFE
CONSERVATION AREA

the prairie to the south. Just beyond **mile 5.0** is a trailhead for a short hiking trail into the conservation area that leads to an excellent area for birding, with egrets, great blue herons, anhingas, and songbirds among the attractions. The creek can also be canoed.

Just beyond the road crossing of C.R. 234 there is a restroom on the right. In less than a mile the trail enters the Lochloosa Wildlife Management Area. The trail crosses Little Lochloosa Creek at **mile 10.0**. Just before **mile marker 12.0** it crosses Lochloosa Creek, then angles to the southeast, crossing C.R. 2082 (Lake Drive). After crossing Southeast 200th Drive the trail comes to the **Lochloosa Trailhead (mile 14.5)**. From here to the south is an extensive network of hiking, biking, and horseback trails to the north and west of Lochloosa Lake. Large communities of bald eagles and wading birds are found here, as are sandhill cranes, wood storks, and black bears. Continue eastward on the trail for another 1.5 miles to the Hawthorne trailhead.

A JOURNEY TO TALAHASOCHTE ON THE LITTLE ST. JUAN RIVER

The object of Bartram's second western trek from Spalding's Lower Store was Talahasochte. Once again in the company of a band of traders, Bartram departed from the Alachua Savanna on the old trail, now approximated by Fla. 24. After camping the first night near Lake Kanapaha, they arrived at their destination on the second day. Talahasochte sat on a bluff more than 30 feet above the Suwannee River, dubbed the "Little St. Juan" by Bartram. Here Bartram found more than "thirty habitations constructed after the mode at Cuscowilla" (T227). The square was more spacious than Cuscowilla's, and the council house was larger. Talahasochte was the Seminoles' largest settlement; it encompassed the area from today's New Clay Landing on both sides of the river to Oldtown, 10 miles upstream. The river sustained a vigorous economy, with its floodplain providing rich soils for growing corn and other produce. The river and the Gulf of Mexico, 20 miles downstream, were important food sources, as both were rich in fish and shellfish. Finally, the Suwannee was an important trade highway to the Atlantic and the Caribbean. The Indians used large cypress canoes capable of seating twenty to thirty for trade expeditions to Cuba, the Bahamas, and settlements on the Atlantic coast.

The chief of the region was the "White King," who unlike Cowkeeper at Cuscowilla had not broken his ties with the Lower Creek Confederacy.[5] The

5. Covington, *Seminoles of Florida*, 13–14.

traders' mission was similar to the one to Cuscowilla in April; they hoped to convince the White King and his council to restore trade between their stores and Talahasochte. On their arrival the traders and Bartram learned that the king was on a hunting expedition. Bartram decided to do some exploring while waiting for him to return. Toward the evening of the first day he joined a young man in the traders' company for a "fishing excursion for trout with a bob" (T228). The next day Bartram and the young man set off for the "admirable Manate Spring, three or four miles down the river," today's Manatee Springs (T230). The third day he and a group of traders and Indians forded the Suwannee River on horseback and traveled north on the west bank to the Old Spanish Road. They followed the road through fields where they saw "plain marks or vestiges of abandoned Spanish plantations and dwellings" (T233).

They returned to Talahasochte the same day, as did the White King. Immediately a feast of bear ribs, hot bread, and honeyed water was prepared. The feast was held in the square and was attended only by the men. The leftovers were distributed to the rest of the town's population. Afterward a calumet ceremony was held in which the chief "with the rest of the white people in town, took their seats according to order." After the calumet pipe was passed and shared, black drink was passed around. The ceremony was followed by entertainment that lasted all night. The next day a council was held at which the chief and his elders "requested to have a trading house again" (T235–236).

Manatee Springs State Park

The park surrounds its most prominent natural feature, a first-magnitude spring that produces more than 80,000 gallons of clear water every minute. The park offers a 0.25-mile boardwalk along the spring run, in which one can still see the "troops and bands of fish"—gar, bream, bass, and others— "... continually ascending and descending, roving and figuring amongst one another" (T230). To the left of the boardwalk are views of the adjoining swamp, with cypress and swamp maples. The spring's constant 72-degree temperature provides a year-round habitat for manatees, although they are best viewed from November to April.

In the park are two hiking trails. Biking is allowed on the 8.5-mile North End Trail. Off the northern leg of the trail, west of Shacklefoot Pond, is a 0.5-mile spur trail that dead-ends at the park's boundary fence. Beyond the fence to the left is New Clay Landing. The site of **Talahasochte** was near here on the

Manatee Springs Run, Manatee Springs State Park, Florida.

river. The trailhead is on the main park road 0.5 mile west of the ranger station. The park offers camping, picnic areas, and swimming in the spring, and canoe rentals.

The park is located on Fla. 320, 6 miles west of Chiefland.

Suwannee River Canoe Trail

The Suwannee River, called the "Little St. Juans" in the eighteenth century, is more than 200 yards wide. From Manatee Springs State Park it is a 23-mile paddle to the Gulf of Mexico. The last good access to the river before the gulf is at Fowler Bluff, a 9-mile float south of the park. Access to the bluff is off U.S. 19, 10 miles south of Chiefland. The put-in for the section upstream from the

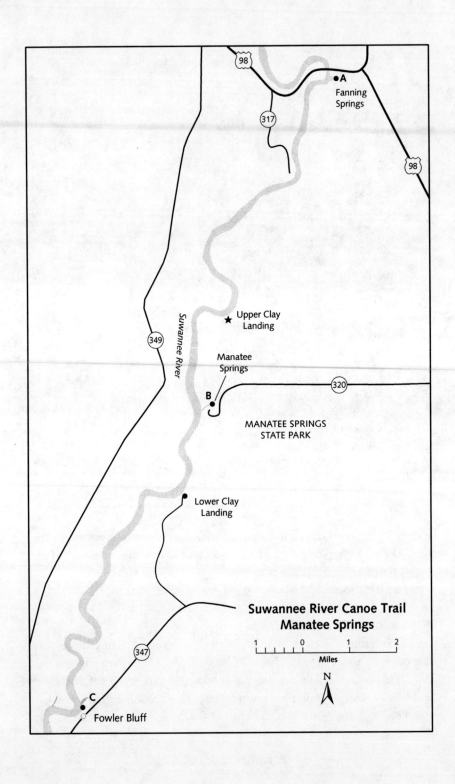

98

•A
Fanning
Springs

317

98

Suwannee River

349

★ Upper Clay
Landing

Manatee
Springs

320

B •

MANATEE SPRINGS
STATE PARK

• Lower Clay
Landing

Suwannee River Canoe Trail
Manatee Springs

1   0   1   2
Miles

N

347

•C
○ Fowler Bluff

park is at Big Fanning Springs State Park. From the boat dock it is a 9.5-mile float to the park. New Clay Landing is en route, 6.5 miles south of Big Fanning Springs.

Fanning Springs State Park

The recreation area surrounds two springs, Big Fanning and Little Fanning. Big Fanning is a first-magnitude spring. Here the Suwannee bends from the south to the west. The bend was the site of the White King's first village.[6] The park offers a nature trail, swimming in Big Fanning Springs, and boat access to the river.

The entrance is at the U.S. 19/98 bridge, on the east bank of the river.

6. Weisman, *Unconquered People,* 142.

Upper St. Johns River

Bartram made two trips from Spalding's Lower Store up the St. Johns River. His narrative of the first trip in the *Travels* is actually a composite of those two journeys. The result is a confusing account with anomalies such as hurricanes in May. The reconstructions of the two St. Johns trips of 1774 that follow are based on the more reliable narrative in Bartram's report to Fothergill. About mid-May 1774 Bartram left the Lower Store on his journey, sailing alone in his "little Vessell" (R1:86). He spent the first night as the guest of Mr. Tucker at an indigo plantation near Mount Royal, an Indian shell mound still visible today just off the east bank of the river. Preparing for the difficult crossing of Lake George, Bartram sought, without success, to hire someone to accompany him on the river. Storms over the lake kept him in the harbor the next day. The following day he departed in the tow of a larger boat with a good sail. Three miles into the lake, they encountered a gale from the southwest that forced a return to the north; they spent the night at the southern tip of Drayton Island. The next day was calm and they were able to cross the lake, arriving at the Upper Store (near Astor) that evening.

Joined by one of the traders from the Upper Store, Bartram continued his journey upstream. His destination was the Beresford plantation, west of today's DeLand, Florida. The two men camped the first night at a "high Orange Grove bluff"—the modern Idlewilde Dock (R1:89; T116). This is the "Battle Lagoon" where Bartram and his companion fought off alligators through the day and evening. The "River monsters" attacked their craft and pursued them onshore to their campsite, where Bartram won a short and uneasy truce by shooting and killing one of his pursuers. The two traveled further upstream to Mosquito Grove, also on the west shore of the St. Johns, about 6 miles above Lake Dexter. They also camped at St. Francis, a shell bluff on the west bank in today's Ocala National Forest. Their next campsite was on the high bluff at Hawkinsville, also on the west bank, north of today's Crows Bluff. The next day they arrived at Lord Beresford's plantation on the eastern shore of today's Lake Beresford, west of DeLand. Bartram's host guided him and his companion to Blue Springs, a dozen miles south of the plantation. Bartram

*Lake George. View from the Lake George Trail at Silver
Glen Springs, Ocala National Forest, Florida.*

then returned to the Upper Store, where he remained for several days before returning to the Lower Store in the first few days of June, bringing to an end the two- or three-week trip (R1:85–102; T185–187).

The second journey up the St. Johns commenced in August 1774 when Bartram joined a trader's party with two canoes headed for the Upper Store. The group camped the first night at Mount Royal and then entered Lake George, following the western shore. At the mouth of Salt Springs Run they followed the run up to the springs, where they camped that evening. Bartram had camped here with his father in 1766. Working down the western shore of the lake, Bartram and the traders camped at Volusia Bar and reached the Upper Store the next day.

The next morning Bartram set off alone up the river. He camped again at

Site of Spalding's Upper Store on the east bank of the St. Johns River near Astor, Florida.

"Battle Lagoon." An "abundance of Monstrous Alegators" gathered about his camp, but he kept them away by firing his gun at them (R1:33). He camped again at St. Francis as well, exploring the nearby lagoon. Here he observed both orange groves and burial grounds, the last remnants of the Yamasees who had been driven out by the Seminoles. He camped again at Hawkinsville before returning to Lake Beresford. A mile before arriving at the plantation, Bartram was forced to seek shelter in a marsh while a hurricane raged. For hours he "beheld with astonishment and terror the strength and fury of the storm" (R1:37). When the storm abated, he continued on to the plantation through the wake of destruction left by the storm. On his return to Spalding's Lower Store he followed the western shore of Lake George and visited Silver

Softshell turtle on the banks of the St. Johns River in Florida.

Glen Springs. Camping there and then again at Drayton Island on the way back, he arrived at the store in September 1774.

Florida's Great Springs: Bartram at the Source

But behold yet something far more admirable, see whole armies descending
into an abyss, into the mouth of the bubbling fountain, they disappear! are
they gone forever? is it real? I raise my eyes with terror and astonishment,—
I look down again to the fountain with anxiety, when behold them as it
were emerging from the blue ether of another world. (T167)

Few of Bartram's many readers seized on the power of his imagination as enthusiastically as did England's Romantic poets, in particular Samuel Taylor Coleridge. His most famous work, *Kubla Khan,* draws directly from Bartram's *Travels,* specifically from Bartram's descriptions of the great springs of central Florida. At Salt Springs, for example, Bartram saw an "inchanting and amazing crystal fountain, which incessantly threw up, from dark, rocky caverns below, tons of water every minute." Coleridge writes in *Kubla Khan:* "And from this chasm, with ceaseless turmoil seething, / As if this earth in fast

Silver Glen Springs, Ocala National Forest, Florida. Bartram visited
the springs on his tour of the upper St. Johns River in 1774.

thick pants were breathing, / A mighty fountain momently was forced." Coleridge cites the *Travels* in his notebooks, his letters, and even in footnotes to his poems. Clearly, Bartram had a strong hold on his vision.

One need only go to the springs around Orlando and Ocala to understand that grip. At Blue Springs, one gazes down into the water bubbling forth from a cleft in the earth and feels in touch with the subterranean world that courses beneath. This world held an endless fascination for Bartram, who wondered if "those who are so fortunate as to effect a retreat into the conductor, and escape the devouring jaws of the fearful alligator and the armed gar, descend into the earth, through the walls and cavities or vast perforations of the rocks, and from thence are conducted and carried away, by secret subterranean conduits and gloomy vaults, to other distant lakes and rivers." As one travels from

Blue Springs to Salt Springs, from Juniper Springs to Alexander Springs, one can feel this underground world pulsing beneath, breaking forth at the source, connecting vast areas of land with an underwater world below (T206).

Here, on and below this land, is Bartram at his most visionary. His admirers across the Atlantic recognized the power of his vision and brought it into their own work as a figure for the imagination, a new world beckoning. The great springs of central Florida still call forth to visitors in this silent song. Canoe Salt Spring and see the bass and gar darting underneath the boat as an osprey circles overhead. The tranquillity of this watery world is broken by motorboats and airboats as they dart up and down the run, yet the fascination Bartram described holds true nonetheless—the water bubbles upward ceaselessly from unknown locations in the earth.

Those lucky enough to canoe the run at Juniper Springs are in for an even more profound experience. One starts just below the spring, near a waterwheel that marks a put-in for canoers attempting the 7-mile trip. The sand that marks the bottom of the river is astonishingly white, the water is perfectly clear, and all around are palms, palmettos, and dense vegetation that bespeak a journey through a tropical forest. No wider than 20 feet, Juniper Springs transports and immerses a paddler in Bartram's green world.

When Bartram visited Florida in 1774, everything about the landscape was new to him, and much of it was uncataloged. But nothing he had yet experienced prepared him for the great springs of central Florida, and he was unabashed in using his imagination to describe the strangeness of the place for his readers. Today, that landscape is just as astonishing. The water pours forth as it has for millions of years, and though one is tempted to see the development of many of these locations as ruining the imaginative power of the landscape, there is yet something powerful and abiding in these springs. One can still choose to gaze upon the current, much as Bartram and Coleridge did, to probe the time and the depth of these sources. Here the imagination, as the great springs invite, can flow deep.

Great Springs Canoe Trails

Juniper Creek

Section: Juniper Springs Recreation Area to Fla. 19
Distance: 7.0 miles; 4–5 hours
Difficulty: 1–2; flat water
Hazards: no access points along the trail
Highlights: spring run; marshes

Salt Springs, Ocala National Forest, Florida.

The trail begins in the Juniper Springs Recreation Area and winds for 7 miles through the Juniper Springs Wilderness Area. For the first 2.5 miles the canoe run traverses a dense forest of palms, cypress, and other southern hardwoods. In this section of the trail the channel is narrow—about 6 feet wide—and shallow. The water is clear and there is a sandy bottom. Below Half-Way Landing the channel widens and the trail loses its canopy as it works through marshes, with alligators of substantial size visible on the banks and in the water. The put-out is at the highway bridge.

Canoe rentals and rehaul service are available from the Juniper Springs concessionaire.

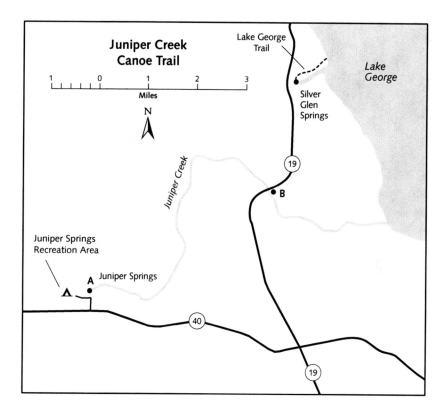

Salt Springs Run

Section: Salt Springs Landing to Lake George
Distance: 10 miles (round-trip); 4–6 hours
Difficulty: 1–2; flat water
Hazards: powerboats, airboats, heavy traffic on weekends
Highlights: Lake George; marshes

The trail begins near the Salt Springs Run Recreation Area, at the boat ramp on the south side of the run. This run is wide and deep. There are few access points along the trail, save for one a mile before the run empties into Lake George. This point is suitable for primitive camping. The best time to canoe the run is Monday through Thursday. On the weekends there is heavy boat traffic.

Alexander Springs Creek

Section: Alexander Springs Recreation Area to Shell Landing
Distance: 8.4 miles; 5–6 hours (one-way)
Difficulty: 1–2; flat water

*Juniper Springs Run, near the start of the canoe trail
at the springs, Ocala National Forest, Florida.*

Hazards: none; water hyacinths may jam the stream

Highlights: abundant wildlife

The trail begins in the Alexander Springs Recreation Area at the spring, which produces 80 million gallons of clear water a day. For the first 4–5 miles the creek is broad and clear, surrounded by hardwood swamp. As the trail approaches Antonio Landing, the creek becomes narrow and winding and may be jammed by water hyacinths. The creek passes the 52B landing at **mile 6.4** (a common put-out) and remains narrow until Shell Landing. For a wilderness canoe trip, it is an additional 4 miles downstream to Horseshoe Landing on the St. Johns River—a trip recommended only for experienced canoeists with proper gear and maps.

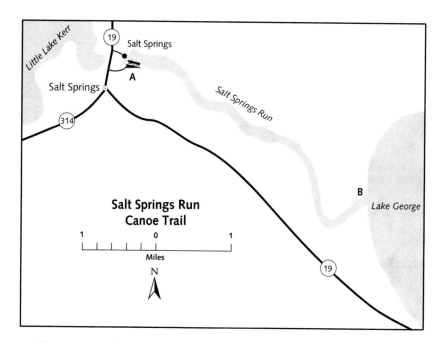

The canoe trail provides numerous opportunities for viewing wildlife. Canoes can be rented at the recreation area; the concessionaire also provides a rehaul service from the 52B landing.

De Leon Springs to Woodruff Lake

Section: De Leon Springs State Park to Lake Woodruff
Distance: 8.4 miles (one-way); 5–6 hours
Difficulty: 1–2; flat water
Hazards: wind on lakes; few access points
Highlights: spring run; Tick Island; site of Bartram's "Battle Lagoon"

The canoe trail begins in De Leon Springs State Park, just north of De-Land. The trail follows the course of the wide spring run for a few hundred feet and then empties into Spring Garden Lake, which extends to the south for several miles. Follow the northern shore of the lake, heading west. To the right, directly west of the spring run, is the entrance to Spring Garden Creek (this is also the eastern boundary of the Lake Woodruff National Wildlife Refuge, a 19,000-acre refuge with Lake Woodruff at its center). Enter the creek and follow its course as it meanders west and then south around Jones Island. Before the creek empties into Lake Woodruff **(mile 3.5)** you paddle by Pontoon Landing—one of the few sections of pine flatwood along the trail.

Lake Woodruff is large, covering more than 2,000 acres and with more

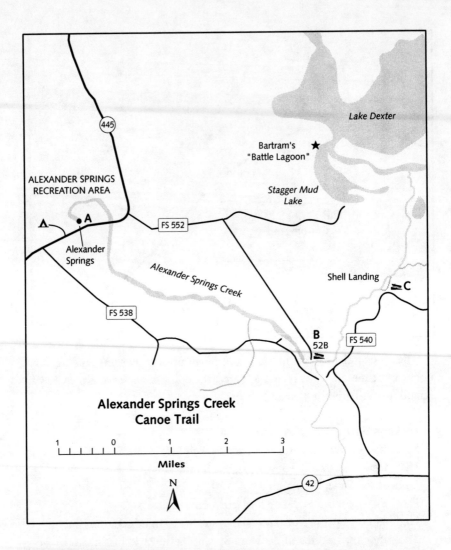

**Alexander Springs Creek
Canoe Trail**

Miles

N

than 11,000 acres of marshland surrounding it. In the lake continue to the west, again along the north shore. Paddle past Cypress Point and then turn to the northwest into the wide mouth of Tick Island Creek **(mile 5.5)**. The wide waterway soon empties into Dexter Lake **(mile 6.5)**. Cross the lake, hugging the southern shore, just below two unnamed islands. Past the mouth of Eph Creek it is a 2-mile paddle to the St. Johns **(mile 10)**. On the west shore of the St. Johns is **Idlewilde Point** near **Bartram's "Battle Lagoon."**

The boat launch is located in De Leon Springs State Park. Canoe and kayak rentals are available year-round. No camping is allowed in either the state

Great White Heron landing in the Alexander Springs Run, Ocala National Forest, Florida.

park or the Woodruff National Wildlife Refuge. The refuge does offer 6 miles of hiking/biking trails with opportunities to view the 200 species of birds that have been identified in the park. Both the park and the refuge close at dusk.

De Leon Springs State Park is located in De Leon Springs, Florida.

Blue Springs State Park

The main feature of the park is a first-magnitude spring producing more than 55,000 gallons of water a minute. The clear 72-degree water is a winter home for manatees, which come into the spring run from the St. Johns River. There is a boardwalk that follows the spring run, less than 0.5 mile, to the St.

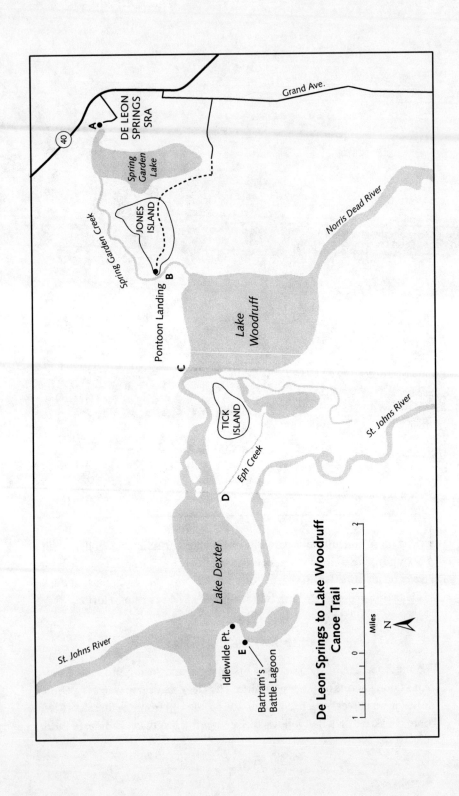

De Leon Springs to Lake Woodruff
Canoe Trail

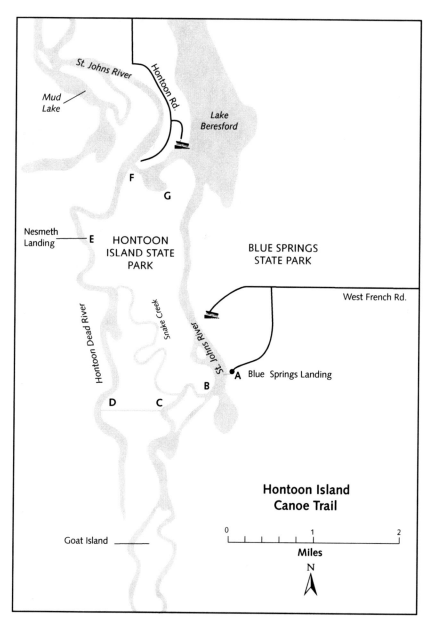

St. Johns River

Mud Lake

Hontoon Rd.

Lake Beresford

F

G

Nesmeth Landing

E

HONTOON
ISLAND STATE
PARK

BLUE SPRINGS
STATE PARK

West French Rd.

Hontoon Dead River

Snake Creek

St. Johns River

A Blue Springs Landing

B

D   C

**Hontoon Island
Canoe Trail**

Goat Island

0   1   2

Miles

N

Johns. At the mouth of the run are a boat ramp and a canoe launch. Downstream it is 4 miles to Hontoon Island State Park, accessible only by boat. There is a 9-mile canoe trail around Hontoon along the course of the dead river—the old St. Johns River—on the west side of the island. The chief hazards for canoeing on the St. Johns are powerboats and commercial barges.

Boils at Blue Springs, Blue Springs State Park, Florida.

Blue Springs also offers a 4-mile hiking trail through pine-shrub, marsh, flatwoods, and swamp, ending at a primitive camping area. The trailhead is near the boat landing, at the Thursby House, a late-nineteenth-century house built on an Indian shell mound. The park also offers a developed campground.

Located west of Orange City. Canoe rentals are available at the park. For information, call 904-775-6888.

Journey to Cherokee Country

Bartram's Cherokee Country

*After crossing this delightful brook and mead, the land rises again
with sublime magnificence, and I am led over hills and vales, groves and high
forests, vocal with the melody of the feathered songsters; the snow-white
cascades glittering on the sides of distant hills. (T342–343)*

Bartram approached the Blue Ridge Mountains in May 1775. At the summit
of Station Mountain (near today's Oconee State Park) he saw hills "appearing regularly undulated as the great ocean after a tempest" (T335). For the past
two months he had journeyed from Charleston, by way of the Savannah River
and Augusta, into Cherokee country. In front of him stood the high ridges of
the "Cherokee mountains," and all around him flowed water. He followed the
trading path into today's Georgia, crossing the Chattooga River at Earls Ford.
He continued along the "Warwoman Trace," upstream along Warwoman
Creek into Warwoman Valley. After crossing Beck Ridge, Bartram entered
the beautiful vale at Martin Creek.

The *Travels* contains a lengthy description of his passage through the valley, his discovery of the "unparalleled cascade" of Martin Creek Falls, and his
observations of the flora he encountered along the way. To read Bartram on
north Georgia is to discover a land rich with mountains and hills providing
magnificent views, deep, dark forests that promise quiet and solitude, and
flowing creeks and rivers that cascade through their rocky beds in spectacular waterfalls.

Perhaps no character of this region's landscape figures more prominently
than the Chattooga River, which Bartram mentions only in passing. James
Dickey's *Deliverance* has earned this river much of its reputation. Named the
nation's first Wild and Scenic River in 1979, the Chattooga today appears
much as it must have looked in Bartram's day. On the Bartram Trail along the
river or the path to Bull Sluice on the Chattooga's Section 3, the quiet but
powerful voice of the river is punctuated by explosive roars as the flow drops
steeply in the streambed. The banks rise abruptly to ridgelines that mark the

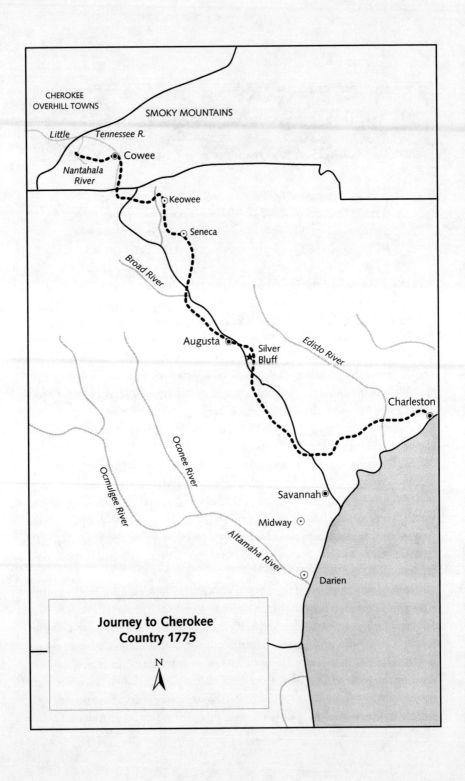

CHEROKEE
OVERHILL TOWNS

SMOKY MOUNTAINS

Little *Tennessee R.*

◉ Cowee

Nantahala
River

◉ Keowee

◉ Seneca

Broad River

Augusta ◉
★ Silver
Bluff

Edisto River

Charleston ◉

Oconee River

Ocmulgee River

Savannah ◉

Midway ◉

Altamaha River

◉ Darien

**Journey to Cherokee
Country 1775**

N

river's course. The waterfalls, cymbals to the river's bass, drop into the Chattooga at Dicks Creek and Fall Creek in tremendous flourishes.

The ridges of this area are but an intimation of what lies beyond the streambed. For as soon as the Bartram Trail parts from the Chattooga, the trail begins to climb—at first gradually, then steeply—to the region's higher peaks. Whether one hikes, rides horseback, or drives through north Georgia, the steep and winding nature of the route characterizes the region. The flow of water that becomes concentrated in the Chattooga begins in the hills and mountains as numerous small streams, many, like Bartram's "Falling Creek," with falls as magnificent as those that line the Chattooga.

As the streams get smaller and the hills get steeper, one cannot help but be enchanted by the vistas that announce themselves through breaks in the forest that lies all around. From the top of Pinnacle Knob, a day hiker has views to the south and east of what Bartram would have seen as he climbed through the Piedmont to the ridges that become this vantage point. Through Windy Gap and Wilson Gap, the laurel and rhododendron so evident in the *Travels* form a canopy around the Bartram Trail, ushering the hiker to higher and higher elevations. By the time one reaches Rabun Bald, either on a day hike or as the terminus of an extended hike that originates along the Chattooga, the roar of the river is far away, replaced by views that take in all of Bartram's north Georgia and beyond. On a clear day, Tennessee's Clingmans Dome and Mount LeConte beckon from the north while Georgia's Brasstown Bald and Blood Mountain loom to the west. Bartram notes in the *Travels* that the "towering mountains seem continually in motion as I pass along, pompously raising their superb crests towards the lofty skies, traversing the far distant horizon" (T346).

All in all, north Georgia remains fertile soil for a traveler's imagination. Whether hiking the Bartram Trail or driving through the countryside that Bartram visited, the lofty summits, swelling hillsides, murmuring creeks, and crashing waterfalls and rapids all speak to a land alive with sights and sounds. Bartram called the landscape "sublime." Each visitor may call it something different, but this much is certain—it does not disappoint.

Bartram entered today's North Carolina on a route that followed the Little Tennessee River. Flanking the river valley were the Nantahala Mountains to the west and the lower Cowee Mountains to the east. That Bartram looked upon this landscape, too, with wonder is hardly a surprise to visitors to this region, who, whether they travel by foot or by car, are immersed in "a sublimely awful scene of power and magnificence, a world of mountains piled upon mountains."

The difference between the prospect from North Carolina and the prospect from north Georgia is subtle. It is not that north Georgia is tumbling falls and soaring mountains and North Carolina is not. The Cullasaja and the Nanta-hala are two magnificent rivers of North Carolina that wind their way through steep gorges and descend in a flurry of whitewater. It is not that North Car-olina lacks dramatic cataracts; a visit to Dry Falls and Cullasaja Falls will surely impress. What is different is that to arrive in this area of North Carolina is to arrive firmly in the mountains, leaving the Piedmont behind: the Snow-bird Mountains lie to the west, the Blue Ridge to the south, and the entire ex-panse of the Nantahala Mountains runs to the north, ending at the southern base of the Great Smoky Mountains. The earth itself shows the effect of mas-sive forces of compression, every feature of the landscape suggesting an up-ward pressure. This is a world where "ridges of hills rising grand and sub-limely one above and beyond another, some boldly and majestically advancing into the verdant plain, their feet bathed with the silver flood of the Tanase, whilst others far distant, veiled in blue mists, sublimely mount aloft, with yet greater majesty lift up their pompous crests and overlook vast regions."

Yet it would be a mistake to think of this landscape only in terms of its mas-sive mountains. Its flora is sublime as well. In the late spring, blooming rho-dodendrons and azaleas crown many of the ridges. Amidst the sea of green that rises with the landscape are pockets of pinks, reds, and oranges—bril-liant colors paint the hillsides. Hiking the Bartram Trail through a canopy of flame azaleas is nearly as overwhelming as looking out upon the surround-ing mountains. The brilliance of the blooms is everywhere, and one wants to linger, to absorb this beauty before facing the next set of ridges, which are surely just a prelude to the next peak. Many USDA Forest Service roads thread through this area and the adventurous driver is never far away from these sights, but the road will surely wind and twist and turn before arriving at any destination.

Another unique feature of this area is its timelessness. Many spots here still resemble the country Bartram traveled 200 years ago. It is less developed, surely less inhabited, than other regions he visited. This is particularly true of the Joyce Kilmer Memorial Forest. "The spacious high forests" that Bartram saw have been logged, but there are still pockets that suggest the old magnif-icence of these woods. The groves at Joyce Kilmer are just such a place, "grand and sublime."

Gone, too, are most of the Native Americans who called this region home. Much of Bartram's description of this part of his journey is marked by his en-counters with the Cherokees: the roving scout he met as he traveled to the

Overhill Towns, a group of frolicking Indian maidens, and, toward the end of his journey, "the great Ata-cul-culla . . . emperor or grand chief of the Cherokees." As he entered North Carolina, Bartram's immediate destination was Cowee, the largest and oldest Cherokee settlement along the river he called the "Tanase." Only traces remain of the landscape Bartram encountered here. Mounds built by the predecessors of the Cherokees still exist in Cowee and Franklin. At Robbinsville is the gravesite of Chief Junaluska. And the Cherokee Museum in Cherokee offers a record of Native American culture. The land itself, however, is still larger than life, and those who visit with Bartram's descriptions in mind will not fail to be awed.

Charleston to Cherokee Country

In the spring of 1775 Bartram set out on horseback from Charleston for a visit to the Cherokee Nation. For 11 miles he followed the road parallel to the Ashley River. Crossing the river at the ferry near **Drayton Hall**, he turned west to join the Charleston Road. From the Stono River to Savannah the route of this colonial road coincides with today's U.S. 17. Bartram chose this route over the more direct course to Keowee—"the Cherokee Path" from Charleston to Fort Ninety-six—so that he could explore the "steep banks, vast swamps, and low grounds" of the Savannah River (T317). On his way to the river he spent three nights on the road, first at Jacksonboro, then at an inn 25 miles farther down the road, and finally near Allison, today's Ridgeland.[1] He left the main road here for the Three Sisters Ferry across the Savannah, 3 miles east of Clyo, Georgia. The ferry was active until the early years of the twentieth century.

In Georgia he followed the "high road" toward Augusta. En route he stopped at a "delightful habitation" at today's Mount Pleasant and recorded the plantation's logging operation in some detail. Slaves cut tall yellow pines, rolled them into the river, and then formed them into rafts, which were floated down to Savannah for sale. He continued northward, taking the familiar detour to South Carolina and **Silver Bluff**. At the river crossing he explored Shell Bluff. On the Georgia side, this bluff stood more than 100 feet above the river. Buried in its soil were fossil oyster shells 15–20 inches long and 6–8 inches wide. At Silver Bluff, George Galphin offered Bartram both hospitality and letters of introduction to traders in the Indian towns.

1. Jacksonboro is "Ponpon" on Faden's 1780 "A Map of South Carolina and a part of Georgia." Ponpon was an Indian village that became the colonial town of Jacksonboro. The "Road to Charleston" from Ponpon to Ashley Ferry is marked on the map.

Bartram's stay at Silver Bluff was brief. He continued northward, crossing the Savannah on the ferry at Fort Moore. In Augusta he conferred with gentlemen "conversant in Indian affairs." Soon he set off for **Fort James Dartmouth**, riding on the "Petersburg Road," or Washington Road. He spent the night at a public house on the Little River and arrived at the fort at the end of the next day. From there he conducted brief explorations of the "remarkable Indian monuments" on the banks of the Savannah (T321, 324). He noted heaps of "white gnawed bones" of elk, deer, and buffalo. Seven miles north of the fort, at today's Calhoun Falls, he crossed the Savannah once more. In South Carolina again, he traveled the high road to "Lough-abber" (Lochaber), Alexander Cameron's plantation on a tributary of Long Cane Creek. Cameron, commended to Bartram by John Stuart, was the "deputy commissary for Indian affairs for the Cherokee nation." Cameron enjoyed favorable relations with the Cherokees and was known for his trustworthiness and fairness. Bartram was Cameron's guest for several days, as heavy rains swelled the rivers and made the fords too dangerous.

On May 15, as the weather cleared, Bartram resumed his trek up the colonial road, noting the beauty of the flame azaleas, which "abound[ed] and illuminate[ed] the hill sides." Cameron provided a slave to pilot his guest as far north as **Seneca**, the site of an ancient city located about a mile south of today's Clemson University. The Seneca that Bartram visited was a "new town" rebuilt in the aftermath of the Cherokee War of 1761, when the Cherokees were defeated by the combined forces of British regulars led by Lieutenant Colonel James Grant and the Carolina militia. Bartram estimated that the "new" Seneca, which consisted of houses on both sides of the river, had a population of 500, with 100 warriors. The next day, Bartram left alone for Keowee 15 miles to the north. He took the road on the west side of the Keowee River to **Fort Prince George** near the mouth of Crow Creek.

He waited nearly a week at the former military post, now a trading center, for a Cherokee guide to lead him into the mountains, then decided to press on without one. Bartram traveled alone along the rocky and uneven trading path out of the Keowee Valley and climbed the ridge that separates this valley from that formed by the Little River. He rode through the Little Valley, then crossed Tomassee Creek. Climbing out of the valley, he ascended the "top of Oconee Mountain"—the southern end of **Station Mountain**. At the base of the mountain were the "ruins of the antient Occonne town" (T335). Here he entered the valley of a large creek, either Jerry Creek or Village Creek—both are headwaters of the Chauga River. Following the Indian path, he passed through Rocky Gap in the Chattooga Ridge about 3.5 miles southeast of the mouth of Warwoman Creek on the Chattooga River. Soon he reached the "main branch of the Tugilo," crossing the Chattooga at today's Earls Ford. After fording the river, he followed the path that paralleled Warwoman Creek into the Warwoman Valley. The trail left the valley, unlike today's road, to climb Beck Ridge. Descending the ridge he visited the celebrated Martin Creek Falls. From here he climbed "Mount Magnolia"—Pinnacle Knob—to Courthouse Gap. He rode from the gap to The Dividings—a junction of Indian paths north of today's Clayton, Georgia.

From the junction he took the rough path to the north through Rabun Gap and camped that evening on one of the headwaters of the Little Tennessee River. Bartram was now in the "vale of Cowe," the Little Tennessee River valley stretching north to the base of the Great Smoky Mountains. He followed the Little Tennessee downstream past a battlefield, near present-day Otto, of the 1761 Cherokee War. That evening he stayed as the guest of a trader and his Indian wife at their hut on the left bank of the river. The next day he visited Echoe, located at the mouth of Cartoogechaye Creek southeast of today's Franklin, North Carolina, where he commented on the number of good houses. He continued northward for 3 miles to the abandoned town of **Nucassee**, and then on to Watauga, farther downstream. Bartram followed the road through the large town into little plantations of corn and beans to a council house "situated on the top of an ancient artificial mount" (T350). The road ended at the mound, and Bartram was not sure how to proceed. The town's chief, Will of Wautauga, saw the lost traveler and took him in as his guest. The next day the chief escorted Bartram to the trail leading to Cowee.

On the morning of May 20 Bartram arrived in **Cowee**, the largest of the Cherokee Middle Towns, where he stayed as the guest of the chief trader at the settlement, Patrick Galahan. The next day Bartram and Galahan set out for a day trip across the Cowee Mountains to present-day Alarka Valley, where the trader kept horses of "all colours, sizes and dispositions." Bartram and his host continued riding through the valley and encountered a group of Cherokee girls gathering strawberries. This "sylvan scene" was the occasion for one of the *Travels'* best-known passages describing the beauty of the "Elysian fields" and the young virgins. The two men crossed the ridge and returned to Cowee that evening. Bartram waited here two days for an Indian guide to take him to the Overhill Towns across the Nantahalas and Smokies in present-day Tennessee.

The guide did not appear, and, against the warnings of the traders, Bartram resolved once again to travel alone. He left Cowee on May 24, joined for the first 15 miles by his host. They rode to the west on a trail bisecting the Iotla

Valley and then turned to the north to pass through the Iotla Gap, also known as Parrish Gap.[2] As they approached Burningtown Creek, the path intersected another road from the Overhill Towns to Cowee. Bartram's host and guide took his leave here, and Bartram continued to the west to the main ridge of the Nantahalas. He forded with difficulty a "large creek, twelve or fifteen yards wide, roaring over a rocky bed"—Burningtown Creek—and entered the narrow valley divided by Burningtown Creek, whose course he followed up the mountain to **Burningtown Gap**.

Bartram descended the main ridge, following the course of Ben Creek, to near present-day Kyle, where he joined a trail that followed Whiteoak Creek downstream.[3] He camped along the path near the mouth of Otter Creek or Partridge Creek. The next day he rode 8 or 10 miles to a large creek or river— no doubt the Nantahala. Entering the river gorge, Bartram "observed at some distance, a company of Indians, all well mounted on horse back," led by Chief Attakullakulla, the leading chief of the Cherokees. The party, which was en route to Charleston to meet with John Stuart, descended into the gorge and approached Bartram. After exchanging pleasantries, the chief welcomed Bartram into his country as a "friend and brother." Bartram continued on his trek to the Overhill Towns, following the downstream course of Tulula Creek, and camped that night in the vicinity of Sweetgum, North Carolina. The next day he decided that the risks of traveling alone were too great and that he should not "range the Overhill settlements until the treaty was over." On May 26 he turned around and rode back to Cowee, arriving on the evening of the next day. After spending two days with Mr. Galahan, Bartram set off on the morning of May 29 for the two-day trip to Fort Prince George and Keowee.

2. According to Harper, Bartram and Galahan did not part company; they continued to ride together following the course of Burningtown Creek. In less than 3 miles they turned south following the course of Falls Creek. Past the falls, they crossed over the eastern ridges of Wayah Bald. From the highest ridge, Trimont Ridge at 3,300 feet, they began their descent to the south. At the base of the ridge they intersected a road, and Galahan departed to the east while Bartram continued to the west up Wayah Creek to Wayah Gap, to the south of Wine Spring Bald (*Travels*, 390–391).

3. According to Harper, Bartram descended the Nantahalas from Wayah Creek down the valley to Jarrett Creek. At the end of the descent he crossed one of the main branches of the "Tanase," the Nantahala River. The crossing was in the vicinity of Aquone, now inundated by Nantahala Lake. From the crossing, he followed a path up Choga Creek to Junaluska Creek. In this area, close to Andrews, North Carolina, he met with the grand chief of the Cherokees, Attakullakulla.

South Carolina Upcountry

Driving Tour: Tamassee Knob to Fort Prince George

This 65-mile driving tour begins and ends in the city of Walhalla, South Carolina. The tour climbs the foothills west of the city and then turns northward on S.C. 107. Passing Oconee State Park, the road joins the Chattooga Ridge, which forms the eastern boundary of the Chattooga River corridor. On the ridge are many opportunities for hiking, notably the Bartram Trail, the Big Bend Trail to the river, and the Tamassee Knob Trail. Along S.C. 107 there are numerous vistas and picnic areas. From the ridge, the tour descends to the Whitewater River valley and then farther south to the Keowee River valley. East of the Keowee River is Keowee-Toxaway State Park, which offers an interpretive trail on the history and culture of the Cherokee Indians. To the south, on the right bank of the river, is Keowee Landing, the site of one of the largest Cherokee towns in the region. From the river the tour heads west, returning to Walhalla.

Walhalla is located at the center of Oconee County, at the northwestern tip of South Carolina. John A. Wagener of the German Colonization Society of Charleston founded this mountain community in 1850. Its first settlers declared that it was as beautiful as the "garden of the Norse gods," Valhalla. To reach the city from the south and west, take I-85 to South Carolina Exit 1, the interchange with S.C. 11, also called the Cherokee Foothills Parkway. The parkway is a scenic highway that arcs to the northeast, skirting the southeastern edge of the Blue Ridge Mountains. From the interstate, take the parkway north for 19 miles to the interchange for S.C. 28. At the interchange, turn left onto the ramp for S.C. 28 North. In less than a mile the highway comes to the center of town.

The driving tour begins in the center of Walhalla on S.C. 28 North. For 5 miles the road climbs the foothills, gaining 700 feet in elevation. Nearing the end of the climb is Yellow Branch, a USDA Forest Service picnic area that overlooks the Piedmont to the east. *Continue north on the state highway,* which soon intersects the approach road **(mile 5.5)** to the Stump House Mountain

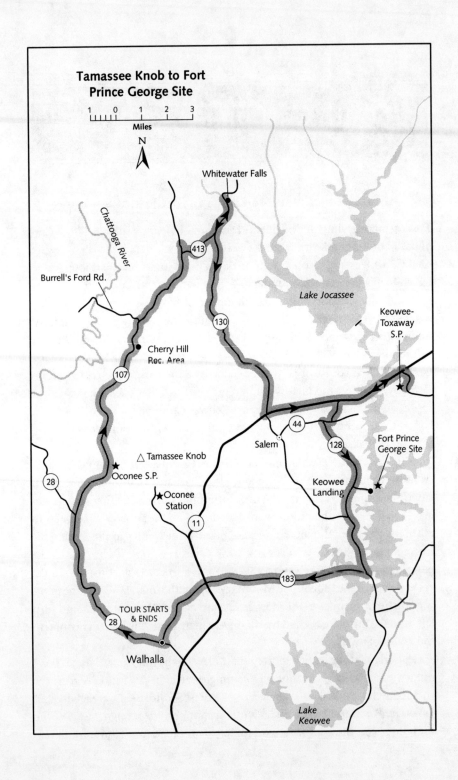

Tamassee Knob to Fort
Prince George Site

1   0   1   2   3
Miles

N

Whitewater Falls

Chattooga River

Burrell's Ford Rd.

413

130

Lake Jocassee

Keowee-
Toxaway
S.P.

107

Cherry Hill
Rec. Area

44

Salem

128

Fort Prince
George Site

△ Tamassee Knob

★ Oconee S.P.

28

★ Oconee
Station

11

Keowee
Landing

183

TOUR STARTS
& ENDS

28

Walhalla

Lake
Keowee

The trailhead for this 2-mile trail to the summit of the knob is near the cabins. The path starts out with the Foothills Trail and shares the same pathway for 0.4 mile. Just past Station Mountain Road, the Foothills Trail turns sharply to the left and the Tamassee Trail continues at a right angle to the right. Station Mountain Road, heading to the southeast, was the route Bartram traveled from today's Oconee Station en route to Earls Ford across the Chattooga (т385). From the junction the trail enters a gap and then begins the steady climb up the knob. As it approaches the summit there are views of the Piedmont to the south and east. The trail crosses over the summit and ends on the eastern face of the knob, offering a vista with spectacular views of the mountains from the west to the north and of the Piedmont directly below. To the south is a view of Station Mountain.

To reach the trailhead (for both the Tamassee Knob Trail and the Foothills Trail): enter the park and follow the signs for the campground. Passing through the campground, the road comes to a junction. Turn left and follow the signs for Cabins 13–19. The parking area for the trails is near Cabin 13.

Tunnel. In 1853 John C. Calhoun tried to connect the Blue Ridge Railroad in Tennessee with the Charleston rail line. The state legislature financed the project with more than $1 million, but after six years only two-thirds of the tunnel had been completed. With the outbreak of the Civil War the project was doomed. Three later attempts to complete the tunnel—in 1876, 1900, and 1940—were also unsuccessful.

Continue north on S.C. 28. In 0.25 mile there is a USDA Forest Service district office on the right offering visitors assistance and information. Two miles past the junction with Long Creek Road, the road forks **(mile 8.2)**. *Bear to the right, taking S.C. 107.* A little more than 2 miles on the right is the entrance to one of South Carolina's oldest state parks—Oconee State Park **(mile 10.6)**. The Civilian Conservation Corps (CCC) built the park in the 1930s on a natural shelf on the ridge. Today the park offers cabins, camping, a 20-acre lake, and more than 6 miles of hiking trails. The park is the southern trailhead for the Foothills Trail, which winds approximately 85 miles to the north and east to Caesar's Head State Park. It is also the trailhead for the Tamassee Knob Trail.

Exiting the park, turn right onto S.C. 107. In less than 1 mile the road intersects Village Green Road to the left **(mile 11.5)**. *Continue north on the state highway,* now on the spine of the Chattooga Ridge. On the right is a parking area providing access to the Foothills Trail. From here, the road begins a steady climb up one of the high points of the ridge, with views to the west and east. The climb ends as the state highway intersects Cheohee Road **(mile 14.3)**

To visit the river, turn left onto Burrell's Ford Road, which reaches the Chattooga in 3 miles. This single-track gravel road is heavily used and is passable by conventional automobiles. A one-lane concrete bridge has replaced the ford over the Chattooga. At the bridge there are views of the upper Chattooga to the north and south. There are two waterfalls, King's Creek and Spoonauger, each within 1.5 miles of the parking area. Adjacent to the river is a Forest Service campground, accessible by foot only. The ford also provides access to the Foothills Trail, the Chattooga River Trail, and to trails leading into the Ellicott Rock Wilderness Area.

and the eastern trailhead of the Bartram Trail. There is a small parking area for hikers at the northeast corner of the intersection. Continue north on S.C. 107, passing the trailhead for the Big Bend Trail, which leads west to the Chattooga River **(mile 16.6)**. Soon the highway passes, on the right, the USDA Forest Service's Cherry Hill Campground, with seasonal camping. As it continues north, the highway passes Moody Springs, named for an early-nineteenth-century settler who drew his water from the spring. Farther northward there is another vista with views to the west of the Blue Ridge Mountains in Georgia. Continuing to the north, S.C. 28 intersects Burrell's Ford Road **(mile 18.3)**.

From the junction of Burrell's Ford Road and S.C. 107 the tour continues straight ahead on the state highway. Less than 0.25 mile on the right is another vista. Less than 2 miles from the junction on the left is the access road leading to the Walhalla Fish Hatchery **(mile 19.8)**. *Continue north on S.C. 107* to the intersection with S.C. 413—Wigington Highway **(mile 22.1)**. *Turn right onto S.C. 413* and begin the 2-mile descent to the Whitewater River. As the road drops, there is an overlook on the right with views of the Piedmont hills extending to the horizon. To the east are views of Lake Jocassee, and in the distance to the south is Lake Keowee. Continue downhill on the connector until the road ends at S.C. 130 **(mile 24.3)**. At the intersection, *turn left and take S.C. 130* to the North Carolina state line. On the right **(mile 25.4)** is the access road to Whitewater Falls.

Whitewater Falls

These falls, cascading more than 400 feet, are the tallest in the eastern United States. There is a short asphalt access trail that leads to an overlook for the falls. The access trail also intersects the Foothills Trail, which offers overlooks of the falls from below and above. The overlook above the falls is the more dangerous of the two; it has claimed sixteen lives since 1990. The recreation area is open during the daylight hours year-round; there is a fee for parking. As you exit the recreation area, turn left to return to South Carolina.

In South Carolina *continue south on S.C. 130*, past the intersection with S.C. 413. In 5 miles the highway intersects North Little River Road, S.C. 37 **(mile 31.5)**. Continue straight ahead. In a little more than 4 miles S.C. 130 comes to the junction with the Foothills Parkway, S.C. 11 **(mile 36)**. *Turn left onto S.C. 11 East.* In approximately 3 miles, S.C. 11 intersects Fall Creek Landing. In another 1.5 miles the highway crosses the Keowee River **(mile 40.4)**, with views of the Blue Ridge Mountains to the north. Another 1.5 miles ahead on the right is the entrance to Keowee-Toxaway State Park **(mile 42)**.

Keowee-Toxaway State Park

Located on the shore of Lake Keowee, this park is approximately 10 miles north of the site of the Cherokee town of Keowee and its accompanying colonial fort, Fort Prince George. The park offers an interpretive center on the life, history, and customs of both the Cherokee Indians and the colonists. The exhibits include a model of the British fort that was reconstructed after a complete archaeological excavation of the fort in the 1960s. Outside the small museum is the trailhead for the 0.25-mile Cherokee Self-Interpretive Trail, featuring four kiosks with information on the Cherokees and their relationship with the early European settlers. The first kiosk is devoted to pottery, dress, hunting, and nonfood plant use. There is also an exhibit on the village of Keowee as it would have been in 1650. Accompanying the exhibit is a reference to Bartram's description of the Native Americans he encountered in this region: "The Cherokees are yet taller and more robust than the Muscogulges, and by far the largest race of men I have seen[,] their complexions brighter and somewhat of the olive cast, especially the adults; and some of their young women are nearly as fair and blooming as European women" (T484–485). The second kiosk is devoted to the early European traders, with a map of early trading paths into Cherokee country and exhibits on the commodities traded and their relative value. The third kiosk is devoted to the conflicts between Cherokees and Europeans. There is also a replica of Fort Prince George, 6 miles to the south. The last kiosk deals with the role of the Cherokees during and after the Revolution and leading up to the Trail of Tears. The trail ends at the interpretive center.

From the parking lot, *exit the park, turning left onto S.C. 11.* As the road approaches the river there are views of the mountains to the right. After crossing the Keowee River the road begins the mile-long climb out of the steep valley. On the plateau, *turn left onto C.R. 127*, Fall Creek Landing Road **(mile 45)**.

Follow the county road for a little less than 1 mile, ending at S.C. 44—Shallowford Road. *Turn right and take Shallowford Road west* to the junction with Nimmons Bridge Road, S.C. 128 **(mile 47)**. At the junction, *turn left onto Nimmons Bridge Road* and take it south for about 3 miles. *At the junction with C.R. 98, turn left.* At the intersection is a sign for **Keowee Landing (mile 50)**. In 0.9 mile the road ends at a boat ramp on the eastern shore of the lake.

Keowee Landing

The road enters the valley described by Bartram as a "fertile vale . . . environed at various distances, by high hills and mountains" (T330) and ends at the public boat landing. Just to the northeast is the site of the once-thriving Cherokee village. By the time of Bartram's visit in 1775 the town had been nearly abandoned for the third time: "There are several Indian mounts or tumuli, and terraces, monuments of the ancients at the site of Keowe, near the fort Prince George, but no Indian habitations at present" (T332). Keowee was first abandoned in the late 1740s after it was destroyed during the Creek-Cherokee War. Rebuilt, it was abandoned again, in the 1750s, when a smallpox epidemic—a regular scourge of both white and Indian populations—swept through the town. On the eve of the Cherokee War (1760–61) the town had fully rebounded as an agricultural and trade center. The brutal war between the colonists and the Cherokees left the town and surrounding farmlands in ruins.[1] The Cherokees returned again to rebuild, but this time, too, the restoration was short-lived. As the Cherokee population declined in general and as white farmers moved closer to the valley, the Cherokees finally abandoned their town for settlements in North Carolina and Tennessee. The only residents Bartram encountered were several white traders.

The site of **Fort Prince George**, which like the town site now lies beneath a lake built by Duke Power Company, is northeast of Keowee Landing, near the small island. The fort was located on the left bank of the river, across from the center of the Indian town. It was constructed in the fall of 1753 as part of the settlement between the Cherokees and the colonial government ending the trade embargo of 1751–52 established by Governor Glen in retaliation for Cherokee raids on northern colonists. The earthen-walled fort was 100 feet square and surrounded by a moat. At each corner was a bastion. Inside the fort were barracks, the commander's house, and a kitchen. The fort

1. Corkran, *The Cherokee Frontier*, 33–36; Smith, "Distribution of Eighteenth-Century Cherokee Settlements," 48–49; King, introduction to *The Cherokee Indian Nation*, xxii–xxiii. See also Hatley's "The Three Lives of Keowee," 227–229.

Blockhouse at Oconee Station, Oconee Station State Park, South Carolina.

was rebuilt twice: in 1756 and again after the Cherokee War. In 1765 the treaty that determined the boundary between the colony and Cherokee lands until the Revolution was signed there. Like the town, the fort had been abandoned by the time Bartram visited: "The old fort Prince George now bears no marks of a fortress, but serves for a trading house" (T332).

From Keowee Landing, *return to the junction with Nimmons Bridge Road. Turn left* and follow the road south for just over 1.5 miles. This road closely approximates the eighteenth-century road Bartram followed from Seneca, 16 miles south of the fort. *At the junction with S.C. 130* **(mile 53.3)**, *turn left* and follow the state highway to the south. In less than 3 miles **(mile 56)** the road ends, intersecting S.C. 183. A quarter mile left of the intersection is a Bartram Trail marker. At the intersection, turn right and follow S.C. 183 for 9 miles into Walhalla **(mile 65)**.

Other Points of Interest

Oconee Station State Park

This park has preserved one of many blockhouses constructed in the 1790s as part of a defense system against the Creeks. Adjacent to the blockhouse was a trading post built by William Richards in 1795. Troops were posted at the site until 1799, and the trading post thrived until the early nineteenth century. Richards's post and the blockhouse were on the site of an earlier trading house built in the 1760s that was on the route Bartram followed from today's Salem northwest to Station Mountain. In addition to the historic buildings and artifacts, the park offers living history demonstrations on the lives of early colonists and the Cherokees. The park also offers a 1-mile nature trail.

ACCESS

The park is approximately 8 miles north of Walhalla, 2 miles off S.C. 11. *From Walhalla:* take S.C. 11 north for 6 miles. At the junction with Oconee Station Road, turn left. The park is 2 miles ahead.

Park hours: Thursday–Sunday, 9 A.M.–6 P.M. The park is closed during January and February.

North Georgia

Driving Tour: The Chattooga Watershed

The Chattooga loop, which begins and ends in Clayton, follows the Chattooga River corridor to numerous points of interest for the Bartram enthusiast. For those preferring short hikes with magnificent scenery, the loop provides access to Becky Branch Falls and Martin Creek Falls near Warwoman Dell. The quick hike to Bull Sluice Rapids on the Chattooga gives a firsthand glimpse of the awesome power of this Wild and Scenic River. There are two short spur trips: the first to Earls Ford on the South Carolina side of the river, the second to Dicks Creek Falls and Dicks Creek Ledge on the Georgia side farther downstream. The driving loop travels 42 miles; none of the short hikes measures much more than 1 mile.

The driving tour begins in Clayton at the intersection of U.S. 441 and U.S. 76. *Take U.S. 76 east out of Clayton.* At **mile 2.0** and **mile 4.5** there are views to the left of Rainy Mountain and the east–west ridges that run from the Blue Ridge to the Chattooga. At **mile 8.1** the road reaches the **Chattooga River**. To the left, on the Georgia side of the river, is a small parking lot. This is the closest parking area to the river. The bridge has sidewalks on both sides for viewing the river upstream and downstream.

Chattooga River

The Chattooga, known to Bartram as the Tugilo, is one of seven Wild and Scenic Rivers in the eastern United States. Many regard it as the crown jewel of southern whitewater rivers. The river begins on the east face of Whiteside Mountain in North Carolina and runs 50 miles to its end in Lake Tugaloo, just south of Tallulah Falls, Georgia. Because it is a Wild and Scenic River, no motorized vehicles are allowed within 0.25 mile of the river except at a select number of bridges and roads built before the river gained its current status. Man-made facilities are minimal, and the area looks much as it must have appeared in 1775 when Bartram crossed the river at **Earls Ford**, approximately 12

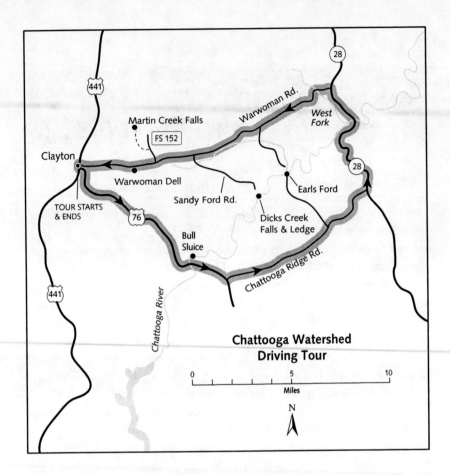

Martin Creek Falls

FS 152

Clayton

Warwoman Dell

TOUR STARTS
& ENDS

76

Bull
Sluice

Warwoman Rd.

West
Fork

28

28

Earls Ford

Sandy Ford Rd.

Dicks Creek
Falls & Ledge

Chattooga Ridge Rd.

441

441

Chattooga River

**Chattooga Watershed
Driving Tour**

0   5   10

Miles

N

miles upstream. As the designation "Wild and Scenic" suggests, this river alternates between calm water and agitated flows.

The river is divided into four sections of increasing difficulty for the whitewater enthusiast from north to south. The U.S. 76 bridge serves as the division point between two of the most difficult sections of the river, Sections 3 and 4. Two-tenths of a mile **(mile 8.3)** after crossing the U.S. 76 bridge there is a drive leading to a large parking area on the east side of the river. This lot is the major put-in site for Section 4. This area is also the trailhead for a short spur trail to the last rapids of Section 3, **Bull Sluice**. This class 5 rapids is one of the river's most dangerous; it has claimed eighteen lives since 1970.

Bull Sluice Access Trail

The trailhead is at the visitors' center on the South Carolina side of the river. From the center, follow the paved path downstream for a few hundred

The parking area on the Georgia side of the river is the southern trailhead for this 10.7-mile trail. To the north, the trail ends at the junction with the Bartram Trail. Although the trail parallels the river, it is for the most part well out of sight and sound of Section 3. The trail intersects the river at **mile 4.1** and follows it for nearly 1.5 miles to **mile 6.3.**

---

feet. The trail leaves the path, turning sharply to the left. Follow the trail for less than 0.2 mile to a series of boulders overlooking the rapids from the east. The boulders are just to the south of one of the most dangerous hydraulics in the rapids. Exercise caution when walking on the boulders, especially when they are wet.

At the exit for the parking area, turn left and continue eastbound on U.S. 76 for 2 miles. *Turn left* **(mile 10.3)** *onto Chattooga Ridge Road.* This road parallels the river on the South Carolina side, following a series of low ridges. In 4.5 miles **(mile 14.8)** there is a small pull-off on the west side of the road that offers views of the river valley and the Blue Ridge Mountains in the distance. The highest peak to the right is Rabun Bald. There are also views of the mountains in North Carolina to the north. Soon the road intersects S.C. 193, Whetstone Gap Road **(mile 16.4)**. To visit Earls Ford, where Bartram forded the Chattooga, turn left.

Earls Ford

From Chattooga Ridge Road it is less than 4 miles to the river. After 1.7 miles the pavement ends and the road becomes a single-track Forest Service road passable by most automobiles. The road ends at a parking area, the trailhead for an access trail to the river and Earls Ford. The 0.25-mile trail follows an old roadbed to the river. Near today's trail was the main east–west road or path connecting the Cherokee Lower Towns in the South Carolina upcountry with the Middle Towns in the Little Tennessee River valley in Georgia and North Carolina. The road or path shows up on both George Hunter's 1730 "Map of the Cherokee Nation" and John Drayton's map from the Revolutionary War.[1] From Keowee Bartram followed this path by present-day Oconee Station, over Station Mountain, and through Rocky Gap in the Chattooga Ridge to Earls Ford.

1. Drayton, *Memoirs of the American Revolution,* 2:343.

From the intersection with Whetstone Gap Road, *continue northward on Chattooga Ridge Road*. In a little more than 3 miles the road ends **(mile 19.7)** at the Highlands Highway, S.C. 28. *Turn left and follow S.C. 28 westward*, winding down a series of coves as it approaches the river. Near the end of the descent **(mile 23.8)** the Chattooga comes into view. A few tenths of a mile ahead **(mile 24.1)**, on the left side of the road, is the northern access for Section 2. There is a parking lot with a number of short spur trails down to the river.

Russell Farmstead

A little more than 0.5 mile from the S.C. 28 access is the Russell Farmstead **(mile 24.7)**, the site of a farm and inn built by Ganaway Russell in 1867. Toward the end of the nineteenth century as many as eighty visitors a night stayed at the Russell Inn, which was located at the halfway point for the two-day coach trip between Walhalla, South Carolina, and Highlands, North Carolina. Summer tourists from the South Carolina low country traveled by train to Walhalla. From there it was another two days to the cool relief of the North Carolina mountains. The road was rocky and rough, and the journey involved fording the Chattooga just beyond the Russell farm. Visitors usually spent one night at the inn before beginning the road trip, more if the river was high. With the expansion of rail lines and the construction of modern highways, the inn was no longer needed. The structure survived until 1988, when vandals burned it down. Still standing are more than eight structures, including two barns, the smokehouse, and the springhouse.

Continue on S.C. 28 to the bridge crossing the Chattooga River **(mile 25.5)**. On the Georgia side of the bridge, on the right, is a small parking area for the trailhead for Section 1 of the Bartram Trail in Georgia. The trail begins on the other side of the road. In 0.4 mile the trail leads to the newly constructed steel bridge over the West Fork of the Chattooga. Two-tenths of a mile from the road is a spur trail leading to the junction of the Chattooga and the West Fork. To the north of the parking area is an example of upper Piedmont wetlands.

From the bridge, continue on Ga. 28. *At the junction with Warwoman Road* **(mile 27.7)**, *turn left*, crossing the West Fork of the Chattooga. For the next 2 miles the road twists and turns as it climbs an unnamed ridge. Passing through Cornpen Gap, the road descends and straightens as it enters the narrow valley formed by Marsengill Creek. The road follows the creek for a few miles and then climbs Goble Gap. Descending from the gap, the highway enters Warwoman Valley, with views to the left of Rainy Mountain and the east–west ridge that forms the southern wall of the valley **(mile 35.1)**. The main path between the Cherokee Lower and Middle Towns continued along Warwoman

From the Ga. 28 bridge, the Bartram Trail parallels the river for 7 miles downstream. In less than 0.5 mile the trail intersects the West Fork of the Chattooga River just upstream from where it enters the main body of the river. This junction is the division between Sections 1 and 2 of the Chattooga River. Section 1 consists entirely of the western branch of the Chattooga; Section 2 is the main branch of the Chattooga south of the bridge. No floating or canoeing is allowed on the main branch north of the Highway 28 bridge. To the north of the bridge, the Bartram Trail follows the Chattooga River 5 miles upstream, on the South Carolina side of the river.

Creek. From today's Earls Ford, the path followed Warwoman Creek upstream into Warwoman Valley. At Finney Creek the road turned northwest, past today's Martin Creek, for Courthouse Gap. After crossing the Blue Ridge Mountains at the gap, the road ended at The Dividings, north of present-day Clayton.[2] This is the route Bartram traveled in 1775.

To visit **Dicks Creek Falls and Ledge**, a beautiful waterfall near one of the Chattooga's most prominent rapids, turn left at Sandy Ford Road **(mile 35.9)**.

Dicks Creek Falls and Ledge

On Sandy Ford Road, formerly known as Dicks Creek Road, bear to the right on the paved road. At **mile 0.6** turn left over the bridge crossing Warwoman Creek. The pavement ends and Sandy Ford Road becomes a single-lane gravel road passable by most conventional automobiles. The road crosses Dicks Creek twice, the first time over a newly built culvert, the second time at a ford **(mile 3.5)** passable by most automobiles. Before the ford, on the left, is a small parking area. This is the trailhead for the Dicks Creek Falls Access Trail. Follow the trail downstream for 0.25 mile to the junction with the Bartram Trail, just above the falls.

At the junction with the Bartram Trail, continue hiking straight ahead. In less than 0.1 mile the first ledge of the falls appears on the right. In less than 100 feet the trail comes to the site of an old Forest Service viewing platform. Walk carefully on the boulder to what remains of the platform foundation for a spectacular view of the falls from the top and Dicks Creek Ledge below.

From the intersection with Sandy Ford Road, *continue west on Warwoman Road* through the valley. The valley ends to the west on a high gap south of

---

2. Mooney, *Myths of the Cherokee*, 532.

Dicks Creek Ledge on the Chattooga River.

Pinnacle Knob. Below the gap is Warwoman Dell, named, as was the creek, for a Cherokee woman who displayed both "valor and stratagem" in a decisive battle against the enemy. After the conflict she "was raised to the dignity and honor of a Queen or chief of the Nation" (0153). Not many Cherokee women participated in battles, but those who did achieved special status. War women participated in the Eagle Dance, sat apart from other women on ceremonial occasions, and were given the privilege of deciding the fate of war captives.[3]

3. Perdue, *Cherokee Women*, 38–39. The prevailing view is that the dell is named for Nancy Morgan Hart of Georgia, a Revolutionary War heroine. According to one of the most often told versions of her heroics, Hart's cabin, north of Augusta, was invaded by six British soldiers. While entertaining her captors with food and drink, she smuggled their weapons outside. When one of the soldiers noticed, she shouldered her own firearm and wounded two of the men. Her husband arrived and proposed

Martin Creek Falls

Two miles after turning off Sandy Ford Road, *turn right on Finney Creek Road*, USDA *Forest Service (F.S.) road 152* **(mile 38.2)**. Take the single-lane dirt road north for 0.5 mile. There is a small, unsigned parking area; to the west is the trailhead for the **Martin Creek Access Trail**. This trail, less than 0.25 mile in length, ends at the Bartram Trail. Turn right onto the Bartram Trail and hike for less than 0.2 mile to the falls.

Unlike the present Warwoman Road, the colonial road that Bartram took did not cut through the dell. It followed a more northerly route out of the valley, crossing Beck Ridge en route to the Blue Ridge Mountains at Courthouse Gap. Although the modern road crosses the mountains at the lower gap, approximately 400 feet below Courthouse Gap, this route was probably an overgrown canebrake when Bartram came through, making travel nearly impossible. Bartram was enchanted by his first view of the land beyond Beck Ridge. "Descending on the other side of the mountain, I perceived at some distance before me, on my right hand, a level plain supporting a grand high forest and groves; the nearer I approached, my steps were the more accelerated from the flattering prospect opening to view; I now entered into the verge of the dark forest, charming solitude!" (T341).[4] Judging from the size of many of the older pines and hemlocks in this valley, this dark forest offers the same solitude today that it offered to Bartram more than 200 years ago. Farther upstream he came upon Martin Creek Falls. "On approaching these shades, between the stately columns of the superb forest trees, presented to view, rushing from rocky precipices under the shade of the pensile hills, the unparalleled cascade of Falling Creek, rolling and leaping off the rocks, which uniting below, spread a broad, glittering sheet of crystal waters" (T341). At the base of these two-tiered falls Bartram discovered the "Mountain Magnolia,"

---

shooting all of them, but Nancy objected, insisting "on hanging the men on the spot." See *The New Georgia Guide*, 7–8. E. Merton Coulter has established that Hart's exploits are "made of legend, tradition, hearsay, inference and myth with a touch of exaggeration." See his "Nancy Hart, Georgia Heroine of the Revolution," 125. Given that Warwoman Creek was named before the Revolution, the view that it was named for Hart's alleged exploits cannot be correct.

4. Beck Ridge is named for the Beck family, early-nineteenth-century European settlers in Rabun County. The Earls, Holdens, Bleckleys, Martins, and Walls, many of whom migrated southward from Pennsylvania, Virginia, and North Carolina in the early 1800s, also gave their names to sites in this region. See Ritchie, *Sketches of Rabun County History*.

Martin Creek Falls near Warwoman Dell, Georgia, Chattahoochee National Forest.

a tree commonly known as the Fraser magnolia, with white to cream-colored fragrant flowers and large leaves up to 18 inches in length.

Warwoman Dell

From the junction with F.S. 152 *continue west on Warwoman Road*. A little more than 0.5 mile on the left is the entrance to the **Warwoman Dell Recreation Area (mile 38.8)**. Turn left at the entrance and proceed down the gravel road to the parking area on the left. The CCC developed the recreation area in the 1930s. Today it offers picnic sites along the banks of Saddle Branch. At the western end of the dell is a 1-mile-long interpretive trail with signs describing the area's flora, the CCC, and the Black Mountain Railroad. The trail follows a railroad cut whose route was intended to run from Clayton, Georgia, to South Carolina as part of the longer Blue Ridge Railroad running from Walhalla, South Carolina, to Knoxville, Tennessee, eventually connecting Cincinnati and Charleston. Many sections of the Black Mountain Railroad were completed in the 1850s, but construction came to a halt when the Civil War began. Another attempt was made after the war to complete the railroad, but it, too, failed. The entrance to the dell is closed from November until the first weekend in April.

Exiting the recreation area, *turn sharply to the left onto Warwoman Road*. It is 3.3 miles to the intersection with U.S. 441 in Clayton. *Turn left* and in 0.1 mile is the intersection with U.S. 76.

Other Points of Interest

Ellicott Rock Wilderness

This wilderness area, with more than 9,000 acres, was named after the surveyor Andrew Ellicott, who surveyed the thirty-fifth parallel forming the boundary between North Carolina and Georgia in 1811. At the junction of the boundaries of Georgia and the two Carolinas, Ellicott chiseled a mark in a stone on the east bank of the Chattooga River. This mark is now the destination of four trails. The wilderness is 19 miles northeast of Clayton and 16 miles north of Walhalla, South Carolina, on S.C. 28.

Tallulah Gorge State Park

A partnership between the Georgia Power Company and the state of Georgia has provided a spectacular new park. The Tallulah River Gorge, more than 2 miles long and 600 feet deep, is one of the deepest gorges in the eastern

United States. A trail approximately 0.3 mile in length descends to the floor of the gorge. On the south and north rims are trails overlooking the gorge's seven waterfalls: Terrora, Ladore, Hawthorne, Tempesta, Hurricane, Caledonia, and Oceana. Before the Tallulah River was dammed and diverted in 1912, the roar of these falls echoed through the gorge. The Cherokees named the river Tallulah, "terrible," for the noise they made. The renewal of Georgia Power's license for the dam in 1997 permits, for the first time since 1912, whitewater releases into the gorge at least five weekends a year.

The park also offers the newly opened Jane Hurt Yarn Interpretive Center, which has exhibits on all aspects of the gorge and its geology, the cultural history of the area, and the wildlife that can be observed in and near it.

ACCESS

Tallulah Gorge State Park is located in the village of Tallulah Falls, 12 miles south of Clayton on U.S. 441. Phone: 706-754-8257.

Sarah's Creek Campsite

This Forest Service campsite is located 2 miles north of Warwoman Road on Sarah's Creek Road **(mile 32.6)**. The campsite has designated areas for pads. No electricity or water.

Willis Knob

Willis Knob offers horse trails, camping, and fishing in the midst of rugged mountain scenery near the Chattooga River. Willis Knob Trail is a 15-mile loop that intersects the Bartram Trail and numerous gravel roads.

ACCESS

From Clayton, go east on Warwoman Road (Ga. 28) for 11.6 miles. Turn right on Willis Knob Road (F.S. 157, formerly known as Goldmine Road). In 0.2 mile the road intersects the horse trail at the Woodall Ridge Day Use Parking Area. From here it is 1.9 miles to the Willis Knob Horse Camp.

Driving Tour: Bartram's Travels in the Mountains

This mountain loop, beginning and ending in Clayton, shadows Bartram's path through some of Georgia's highest ridges and peaks. The winding route offers spectacular views of the countryside, including Estatoah Falls and Sky Valley. Along the drive, trails to the summits of Pinnacle Knob and Rabun

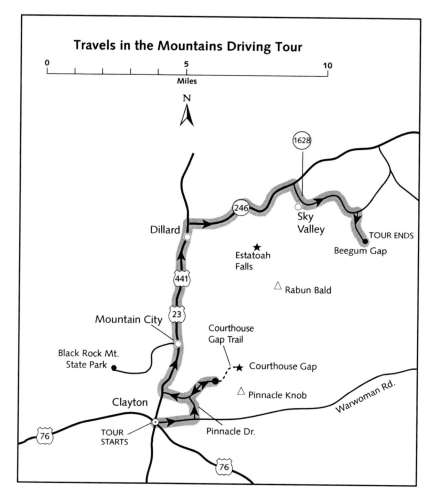

Travels in the Mountains Driving Tour

Bald are demanding hikes, but they pay back amply for the effort. On a clear day, the views from either peak are fabulous. The drive measures approximately 30 miles round-trip; each of the hikes is less than 4 miles long but ascends through ruggedly beautiful terrain.

The tour begins in Clayton at the intersection of U.S. 441 and U.S. 76. *Take U.S. 441 North for 0.1 mile* to the intersection with Rickman Drive. *Turn right onto Rickman* and in 0.3 mile the road intersects Warwoman Road. *Turn right onto Warwoman Road* and at **mile 1.5** *turn left onto Pinnacle Drive.* In 0.1 mile Wayah Road joins the road from the right. Continue straight ahead on Pinnacle Drive. The road enters the gate for Camp Pinnacle, a Baptist mission camp. Continue on Pinnacle Drive until it intersects Courthouse Trail **(mile**

2.3). *Turn right* at the intersection and follow the gravel road for 0.2 mile, past the last house on the left. Park in the small gravel lot near the power-line standard. Do not block the road, which is still in use.

Courthouse Gap Access Trail

This 0.6-mile trail provides access to the Bartram Trail and Courthouse Gap from Courthouse Gap Road. The trail begins as an old road, which the USDA Forest Service will soon close. In a little more than 0.1 mile, before the second stream crossing, the trail leaves the road, turning sharply to the left. At the turn, the trail enters a large thicket of rhododendrons. In the next 0.5 mile the trail steadily gains approximately 400 feet in elevation, hugging **Pinnacle Knob** on the south side of the cove. The trail crosses a small streamlet **(mile 0.4)** with water in the springtime. For the last 0.2 mile the trail alternates between moderate ascents and level stretches as it enters the gap. As Bartram crossed this gap he encountered the terror of a mountain thunderstorm, recounted in his famous description: "the mountains tremble and seem to reel about, and the ancient hills to be shaken to their foundations" (T343). As the storm ended, he took shelter in an abandoned Indian hunting cabin on the west side of the gap.

The contemporary trail parallels the road Bartram traversed in 1775. To the right is **Pinnacle Knob**, "the highest ridge of the Cherokee mountains, which separates the waters of the Savanna river from those of the Tanase" (T339). Bartram named this mountain "Mount Magnolia" for the tree (Fraser magnolia) he discovered at the base of Martin Creek Falls. After spending the night at the abandoned cabin Bartram followed the road to its end at The Dividings—a junction of Indian trails at a spur of Black Rock Mountain. Facing north, to the left of this divide was the path to the Hiwassee River. To the right, the path Bartram followed, was the path to the Cherokee Middle Towns in today's North Carolina (T388).

Pinnacle Knob Trail

A spur trail from the Bartram Trail leads to the summit of "Mount Magnolia." The trailhead for the 0.5-mile spur is a little more than 0.25 mile south of Courthouse Gap. Although it follows the bed of an old jeep road, the trail is steep and a strenuous climb (climbing 500 feet in 0.5 mile). The rewards are equally great, with excellent views from the summit (elevation 3,140 feet). Directly to the west is Black Rock Mountain; to the southwest, Clayton; to the far west, Tray Mountain. To the northwest there are excellent views of the Nantahala Mountains. To the far north are the Cowee Mountains north of Franklin.

Immediately to the north is a view of Stekoa Creek valley, the "pretty grassy vale" on Bartram's right as he descended from Courthouse Gap.

After returning to the parking area at the base of Courthouse Gap, take Courthouse Gap Road 0.2 mile to the intersection with Pinnacle Drive. *Turn right onto the paved road.* In 0.6 mile the road intersects U.S. 441 **(mile 3.3)**. *Turn right onto the highway.*

Ancient Town of Sticoe

Just before the intersection with U.S. 441, the road crossed Stekoa Creek. In this valley, surrounded by hills, stood the "ancient famous town of Sticoe," or Stecoe, where Bartram witnessed "a vast Indian mount or tumulus and great terrace, on which stood the council house, with banks encompassing their circus" (T345). The town was already in ruins by that time. In 1760 Colonel Montgomery destroyed most of the Cherokee Lower Towns as part of a British offensive in the Seven Years' War (1756–63). No trace of the town or its ruins survives. *At U.S. 441, turn right.* Soon the highway climbs through Rabun Gap to the south of Mountain City; as the road levels it enters the Little Tennessee River valley. Continue on the highway into Dillard as the valley continues to widen. Immediately before the North Carolina state line, *at the junction with Ga. 246, turn right toward Sky Valley* **(mile 10.3)**.

Estatoah Falls

A short distance after the turn, a little more than 0.5 mile, there is a view straight ahead of Estatoah Falls. The falls today are not the "unparalleled water fall" that Bartram saw in 1775 "as a vast edifice with a crystal font, or a field of ice lying on the bosom of the hill" (T347). Early this century the headwaters were dammed for hydroelectric power. Only after heavy rains do the falls show any of the majesty seen by Bartram. The falls are in private hands. The only public land where they can be viewed is on the side of Ga. 246 (1 mile east of U.S. 441). From here Bartram continued his journey northward into North Carolina.

Sky Valley

Continue on Ga. 246 as it begins a steep climb. A mile and a half into the climb there is a scenic overlook of the valley to the southwest **(mile 13.3)**. Continue on Highway 246 as it enters North Carolina and becomes N.C. 106. *At the junction with Old Mud Creek Road, N.C. 1628, turn right* **(mile 14.5)**. Continue on the road for just under 3 miles as it enters Georgia again. The main entrance for the city of Sky Valley will be on the right. Sky Valley is both the highest city in Georgia—more than 4,000 feet—and the southernmost ski re-

Estatoah Falls near Dillard, Georgia.

sort in the United States. Continue on the road. *Turn right onto Kelsey Mountain Road* **(mile 17.3)**, also marked with a USDA Forest Service Hiking Trails sign. The turn is very sharp, and the road is steep. In 0.4 mile the road ends at Beegum Gap. Park on the side of the road. Do not block any of the roads; three of them are still in use.

Rabun Bald

From the gap, take the road farthest to the left. On the left are a number of houses; to the right are the red boundary markers for the national forest. In 0.2 mile the road intersects the Bartram Trail. To hike to the summit of Rabun Bald, turn to the right; in 1.7 miles the Bartram Trail reaches the top of the second-highest mountain in Georgia (4,696 feet). The climb is a steady ascent over a series of old logging roads that approach the northern face of the summit. Although this mountain is called a bald, only a small clearing on the north face offers any vistas. Nonetheless, the summit does offer a panoramic 360-degree view from an observation deck at the site of a former Forest Service fire tower. The deck was reconstructed in the winter of 1995.

From the deck, the mountain directly to the west is Eagle Mountain. The prominent range of mountains to the west is the main line of the Blue Ridge, from Tray Mountain to Standing Indian Mountain in North Carolina. Southwest is Lake Lanier and the Georgia Piedmont. To the southeast is Hartwell and views of the South Carolina Piedmont. To the north (due north) is Fishhawk Mountain. Just behind Fishhawk, in the distance, are the Cowee Mountains. Slightly northwest of the Cowees, Clingmans Dome and Mount LeConte in the Great Smoky Mountains National Park are visible on clear days. Immediately to the northwest is the city of Sky Valley. Just to the west of Sky Valley is Bartram's "unparalleled" Estatoah Falls. He saw the falls from the valley to the west as he traveled northward from present-day Clayton to the Little Tennessee River.

Other Points of Interest

Black Rock Mountain State Park

Georgia's highest state park (3,640 feet) derives its name from the sheer cliffs of dark granite that are some of the oldest geologic formations on earth. Numerous scenic overlooks provide spectacular views of the Appalachians. The park offers nearly 10 miles of hiking trails as well as four overlooks accessible by car. The Cowee overlook, just below the junction for the road to the campground, offers outstanding views of the Blue Ridge to the east and northeast, from Rabun Bald to Pinnacle Knob.

ACCESS

The park is 3 miles north of Clayton via U.S. 441. Phone: 706-746-2141.

Foxfire Museum

This small museum is devoted to artifacts of Appalachian living. The various contributors and editors of the Foxfire series—more than ten volumes devoted to chronicling Appalachian culture—collected these housewares, games, and farm implements. There is also a bookstore and gift shop. Open Monday–Friday, 9 A.M.–5 P.M.; Saturday, 10 A.M.–4 P.M.

North Carolina

Driving Tour: Cowee to the Nantahalas

This 65-mile loop, beginning and ending in Franklin, North Carolina, shadows Bartram's trek up the Little Tennessee River to the Cherokee Middle Towns, then across the Nantahala Mountains—called the Jore mountains by Bartram—to the Nantahala River. From Franklin the tour follows the route of an old Indian path to Wayah Gap. An 8-mile loop goes to the lookout tower at the summit of Wayah Bald. Returning to Wayah Road, the route descends to Nantahala Lake. Past the lake, at Kyle, is a 6-mile loop road to Burningtown Gap, where Bartram crossed the Nantahala Ridge. From Kyle the road follows Whiteoak Creek to the Nantahala River. The road follows the mountain river, past numerous rapids and cascades, into the Nantahala Gorge. At the southern entrance to the gorge, Bartram ended his journey to the Overhill Towns. The tour continues through the gorge to Wesser and then arcs to the east to join the Little Tennessee River. As the tour returns to Franklin, it passes by Cowee, the largest of the Cherokee Middle Towns.

From the junction of U.S. 64 and U.S. 441, *take U.S. 64 West*. Immediately outside Franklin there are impressive views of the Nantahala Mountains farther to the west, with Wayah Bald straight ahead and Standing Indian Mountain to the left. To the right are views of Trimont Ridge, the difficult route taken by the Bartram Recreation Trail to the summit of Wayah Bald. At **mile 3.8** *turn right* onto **Old Murphy Road** (N.C. 1442); the turn is marked with signs for Wayah Bald and the LBJ CCC Center. In less than 0.2 mile *turn left* onto **Wayah Road, N.C. 1310,** also marked with signs for Wayah Bald. For the next 2 miles the road crosses through farmlands in the upper Cartoogechaye Valley. At **mile 6.0** N.C. 1310 intersects on the right F.S. 713—a single-track gravel road leading to Harrison Gap and the Bartram Trail on Trimont Ridge. Soon the road joins Wayah Creek, which it will follow up to Wayah Gap.

A mile past the F.S. 713 intersection, N.C. 1310 passes the **Arrowwood Glade Picnic Area (mile 7.2)**—a USDA Forest Service recreation area with picnic sites along Arrowwood Creek. Immediately across from the area is the LBJ Civil-

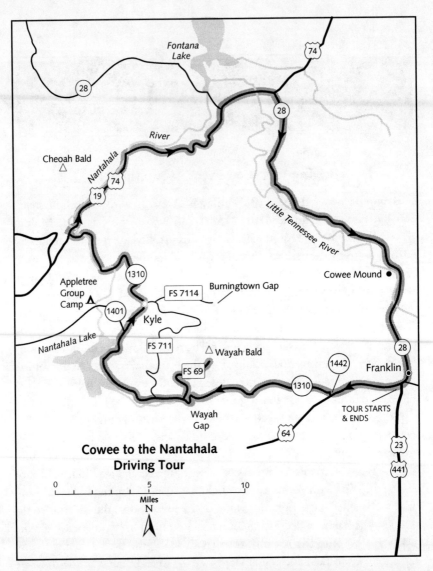

Fontana
Lake

74

28

Cheoah Bald
△

River

Nantahala

74

19

Little Tennessee River

Cowee Mound ●

1310

Appletree
Group
Camp △

1401

FS 7114

Burningtown Gap

Kyle

Nantahala Lake

FS 711

△ Wayah Bald

FS 69

28

1442

Franklin

1310

TOUR STARTS
& ENDS

Wayah
Gap

64

**Cowee to the Nantahala
Driving Tour**

23

441

0   5   10
Miles
N

ian Conservation Corps Center, with an outdoor public swimming pool that is open in the summer. Less than 2 miles past the picnic area the road intersects F.S. 316 **(mile 9.5)**, which leads to the trailheads for Trails 16 and 16A. Both trails climb Trimont Ridge, joining the Bartram Trail west of Locust Tree Gap. Shortly after the junction with F.S. 316 the Wayah Creek floodplain disappears as the road begins the climb to Wayah Crest.

The pitched climb is braced by a series of hairpin turns. As the climb ends, the road enters **Wayah Gap (mile 12.9)** at an elevation of 4,180 feet. Francis

Harper believes this is the gap Bartram crossed en route to the Overhill Towns. We think Bartram crossed the main ridge of the Nantahalas at Burningtown Gap, north of Wayah Bald. In 1776 Wayah Gap was the site of a battle between the Cherokees and patriot forces led by Gen. Griffith Rutherford. The Cherokees rallied in the gap as Rutherford's forces advanced, attempting to retaliate for recent Indian attacks on the frontiers of Virginia, the Carolinas, and Georgia. Today there is a Forest Service recreation area, Wayah Crest, immediately to the south of the gap that offers picnic tables, restrooms, and access to the Appalachian Trail.

Wayah Bald Overlook

To reach the summit of Wayah Bald, turn right onto F.S. 69. In less than a mile the road intersects the white-blazed Appalachian Trail **(mile 0.6)**. The small parking area has views of the valleys below to the southeast. Continuing northward, F.S. 69 comes to the trailhead for the Shot Pouch Trail, another access trail to the Appalachian Trail **(mile 1.2)**. In a little more than 0.25 mile the road passes the **Wilson Lick Ranger Station**, built in 1913 by the Forest Service as the first ranger station in the Nantahala Forest. Unlike modern stations, Wilson Lick was a residence for rangers, who staffed fire towers and administered grazing permits. There are several exhibits at the restored station on the history of Nantahala National Forest and the early years of Forest Service work.

At **mile 4.4** F.S. 69 ends at the parking area for **Wayah Bald Overlook**. This mountain, named "Wolf" by the Cherokees, is one of the highest summits in North Carolina at 5,342 feet. From the pull-around there are views to the east and north. At the entrance to the parking area is the access trail to the old ranger station on Wayah Bald. The paved access trail is also the Bartram Trail and Appalachian Trail. The trail, less than 0.25 mile long, leads to one of the most spectacular views in the Appalachians. The Cowee Mountains and the Little Tennessee River valley in front of them are visible to the northeast. To the north is Copper Ridge Bald, and just to its right in the distance are the Great Smoky Mountains. To the northwest is Cheoah Bald, the western terminus of the Bartram Trail. To the west are the Snowbird Mountains.

From the overlook parking area return on F.S. 69 to Wayah Road, N.C. 1310. At the intersection with N.C. 1310, turn right. From Wayah Gap, S.R. 1310 begins a steady descent down the west side of the ridge. South of the road is Jarrett Creek; in Harper's view, Bartram took an Indian path that followed the course of the creek. Bartram's descent was "remarkably gradual, easy and pleasant, through grassy open forests for the distance of two or three miles"

(T363). At **mile 14.6** the road intersects Sawmill Gap Road, F.S. 711, and then quickly descends. To the right are views of Jarrett Bald, the highest peak on McDonald Ridge to the north. Before the road reaches Nantahala Lake there is a junction with Rainbow Springs Road **(mile 16.6)**—a Forest Service road that leads to a village built by a lumber company in the 1920s. N.C. 1310 reaches the lake, with views across the water to the dam that impounded the Nantahala River in the 1940s. As the road works around the eastern shoreline it crosses the Bartram Trail **(mile 21.1)**. This crossing is the trailhead for Section 5, leading to Wayah Bald, and for Section 6, to Appletree Group Camp. At **mile 22.1** the road intersects Junaluska Road, N.C. 1401. To visit the Appletree Group Camp, the trailhead for a system of trails west of the Nantahala River, turn left at the junction and follow Junaluska Road for 2.3 miles. Otherwise, *continue straight ahead on N.C. 1310.*

Appletree Group Camp

To reach the parking area for the trails from the Appletree Group Camp, cross the bridge and turn right onto the driveway into the camp. The parking area for the trails is immediately outside the gate. To hike the Bartram Trail, cross the post-and-rail fence marked with a Hiking Trail sign. To reach the trailheads for the Yellow Mountain, Laurel Creek, and Junaluska Trails, enter the camp's driveway on foot. The trailheads are located in Group Camp A. Several archaeological digs in this area, which is on a wide floodplain of the Nantahala, have uncovered evidence of human habitation dating back several centuries.

From the junction with Junaluska Road, continue on S.R. 1310 through the small villages of Aquone and Kyle. At Kyle **(mile 23.6)** the road intersects Whiteoak Lane, which ends at N.C. 1397. Turning right, N.C. 1397 intersects F.S. 7114—a single-track road that climbs the main ridge of the Nantahalas for 2 miles to **Burningtown Gap**.

From Kyle continue on N.C. 1310, now following the course of Whiteoak Creek. Before the junction with River Road **(mile 27.6)** there is an unnamed two-stage waterfall on the left. Here Whiteoak Creek enters the Nantahala River, and N.C. 1310 follows the course of the Nantahala downstream into the Nantahala Gorge. At **mile 28.9** is Camp Branch Falls, a 200-foot waterfall from a small stream that empties into the Nantahala River. The road crosses the river several times as the gorge deepens. After passing the put-ins for the whitewater run on the Nantahala, N.C. 1310 ends at U.S. 19 **(mile 31.6)**.

At the junction, *turn right onto U.S. 19.* On the right is a historical marker indicating that this was the site of Bartram's meeting with Chief Attakulla-

Bartram left Cowee on a trail to the west through Iotla Valley and soon began the steep climb up the Nantahala Mountains on a trail that followed the course of Burningtown Creek. The climb ended at Burningtown Gap (4,236 feet), where he and his horse rested. Here Bartram met a young Cherokee with whom he exchanged choice tobacco for answers to his inquiries regarding the roads and distance to the Overhill Towns. Bartram lingered on the main ridge of the Nantahalas, taking a side trail to one of the summits nearby. The peak he climbed was most likely Burningtown Bald (more than 5,100 feet in elevation). On the summit he looked out to the east and north to the Cowee Mountains and the Great Smoky Mountains, "a sublimely awful scene of power and magnificence, a world of mountains piled upon mountains" (T362). Overlooks such as those at Wayah Bald and on the Appalachian Trail offer a similar view. From the gap, Bartram descended to the west on a trail that followed Ben Creek to Cold Spring Creek. F.S. 711, the access road to the gap, follows the same route.

From Burningtown Gap, the Appalachian Trail steadily climbs the southwestern face of Burningtown Bald. On the western side, considerably below the summit, the trail crosses a ridge as it begins to climb Copper Ridge Bald. Again the trail arcs around the west side of the mountain. The 2-mile climb stops, and the trail dips down to a narrow gap north of the summit. To the east the view looks out over the mountains surrounding the Little Tennessee River.

---

kulla.[1] "Soon after crossing this large branch of the Tanase" Bartram "observed descending the heights at some distance, a company of Indians, all well mounted on horse back." As the party approached, Bartram "observed a chief at the head of the caravan, and apprehending him to be the Little Carpenter, emperor or grand chief of the Cherokees" (T365). The grand chief introduced himself to Bartram, shook his hand, and then asked Bartram if he knew of his name. Bartram, who had seen the chief at the Indian Congress in Augusta two years earlier, replied that the name of Attakullakulla was "dear to his white brothers in Pennsylvania." The two talked about their mutual friend in Charleston, the British superintendent for Indian affairs, John Stuart, whose life Attakullakulla had saved after the disastrous British retreat from Fort Loudoun in 1760. The chief told Bartram that he was on his way to see their friend.

1. According to Harper, Bartram met the Cherokee chief near the present-day Junaluska Gap. According to other authorities, Bartram met the chief en route to the Overhill Towns, near present-day Tellico, Tennessee. This valley constituted a major Cherokee settlement in the 1770s. See Mails, *The Cherokee People*, 20.

Nantahala Gorge

The river takes its name from this gorge. Nantahala is the Cherokee term for "land of the noon-day sun." The steep walls of the gorge permit sunlight to reach the river plain only when the sun is high in the sky. Immediately to the north of the historical marker is a USDA Forest Service overlook with a view of the first major rapids of the Nantahala River, the class 3–rated Patton's Run. At this point the river has fully entered the steep gorge. This 8.3-mile section of river, ending just below Nantahala Falls, is the most popular whitewater rafting river in the Southeast (as the presence of more than twenty outfitters on U.S. 19 indicates). Because the river is dam-controlled, there is, during daylight hours, sufficient flow for whitewater enthusiasts. For the next 10 miles U.S. 19 parallels the river as it cuts through this impressive gorge. The road crosses the river only once **(mile 34.2)**; immediately on the left past the bridge is the Ferebee Memorial—a Forest Service recreation area offering both picnic areas and places to view rafters and canoeists on the Nantahala. The Forest Service has built another observation area for this class 3 rapids at a spot where the road approaches Nantahala Falls. Just above the falls is a take-out for those who choose not to run the rapids. Parking is available at the wide turn a few hundred feet upstream.

As the road exits the gorge, it is 3 miles to the junction with U.S. 74 **(mile 43.5)**. *Turn right onto the divided highway* that descends to the Little Tennessee River. On the east side of the river U.S. 74 intersects N.C. 28 **(mile 46.8)**. *Turn right* and follow the road for 8 twisting, turning miles toward Franklin along the low ridges of the Cowee Mountains. As the road enters the Little Tennessee River valley it begins to level and straighten. At **mile 59.4**, north of Wests Mill, is a historical marker for the Cherokee settlement of **Cowee**. Bartram visited the settlement twice.

Cowee

Near the Horseshoe Bend of the Little Tennessee River stood Cowee, one of oldest and largest of the Cherokee settlements. Bartram arrived in Cowee on May 22 en route to the Overhill Towns. Several of the town's traders directed him to Mr. Galahan, who for the next week was Bartram's host. Bartram described Cowee as a town of "about one hundred dwellings" on both sides of the Little Tennessee River (T366). Most of these "oblong four square buildings" were one story tall with walls built of tree trunks or logs, and roofs made from chestnut bark or long, broad shingles. The town's council house, a rotunda "large enough to accompany several hundred people," sat atop an "ancient mount of earth" about 20 feet in height. Bartram reported that nei-

*Cowee Mound, on the west bank of the Little Tennessee
River north of Franklin, North Carolina. This was the site of the
council house for the largest of the Cherokee Middle Towns.*

ther he nor the Cherokees understood "by what people or for what purpose
these artificial hills were raised" (T367).

The next day Bartram and a young trader who lived on the east side of the
river set off on horseback for a one-day excursion over the Cowee Mountains.
The two riders crossed the ridge at Leatherman Gap and descended into today's Alarka Valley. After crossing a shallow gap in the vicinity of the present-
day Parrish, about a mile northeast of Burningtown, Bartram and his companion encountered "companies of young, innocent Cherokee virgins" gathering
strawberries. "Some [were] busily gathering the rich fragrant fruit, others
having already filled their baskets, lay reclined under the shade of floriferous

and fragrant native bowers of Magnolia, Azalea, Philadelphus, perfumed Ca-lycanthus, sweet Yellow Jessamine and cerulian Glycine frutescens, disclosing their beauties to the fluttering breeze, and bathing their limbs in the cool fleeting streams" (T357). This scene being "perhaps too enticing for hearty young men long to continue idle spectators," Bartram and his companion re-turned to Cowee, crossing the mountains to the west of Leatherman Gap. The next day, May 25, Bartram, set off for the Overhill Towns.

On his return trip to Georgia, Bartram stayed in Cowee for three days. He met Cowee's chieftain and attended a festival with music and dance that was the prelude to a game of stickball. The game was a civic endeavor; Cowee was playing the team from a nearby Cherokee settlement. As part of the opening ceremony, the local chief recounted Cowee's accomplishments in the sport. A year after Bartram's second visit, Cowee was destroyed in Rutherford's cam-paign.[2] The town was rebuilt and destroyed again in 1783. It was occupied again until 1819, when the Cherokees gave the land away. All that remains to-day is the ancient mound near the Little Tennessee River, on the west side of the highway. The land is private property and the mound is visible only when the foliage allows a view.

From the Cowee site, *continue south on N.C. 28* for 6 miles to Franklin **(mile 65.4)**. In downtown Franklin, continue south on N.C. 28, past the Nikwasi Indian mound. From there it is 1.3 miles to U.S. 64. At the inter-change, *take U.S. 64 West*, returning to the junction with U.S. 441.

Other Points of Interest

Oconaluftee Indian Village

This museum, operated by the Cherokee Historical Association, features a reconstructed 1750s Cherokee village with typical residences and a seven-sided council house. Cherokee guides in native costumes take visitors through the village explaining their history and culture. Artisans demonstrate arts and crafts, including making arrowheads, baskets, ceremonial masks, and dugout canoes. In the village are displays with artifacts similar to those Bar-tram would have seen in the late eighteenth century, including farming uten-sils, weapons of hunting and war, clothing, pottery, baskets, and other items of historical interest.

2. Dickens, "The Route of Rutherford's Expedition against the North Carolina Cherokees."

The museum is in Cherokee, North Carolina, on U.S. 441 North. Open daily, 9 A.M.–5:30 P.M. Admission fee. For more information, call 828-497-2315. Web site: www.dnet.net/~cheratt

Museum of the Cherokee Indian

Also located in Cherokee, this museum was completely renovated in 1998. It features a self-guided tour with computer-generated imagery, special effects, and audio relating the history of the Cherokees from their "prehistory" through the colonial period and the Trail of Tears to the present day. The museum also houses an extensive archive with documents and artifacts created by the Cherokee Indians.

ACCESS

Open daily except for Christmas, New Year's Day, and Thanksgiving. Admission fee. For more information, call 828-497-3481. The museum is located at U.S. 441 and Drama Road in Cherokee. Web site: www.cherokeemuseum.org

Driving Tour: Joyce Kilmer Memorial Forest and the Cherohala Skyway

This loop begins near the southern base of Cheoah Bald, most likely the spot where Bartram decided to abandon his journey to the Overhill Cherokee settlements and return to Augusta. The tour follows U.S. 129 North through Robbinsville and then arcs to the northwest around Santeetlah Lake. From the lake, the tour enters the Joyce Kilmer Wilderness Area. The highlight of this area is the Joyce Kilmer Memorial Forest, one of the largest virgin stands of hardwood left in the eastern United States. From the forest, the tour follows N.C. 1127 to Santeetlah Gap. To the west of the gap is one of the most beautiful parkways in the eastern United States—the Cherohala Skyway. The skyway, maintained by the USDA Forest Service, rivals the Blue Ridge Parkway for both views and recreational opportunities. The tour completes the loop, returning to Robbinsville and then to U.S. 19.

The driving tour begins at the junction of U.S. 19 and U.S. 129, just north of Topton, North Carolina—10 miles north of Andrews, North Carolina (on the combined U.S. 19/129). *From the junction, follow U.S. 129 to the north.* The road crosses over the high plateau between the Snowbird Mountains and the Cheoah Mountains. In 11.4 miles U.S. 129 reaches the junction with N.C. 143 East in Robbinsville, North Carolina. This town, the county seat of Graham

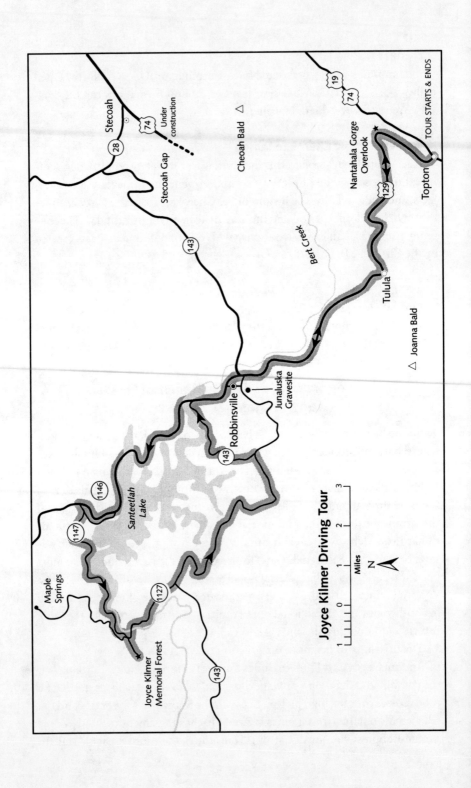

Joyce Kilmer Driving Tour

N

Miles

0   1   2   3

Maple
Springs

Joyce Kilmer
Memorial Forest

143

1127

1147

1146

Santeetlah
Lake

143

Robbinsville

143

Junaluska
Gravesite

Bert Creek

Stecoah

28

74

Stecoah Gap

Under
construction

143

Cheoah Bald △

Tulula

△ Joanna Bald

Nantahala Gorge
Overlook

129

19

74

TOUR STARTS & ENDS

Topton

County, is the **burial site of Junaluska**, a famous Cherokee chief. Junaluska, who was alive during Bartram's visit, fought with the Americans in the Creek War in 1814. In 1838, during the Great Removal of the Cherokee Nation, he was forced to leave his homeland. He returned to North Carolina nine years later and was granted citizenship by the North Carolina Legislature because of his heroism against the Creeks. Junaluska lived the remainder of his years in Robbinsville. To reach the gravesite, turn left at the junction with N.C. 143. At the Graham County Courthouse, continue straight ahead on Main Street. The grave is on the left, 0.2 mile past the courthouse. Continue on the Robbinsville Bypass for 1.5 miles to the junction with N.C. 143 West **(mile 12.9)**. If driving directly to the Cherohala Skyway, turn left here. Otherwise, *continue driving straight ahead on U.S. 129 North.*

North of Robbinsville there are views to the northeast of the Cheoah Mountains, the range immediately south of the Great Smoky Mountains. To the left there are occasional views of Lake Santeetlah, which was built for hydroelectric power in the late 1940s. Continuing north, there is a scenic overlook on the left with ample parking **(mile 17.5)**. A mile beyond the overlook the road intersects the Wauchecha Bald Trail—an 8.3-mile trail leading to the Appalachian Trail crossing over Wauchecha Bald. Less than 0.25 mile from the trail, *turn left on N.C. 1146* **(mile 18.7)**.

The road, old U.S. 29, winds to the north past the dam for Lake Santeetlah. As the road loses elevation, Cheoah Point Recreation area is to the left. Continue on the road to the *junction with N.C. 1146* **(mile 20.3)**. *Turn left* onto the road and in less than 0.1 mile *turn right onto Joyce Kilmer Road, N.C. 1147.* Cross the bridge over the Cheoah River and continue west, working in and out of coves along the northern shore of Santeetlah Lake. After passing Avey Branch, one of the lake's public boat launches **(mile 24.2)**, the road reaches the western limit of the lake. In a mile the road bisects the Horse Cove Campground **(mile 25.2)**. From the campground it is less than 0.5 mile to the junction with Maple Springs Road **(mile 25.6)**. *From the intersection, continue straight ahead for the old forest.*

Immediately to the left is the parking area for the Jenkins Meadow Trail. The road to the north parallels Little Santeetlah Creek, which has its headwaters near the base of Bob Stratton Bald. Continue on the paved road until it comes to the parking area for the old forest **(mile 26.2)**.

Joyce Kilmer Memorial Forest

This 3,800-acre area was set aside in 1938 to memorialize Joyce Kilmer, journalist, soldier, and poet—the author of the poem "Trees"—who was killed in

From the intersection with Joyce Kilmer Road, take Maple Springs Observation Road, N.C. 1127, north. The road, a two-lane paved highway, climbs more than 1,500 feet in 4 miles. It was originally planned as a state highway that would arc to the left, cutting through the Slickrock watershed to Tennessee. The road was stopped in the late 1960s with the creation of the Joyce Kilmer–Slickrock Wilderness.

At the end of the road is a small turnaround with parking. Approximately 0.25 mile from the circle is another parking area with picnic tables. This area is the trailhead for the Haoe Lead Trail. At the end of the road is a path leading to the wooden observation deck, which offers a panoramic view of the Smoky Mountains from Lake Fontana to Mount LeConte and other summits to the east.

---

action in World War I. This forest is one of the most impressive remnants of old-growth forests in the United States. Some of the poplars, hemlocks, oaks, basswoods, and sycamores in Poplar Cove are more than 20 feet in diameter and 100 feet in height. These giants are more than 300–400 years old.

A 2.25-mile trail climbs through the cove. The trail is divided into two loops, each approximately 1 mile in length. Most of the old-growth trees are on the second loop, just past the memorial to Joyce Kilmer. The trail does not connect with any other trail. It is for day use only; no camping is permitted in the cove.

Leaving the parking area, follow Joyce Kilmer Road to the intersection with N.C. 1127 **(mile 27)**. *Turn right and take N.C. 1127 to the south.* In less than 0.25 mile the road crosses over the Santeetlah River. To the right is the Rattler Ford Group Camp. This is the parking area for the eastern trailhead for the Bob Stratton Trail. From the river the road climbs for more than 2 miles to **Santeetlah Gap** and the junction with the **Cherohala Scenic Skyway (mile 29)**.

To conclude the driving tour from Santeetlah Gap, *turn left onto N.C. 1127,* toward Robbinsville. The road descends for more than 2 miles to Lake Santeetlah. As the road descends, Santeetlah Creek is to the right. The road passes the Snowbird Picnic Area **(mile 34.4)**. Continue east on N.C. 143 for 10 miles to U.S. 129, just north of Robbinsville. *Turn right on U.S. 129.* It is 12 miles to the junction of U.S. 129 and U.S. 19, near Topton **(mile 51.0)**.

Cherohala Scenic Skyway: North Carolina Section

The name of this road represents the combination of "Cherokee" and "Nantahala," because it runs along the boundary between the two national forests.

The skyway is 44 miles long in its entirety, from Robbinsville, North Carolina, to Tellico Plains, Tennessee. Although it was conceived in 1958 and construction began in 1965, the road was not completed until October 1996. The high cost of building such a highway coupled with the many environmental controversies that swirled around it delayed construction on several occasions. The section described below is the 18-mile North Carolina section, N.C. 143, the last section of the highway to be completed. It is also the highest section, crossing over the east–west ridges from Cedar Top to just north of Hooper Bald. West of Hooper the parkway curls to the northwest to the main ridge of the north–south Unicoi Mountains. Just west of the ridge this section ends. The skyway continues into Tennessee as Tenn. 165. The North Carolina section of the highway features fifteen overlooks and picnic areas; several of these are also trailheads for short trails to summits or other vistas. The overlooks and pull-offs are listed below from east to west. Although only the North Carolina section described below was constructed by the USDA Forest Service, the entire skyway is managed by the service as a scenic parkway.

Snow is common on the parkway from November through mid-April. There are no services—filling stations, restaurants, etc.—on the highway.

Mile 0.0 Santeetlah Gap

Views of the Unicoi Mountains. To the right are views of Bob Stratton Bald and Horse Cove. At the overlook is a bulletin board with information on the parkway.

Mile 1.9 Hooper Cove

A small picnic area overlooks the drainage for Santeetlah Creek.

Mile 3.0 Shute Cove

At 3,550 feet there is a platform with views of the valley below.

Mile 3.9 Obadhiah Gap (elevation 3,740 feet)

There are views from here of the southern boundary of the Joyce Kilmer–Slickrock Wilderness Area.

Mile 5.4 Wright Cove (elevation 4,150 feet)

Mile 8.4 Spirit Ridge

This pull-off offers a picnic area with tables. There is a 0.3-mile shore trail to an overlook with sweeping views of the area.

Mile 9.2 Huckleberry Knob Trail

This pull-off at 5,300 feet with a small parking area is the trailhead for the Huckleberry Knob Trail. This trail, 2.5 miles one way, follows the ridge to the summit of its namesake. The trail continues to Little Huckleberry Knob and Oak Knob.

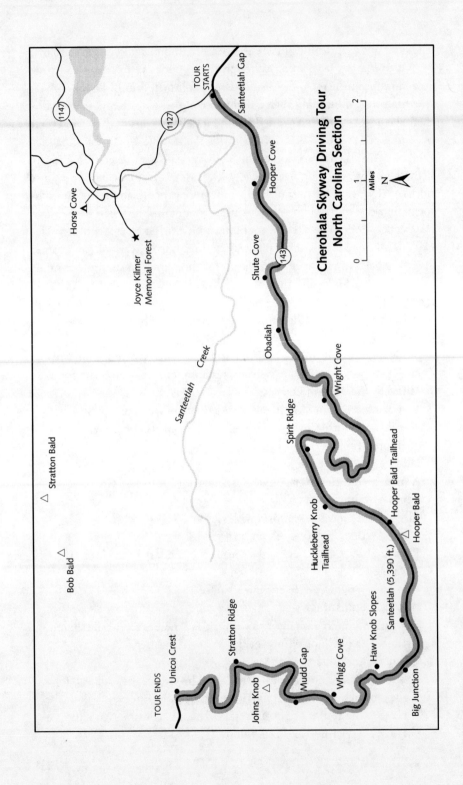

Horse Cove

Joyce Kilmer
Memorial Forest

(1147)

(1127)

TOUR
STARTS

Santeetlah Gap

Hooper Cove

Shute Cove

(143)

Obadiah

Wright Cove

Santeetlah
Creek

Spirit Ridge

Stratton Bald

Bob Bald

Huckleberry Knob
Trailhead

Hooper Bald Trailhead

Hooper Bald

Santeetlah (5,390 ft.)

Haw Knob Slopes

Big Junction

Stratton Ridge

Johns Knob

Mudd Gap

Whigg Cove

Unicoi Crest

TOUR ENDS

Cherohala Skyway Driving Tour
North Carolina Section

N

0   1   2

Miles

Mile 10.2   Hooper Bald Trailhead

To the left there is a short drive to a parking area that is the trailhead for
Hooper Bald Trail, a 0.25-mile-long trail to the summit. At the
trailhead are restrooms and picnic tables.

Mile 10.9   Santeetlah Picnic Area

This picnic area is the highest point on the skyway at 5,390 feet.

Mile 11.7   Big Junction

This overlook, located on one of Unicoi's ridges, is on the North
Carolina–Tennessee state line. The overlook provides the first views of
the mountains in Tennessee, with a view of Huckleberry Knob to the
north.

Mile 12.9   Haw Knob Slopes

There is an overlook on the ridge between Santeetlah Creek and Whigg
Creek.

Mile 13.9   Whigg Cove

There is a picnic area here near the headwaters of Whigg Branch.

Mile 14.2   Mudd Gap

This pull-off area, also located on the state line, is the trailhead for the
trail to Whigg Meadows. The trail follows the path of an old road.

Mile 15.8   Stratton Ridge

This picnic area with restrooms overlooks the mountains to the east and
north.

Mile 17.1   No Name Gap

There is a pull-off area here with parking.

Mile 17.5   Unicoi Crest

This is the last pull-off for the North Carolina section of the Cherohala
Skyway. From here there are views of mountains to the east and west
in North Carolina and Tennessee. A little more than 0.25 mile west of
the overlook is the North Carolina–Tennessee state line.

Little Tennessee River Canoe Trails

South of Franklin

Section:	Otto to Franklin
Distance:	11 miles
Difficulty:	1–2; time, 4–5 hours
Hazards:	class 2 rapids; strainers
Highlights:	woodlands and pastures
Minimum Level:	1.5 feet; USGS gauge north of Prentiss Bridge

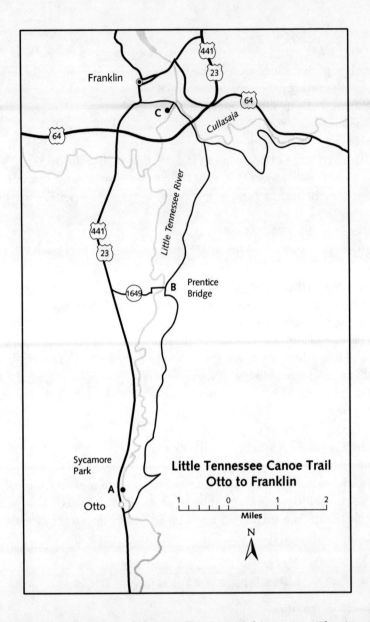

The Little Tennessee River is a small stream in this section. The river cuts through the wide and flat floodplain as it continues its northerly flow, twisting and turning through farmland and pastures. The only class 2 rapids are below the gauging station. The most common hazards are strainers from blowdowns or other debris. Some of the strainers will require portaging.

JOURNEY TO CHEROKEE COUNTRY

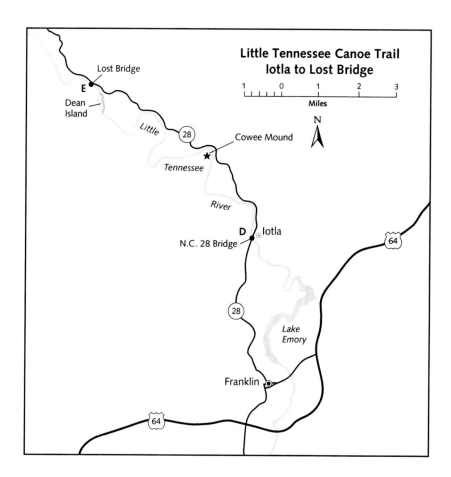

Little Tennessee Canoe Trail
Iotla to Lost Bridge

ACCESS POINTS

There are four public access areas: two in Otto, one at the Prentiss Bridge, and one in Franklin. The Sycamore Park put-in in Otto is in a private park 0.3 mile south of Otto on U.S. 441. The park is open to the public; please make a donation at the canister at the gravel parking area. The second Otto put-in is also on the east side of U.S. 441. The Prentiss Bridge put-in is on N.C. 1651, 1.3 miles east of U.S. 441. The last area is the put-out in Franklin, southeast of downtown on Ulco Drive, off Wayah Street.

North of Franklin

Section: Iotla to Lost Bridge (off N.C. 28)
Distance: 13 miles
Difficulty: 2–3

Hazards: class 2 rapids
Highlights: Cowee; farmlands
Minimum level: 2.0 feet; USGS gauge 0.8 mile north of Needmore

Below Franklin and Lake Emory, the Little Tennessee emerges as a mountain river. The first few miles of the river, past Cowee Mound, are relatively flat as the river continues to work its way through the valley. The valley is much narrower here, but the river is also wider. The last half of this section does offer a few shallow ledges that may be at class 2. The only hazards are these rapids and strainers near the shore.

ACCESS POINTS
The put-in is at the N.C. 28 bridge in Iotla, about 4 miles north of Franklin. The put-out is Lost Bridge, immediately west of N.C. 28, 5 miles north of Iotla.

Bartram Recreation Trail
Mountains

SOUTH CAROLINA

Section 1

Section: S.C. 107 to the Chattooga River
Distance: 7.1 miles
Difficulty: easy to moderate (both directions)
Hazards: none
Highlights: falls on Lick Log Creek; Chattooga River
Maps: Tamasee, South Carolina–Georgia; Sataloah (USGS)

This 7-mile section of trail starts at S.C. 107. For 2.5 miles the Bartram Trail and the Foothills Trail share the same path as they descend the Chattooga Ridge into the river's wide floodplain. Near the mouth of Lick Log Creek, the Bartram Trail turns to the southwest and joins the Chattooga River Trail. These two paths follow the river downstream for 1.5 miles past two sets of waterfalls on Lick Log Creek. The Bartram Trail leaves the river to climb the northern ridges of Hickory Mountain, then descends again to the river near the Highway 28 bridge into Georgia.

The Bartram Trail begins at the junction of S.C. 107 and Cheohee Road. The footpath begins a steady descent into a southwest-facing cove on the southern base of Morton Mountain, part of the Chattooga Ridge. As the trail levels off **(mile 0.4)**, the stream that cuts through the cove becomes visible 20–30 feet below the footpath. The descent continues down a series of wooden steps **(mile 0.5)**. To the left is a rock ledge over the unnamed stream below. Within a few hundred feet the path levels off as it continues to work along the ridge. Passing through a grove of mountain laurel, the trail begins a long, north-westerly descent of the Chattooga Ridge. As the descent ends, the footpath crosses a stream—dry in late summer—on a wooden footbridge **(mile 0.8)**.

After crossing the unnamed branch, the Bartram begins a short climb of less than 0.1 mile. To the left, Nicholson Ford Road comes into view. As the

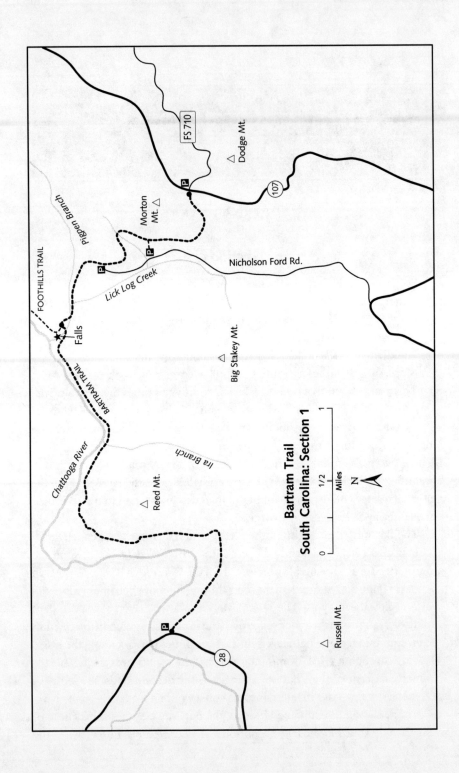

Bartram Trail
South Carolina: Section 1

FOOTHILLS TRAIL

Pigpen Branch

FS 710

Morton
Mt. △

Dodge Mt. △

107

Falls

Lick Log Creek

Nicholson Ford Rd.

BARTRAM TRAIL

Chattooga River

Big Stakey Mt. △

Ira Branch

Reed Mt. △

Russell Mt. △

28

N

Miles

0   1/2   1

trail rolls over one of the southwest ridges of Morton Mountain, it descends to another small stream. After the crossing, on another wooden footbridge, the trail intersects the spur trail to the Thrift Lake Parking Area **(mile 0.9)**. To the left this trail leads in a few hundred yards to the first of two parking areas off Nicholson Ford Road. The Bartram Trail continues straight ahead, with another short rise, then descends again to another small stream, crossing it on a wooden footbridge **(mile 1.2)**. From the stream, the path climbs another shallow ridge. After a brief leveling, the descent, sometimes steep, resumes to Nicholson Ford Road. Before reaching the gravel road, the descent ends on a series of wooden steps **(mile 1.6)**.

In the small parking area at the end of the road, bear to the right; the Bartram Trail exits straight ahead. At first the footpath is level, then it begins a steady descent toward Lick Log Creek. As the path loses elevation, it passes through a grove of hemlocks with some notably old white pines **(mile 1.9)**. In less than 0.25 mile the trail reaches the creek. Just before the crossing, on a wooden footbridge, there is a camping area to the right **(mile 2.1)**. The trail then cuts across the floodplain, crossing the creek a second time. Through this area are numerous level sites for camping. After the second crossing **(mile 2.3)** the Bartram Trail begins a 0.1-mile descent into the Chattooga River floodplain. As the path descends, there are views to the left of the Upper Falls of Lick Log Creek. The descent ends at the junction with the Chattooga River Trail **(mile 2.4)**. This trail, blazed in black, and the Foothills Trail continue to the right as they head northward. The Bartram Trail, joined by the Chattooga River Trail, turns to the left. On the river side of the trail are large flat areas suitable for camping.

The Bartram leaves the Chattooga River and follows Lick Log Creek upstream. The stream and the Lower Falls can be heard to the right, but they are out of view. Heading upstream, the footpath approaches the creek at the base of the Upper Falls of Lick Log Creek **(mile 2.5)**. The Upper Falls cascade down in two tiers, each 10–15 feet in height, into a pool surrounded by a number of boulders suitable for picnic rocks. Crossing the creek on a wooden footbridge, the trail follows the stream back downstream toward the Chattooga. As the path exits the floodplain, there is a small waterfall to the right. From here the trail climbs a ridge on the southern edge of the creek. To the right are the Lower Falls of Lick Log Creek **(mile 2.7)**, a 25-foot cascade that empties into the Chattooga. Bearing to the left, the trail begins a steady descent to the Chattooga River floodplain. Immediately to the left is a camping area.

The trail rises to 50 feet above the river, then descends to the floodplain again. After the trail crosses a small stream there is a large camping area adjacent to the river **(mile 3.0)**. The Bartram continues to follow the river downstream, although more than 100 feet from the shore. To the right is a spur trail to another large camping area near the river **(mile 3.3)**. In less than 0.1 mile the footpath crosses another small tributary of the Chattooga, then follows the bed of an old road. The path then curls to the right **(mile 3.5)** and begins a short, steep climb up a rock ledge overlooking the river. After a level stretch of a few hundred feet, the trail returns to the shore via a sharp descent. Level again in the floodplain, the path approaches Ira Branch and crosses it on a wooden footbridge **(mile 3.6)**. On both sides of the branch are large areas for camping.

A few hundred feet from the branch, the trail bends to the west, providing views of the river both upstream and downstream. The Bartram Trail joins an old road running parallel to the Chattooga. The trail begins to rise and then turns sharply to the left, leaving the roadbed **(mile 4.0)**, and climbs through a rhododendron grove and then through a large field of lady fern. The climb ends at a wide ridge **(mile 4.1)** that is part of the northern spine of Reed Mountain. The path becomes fairly straight here, rising at it cuts through a horseshoe-shaped cove facing west. Exiting the cove, the trail heads northwest, then turns left, crossing over another of Reed Mountain's ridges **(mile 4.5)**. Just beyond the ridge is a small area suitable for camping. After a brief level section, the ascent continues for nearly 0.5 mile as the trail winds in and out of a series of west-facing coves.

The ascent ends **(mile 5.0)** and the trail begins a short descent to an unnamed stream. Crossing the stream **(mile 5.2)**, which has water in both summer and fall, the footpath levels as it rejoins another old road. Then it begins to roll gently up and down, roughly holding the contour line. Turning sharply to the left and heading due east, the trail leaves the old road. Winding in and out of a series of shallow coves, it crosses another stream with water in the fall **(mile 5.4)**. Joining another old road, the path passes through a stand of hemlocks and white pines, then crosses another small stream **(mile 5.6)** which has a trickle of water in late summer. Shortly, the trail leaves the road and begins to climb for the next 0.5 mile through a series of coves open to the west and northwest.

At **mile 6.0** the trail crosses a large stream with ample water year-round. In rapid succession the footpath crosses two more streams in the next hundred feet. Immediately below the trail can be heard and seen a large unnamed tributary of the Chattooga. From here the path rolls up and down as it approaches one of the northern ridges **(mile 6.3)** of Hickory Mountain, just to the southeast. After leveling, the path intersects an old road **(mile 6.4)** that descends to the Chattooga, immediately across from Brack Hill on the Georgia side. To the right is a small level area suitable for camping. The trail turns left and enters a cove that opens to the northeast. It ascends out of the cove and continues the pattern of winding in and out of shallow coves for the next 0.25 mile, crossing over small streams **(miles 6.6 and 6.7)**.

The Bartram Trail leaves the coves at **mile 6.8** and begins a steady descent to the Chattooga. As it descends, there are numerous views of the floodplain, still clear of trees from the farming that occurred on this land nearly forty years ago. Near the end of the descent the trail works down a series of wooden stairs. Off to the side of the steps is a sign indicating 3.7 miles to Pigpen and 12.6 miles to Oconee State Park. At the end of the descent the path rejoins an old farm road, turning to the left. For hikers traveling from north to south, this turn is easy to miss. In 200 feet the trail reaches a Forest Service gate. Immediately beyond is the parking area for the trailhead. To continue on the Bartram Trail into Georgia, cut across the parking area to S.C. 28. Turn right and follow the road as it heads for the Chattooga River bridge. Walk on the right side of the road, which has a wider shoulder. In less than 0.2 mile the trail crosses the river on the narrow highway bridge. The Georgia section begins to the left of the road, immediately past the bridge.

ACCESS POINTS

S.C. 107: From the junction of S.C. 28 and S.C. 107, take S.C. 107 to the north and pass Oconee State Park, on the left. At the junction with Cheohee Road **(mile 6.1)**, the highway intersects the Foothills Trail. Turn right onto Cheohee Road. Immediately to the left is a parking area for the Bartram and Foothills Trails.

Nicholson Ford Road: From the junction of S.C. 28 and S.C. 107, take S.C. 107 to the north. In 3.5 miles, turn left onto Village Creek Road. Follow this paved two-lane county road for 1.75 miles to the junction with Nicholson Ford Road. Turn right onto the unpaved road, F.S. 715. At **mile 1.8** there is a short driveway to the right leading to the first of two parking areas for the Bartram and Foothills Trails. To reach the second parking area, continue on F.S. 715. In less than 0.25 mile the road fords a small stream **(mile 2.0)** and then forks. Take the road to the right, which ends in 0.25 mile at a small parking area. This road is passable by conventional autos, although muddy after heavy rains.

S.C. 28: From the junction of S.C. 28 and S.C. 107, take S.C. 28—also known as the Highlands Highway—to the north. The road winds for 5.8 miles to the Chattooga River. Just before the bridge, turn to the right for the gravel parking area for the northern trailhead.

GEORGIA

The Bartram Trail in Georgia spans nearly 40 miles from the Chattooga River to the North Carolina state line north of Rabun Bald. Most of the trail was located and constructed by the USDA Forest Service and the Georgia Bartram Trail Society between 1970 and 1976. The trail enters Georgia across the bridge for Ga. 28. For the first 9 miles the trail parallels the Chattooga River on its west bank. Shortly after Dicks Creek Falls the trail leaves the river and for the next 10 miles heads in a westerly direction, crossing over several east–west ridges. Just northwest of Rainy Mountain the trail begins its descent into Warwoman Dell. Out of the dell, the trail crosses Warwoman Dell Road to Becky Branch Falls. From there the trail forms a large, inverted C, heading east, then northeast, to Martin Creek Falls. The trail then proceeds to the northwest to Courthouse Gap. In its approach to the gap, the trail joins the spine of the Blue Ridge Mountains. Out of the gap the trail follows the Blue Ridge to Rabun Bald, the second-highest mountain in Georgia. The trail quickly descends to Hale Ridge Road, near the North Carolina state line. Throughout Georgia the trail is blazed with plastic yellow diamonds approximately every 0.2 mile. In laying out the trail, both the Forest Service and the Bartram Trail Society sought to follow the ground contour and ridge tops as much as possible.

Section 1

Section: Ga. 28 to Sandy Ford Road
Distance: 9.6 miles
Difficulty: moderate (both directions)
Hazards: none
Highlights: Dicks Creek Falls; West Fork of the Chattooga
Maps: Sataloah; Whetstone; Rainy Mountain (USGS)

Highway 28 Trailhead

The Bartram Trail begins on the south side of Ga. 28, just before the guardrail for the bridge across the Chattooga. The footpath descends down the southeast flank of Alf Hill Mountain for 0.2 mile and then bears to the right, following the West Fork of the Chattooga upstream. To the left are the foundations of the old highway bridge across the Chattooga River. In 0.1 mile the trail crosses the West Fork of the Chattooga on a metal footbridge **(mile 0.3)**.

The Forest Service built the bridge in 1998, replacing an often-dangerous

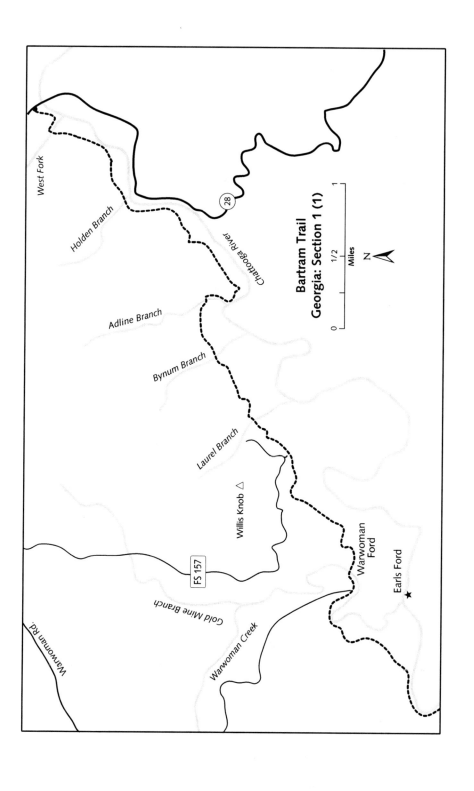

Bartram Trail
Georgia: Section 1 (1)

West Fork

Holden Branch

Chattooga River

28

Adline Branch

Bynum Branch

Laurel Branch

Willis Knob △

FS 157

Gold Mine Branch

Warwoman Creek

Warwoman Rd.

Warwoman Ford

Earls Ford ★

N

0   1/2   1
Miles

ford across the river. From the bridge are views upstream of Big Slide rapids, rated class 2. Downstream, you can follow the course of the West Fork as it empties into the Chattooga River. On the south bank of this branch are many clearings suitable for campsites.

For the next 2 miles the Bartram Trail works its way to the south, traversing the area known as Long Bottom. This wide floodplain, aptly named for its length, was farmed until the 1960s. Evidence of farming still exists throughout the area: barbwire fences, farm machinery, the foundations of several farmhouses, and the Holden Cemetery. From the bridge, the Bartram Trail turns to the left for a few hundred feet and then bears to the right to follow the bed of an old farm road for the next 2 miles. Hugging the western boundary of the floodplain, the road is for the most part out of sight and sound of the Chattooga River. After working up and down the southeast flank of Holden Mountain, the trail briefly returns to the floodplain **(mile 0.6)**. The path then curls to the right and rejoins the old road. In less than 0.5 mile the floodplain narrows and the trail descends to the river, which it follows for only a few feet. Out of the narrows, the Bartram turns to the right, onto the farm road, for nearly 0.5 mile.

The trail leaves the old road and descends to a footbridge crossing **Holden Branch (mile 1.2)**, then climbs steps to a road on the south side of the stream. South of the branch the floodplain narrows again and the Bartram closely follows the course of the Chattooga for 0.25 mile. Across the river is a boat ramp on the South Carolina side—a put-in for Section 2 providing access to a very popular area for trout fishing. As the floodplain widens, the trail veers southwest, away from the river. Soon it crosses an unnamed branch over a wooden footbridge **(mile 1.5)**, again on the bed of the old road. In less than 0.5 mile the footpath approaches a fork and turns to the left, reentering the floodplain on another farm road. Just before a streamlet **(mile 2.1)**, to the right, are the foundations and chimney of an old farmhouse. To the left is a rusting baler. After the trail crosses the unnamed stream there is a large tree plantation on the left.

The Bartram Trail leaves Long Bottom and climbs to the west over a ridge into a southwest-facing cove. In the cove the trail holds to the contour line working from east to west. Exiting the cove, it descends to a horse trail **(mile 2.6)** marked with orange blazes. The trail follows the course of the horse trail for a few feet and then turns sharply left for a brief descent. In a little more than 0.1 mile the descent ends at **Adline Branch (mile 2.7)**.

After crossing the stream on a wooden footbridge the trail turns sharply to the left and begins a moderate ascent of a shallow ridge. After the climb,

"BIG SHOALS TRAIL"

This footpath, not formally designated a trail, is an old road descending from the jeep mound to the Chattooga River. After a 0.4-mile descent, rugged in some sections, the path intersects the Willis Knob Horse Trail just above Laurel Branch. Turn to the right and follow the horse trail. In 0.1 mile the trail approaches the banks of the Chattooga River. To the left are sandy beaches and areas suitable for a picnic. Continue downstream for an additional 0.2 mile for views of Big Shoals Rapids, rated class 3.

---

the trail turns west, entering a cove where it intersects another old road **(mile 2.9)**. Holding to the contour line, the trail exits and enters a second cove. Following a brief descent the path enters a stand of hemlocks and then a third cove before descending to **Bynum Branch (mile 3.3)**, which it crosses on another wooden footbridge immediately below a fork in the stream. On the western bank of the stream are plentiful areas for camping.

A few hundred feet past the stream the path climbs to an old jeep trail, crosses it, and continues the ascent. In a few hundred feet the trail intersects a second jeep road 0.1 mile from Bynum Branch. From here the moderate climb continues. In 0.2 mile the ascent ends via a short switchback at the junction with the Willis Knob Access Trail **(mile 3.7)**. The trail is an old road that connects the Bartram Trail with Gold Mine Road (F.S. 157), also known as Willis Knob Road. The connector is 200 feet long. Warwoman Road is 4.7 miles down the road to the left.

After the junction with the Willis Knob Trail, the Bartram Trail descends for a few hundred feet and then turns very sharply to the right, leaving the old road, immediately before a jeep mound, a barrier placed to bar car and jeep traffic. This is also the junction for the "Big Shoals Trail."

After the sharp turn, the Bartram Trail enters a cove and then begins to descend via a switchback. The footpath levels off and follows the contour line through a series of three coves. In the third cove it begins a steady descent to **Laurel Branch (mile 4.2)**, which it crosses on a wooden footbridge. The trail begins to climb out of the cove and soon turns to the right, crossing over a ridge. After a very brief descent, the path levels and then dips to an unnamed branch. Near the branch are flat areas suitable for camping.

The descent ends at an old road that the path joins for a short distance. After a short rise the Bartram turns sharply to the left, leaving the road **(mile 4.4)**. The trail continues to climb for nearly 0.25 mile before reaching a small gap. Through the gap, it joins another old road for a few hundred feet, then turns sharply to the left on a footpath. From the turn, the Bartram descends and then begins to roll up and down a series of shallow ridges that form the southeastern base of Willis Knob (elevation 2,417 feet). The path drops to an unnamed stream and crosses it on a wooden footbridge **(mile 5.1)**, climbs out of the cove over a long north–south ridge, and descends again to a small streamlet with water in the winter **(mile 5.5)**.

After crossing the stream, the trail turns sharply to the left and climbs toward a large stand of young pine trees, evidence of a forest fire in the late 1970s. At this point the trail is near the head of a long cove facing the Chattooga. As the path leaves the cove, it continues to climb. On the left the trail approaches the boundary of the Chattooga River Wild and Scenic Area (CWSR), which is marked with blue blazes. The ascent ends at a level area, intersecting a footpath to the left and an old road to the right **(mile 5.6)**. It is difficult to follow the course of the trail in this area. The path to the far left follows the boundary markers of the CWSR. The Bartram Trail, marked with metal blazes, continues to the right of this footpath.

From the junction the trail begins the downward trek to **Warwoman Creek**. In 0.1 mile the path crosses an unnamed branch and then gently slopes for 0.25 mile to the Willis Knob Horse Trail **(mile 6.0)**. From the junction, the Bartram continues straight ahead, continuing its descent. After leveling, the trail bears to the left, cutting across a shallow ridge, then enters a cove and begins to work down the left side and then the right. As the path exits the cove, there are views of Warwoman Creek straight ahead. Bearing to the left, the trail comes within clear view of the creek's wide floodplain, which offers numerous campsites. The descent ends at the north bank of the creek. The trail follows the creek downstream for a short distance, then crosses it on a steel and concrete bridge **(mile 6.4)** with good views of this beautiful mountain river.

After crossing the bridge, the path turns to the left and continues to follow Warwoman Creek downstream. Several old hemlocks are scattered throughout this area. In less than 0.5 mile the trail intersects **Earls Ford Road (mile 6.8)** just north of the road's ford over the creek. The trail crosses the road and continues along the creek's right bank for 0.25 mile to a wooden footbridge **(mile 7.1)** crossing an unnamed branch. From the bridge, the path continues downstream for a short distance and then turns sharply to the right, leaving the old road, which is severely eroded in many sections. The newly constructed path winds up an unnamed ridge and rejoins the old road at the top **(mile 7.6)**.

The trail turns to the right and follows the old road for a 0.25-mile descent to the Chattooga. Approaching the river, the Bartram crosses an unnamed

A few hundred feet after leaving the Bartram Trail, the spur trail comes to the first ledge of Dicks Creek Falls. Another 50 feet downstream, the trail comes to the site of an old viewing platform that offers a panoramic view of Dicks Creek Falls cascading 50 feet into the Chattooga below and Dicks Creek Ledge, a class 4 rapids. Less than 0.1 mile downstream there is a faint trail to the right. This little spur leads to the base of Dicks Creek Falls. The hike is something of a root climb, just above a portion of the ledge. Exercise caution. At the base of the falls are several large boulders for enjoying the waterfall and river. To the left, the main track of the spur trail leads to sandy beaches just above the rapids. There is a large pool suitable for swimming. Exercise caution if the water is high; the rapids are immediately downstream!

---

branch **(mile 7.8)** and then for 0.5 mile continues on the road just above the river. Throughout this area are many sites for camping. The trail leaves the river again **(mile 8.3)** and begins a steady climb up the ridge to the right.

From the old road, the Bartram climbs for more than 0.25 mile and intersects an unnamed footpath to the left at the top of the ridge. The trail then gradually descends in and out of a series of coves. As the path levels, the Bartram crosses an unnamed stream **(mile 8.9)** on a wooden footbridge. A tenth of a mile from the crossing there is a junction with an unmarked footpath to the right. The Bartram turns to the left, slightly descending to the banks of **Dicks Creek (mile 9.2)**. Just before the trail reaches the near bank of the creek there is a junction with the Dicks Creek Spur Trail. To the left, this path ends in 0.25 mile at the Chattooga near the base of Dicks Creek Falls. To the right, it is 0.25 mile to Sandy Ford Road. The Bartram continues straight ahead, crossing the wooden footbridge. This junction offers numerous flat areas for camping.

From the falls the trail crosses a small wooden footbridge and continues to ascend. In a little more than 0.25 mile the trail reaches the junction with the **Chattooga River Trail (mile 9.5)**. The Bartram Trail continues to the right while the black-blazed Chattooga River Trail veers to the left. The Bartram Trail continues to ascend until its intersection with **Sandy Ford Road (mile 9.6)**.

WATER AND CAMPING

Section 1 of the Bartram Trail in Georgia offers numerous sites for water and for camping. Listed below are selected sites.

Water: mile 0.3, West Fork of the Chattooga; mile 4.2, Laurel Branch; mile 5.1; miles 6.5–7.3, Warwoman Creek; mile 9.2, Dicks Creek.

Camping: mile 0.4, south side of the West Fork of the Chattooga; miles 6.5–7.3, Warwoman Creek; mile 9.4, Dicks Creek Spur Trailhead.

ACCESS POINTS

Ga. 28: Approximately 14.2 miles from Clayton on Warwoman Road, turn right onto Ga. 28. Take Ga. 28 for 2.2 miles. Just before the bridge crossing the Chattooga into South Carolina there is a moderate-sized parking area on the left. The trailhead is across the road, just before the guardrail on the south side of the road.

Willis Knob Road: Approximately 11.7 miles from Clayton on Warwoman Road, turn right onto Willis Knob Road, F.S. 157. Take the gravel road, passable for most cars, 4.7 miles to the trailhead for the Willis Knob Road Access Trail. There is adequate space for two or three cars; approximately 0.2 mile before that parking area is a larger parking area. Take the trail over a series of jeep mounds. In 200 feet the trail intersects the Bartram Trail.

Earls Ford Road: From Clayton (U.S. 441) take Warwoman Road 8.0 miles to the east. Turn right onto Earls Ford Road and follow the paved road to the southeast. The pavement ends shortly after the bridge over Warwoman Creek. The single-track gravel road continues to follow the creek downstream, crossing it again on a narrow concrete bridge. The road leaves the creek, returning to it at Warwoman Ford (4.0 miles from Warwoman Creek Road). Before the ford there are small parking areas on both sides of the road. The ford is still crossed by automobiles, so be certain not to block the road.

Sandy Ford Road (formerly known as Dicks Creek Road): From Clayton (U.S. 441) take Warwoman Road approximately 6 miles to the east. Turn right onto Sandy Ford Road and bear to the right on the paved road. At **mile 0.6** from the turn-off on Warwoman Road, the road turns sharply to the left over a bridge crossing Warwoman Creek. Follow the road, now gravel, for another 3 miles. The road crosses Dicks Creek twice, the first time on a newly build culvert, the second time at a ford **(mile 3.5)**. After the ford the road becomes rutted and, depending on weather conditions, may be impassable for conventional cars. At **mile 3.7** Sandy Ford Road intersects the Bartram Trail. There is a small parking area to the left. If the water level of Dicks Creek prevents fording by automobile, there is an access trail on the near side of the creek. This trail is approximately 0.25 mile long and follows Dicks Creek to the trailhead for the spur trail.

Section 2

Section: Sandy Ford Road to Warwoman Dell
Distance: 9.4 miles
Difficulty: moderate (both directions)
Hazards: none
Highlights: Rainy Mountain; Warwoman Dell
Maps: Rainy Mountain; Rabun Bald (USGS)

From Sandy Ford Road, this section continues to head in a westerly direction, leaving the Chattooga watershed. The trail works its way to the west along the spine of a series of east–west ridges that offer numerous overlooks of the mountains south and north of the trail. The trail leaves the ridges as it crosses the northern shoulder of Rainy Mountain. Then it begins its descent into Warwoman Dell. The path alternates between old jeep or logging roads and well-constructed trail.

The trailhead at **Sandy Ford Road** is marked with one of the distinctive granite Bartram Trail signs, which incorrectly gives the distance to Warwoman Dell as 12 miles. For the next 0.2 mile the Bartram gradually ascends, via a wide switchback, to a shoulder of an unnamed ridge. From the shoulder, the footpath continues to climb for another 0.1 mile. The trail veers to the left before it reaches the top of the ridge and then begins to descend, crossing over the northern spine of the ridge. At that point there is a steep cove opening to the north that provides a view of Wall Mountain just south of Warwoman Creek.

The trail continues in a westerly direction, intersecting an old jeep road **(mile 0.6)**. At this junction the trail continues with a very sharp turn to the right (about 35 degrees). In less than 100 feet the trail forks; the Bartram Trail follows the path to the right. For nearly a mile the footpath turns in and out of a series of coves on the north side of an unnamed ridge, holding for the most part to the contour line. The trail reaches an unnamed stream **(mile 1.5)** and crosses it on a wooden footbridge. This is the last reliable water for several miles. In approximately 0.1 mile there are views of the Blue Ridge Mountains to the north and northeast. Immediately in front of the ridgeline is a view of Beck Ridge, which Bartram crossed en route to the valley just below Martin Creek Falls.

The trail descends into **Speed Gap (mile 1.9)**, marked with one of the granite Bartram Trail signs. An unmarked path and two old jeep roads also intersect the gap. The jeep road that turns sharply to the right proceeds north to Sandy Ford Road. Both roads are now closed. From this intersection the trail

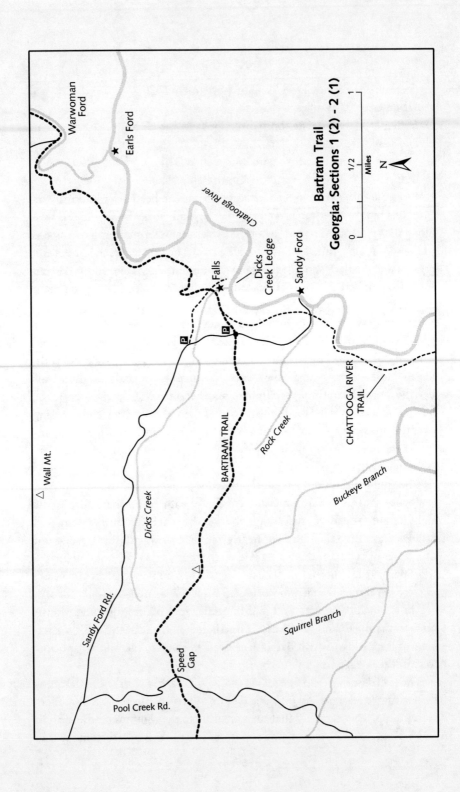

Bartram Trail
Georgia: Sections 1 (2) - 2 (1)

Warwoman Ford

Earls Ford

Chattooga River

Falls

Dicks
Creek Ledge

Sandy Ford

CHATTOOGA RIVER
TRAIL

Rock Creek

BARTRAM TRAIL

Buckeye Branch

Dicks Creek

Wall Mt.

Squirrel Branch

Speed Gap

Sandy Ford Rd.

Pool Creek Rd.

N

0   1/2   1
Miles

continues straight ahead. In approximately 0.25 mile there is another intersection with a closed jeep road **(mile 2.2)**. The trail turns right and follows the track of the road. After sharing the roadbed for 0.2 mile, the Bartram Trail turns off the road sharply to the left, veering south of a high point on the ridge. Shortly afterward the trail reaches a narrow shoulder at 2,160 feet. In less than 0.1 mile the trail begins to turn to the northwest, running along the top of a ridgeline.

The trail begins a series of steady ascents, eventually reaching the first of two high points on the ridge **(mile 2.7)**. After a descent of less than 0.1 mile, the footpath begins a 0.25-mile climb to the second high point **(mile 3.0)**. Afterward it descends for nearly 0.5 mile to Bob Gap **(mile 3.4)** through a forest of blackjack oak.

This small gap (elevation 2,056 feet) offers no places for camping. In the gap, the trail intersects Pool Creek Road. To the north this road ends at Warwoman Road, to the south at Ga. 76. The Bartram Trail crosses the road and ascends a series of stairs to the right. For nearly 0.5 mile the footpath returns to the pattern of moving in and out of coves, maintaining a relatively constant elevation at 2,200 feet. These coves have large groves of mountain laurel. The trail intersects another old jeep road **(mile 3.8)** and, turning to the right, joins the road, running along the top of the ridge for more than a mile.

The Bartram reaches the highest point on the ridge at an elevation of 2,745 feet **(mile 4.9)**, then follows a steady down grade to an old jeep road that will begin to approach the northeast base of **Rainy Mountain**. Throughout this descent are views of the South Carolina mountains and piedmont. The trail makes an abrupt turn to the right and leaves the road **(mile 5.3)**, which continues straight ahead and in approximately 0.5 mile intersects an unmarked trail that approaches the summit of Rainy Mountain. The Bartram begins a short climb of approximately 0.1 mile, crossing over the northeast shoulder of Rainy Mountain. The footpath begins to descend across the north base of the mountain through long stretches of mountain laurels and rhododendrons. In 0.2 mile there is a small rivulet—the first reliable water in 4 miles. From the stream, the path resumes the familiar pattern of moving in and out of a series of north-facing coves, several with rivulets or springs in the middle. The trail rises to the northwest shoulder of Rainy Mountain and then begins gradually to descend. To the right is a deep and wide northwest-facing cove. In the fall and winter there are views of Rabun Bald to the north. As the trail descends, it intersects the **Red Trail (mile 6.4)**.

From the junction the trail continues to lose elevation on the old road. In

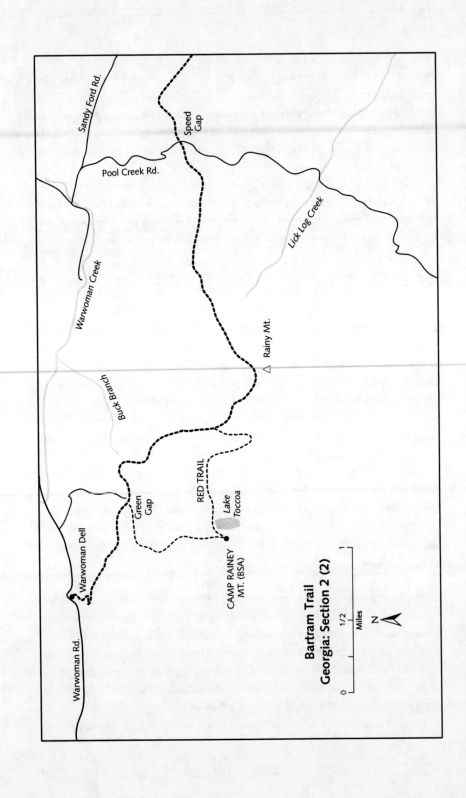

**Bartram Trail
Georgia: Section 2 (2)**

Sandy Ford Rd.

Speed
Gap

Pool Creek Rd.

Lick Log Creek

Warwoman Creek

Buck Branch

Rainy Mt.

Green
Gap

RED TRAIL

Lake
Toccoa

Warwoman Dell

CAMP RAINEY
MT. (BSA)

Warwoman Rd.

N

0   1/2   1

Miles

This trail, blazed in red, is a 5-mile loop that begins and ends at Camp Rainey Mountain, a Boy Scout camp. To the left, this trail follows the main ridge of Rainy Mountain for 0.1 mile. The trail turns abruptly to the right and begins a 1.5-mile descent of the ridge. The grade of the descent is steep and is not broken by switchbacks. From the turn on the ridge, if you continue straight ahead on the old road, it is 0.4 mile to the summit of Rainy Mountain. There are panoramic views of the region in the fall and winter, as well as small areas for camping. From the junction with the Bartram Trail, the Red Trail parallels the Bartram until Green Gap. At the gap, the Red Trail begins a 1.25-mile descent following an old logging road. The trail ends at the camp's dining hall.

0.2 mile **(mile 6.6)** the trail leaves the road, making an abrupt turn to the right. After the turn there is a level camping area to the left. The trail descends for less than 0.1 mile, then makes a steady ascent to a small unnamed gap **(mile 7.0)**, resuming the established pattern of passing in and out of coves. After the gap, the trail curls to the northeast, crossing over the east–west ridge onto its northern side. The ridge offers views of the Blue Ridge Mountains to the north. The footpath crosses a small boulder field, then curls across the ridge into a shallow cove with a dried-out streambed. From there the trail ascends to intersect a jeep road **(mile 7.4)**. After crossing the road, the trail rises for a few hundred feet and then begins a 0.3-mile descent through groves of mountain laurels to **Green Gap (mile 7.8)**.

The gap, marked with a granite Bartram Trail sign, is named after the Green family, original settlers of Rabun County from Europe, who have lived on land just north of the gap since 1829. The gap is intersected by a one-lane road that ends at Warwoman Road. In the gap, the trail follows the road to the west. After a little more than 200 feet the trail turns to the left and leaves the old road. At this turn the **Red Trail** heads to the left for its descent into Camp Rainey Mountain. As the Bartram Trail leaves the gap, it begins a 0.4-mile climb of the east shoulder of Bleckley Mountain. This climb does not reach the top of the shoulder, but instead veers to the left, staying on the south face of the ridge. To the south are views of Camp Rainey Mountain Boy Scout Camp and Lake Toccoa **(mile 8.4)**. For the next 0.4 mile the footpath begins to descend to the north. The trail crosses a small footbridge **(mile 8.8)**, then continues its descent through a small boulder field. The descent continues for almost 0.5 mile, ending at Warwoman Dell **(mile 9.2)**.

Warwoman Dell

As mentioned above, this USDA Forest Service recreation area was built by the Civilian Conservation Corps in the 1930s. Today it offers picnic areas, restrooms, and water. At the west end of the dell is a self-guided interpretive trail on the area's history and flora. Sections of the trail follow a cut of the nineteenth-century Black Mountain Railroad. The entrance to the dell is closed by a gate from November until the first weekend in April. Near the gate, on the inside, is a parking area for Bartram Trail hikers.

To continue on the trail northward, follow the gravel road to the east (to the right). In approximately 0.1 mile the trail turns left, leaving the road, and in another 0.1 mile reaches **Warwoman Road (mile 9.4)**. Section 3 continues across the road.

WATER AND CAMPING
Water: mile 5.6, streamlet; mile 9.25, Warwoman Dell.
Camping: mile 4.5; mile 6.6 (near junction with Rainy Mountain Trail).

ACCESS POINTS
Sandy Ford Road: Approximately 6 miles from U.S. 441 in Clayton turn right onto Sandy Ford Road. The road is paved for 0.7 mile. The road then turns sharply to the left over a bridge crossing Warwoman Creek. Follow the road, now gravel, for another 3.0 miles. The road fords two streams, the second over Dicks Creek. After the second ford the road becomes rutted and, depending on weather conditions, may be impassable for conventional cars. At **mile 3.7** Sandy Ford Road intersects the Bartram Trail. There is a small parking area to the left.

Warwoman Dell Recreation Area: The recreation area is approximately 3 miles from U.S. 441 in Clayton. There is parking in the recreation area. When the area is closed (from the end of October to early April) there is pullout parking at the trail crossing, just a few hundred yards west of the entrance to the parking area.

Pool Creek Road: Approximately 6 miles from U.S. 441 in Clayton turn right onto Sandy Ford Road. The road is paved for 0.7 mile. The road then turns sharply to the left over a bridge crossing Warwoman Creek. On the opposite side of the creek, turn right on Pool Creek Road. In 2.2 miles the road intersects the Bartram Trail. There is a small parking area with room for a few cars.

Section 3

Section: Warwoman Dell to Wilson Gap
Distance: 8.4 miles
Difficulty: south to north: moderate to difficult; north to south: moderate
Hazards: none
Highlights: Courthouse Gap; Pinnacle Knob; Martin Creek Falls
Maps: Rabun Bald (USGS)

The first 4-mile segment of this section forms a large inverted C, beginning at Warwoman Dell and ending at Courthouse Gap. At the middle of the C are Martin Creek and Martin Creek Falls, described at length in Bartram's *Travels*. From the waterfall the trail makes a long, steady climb to the gap. There the trail joins the main spine of the Blue Ridge, which it follows northward for approximately 4.5 miles. This spine is also the western boundary of the Warwoman Wildlife Management Area. From Courthouse Gap to Rabun Bald, the trail is also marked with yellow boundary signs for the wildlife area. The footpath alternates between old jeep and logging roads and well-constructed trail. At Courthouse Gap the trail is intersected by an access trail. There are spur trails to Pinnacle Knob and Rock Mountain, which offer outstanding views.

The Bartram Trail leaves Warwoman Dell on the gravel access road. After a few hundred feet the trail leaves the road, turning to the left. The footpath climbs, via a short switchback, to Warwoman Dell Road. The path crosses the road and begins a steep climb of the west side of the cove, which is bisected by Becky Branch. In the middle of the cove there is a large hemlock that is approximately 200 years old. The ascent stops at the base of **Becky Branch Falls (mile 0.2)**, a beautiful cascade of 25 feet. The trail crosses the stream on a wooden footbridge at the base of the falls. In a little more than 100 feet the trail intersects a blue-blazed trail to the right. This path descends on the east side of the cove, returning to Warwoman Road. The Bartram continues on the path to the left.

For the next 0.5 mile the Bartram Trail begins to level at an elevation of approximately 2,000 feet and turns to the east, following the southern side of one of the unnamed ridges of Pinnacle Knob. The prominent mountain in the distance to the east is Wall Mountain, with views of Warwoman Valley to the right. After a brief descent, the footpath levels again and intersects an old jeep road **(mile 0.8)**; to the right (south), this road returns to Warwoman

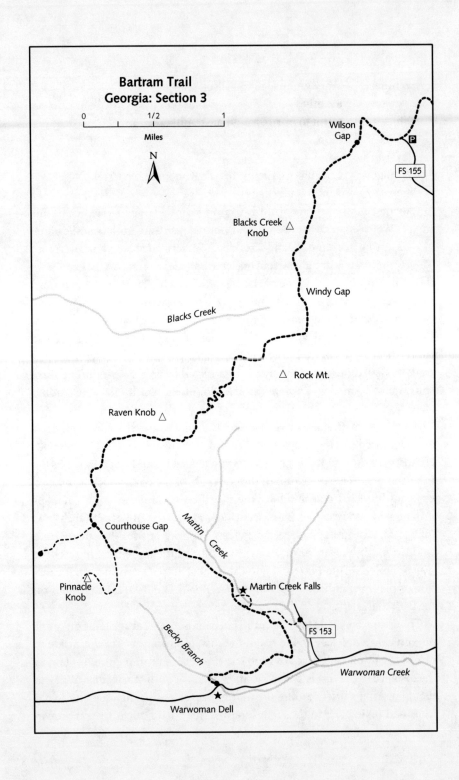

Bartram Trail
Georgia: Section 3

0   1/2   1

Miles

N

Wilson Gap

P

FS 155

Blacks Creek
Knob △

Windy Gap

Blacks Creek

△ Rock Mt.

Raven Knob △

Courthouse Gap

Martin Creek

△
Pinnacle
Knob

★ Martin Creek Falls

FS 153

Becky Branch

Warwoman Creek

★
Warwoman Dell

Road near the intersection with F.S. 153. From the jeep road, the Bartram Trail descends into a small vale divided by an unnamed creek that feeds into Warwoman Creek. The footpath follows this creek for a short distance **(mile 1.0)** and then crosses it. Throughout this small valley are several large white pines.

The trail leaves the cove and begins to climb again for 0.25 mile, then returns to the familiar pattern of moving in and out of a series of coves, along a ridge of Pinnacle Knob heading north-northeast paralleling Finney Creek. The trail enters a stand of old hemlocks and pine trees **(mile 1.5)** and in less than 0.1 mile crosses a small stream and then intersects an old road **(mile 1.7)** from the south. The Bartram continues to the left. The path to the right is the Martin Creek Access Trail, which follows Martin Creek downstream for 0.25 mile, fords the creek, climbs through a small camping area, and ends at F.S. 153.

Approximately 0.1 mile from the junction, the Bartram Trail reaches the west bank of **Martin Creek**. The footpath follows the creek upstream for more than 0.25 mile. Originating on the upper reaches of Pinnacle Knob, Martin Creek is for nearly 0.5 mile a mountain whitewater stream. Highlighting the many falls and ledges in this steep-sided sluice are three prominent cascades. Although the plain is chiefly a second-growth forest, a few of the older pines and hemlocks provide some sense of the grandeur of this forest back when Bartram entered Martin Creek valley. The floodplain offers many areas for camping on either side of the stream. As is true of all mountain streams, camping close to the stream is risky in rainy weather. Exercise caution.

As the Bartram Trail begins to climb out of the floodplain, it reaches the trailhead for a loop trail to the base of **Martin Creek Falls**, Bartram's "unparalleled cascade of Falling Creek." Although only 45 feet in height, this two-tiered waterfall is among the most beautiful in the north Georgia mountains. The loop trail, working counterclockwise, crosses Martin Creek on a 30-foot bridge and then follows the creek upstream to the falls. There it returns to the west side on another bridge, working downstream on a boardwalk to the Bartram Trail.

The trail leaves the flat, climbing to a side hill to the west. It then turns to the east to join an old roadbed, forming a gentle switchback to the east **(mile 2.3)**. In 0.2 mile the trail crosses a streamlet with water in the spring and early summer **(mile 2.5)**. In November, water is still available, but only as a trickle. For the next 0.8 mile the footpath begins the gradual ascent to Courthouse Gap, climbing from 2,100 to 2,600 feet on the northeast base of Pinnacle Knob. The ascent is moderate, in many sections following old roads, and the trail passes in and out of a series of rhododendron thickets. As the ascent of

Although this 0.5-mile trail is an old jeep road, the footpath is steep and a strenuous climb (climbing 500 feet in 0.5 mile). The rewards for the climb are equally great, for there are excellent views from the summit (3,140 feet). Directly to the west is Black Rock Mountain; to the southwest is Clayton; to the far west is Tray Mountain; to the northwest there are excellent views of the Nantahala Mountains. To the far north are the Cowee Mountains north of Franklin. Immediately to the north is the Stekoa Creek valley, the "pretty grassy vale" on Bartram's right as he descended from Courthouse Gap.

---

the mountain continues, the path crosses another spring (mile 3.2). This is the last source of water before the gap. At the highest point of the ascent to the gap, approximately 0.3 mile before the gap, the Bartram intersects the Pinnacle Knob Trail (mile 3.3).

The Bartram Trail begins a steady down grade for 0.3 mile to **Courthouse Gap (mile 3.6)**. The gap, at an elevation of 2,540 feet, is marked with a sign. To the left is the access trail to Courthouse Gap Road, paralleling Bartram's route from the gap to the valley north of Clayton.

The Bartram Trail continues to the north with a steep climb of Hogback Mountain. It departs from the gap on an old road. Within 200 feet the trail leaves the road, turning sharply to the left. After a long switchback the footpath returns to the same road to continue the steep climb (mile 3.7). For hikers traveling from north to south, this turn is especially easy to miss. Immediately past the turn, the climb becomes rugged for nearly 0.1 mile. After a brief respite, the climb continues. The ascent moderates as the trail resumes the pattern of climbing in and out of a series of coves. As the trail levels, it passes just below a gap (mile 4.6) southwest of Raven Knob (elevation 2,900 feet). The trail begins to head in an easterly direction, maintaining a fairly constant elevation. Soon after the gap, to the left, cliff formations on the south face of Raven Knob come into view. To the right are views of Pinnacle Knob and other mountains to the south.

The Bartram Trail crosses a small streamlet (mile 5.0) with water in early summer. To the right are views of the cliffs on Wild Hog Ridge. The footpath begins a moderate climb (mile 5.3) inside the cove on the northeast side of Raven Knob. As the trail approaches the gap, it stays just to the east and passes through a small boulder field (mile 5.3). For the next 0.8 mile the path begins a steep ascent up the southwest shoulder of Rock Mountain via more than

This 0.6-mile trail provides access to the Bartram Trail from Courthouse Gap Road. The trail begins on an old road, still passable by four-wheel-drive vehicles. In a little more than 0.1 mile, before the second stream crossing, the trail turns sharply to the left, leaves the roadway, and enters a large grove of rhododendrons. In the next 0.5 mile the trail steadily gains approximately 400 feet in elevation, hugging Pinnacle Mountain on the south side of the cove. The trail crosses a small streamlet (mile 0.4) with water in the spring. For the last 0.2 mile the trail alternates between moderate ascents and level stretches.

---

half a dozen switchbacks. Afterward, the trail twists and turns for 0.2 mile before reaching the highest point of the ascent (mile 6.1) at 3,160 feet.

After a brief leveling, the Bartram veers to the left onto an old jeep road. The trail descends steadily for more than 0.5 mile, moving in and out of northwest-facing coves. This section is almost one continuous grove of mountain laurels and rhododendrons, which form a canopy over the path. In the summer of 1996 we encountered boar rootings and an eastern diamondback rattlesnake here. After crossing a small streamlet (mile 6.6), the footpath gently descends to an unnamed gap on the north side of Rock Mountain. This gap offers a large, flat area suitable for camping. In another 0.1 mile (mile 6.8) the trail ascends to the top of the ridgeline before descending into Windy Gap (mile 7.0).

Windy Gap is very small and aptly named. The gap offers neither water nor level ground for campsites. Out of the gap, the trail begins a steady climb on the east side of Blacks Creek Knob for nearly a mile. After leveling, the path crosses two streams (mile 7.8) within a few hundred yards; both carry water in summer and winter. After the second crossing, the climb continues. The trail briefly levels (mile 8.0) on the east side of the ridge, at approximately 3,500 feet, then begins a steady but gradual descent to Wilson Gap (mile 8.4). The gap, marked with a granite Bartram Trail sign, offers a large camping area. The trail continues northward, following the roadbed of F.S. 155. There are springs on either side of the gap with water in summer and winter.

WATER AND CAMPING

Water: mile 0.3, Becky Branch; mile 1.5, Finney Creek; mile 1.8, Martin Creek; mile 2.5; mile 5.0; mile 6.6; mile 7.8; mile 8.4, Wilson Gap.

Camping: mile 1.8, Martin Creek; mile 6.7; mile 8.4, Wilson Gap.

Courthouse Gap north of Clayton, Georgia. Pinnacle
Knob (Bartram's Mount Magnolia) is to the right.

ACCESS POINTS

Warwoman Dell Recreation Area: The recreation area is approximately 3
miles from U.S. 441 in Clayton. Parking is available in the recreation
area. When the area is closed (from the end of October to early April),
there is pullout parking at the trail crossing just a few hundred yards
west of the entrance to the parking area.

Tuckaluge Road (seasonally closed): Approximately 5.3 miles from U.S.
441 in Clayton turn left onto Tuckaluge Road. Follow the road for 2.5
miles to the junction with F.S. 153A. At the junction, drive straight
ahead on what becomes 153A. Continue on this road for 2.6 miles. At
the junction with F.S. 155, turn left. Follow F.S. 155 west for 1.5 miles
until you reach the intersection with the Bartram Trail. The
intersection is marked with a granite sign indicating 4.3 miles to
Rabun Bald. To the left of the sign, and on the right side of the road, is
a small parking area. To reach the northern trailhead for Section 3
continue down the roadway for an additional 0.6 mile. This last
section is passable only by high-clearance vehicles, and after rain only
by four-wheel-drive vehicles.

Courthouse Gap: Approximately 1.5 miles from U.S. 441 in Clayton turn left onto Pinnacle Drive. In 0.1 mile Wayah Road joins the road from the right. Continue straight ahead on Pinnacle Road. The road enters the gate for Camp Pinnacle, a Baptist mission camp. Continue on Pinnacle Drive for 0.5 mile until it intersects Courthouse Gap Road. Turn right at the intersection and follow the gravel road for 0.2 mile, past the last house. Park in the small gravel lot near the power-line standard. Do not block the road, which is still in use.

Section 4

Section: Wilson Gap to Hale Ridge Road
Distance: 9.3 miles
Difficulty: north to south: moderate to easy; south to north: moderate to difficult
Hazards: none
Highlights: views from Rabun Bald
Map: Rabun Bald (USGS)

For approximately 5 miles the trail continues to follow the main spine of the Blue Ridge Mountains. In this section the trail gains elevation from 3,220 feet in Wilson Gap to 4,696 feet at Rabun Bald. From the summit, the trail descends via an old fire-tower road to Beegum Gap. From the gap to Hale Ridge Road the trail remains level, winding in and out of a series of coves. Cutting through most of the coves are small streams that are the headwaters for the West Fork of the Chattooga River.

The Bartram Trail leaves Wilson Gap and turns north on the right-of-way of F.S. 155. This 0.6-mile section of the trail will soon be rerouted east of the road. Although the footpath now follows a road, the climb is both long and steady. After bearing to the east and to the right, the trail levels off and leaves the roadbed **(mile 0.6)**, turning sharply to the left. This turn is marked with a granite Bartram Trail sign indicating 5.0 miles to Rabun Bald. After a short ascent, the path levels, reaching a clearing in less than 0.25 mile **(mile 0.9)**. The clearing offers views of the valley below and the Nantahala Mountains to the northwest. The trail continues to roll gently up and down as it turns into the cove separating the two summits of Double Knob Mountain. In the middle of the cove the trail crosses a small streamlet with water in late March **(mile 1.1)**.

Out of the cove, the trail descends for nearly 0.5 mile as it curls around the second peak. After briefly leveling off, it begins a steady ascent up the west

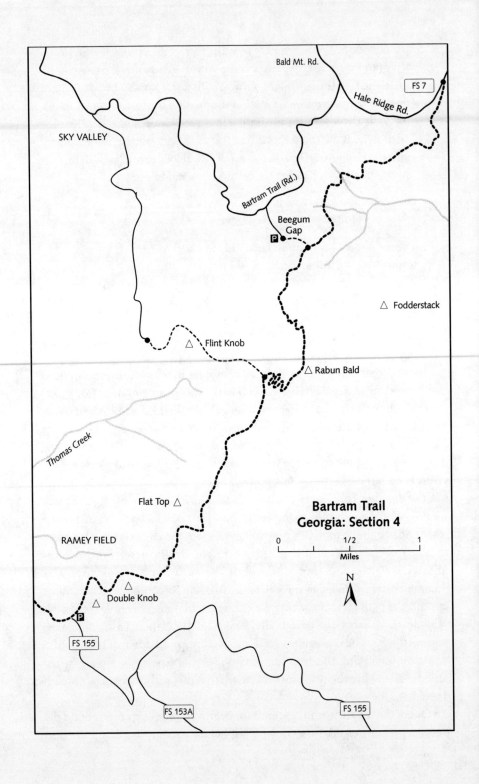

Bald Mt. Rd.

FS 7

Hale Ridge Rd.

SKY VALLEY

Bartram Trail (Rd.)

Beegum
Gap

P

△ Fodderstack

● △ Flint Knob

△ Rabun Bald

Thomas Creek

Flat Top △

**Bartram Trail
Georgia: Section 4**

RAMEY FIELD

0   1/2   1
Miles

△
Double Knob

N

P

FS 155

FS 153A

FS 155

face of Wilson Knob. Before reaching the summit the path veers to the left, into the gap on the north side **(mile 1.7)**, which offers a small level area for camping. In a few hundred feet the trail reaches the first of eight switchbacks up the southwest base of Flat Top Mountain. An open area after the seventh switchback **(mile 1.9)** offers panoramic views of the Blue Ridge to the south and the mountains to the southeast in South Carolina. In another 0.1 mile the trail reaches an intersection with a faint trail to the left. This short spur trail, 20 feet to the west, leads to an overlook of Ramey Field to the northeast. The field, now overgrown with a second-growth forest, was the site of a nineteenth-century farm.

The Bartram Trail continues to ascend, although for the next 0.25 mile the climb becomes more gradual. As the path turns to the right, there is a small stream straight ahead **(mile 2.1)**. This stream, part of the headwaters of Ramey Creek, is the last reliable water on the south side of Rabun Bald. The trail continues to climb as it curls around the southeast side of Flat Top Mountain. On reaching the southeast shoulder of the mountain, the footpath begins a steady ascent of the ridge. Shortly afterward, the trail reaches the highest point of its climb, just below 4,000 feet **(mile 2.5)**. Rabun Bald is visible to the north. The Bartram begins a rapid descent of Flat Top via a series of switchbacks through large groves of rhododendrons. Passing through a small boulder field, the trail straightens as it approaches Salt Rock Gap (elevation 3,680 feet). The gap has flat areas for camping, but no water.

Out of the gap, the Bartram Trail follows a wide trail to the north, then makes a sharp turn to the right, off the trail. The footpath makes a shallow switchback as it begins its long ascent of Rabun Bald. In 0.1 mile the trail turns right again, joining another old jeep road. Just to the left of the turn, approximately 100 feet from the trail, is a small stream with water in the spring **(mile 3.5)**. The trail continues to ascend via another long and steep switchback, which in sections becomes rugged. Afterward the climb becomes more gradual as the trail curls, from left to right, up the shoulder of the mountain. As the elevation increases there are views of the cliff faces of Flint Knob and the Blue Ridge to the far west **(mile 3.8)**. The steady rise continues for nearly 0.5 mile to **Flint Gap (mile 4.2)**, where the Bartram Trail intersects the Alex Mountain Trail. The gap, marked with a granite Bartram Trail sign, is small and does not offer any level areas for camping.

From Flint Gap, the Bartram Trail begins a series of more than eight long and well-graded switchbacks up the southwest shoulder of Rabun Bald. The footpath passes through a long grove **(mile 4.8)** of mountain laurel and purple rhododendron and shortly afterward reaches the south shoulder of

From its junction with the Bartram Trail, the Alex Mountain Trail goes west for 1.8 miles to Alex Mountain. The trail is not marked or blazed. The trail rises steadily out of the small gap to the summit of an unnamed mountain and crosses to the north side of the ridge, offering views of Sky Valley and the mountains in North Carolina to the north. The trail winds down to an unnamed gap, and from there begins a steady ascent to the summit of another unnamed peak. The trail passes through a thicket of mountain laurels and then begins its descent to another gap. This descent, although longer, is over a series of switchbacks. The trail intersects a parking area.

---

the mountain, with views to the east and west. The climb continues, ending in another 0.1 mile at the summit of Rabun Bald **(mile 5.0)**.

Rabun Bald

With its elevation of 4,696 feet, this is the second-highest mountain in Georgia. Although it is called a bald, only a small clearing on the north face offers noteworthy views. The summit does offer a 360-degree panoramic view from an observation deck at the site of a former Forest Service fire tower. The deck was reconstructed in the winter of 1995.

From the deck, the mountain directly to the west is Eagle Mountain. The prominent mountains to the west are the main line of the Blue Ridge, from Tray Mountain to Standing Indian Mountain in North Carolina. Southwest is Lake Lanier and the Georgia Piedmont. To the southeast is Hartwell and views of the South Carolina Piedmont. To the north (due north) is Fishhawk Mountain. Just behind Fishhawk in the distance are the Cowee Mountains. On clear days, Clingmans Dome and Mount LeConte in Great Smoky Mountains National Park are visible northwest of the Cowees.

To the east of the tower, the Bartram Trail intersects the newly named **Rabun Bald Trail**, which drops sharply for 3 miles to the east to its end at Hale Ridge Road, F.S. 7. The Bartram continues on the west side of the tower, where it begins a steady descent on the straight and gradual track of an old road for 0.6 mile. Then the footpath continues to lose elevation via a series of short switchbacks. As the path descends, there are two springs **(mile 5.6 and 5.7)** offering water (and ice!) in the winter. Soon afterward the trail intersects **(mile 5.8)** an old jeep road to the left. The road, although not passable by conventional cars, is still open. The Bartram continues to the right, bearing to the east on the bed of another old road. In a little more than 0.25 mile it passes near a spring that runs through some living-room-size boulders. This area offers views of the cliff face of Rabun Bald, which was covered in ice in the winter of 1996. As the path continues to curl down the north face of the mountain, there is a view of Fodderstack Mountain to the east. The trail levels and intersects an old road to the left **(mile 6.5)**. From the junction, the Bartram leaves the roadbed and continues straight ahead. In a few hundred yards, as the footpath crosses a shallow shoulder, there is a camping area to the left. Just to the east in a grove of rhododendrons is a small stream with water year-round **(mile 6.6)**. From the camping area, the path continues to descend to the junction with the **Beegum Gap Access Trail (mile 6.7)**. From the gap, take the road farthest to the left. On the left are a number of houses; to the right are the red boundary markers for the national forest. In 0.2 mile the road intersects the Bartram Trail. To hike to the summit of Rabun Bald, turn to the right.

For the next 1.5 miles after the junction with the Beegum Gap Access Trail the Bartram Trail remains level, following the contour line in and out of southeast-facing coves. Small streams, all part of the watershed for the West Fork of the Chattooga River, bisect most of the coves. The Bartram crosses the first of several streams approximately 0.5 mile from the Access Trail. In the next 0.5 mile the footpath crosses four small streams as well as a number of springs. After the trail passes through a small boulder field **(mile 7.9)**, there is a large exposed area of the mountain immediately to the left. In 0.1 mile there is a small camping area. From here, turning southward, are views of the cliffs of Rabun Bald. In the next 0.3 mile the footpath crosses two footbridges over small streams with plentiful water in the winter. As the trail exits the cove, there are views to the north of Scaly Mountain and Osage Mountain in North Carolina.

The Bartram crosses another stream on a footbridge at the base of a small waterfall, approximately 25 feet in height, cascading over a series of rocks **(mile 8.2)**. A few hundred feet beyond the waterfall, the trail crosses another small stream on a wooden footbridge with the stream sluicing through the rocks immediately above. Within 0.25 mile the footpath intersects three more streams. Soon after the third stream there are views to the southeast of the West Fork watershed **(mile 9.0)**. Before the end of the section the path crosses two more small streams, the second via a wooden footbridge, then rises gently to the intersection with **Hale Ridge Road (mile 9.3)**, F.S. 7.

WATER AND CAMPING

The first 5.4 miles of this section are without water.

Water: miles 5.4 and 5.5, on the north face of Rabun Bald; numerous springs and small streams from Beegum Gap Trail, mile 6.4, to Hale Ridge Road, mile 9.1.

Camping: mile 0.0, Wilson Gap; mile 3.2, Salt Rock Gap; mile 6.4, near junction with Beegum Gap Trail; mile 7.8, near the boulder field.

ACCESS POINTS

Hale Ridge Road: From Clayton take U.S. 441 to the north. A mile past Dillard turn right onto Ga. 246. Crossing the state line the road becomes N.C. 106. At the junction with Bald Mountain Road turn right. Continue south, returning to Georgia. Past the state line Bald Mountain Road ends at a fork. Take the road to the left—Hale Ridge Road, F.S. 7. Follow the gravel road 1.1 miles to the junction with the trail. There is a small parking area, for two to three cars, on the right side of the road.

Beegum Gap: Follow the directions above for Hale Ridge Road for the route from Clayton to the end of Bald Mountain Road. At the fork, turn right onto the paved road, named Bartram Trail. Take the paved road for 1.3 miles. Turn left onto the steep gravel road, Kelsey Mountain Road. Stay on the road for 0.2 mile to Beegum Gap. In the gap is a small parking area. From Sky Valley, turn right onto N.C. 1628 and go 2.8 miles. Turn right onto the steep road, Kelsey Mountain Road, marked with a Forest Service Hiking Trails sign.

From the parking area, there are two roads and one trail heading to the south. To the far left is a gravel road that intersects the Bartram Trail in 0.2 mile. Directly ahead is a road that forks in less than 200 feet. To the far right is the jeep road to the north shoulder of Rabun Bald. This road, passable only by four-wheel-drive vehicles, is still open. The road on the left side of the fork is the Beegum Gap Trail. This unblazed trail heads north for 0.2 miles to its junction with the Bartram Trail.

Sky Valley, Georgia (Alex Mountain Trail): Enter the city of Sky Valley. Immediately past the police station at the entrance gate, turn left onto Sky Valley Road. Continue on the road past the golf course. Turn left onto Overlook Way. Continue on Overlook Way until the next intersection. Turn right onto Tanglewood Road. At the next intersection continue straight ahead onto Flint Lake Lane. This road becomes Flint Knob Lane, then, as a gravel road, Flint Knob Drive. Turn right at the first asphalt drive on the right. This drive, marked "Hiking Entrance," leads to the small parking area for Alex Mountain Trail.

The Bartram Trail in North Carolina is more than 80 miles long and is divided into two segments. The trail was built and blazed by members of the North Carolina Bartram Society working with the USDA Forest Service. The first segment, Sections 1–2, begins at Hale Ridge Road (in Georgia) and works along the Blue Ridge Mountains to the summit of Scaly Mountain. The footpath descends the north face of Scaly to Tessentee Creek and then begins the long climb up Jones Mountain. After crossing the summit, the trail works along the ridge, turning to the northwest, past Whiterock Mountain and over Fishhawk Mountain. The trail turns west and southwest for a twisting descent to Buckeye Creek, the temporary end of this trail segment. The North Carolina Bartram Trail Society plans to build a Section 3 that will approach the city limits of Franklin.

The second segment, Sections 4–8, spans a line from the western edge of Franklin to Cheoah Bald. From Franklin, the trail follows the course of the old Trimont Ridge Trail, a scenic but very challenging trail to Wayah Bald. From Wayah, the trail works down over Rock Bald Ridge to Nantahala Lake. From the lake to the Appletree Camp, more than half of the trail is on county roads. Leaving the camp, the trail follows the Nantahala River downstream, on its left bank, but soon leaves the river to climb Rattlesnake Rock. At the eastern edge of the Nantahala Gorge the trail begins a steep descent to the river. From the gorge, the last section, completed in 1997, climbs Cheoah Bald to its end at the junction with the Appalachian Trail.

Section 1

Section:	Hale Ridge Road to Jones Gap
Distance:	10.8 miles
Difficulty:	south to north: moderate with difficult sections; north to south: moderate
Hazards:	none
Highlights:	views from Scaly Mountain
Maps:	Rabun Bald; Scaly Mountain (USGS); North Carolina Bartram Trail Society (NCBTS), 1

From the Georgia state line, this section continues north into North Carolina. Skirting around the eastern shoulder of Osage Mountain, the trail descends and then rises to the Osage Mountain Overlook. From here it climbs

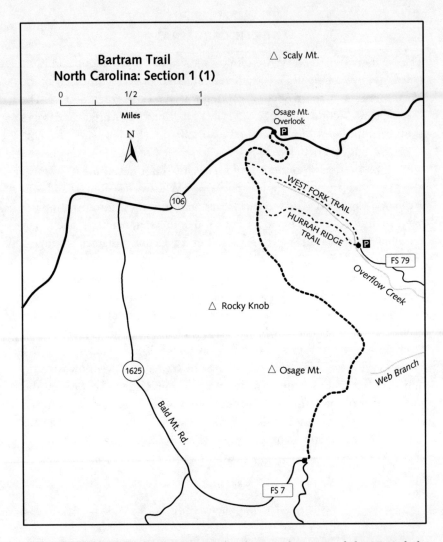

Bartram Trail
North Carolina: Section 1 (1)

△ Scaly Mt.

0   1/2   1

Miles

N

Osage Mt.
Overlook

P

106

WEST FORK TRAIL

HURRAH RIDGE
TRAIL

P

FS 79

Overflow Creek

△ Rocky Knob

1625

△ Osage Mt.

Web Branch

Bald Mt. Rd.

FS 7

Scaly Mountain, offering a panoramic view to the west of the Nantahala Mountains and the Little Tennessee River valley. The trail descends the northwest shoulder of the mountain to Tessentee Creek, and then rises to cross over the western ridge of Peggy Knob. The trail continues to climb via a series of switchbacks to Hickory Gap. From the gap, the trail begins the ascent of "Keith Day Knob," then dips, through fields of wildflowers, to Jones Gap.

This section begins on the north side of Hale Ridge Road, down and across from the trailhead for Georgia's Section 4. In a little more than 0.1 mile the trail enters North Carolina. After a steady rise the path levels, providing views of the mountains to the east, and enters a cove, with a stream crossing fol-

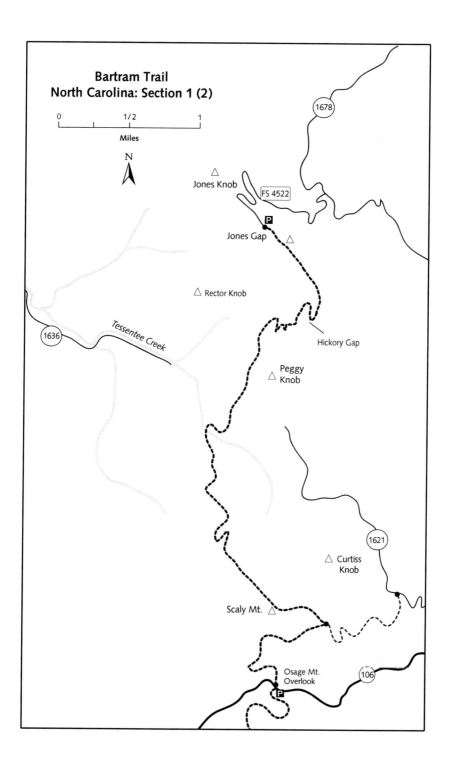

Bartram Trail
North Carolina: Section 1 (2)

0   1/2   1
Miles

N

1678

Jones Knob

FS 4522

P
Jones Gap

Rector Knob

1636

Tessentee Creek

Hickory Gap

Peggy
Knob

1621

Curtiss
Knob

Scaly Mt.

Osage Mt.
Overlook

106

P

lowed by a second crossing within 100 feet. From here the familiar pattern resumes, with the trail following the contour lines as it enters and exits coves. These coves offer numerous streams and rivulets, many with substantial water in late winter and spring. The trail crosses a third stream with water flowing over exposed rocks. Within a few hundred feet a log bridge **(mile 0.6)** crosses another stream with whitewater in early spring. From here the path ascends the ridge and then enters the next cove. In less than 0.1 mile there are two more stream crossings, both over wooden bridges. As the trail continues to the north, there is a stream crossing **(mile 0.8)** with a small waterfall upstream and a sweeping view of the east-facing cove. The trail descends slightly before a moderate climb to the next ridge **(mile 1.0)**, the main east–west ridge of Osage Mountain. On the ridge is a small level area suitable for camping.

Off the ridge, the trail crosses two streams within a few hundred feet. Although the path attempts to hold its elevation, following the contour line, it is not level, and there are several very sharp ascents and descents. The trail crosses a large stream **(mile 1.5)** and soon afterward two additional rivulets. After a brief ascent of a few hundred feet, the Bartram begins a gradual descent. A series of wooden steps brings the trail down to another stream crossing on a wooden bridge **(mile 1.7)**. Afterward there is another crossing and then another set of steps down to a stream sluicing over rocks. As the footpath curls in and out of shallow coves, it begins to slope through a boulder field; after it crosses a small stream **(mile 2.0)** the drop becomes steady. In 0.1 mile there is another stream, crossed by a wooden footbridge. From here the footpath begins to work its way up to the ridge. A few hundred feet after another stream crossing, the trail reaches the crest and follows it for a short distance. It then leaves the ridge for a short drop-off to another creek, crossed by a wooden bridge. Shortly afterward the path comes to another small creek, also crossed by a footbridge **(mile 2.5)**. After the crossing there is a sharp drop-off to the right offering views of the distant mountains to the southeast. The trail then comes to the junction for the **Hurrah Ridge Trail (mile 2.6)**.

The Bartram Trail continues to the left. In a few feet, directly to the north, Scaly Mountain comes into view. The path continues to lose elevation, crossing a stream on a wooden bridge (broken in the spring of 1997) **(mile 2.8)**. From the crossing, there is a slight climb, followed by a descent into a cove passing through a small boulder field. The trail then drops to another stream. At the crossing the stream is divided by a small island, with wooden bridges over each channel **(mile 3.0)**. In a few feet the Bartram Trail intersects the **West Fork Trail**. The Bartram climbs to the left to a small level area suitable for camping. The footpath continues to curl from the north to the east on the inside of the cove, then climbs via a switchback to the north. It approaches a stream and continues to climb on its southern bank. The climb stops as the trail crosses the stream **(mile 3.6)**. In a few hundred feet the trail crosses a second stream and then begins its final rise to the road and the **Osage Mountain Overlook (mile 3.7)**.

The Bartram Trail continues on the north side of N.C. 106 on a series of wooden steps. After a climb of 0.2 mile the trail levels off as it turns to the west. The climb resumes, and the trail intersects a spur trail to the left **(mile 3.9)**. The trail levels again, passes through a grove of rhododendrons, and then crosses a stream with water in late summer. Via a switchback the trail turns to the northeast and then curls to the left. As the trail returns to the northeast, Scaly Mountain once again comes into view. The path comes to another trail junction **(mile 4.5)** and the Bartram Trail continues to the right. After a brief level section the trail begins a steady descent to the junction with the spur trail to **Hickory Gap Road (mile 5.1)**.

From the junction, the Bartram Trail goes left, heading in a westerly direction toward the summit of Scaly Mountain. In less than 0.5 mile there is a rock outcrop **(mile 5.5)** offering views to the south. In 0.2 mile there is a second overlook, also on Scaly's south summit. At **mile 5.9** the trail reaches the western edge of the summit, with views of the Nantahala Mountains and the Little Tennessee River valley to the west. From the summit the path begins a long descent, winding down the northwest face of the mountain for more than 2 miles. As the path works its way down, it crosses over an east–west road **(mile 7.1)**—F.S. 4620—leading back to the west and the south to N.C. 106. On the other side of the road the path enters a rhododendron grove, which is soon followed by a stand of hemlocks. As the down grade continues, the trail angles to the left and begins to follow the course of Tessentee Creek. The small stream is 30–40 feet below as the trail follows it downstream. The trail works its way down to the creek and crosses it **(mile 8.0)**. The stream's floodplain offers a flat area suitable for camping.

On the east side of Tessentee Creek the Bartram Trail follows an old road to the northwest. In approximately 0.25 mile the trail turns very sharply to the right and begins a steep climb, working its way through a boulder field **(mile 8.6)**. The path then reverses direction from southeast to northwest and crosses a dried-out streambed (in late summer) that bisects a northwest-facing cove. Exiting the cove, the trail crosses an east–west ridge off Peggy Knob **(mile 9.3)**. It continues northward on a level section, then, for the next 0.3 mile, climbs up to **Hickory Gap (mile 9.7)** via a series of switchbacks.

From the gap, the trail angles to the left, climbing a series of wooden steps.

This leg forms the base of a long switchback approaching the southern ridge of a knob named "Keith Day Knob" by the North Carolina Bartram Trail Society. The switchback reaches the north–south ridge **(mile 9.85)** and begins a steep climb up "Keith Day Knob." As the trail climbs, there is a rock outcrop on the right that offers views of the mountains to the east and south **(mile 10.0)**. The path climbs through a boulder field and then begins a steep climb up the rock face of the ridge, reaching the highest point of the ascent in a little more than 0.5 mile **(mile 10.6)**. As the trail descends to the gap, it enters a USDA Forest Service wildlife area for a little more than 200 feet. From here the down grade continues into **Jones Gap (mile 10.8)**.

ACCESS POINTS

Hale Ridge Road: From Clayton take U.S. 441 to the north. A mile past Dillard turn right onto Ga. 246. Crossing the state line the road becomes N.C. 106. At the junction with Bald Mountain Road turn right. Continue south, returning to Georgia. Past the state line Bald Mountain Road ends at a fork. Take the road to the left—Hale Ridge Road, F.S. 7. Follow the gravel road 1.1 miles to the junction with the trail. There is a small parking area, for two to three cars, on the right side of the road.

Osage Mountain Overlook: This Forest Service overlook on N.C. 106 offers a paved parking area. The overlook is 5.7 miles southwest of Highlands, North Carolina.

Jones Gap: From the junction of U.S. 64 and Turtle Pond Road, take Turtle Pond Road to the west. In 1.1 miles the road intersects N.C. 1678. Turn right and follow the paved road. Continue on the road as it becomes a gravel road and begins a steep ascent (passable by conventional vehicles). At the junction with F.S. 4522, turn left. Follow the single-track road to its end at the gap. There is a small parking area and a turnaround.

Section 2

Section:	Jones Gap to Buckeye Creek
Distance:	8.4 miles
Difficulty:	moderate (both directions)
Hazards:	north of Wolf Rock the trail is difficult to follow
Highlights:	views from Jones Knob and Whiterock Mountain
Map:	Scaly Mountain (USGS); NCBTS, 2

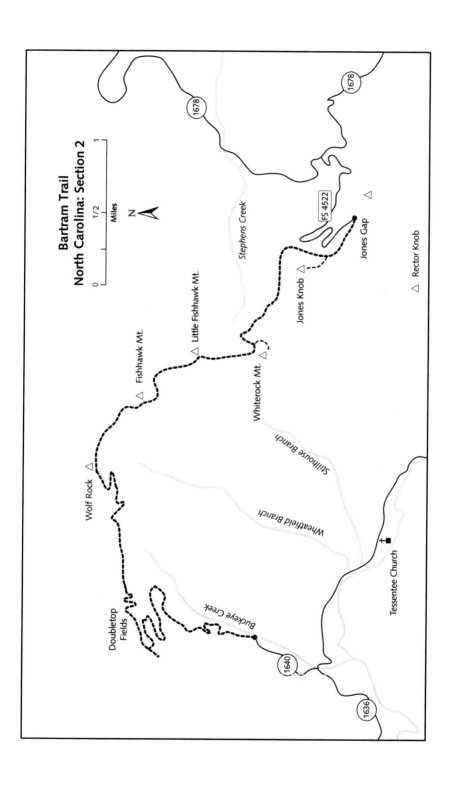

Bartram Trail
North Carolina: Section 2

N

0   1/2   1
Miles

1678

1678

Stephens Creek

FS 4522

Jones Knob △

Jones Gap

△ Rector Knob

△ Fishhawk Mt.

△ Little Fishhawk Mt.

Whiterock Mt. △

Stillhouse Branch

Wheatfield Branch

Wolf Rock △

Doubletop
Fields

Buckeye Creek

Tessentee Church

1640

1636

This blue-blazed trail, less than 0.5 mile long, leads to the summit of the knob. Along the trail are thickets of mountain laurels and flame azaleas. After 0.2 mile the ascent becomes steeper. In a few hundred feet there is a fork; to the left is an overlook. The blue-blazed path continues straight ahead, continuing to ascend, but more gradually. At 200 degrees south there is a clear view of Rabun Bald in Georgia; to the west are the Nantahala Mountains. Beyond the overlook, the path ends at the rocky summit of Jones Knob (mile 0.4).

From Jones Gap, the trail continues northward on the ridge. In the first 2 miles there are blue-blazed spur trails that lead to the summits of Jones Knob and Whiterock Mountain. Both peaks offer outstanding vistas of the mountains to the west, from the Nantahalas to the Great Smoky Mountains on clear days. The trail climbs over Little Fishhawk Mountain and veers to the west of Fishhawk; a third spur trail scales the summit. The Bartram Trail then arcs to the west, over Wolf Rock and down into the Doubletop Fields. The trail ends, and the path continues on the blue connector trail to the south to Buckeye Creek.

The trail begins on the north side of the gap on an old jeep road. Immediately beyond the parking lot is an area rich with wildflowers, with false Solomon's seal, spiderwort, and flame azalea in full bloom in the late spring. Two-tenths of a mile from the gap the trail enters a Forest Service wildlife area. As the trail exits the area it descends slightly, then reaches the junction with the Jones Knob Spur Trail (mile 0.2).

From the junction, the Bartram Trail turns sharply to the right and continues to the north, skirting the eastern edge of Jones Knob. From here the trail begins a gentle descent with views of Shortoff Mountain and Whiteside due east. Leveling off, the footpath enters a long grove of rhododendrons, then rolls slightly as it rounds the northeast shoulder of the knob (mile 0.75). As the trail cuts across the north face of the mountain, it passes over rock shelves and small boulder fields. Soon the path ends its circuit around the knob at the main north–south ridge (mile 1.1).

On the ridge the trail descends into a gap with views of Whiterock Mountain to the northwest and Albert Mountain (250 degrees west-southwest) on the western side of the Little Tennessee River valley. The path then descends via a short switchback down the western side of the ridge. After a short rise, the footpath enters Whiterock Gap (mile 1.35). The gap offers a good but small

The trail climbs through rock outcroppings on the northeast face of the mountain for more than 0.1 mile. The climb stops then, and the trail begins a slight dip, working its way to the rock face on the western side of the mountain. From here there are outstanding views of the Nantahala Mountains to the west and, on clear days, the Great Smoky Mountains to the northwest.

---

camping area and the last reliable water on the ridge. The water source is on the eastern side of the ridge, down **Stephens Creek Trail**. From the gap, the trail begins a moderate ascent through a grove of mountain laurels. The climb continues and becomes much more pitched **(mile 1.7)**. As the trail levels, it reaches the junction with the second spur trail **(mile 1.85)**.

From the junction, the Bartram Trail continues in a westerly direction to a small rock outcrop on the ridge. Turning again to the north, the trail begins a steady climb up the southern shoulder of Little Fishhawk Mountain via a series of very short switchbacks. The climb ends **(mile 2.2)** as the path skirts to the west of the summit. The trail then rejoins the ridge and begins to lose elevation through a mature grove of rhododendrons. At the right time of year, Bowman's root, bluets, and flame azalea can be seen blooming to the northwest. The descent ends in a small gap **(mile 2.75)** with views to the east and west.

From the gap, the trail climbs for less than 0.1 mile, angling from the north to the west. The climb ends as the path joins the bed of an old road, beginning a descent of nearly 0.5 mile. Immediately to the right as the trail loses elevation is the summit of Fishhawk Mountain. The descent ends as the path crosses over Fishhawk's northern face **(mile 3.25)**, then resumes past a rock escarpment and through another long rhododendron grove. As the path turns more to the northwest, the descent continues via a switchback. In a few hundred feet the descent ends at an unnamed gap **(mile 3.7)**.

The trail begins to climb again. In less than 0.2 mile it crosses over Wolf Rock **(mile 3.9)**, the last summit on this section. As the steep descent begins, there are views to the left of the ridge all the way from Scaly Mountain to Whiterock. The trail then turns to the southeast and continues to descend via switchbacks, first to the southeast and then to the west. In this section the path is more than 100 feet below the top of the east–west ridge as it rolls up and down to the west. In the summer of 1997, this section was well blazed but the path was overgrown. The path reaches a rock outcrop **(mile 5.0)** and then begins to scramble down the ridge via a series of short switchbacks. The descent is steep as the trail works its way through boulder fields. The climb down ends as the Bartram enters the Old Orchard Fields **(mile 5.6)** (also the location of an old school bus). The path leaves the fields and begins another descent via a switchback. As the descent continues, the trail curls to the west as it passes a rock outcrop **(mile 5.8)**. From here the down grade continues until the trail reaches a saddle in the ridge. Here the Bartram Trail ends. Immediately to the left is a blue-blazed trail that connects this temporary end of the trail to Buckeye Creek. This saddle has served as the end of the trail since 1991. The North Carolina Bartram Trail Society plans to complete the trail, on the ridge, to The Pinnacle and then into the valley southeast of Franklin.

At the junction, turn left and follow the connector trail off the ridge. The path enters a boulder field via a series of short switchbacks. As the descent continues there is a spring just off the trail **(mile 6.4)**, the first reliable water source since Whiterock Gap. The down grade continues as the trail crosses a stream **(mile 6.9)** and then another within a little more than 50 feet. Soon afterward the path joins an old rock road and continues southward. The rock road descends, crossing over a stream **(mile 7.2)**. The road continues southward and downward, crossing Buckeye Creek **(mile 8.0)**. As the rock road approaches the trailhead, there is a Forest Service gate blocking traffic from the connector. In 0.1 mile the trail reaches the parking area.

ACCESS POINTS

Jones Gap: From the junction of U.S. 64 and Turtle Pond Road, take Turtle Pond Road to the west. In 1.1 miles the road intersects N.C. 1678. Turn right and follow the paved road. Continue on the road as it becomes a gravel road and begins a steep ascent (passable by conventional vehicles). At the junction with F.S. 4522, turn left. Follow the single-track road to its end at the gap. There is a small parking area and a turnaround.

Buckeye Creek: From the junction of U.S. 441 and Tessentee Road (north of Otto), turn right onto Tessentee Road. Follow the paved road for 3.8 miles. At the junction with N.C. 1640, turn left. Follow the dirt road, passable for conventional autos, a little more than 0.5 mile to the trailhead.

Section 4

Section:	Wallace Branch to Wayah Bald
Distance:	10.9 miles

Difficulty:	south to north: difficult with strenuous sections; north to south: difficult
Hazards:	difficult ascents; trail is for the most part without water sources
Highlights:	views along Trimont Ridge
Maps:	Wayah Bald; Franklin (USGS); NCBTS, 4

The first 0.5 mile of this section parallels Wallace Branch upstream. From there the trail begins a steady climb of Trimont Ridge—one of the main east–west ridges of the Nantahala Mountains—ending at the eastern base of Wayah Bald. On the crest, the Bartram Trail rolls up and down a series of summits and gaps. Many of the summits offer spectacular views of the mountains to the south, east, and north. As the trail climbs toward Wayah it generally follows old Forest Service roads, many of which are steep, interspersed with newer sections of foot trail.

From the small parking area, the trail follows Wallace Branch upstream. Within 0.1 mile from the trailhead is a long cascade to the left. The footpath parallels the stream for close to 0.5 mile. At a fork in the stream, the path crosses the right branch **(mile 0.5)** and begins the steady climb up Trimont Ridge. This is the first of many such climbs on this section. In 0.8 mile the trail gains 500 feet in elevation, from 2,700 feet to 3,200. During this climb the trail crosses one of the last reliable water sources in this section, a small stream with water in November **(mile 1.1)**. Two-tenths of a mile beyond the stream the climb ends in a junction with the old Trimont Trail **(mile 1.3)**, which returns to Franklin by way of Trimont Mountain.

The Bartram Trail continues to the left. From the junction, the path undulates and then begins a moderate climb of the southern shoulder of Bruce Knob. At this ridge is another junction with an unmarked trail to the left **(mile 1.7)** that leads south to Gibson Knob. The Bartram continues to the right, beginning a slight descent that lasts for nearly 0.25 mile. In this section there are views of steep Mint Branch Cove to the south. After a brief leveling, the path makes its second long ascent in three stages. The first stage lasts nearly 0.5 mile **(mile 2.4)**. After a level section of less than 0.2 mile, the second climb begins, ending at the small gap to the west of Bruce Knob **(mile 2.8)**. From the gap, the footpath begins its final ascent of the unnamed peak to the west. A little more than 0.1 mile from the gap there is a short spur trail to William's Pulpit—a 100-foot rock shelf that overlooks the Mill Creek watershed to the south. Farther to the southwest are views of the Nantahala Mountains. Climbing the ridge, the path approaches then veers to the right of the summit (elevation 3,520 feet). As the trail levels there are views of Wayah Bald in

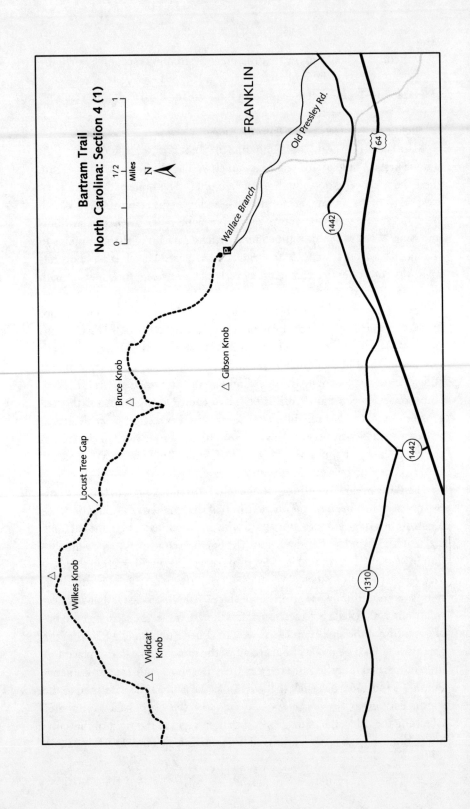

Bartram Trail
North Carolina: Section 4 (1)

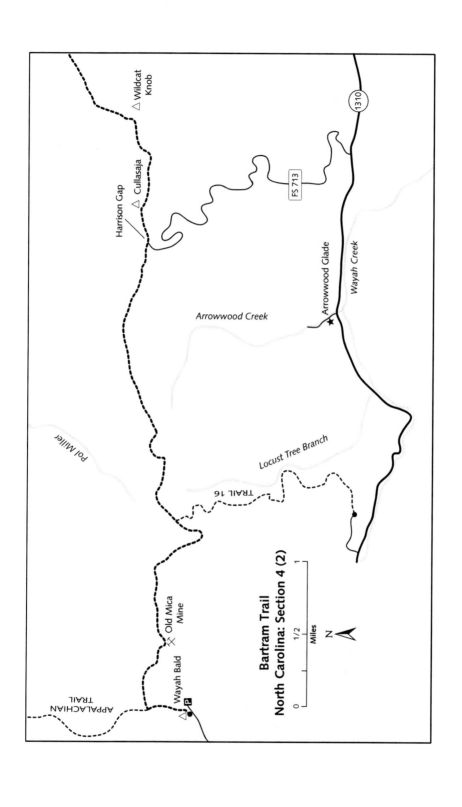

Bartram Trail
North Carolina: Section 4 (2)

Wildcat Knob
Cullasaja
Harrison Gap
1310
FS 713
Arrowwood Glade
Wayah Creek
Arrowwood Creek
Pol Miller
Locust Tree Branch
TRAIL 16
Old Mica Mine
Wayah Bald
APPALACHIAN TRAIL
P

N
0   1/2   1
Miles

the distance. Immediately to the west are views of Trimont Ridge, which forms an arc to the north from Bruce Knob to Wildcat Knob (elevation 3,588 feet).

The trail then quickly descends for 0.1 mile to **Locust Tree Gap (mile 3.1)**. The gap is small and offers only a few spots for camping. An occasional spring can be found a few hundred feet down the north slope from the gap. This is the last reliable source of water for several miles. From the gap, the footpath climbs for nearly 0.2 mile on the southeast shoulder of Wilkes Knob. Again, the path veers south as it approaches the summit. As the trail levels on the south face of the knob it begins a descent to the western gap of the mountain **(mile 3.6)**. A large poplar tree dominates the gap.

Out of the gap, the trail begins a steady 0.3-mile climb on the northeast shoulder of Wildcat Knob. After reaching a small gap on the ridge, it makes another brief climb and then descends for 0.75 mile to Poplar Cove Gap. As the path loses elevation, it passes through a shallow gap on the ridge **(mile 4.3)** with views to the south and east of Trimont Ridge and Mill Creek Cove to the south. In less than 0.3 mile there are views of the rock face of Wildcat Knob immediately to the left. The trail leaves the main spine of the mountain for the western shoulder of the knob and then continues to descend on this spur to **Poplar Cove Gap (mile 4.9)**.

From the gap, the Bartram Trail climbs to the south shoulder of Cullasaja Mountain. Again, the pattern repeats; as the trail approaches the summit, it veers off to the south. From the south face of the mountain, the footpath begins a descent to **Harrison Gap (mile 5.5)**, which is intersected by F.S. 713 (see map 58). From the intersection, the road winds south 4.2 miles, ending at N.C. 1310. The gap does not offer any water or level areas for camping. Out of the gap, the trail rises sharply to the west on an old road for more than 0.1 mile. After a brief level section, it continues the pitched ascent for the next 0.5 mile, passing through an old stand of hardwoods. Lining the trail are many spring wildflowers, including false Solomon's seal, bluets, and hawkweed. The climb continues as the path enters a large grove of mountain laurels. A few hundred feet after the path exits the grove, the ascent ends **(mile 6.3)** at one of the many unnamed peaks on Trimont Ridge.

For 0.1 mile the trail quickly descends, then begins the first stage of another long ascent. This first stage lasts a little more than 0.1 mile. The footpath descends briefly and then levels. In this level section there is a small area to the left suitable for camping **(mile 6.5)**. Within 0.2 mile the path begins another sharp ascent, passing through a stand of older hardwoods dominated by white oaks. In a few hundred feet the path becomes level again, entering a grove of mountain laurels. Quickly the next ascent stage begins with another

Trail 16 heads to the south, ending at N.C. 1310 just west of the Arrowwood Glade Picnic Area. As the trail descends Trimont Ridge it forks into two trails. The southwest branch, Trail 16A, descends to N.C. 1310 via Camp Branch. The southeast branch, the continuation of Trail 16, descends via Locust Tree Branch. Curling to the southwest, this trail joins Trail 16A just before reaching N.C. 1310.

0.1-mile rise. The trail then loses elevation for a few hundred feet before climbing again for 0.2 mile. After leveling off, the path continues the ascent for another 0.25 mile, ending at the first of two wildlife openings—clearings maintained by the Forest Service that provide wildlife with food and cover **(mile 7.5)**—at **Locust Tree Gap**.

The Bartram Trail picks up again on the west side of the wildlife opening, to the left. Just beyond the area there is a spring with occasional water; we found a small trickle in May 1997 **(mile 7.7)**. In 0.1 mile the footpath leaves the old road that it has been following from the wildlife opening and begins a very steep ascent, heading to the southwest on a southern shoulder of Trimont Ridge. As the trail veers to the south, it intersects an unmarked trail to the left, **Trail 16 (mile 8.1)**.

From the junction, the Bartram Trail continues to the right. As the steep ascent continues, there is a small boulder field to the right. The ascent becomes even more pitched as the trail crosses the north–south ridge and returns to Trimont Ridge. Two switchbacks **(miles 8.3 and 8.5)** moderate the final climb to the main ridge. After the path rejoins the main ridge it begins a slight descent and then enters the second wildlife opening **(mile 8.6)**. Bearing to the left, the trail picks up again on the west side of the opening. Out of this unnamed gap, the long ascent continues for more than 0.25 mile. Afterward the trail levels briefly, joining the bed of an old road. There are areas suitable for camping here **(mile 8.9)**, but we found no evidence of recent campers. Beyond the camping area the trail begins a strenuous ascent for more than 0.1 mile. The ascent moderates and then the path begins another climb for 0.2 mile. As the ascent continues, the trail reaches the first switchback on the eastern face of Wayah Bald **(mile 9.3)**. At this switchback, to the left, is a metal fence securing the site of an old mica mine—a fissure more than 100 feet long and 75 feet deep.

As the trail continues to rise along the long switchback it passes through long thickets of mountain laurels and rhododendrons. There are also many wildflowers in this area, notably large patches of bluets. As the trail continues to ascend, it crosses an old road **(mile 9.5)**. The trail continues to the left, levels off, and then begins a descent toward the northern base of Wayah Bald. As the trail descends, it passes a year-round stream **(mile 10.0)**. In less than 0.25 mile the Bartram Trail reaches the junction with the Appalachian Trail **(mile 10.2)**. To the right of the junction is a large camping area.

The Bartram Trail continues to the left, joining the Appalachian Trail. The next 0.75 mile is a steady, but not strenuous, climb up the northern face of Wayah Bald. From the camping area, the path crosses a small streamlet in 0.1 mile. The climb continues, and the footpath crosses an old road in 0.2 mile **(mile 10.5)**. As the conjoined trails approach the summit of Wayah, the trees become shorter and increasingly more stunted. At the very summit of the mountain is an observation tower. In the early 1900s the top of the mountain was already a popular place for picnics and camping. In 1912 the mountain was purchased as a part of the Nantahala National Forest. The summit became a fire lookout station in 1927, and the Forest Service cabin at Wine Spring Bald was relocated to Wayah. Two years later a wooden tower was constructed beside the cabin. In 1935 the CCC began construction on a three-story replacement tower made of stone, which was completed in 1937. With the construction of towers on the summits of surrounding mountains, the Wayah tower was no longer needed, and in 1945 the observation tower was closed. Over the course of the next thirty-eight years the tower fell into disrepair, but the Forest Service restored the structure in 1983. Today the second story stands as an observation tower providing panoramic views of the mountains in all directions. To the north there are clear views of Mount LeConte and Clingmans Dome, with the Great Smoky Mountains extending to the left and right of them. To the northwest stands Cheoah Bald, the western terminus of the Bartram Trail; the Snowbird Mountains are visible to the west. To the south are views of the Nantahala Mountains, including Wine Spring Bald less than 2 miles away. To the east are the Cowee Mountains northeast of the city of Franklin.

Immediately to the south of the tower is an information center with maps and information about the immediate area. From here the trail becomes an asphalt path to the parking lot **(mile 10.9)**. Toward the end of the path are restrooms.

WATER AND CAMPING

Water: mile 0.5, at Wallace Branch; mile 3.1, Locust Tree Gap (down the north side of the gap); mile 7.7, seasonal spring; 10.0, near junction with the Appalachian Trail.

Camping: mile 3.1, Locust Tree Gap; mile 8.9; mile 10.0, at the junction with the Appalachian Trail.

ACCESS POINTS

Wallace Branch: From the junction of U.S. 441 and U.S. 64 south of Franklin, travel west on U.S. 64 for 1 mile. Turn right onto N.C. 1153 (follow the signs for the USDA Forest Service Wayah Ranger Station). Continue on N.C. 1153 for 0.4 mile, then turn left onto Pressley Road. Follow this road for 1.6 miles, ending at the Wallace Branch trailhead. There is a very small parking lot, which is immediately adjacent to private property.

Harrison Gap: From the junction of U.S. 441 and U.S. 64 south of Franklin, travel west on U.S. 64 for 3.5 miles. Turn right onto N.C. 1442, Old Murphy Road. In a little more than 0.1 mile turn left onto N.C. 1310. Continue on this road for 2.0 miles. Turn right onto F.S. 713. Take this single-track gravel road 4.2 miles to the gap, where the road ends. This road is passable by conventional autos.

Wayah Bald: From the junction of U.S. 441 and U.S. 64 south of Franklin, travel west on U.S. 64 for 3.5 miles. Turn right onto N.C. 1442, Old Murphy Road. In a little more than 0.1 mile, turn left onto N.C. 1310. Continue on this road for 9.0 miles. As the road passes over the crest of the gap, turn right onto F.S. 69, Wayah Bald Road. In 4.5 miles the gravel road ends at a large parking circle. The trailheads for Sections 4 and 5 are at the bottom of the parking lot.

Section 5

Section:	Wayah Bald to Nantahala Lake
Distance:	7.4 miles
Difficulty:	south to north: moderate; north to south: difficult
Hazards:	steep descents
Highlights:	views from Wayah Bald and Jarrett Bald
Maps:	Wayah Bald; Topton (USGS); NCBTS, 5

From the summit of Wayah Bald, the Bartram Trail and Appalachian Trail share the same pathway as they head toward Wine Spring Bald. At the bald the Bartram leaves the Appalachian Trail and begins a 5.5-mile westerly descent toward Nantahala Lake. Numerous views of the mountains to the south and north offer as the footpath descends on McDonald Ridge. As the trail leaves the ridge, there is a short spur trail to the summit of Jarrett Bald, which

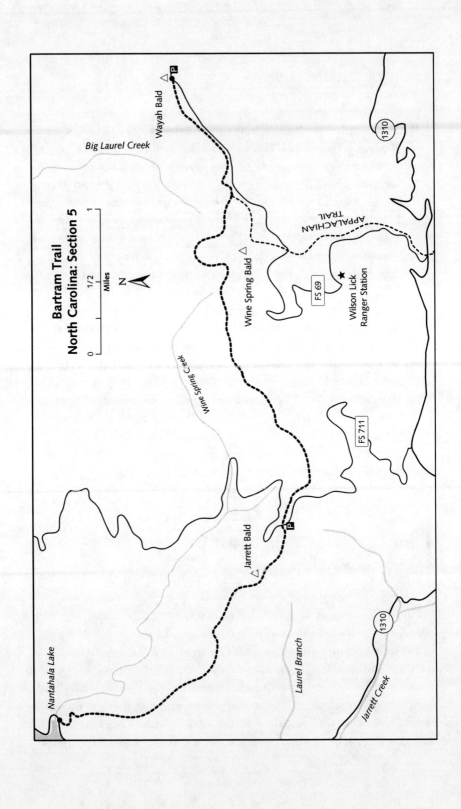

Wayah Bald

Big Laurel Creek

1310

APPALACHIAN TRAIL

Wine Spring Bald

FS 69

★

Wilson Lick
Ranger Station

Wine Spring Creek

FS 711

Jarrett Bald

P

Nantahala Lake

Laurel Branch

1310

Jarrett Creek

offers panoramic views of the surrounding mountains. From Wine Spring Bald to Jarrett Bald, the trail alternates between footpath and old roads. From Jarrett, the Bartram is mostly footpath as it drops off to Nantahala Lake. Section 5 is bisected by Sawmill Gap Road, a paved two-lane highway, providing opportunities for short day hikes.

Section 5 begins at the post at the beginning of the asphalt path to the observation tower on Wayah Bald. From here, the Bartram and Appalachian Trails head southwest, quickly descending from the main ridge running between Wayah Bald and Wine Spring Bald. After intersecting a gravel road (**mile 0.2**), accessible by car, the path descends for nearly 0.25 mile. As the trail loses elevation, it begins to run parallel to the ridgeline above. The path levels off and then begins a 0.25-mile ascent of the same ridge. After crossing a stream (**mile 1.0**) with flowing water in late May, the footpath loses elevation and then begins another sustained climb. Approaching the top of the ridge, it turns to the west as it begins to loop around the north and west sides of Wine Spring Bald for the next 0.5 mile. The ascent continues and the path crosses another small stream that is the headwaters for Laurel Creek (**mile 1.2**). Just after the stream crossing there is a large American beech to the left. The trail continues to climb to the top of Rocky Bald Ridge, the northern base of Wine Spring Bald. At the top of the ridge are views of Wayah Bald to the east and ridges to the north and west. In little more than 0.1 mile the long ascent ends and the trail joins an old road (**mile 1.6**).

The Bartram and Appalachian Trails follow the old road for more than 0.25 mile; 0.1 mile down the road (**mile 1.7**) the two trails intersect a grassy road to the left. This road connects in 0.1 mile with Wine Springs Bald Road, F.S. 69B, leading to the summit. The combined Bartram and Appalachian Trails continue straight ahead. In less than 0.1 mile there is a camping area to the right (**mile 1.8**) intersected by a small streamlet.

Just past the campsites the Bartram Trail and the Appalachian Trail separate. The Appalachian continues straight ahead (south) while the Bartram, turning to the right, begins a steady descent of McDonald Ridge. This junction is marked by a sign. For 0.25 mile the footpath begins a moderate descent down the upper part of the ridge, then levels off and enters the first of three wildlife openings (**mile 2.1**) on this section. Bearing to the right, the trail exits the opening just beyond an old stump marked with a yellow Bartram Trail blaze and continues its descent on a very narrow section of the ridge. Throughout this section the drop-offs to the south are considerable. From here there are views of the ranges to the north and south (**mile 2.3**). The path levels and then begins a series of steps down for more than half a mile. Bluets and false Solomon's seal bloom throughout this area in late May.

The descent ends as the Bartram Trail enters the second wildlife opening **(mile 2.9)**. As the trail leaves the opening it rises briefly and then descends into another shallow gap. From here, the footpath crosses to the south side of the ridge and begins a moderate climb. As it climbs, there are views of the mountains to the south. Crossing back to the north side of the ridge, the path joins another old road **(mile 3.4)** to begin a 0.25-plus-mile descent into the third wildlife opening **(mile 3.7)**. The trail picks up again directly on the other side of the opening, following an old roadbed. After a steep 0.1-mile descent the footpath intersects a gated gravel road. The Bartram Trail continues to the left, in approximately 200 feet intersecting F.S. 711, a paved two-lane highway. Turning again to the left, the trail follows the asphalt road into Sawmill Gap **(mile 3.9)**. From here there are views of the mountains to the south and southwest. The gap has a large parking area but neither water nor campsites.

The trail turns to the right just before reaching the north side of the parking area. At the turn, the trail joins another old road for a 0.1-mile climb. On the left there are views of Siler Bald to the southeast. After leveling, the path enters another small gap and then begins the ascent of the southern base of Jarrett Bald, with views of Fire Ridge, Goat Bald, and Rocky Bald Ridge to the north. Approximately halfway up the mountain the trail leaves the old road **(mile 4.4)**, turning to the left. From here the footpath continues the ascent, but not as sharply. Two-tenths of a mile later the path intersects a blue-blazed spur trail that leads to the summit of the mountain.

The Bartram Trail continues to veer to the west of the bald, heading in a northerly direction. Immediately to the west of the bald's summit the footpath winds through a considerable boulder field **(mile 4.8)**, then enters a gap with a small camping area with room for one to two tents. A tenth of a mile beyond the gap the trail begins its 2.5-mile descent to Nantahala Lake. It will lose 1,700 feet in elevation along the way, from 4,700 feet to about 3,000 feet. As the descent begins, the trail curls in and out of a series of mountain laurel groves. As the ridge narrows, the path winds through a patch of boulders and then drops sharply, making the descent more of a rock scramble downward. Nantahala Lake is visible to the west **(mile 5.1)** during the descent. The path enters a large grove of rhododendrons and then curls left and continues to descend on the south side of the ridge.

The trail continues to lose elevation on the south side via a series of half a dozen short, steep switchbacks. After leveling off **(mile 5.4)**, it climbs up and over two short knobs in the next 0.2 mile and then resumes the descent. As the footpath drops, there are views of the ridges to the north and south **(mile 5.9)**. The path begins a short climb and then levels again as it enters another small gap **(mile 6.3)**. From the gap, the trail climbs a few hundred feet to the top of another small knob and then resumes the descent on a narrow section of the ridge. In some areas the gradient of the descent is very steep, making the climb down treacherous in wet weather. Just below this area, the descent continues via a series of steep and eroded switchbacks **(mile 7.2)**. Immediately northwest of the switchbacks is Wine Spring Creek, which is clearly audible. As the trail approaches the final descent of this section, it comes within 20 feet of the creek. In less than 0.1 mile, Section 5 ends at N.C. 1310 and **Nantahala Lake (mile 7.4)**.

WATER AND CAMPING

Water: mile 1.2, Laurel Creek; mile 1.8, near campsite.

Camping: mile 1.8, near the junction of the Appalachian and Bartram Trails; mile 4.8, gap west of Jarrett Bald.

ACCESS POINTS

Wayah Bald: From the junction of U.S. 441 and U.S. 64 south of Franklin, travel west on U.S. 64 for 3.5 miles. Turn right onto N.C. 1442, Old Murphy Road. In a little more than 0.1 mile, turn left onto N.C. 1310. Continue on this road for 9.0 miles. As the road passes over the crest of the gap, turn right onto F.S. 69, Wayah Bald Road. In 4.5 miles the gravel road ends at a large parking circle. The trailheads for Sections 4 and 5 are at the bottom of the parking lot.

Wine Spring Bald: Follow the directions above for Wayah Bald access. Turn right onto F.S. 69, Wayah Bald Road. Follow this road for 3.5 miles and then turn left onto the gravel road with a sign for Wine Spring Bald. In 0.7 mile the road intersects an old grassy road to the right, now closed to vehicles. Park and walk down the grassy road; in 500 feet it intersects both the Bartram Trail and the Appalachian Trail.

Sawmill Gap: Follow the directions above for Wayah Bald access to Wayah Gap and the intersection with F.S. 69. Continue on Wayah Road (N.C. 1310) through the gap. After descending 1.7 miles, turn right onto F.S. 711, a two-lane paved road. Follow this road for 2.5 miles to Sawmill Gap. There is a large paved parking lot at the gap. The trail is at the far end of the lot.

Nantahala Lake: Follow the directions above for Wayah Bald access to the intersection with F.S. 69. Continue on Wayah Bald Road (N.C. 1310) through the gap for 10 miles to the shore of Nantahala Lake. To the left are two small parking areas next to a large metal Bartram Trail sign.

Section 6

Section: Nantahala Lake (N.C. 1310) to Appletree Group Camp
Distance: 5.6 miles
Difficulty: moderate to easy (both directions)
Hazards: none
Highlights: Nantahala Lake
Maps: Topton (USGS); NCBTS, 6

The trail follows N.C. 1310 for more than 0.5 mile along the northern shoreline of Nantahala Lake. For just over 2 miles the trail winds up and down a series of ridges toward the Nantahala Dam. At the dam's spillway, the Bartram Trail descends quickly to the Nantahala River. After crossing the river on a concrete ford, the trail follows a private road that follows the river downstream. This section ends at the public parking area immediately outside the gate to the Forest Service group camp. The camp is the trailhead for several trails that can be used with the Bartram for a variety of loop hikes of varying lengths.

The trail begins at the small parking area on the side of N.C. 1310 marked with a brown metal Bartram Trail sign. Facing Nantahala Lake, the Bartram turns to the right and follows N.C. 1310 for 0.6 mile, skirting the northeastern shore of the lake. The 1,605-acre lake holds the river water impounded by the dam built in 1942. From the dam, water is pumped by aqueduct and tunnel to the hydroelectric plant located nearly 10 miles downstream. The Bartram Trail leaves the highway immediately past Owenby's Lakeside Store. This store, open year-round, has groceries, camping supplies, a telephone, and water. Two hundred feet past the store, turn to the left and follow the gravel driveway. Although it is on private property, the trail is marked with a USDA Forest Service trail sign.

The gravel drive descends, crossing Lee Branch, and then quickly rises to a junction with an old road **(mile 0.8)**. The trail turns left at the junction and follows another old road as it begins a climb. In a less than 0.1 mile the trail begins to level. Shortly afterward it begins another ascent and then crosses a stream with flowing water in late May **(mile 1.2)**. This area is a second-growth forest dominated by young poplars. In less than 0.1 mile the long ascent ends as the footpath begins a slight descent, still on the old road. Within the span of 0.1 mile the Bartram intersects two roads. At the first intersection **(mile 1.3)**

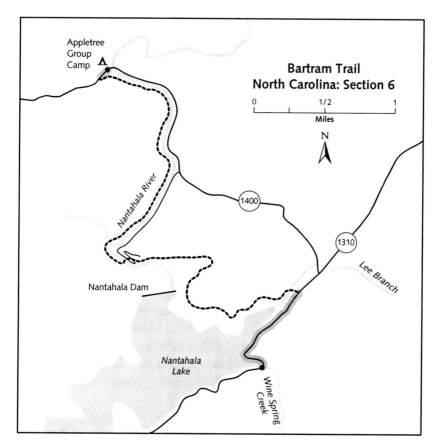

Bartram Trail
North Carolina: Section 6

0   1/2   1
       Miles

N

Appletree
Group
Camp

Nantahala River

1400

1310

Lee Branch

Nantahala Dam

Nantahala
Lake

Wine Spring
Creek

it continues straight ahead. In 100 feet the trail leaves the old road for another road, angling to the right. Almost immediately the trail leaves this road, which is still open to traffic, and turns to the left **(mile 1.4)**, becoming a footpath again. Climbing a ridge, the path curls around to the right and then, in 0.1 mile, enters a switchback. The path ends at a T intersection with another gravel road, also open to vehicle traffic **(mile 1.5)**.

From this intersection, the Bartram turns to the left and follows the gravel road downhill. As the road curves to the left, in approximately 0.1 mile, the trail veers off to the right to become a footpath again. The path briefly parallels the road and then begins to climb an unnamed ridge. After reaching its highest point on the ridge **(mile 1.8)**, the footpath descends into a south-facing cove. For the next 0.5 mile it winds in and out of a series of coves, more or less following the contour line. Nantahala Lake is visible to the left as the path descends from the ridge. The trail then cuts through a small boulder field and small groves of rhododendrons and mountain laurel, and begins a gentle descent for approximately 0.25 mile. As the trail approaches a stream, the path turns sharply to the left onto an old road **(mile 2.4)**. At the turn is a large poplar tree. The descent continues on the old road, paralleling a small stream that empties into the lake. As the path loses elevation, it passes through groves of rhododendrons, crossing another small stream in 0.2 mile **(mile 2.6)**. In a little more than 0.1 mile the trail leaves the old road, turning sharply right (to the west) **(mile 2.7)**. Just to the right is a small level area suitable for camping.

A tenth of a mile after the turn the trail resumes the descent. In another 0.1 mile an old road intersects the trail on the right. The trail continues straight ahead through a grove of rhododendrons. Shortly after the junction, the trail comes to another fork and takes the path to the left. In less than 300 feet this footpath leads to another old road, turning sharply to the right. At the turn there are views of the water sluice from the Nantahala Dam **(mile 3.0)**. Since the dam itself is not visible from this overlook, the sluice takes on the appearance of a 250-foot waterfall cascading over a number of steps through this man-made gorge. Just to the left of the turn is another small area for camping. This area is immediately adjacent to the rim of the gorge, so exercise caution. The Bartram continues to descend on the old road, at a much steeper rate. In 0.25 mile the trail leaves the road to become a footpath again. The descent resumes on two switchbacks over the course of 0.1 mile. After the second switchback the path quickly descends to a gravel road, Nantahala Dam Road **(mile 3.4)**.

At the road the trail turns to the left and in a few feet crosses the concrete ford, which is submerged only in high water. After crossing the river the trail continues on the road until the junction, marked with a sign, with another gravel road to the right, High Water Trail. The Bartram Trail turns to the right and follows this private road downstream for just over 2 miles. After crossing a stream the road and trail intersect another road to the left **(mile 3.7)**; the trail turns to the right. Occasionally there are views of the river to the right, but for the most part the trail is well above and away from it. In 1 mile there is another intersection with a gravel road to the left **(mile 4.7)**; the trail continues straight ahead. After the junction, the trail begins a gradual rise for the next 0.25 mile. In May 1997 there were a number of bear tracks here crossing the road from the wooded area on the left to the river below. After the ascent, the trail crosses another small stream **(mile 5.1)**. In 0.4 mile the trail passes underneath one of the penstocks for the Nantahala Dam aqueduct **(mile 5.5)** and shortly afterward intersects another gravel road. The trail takes a right turn here and follows this road for a few hundred feet until it ends at Junaluska Road (N.C. 1400), then crosses the paved highway and turns to the right. Immediately ahead is the paved entrance to the Appletree Group Camp **(mile 5.6)**. The trail angles to the right, crossing over the lawn, to the post-and-rail fence. Section 7 begins on the other side of the fence.

Appletree Group Camp

This USDA Forest Service group camp is located in the floodplain of a wide bend in the Nantahala River. The camp is the center of a trail system totaling more than 25 miles of trail. Described below are two loop hikes, both including parts of the Bartram Trail.

Laurel Creek Loop

Distance: 8.4 miles (loop following the course of three trails)
Difficulty: moderate (both directions)
Hazards: trails not well blazed
Highlights: wildflowers

Take the Bartram Trail downstream along the Nantahala River. After crossing Piercy Creek **(mile 5.9)** the trail will intersect the northern trailhead for the Laurel Creek Trail in 0.1 mile **(mile 6.0)**. Turn left and ascend on the blue-blazed Laurel Creek Trail for 1.3 miles, where it intersects the yellow-blazed Apple Tree Trail **(mile 7.3)**. Turn left and follow the Apple Tree Trail for 1.1 miles back to the camp **(mile 8.4)**. The Laurel Creek and Apple Tree Trails offer opportunities to see numerous wildflowers and ferns.

London Bald–Junaluska Trail

Distance: 21.2 miles (following the course of three different trails)
Difficulty: moderate to difficult (both directions)
Hazards: trails not well blazed
Highlights: stands of trees more than a century old in the Junaluska Gap area

Take the Bartram Trail downstream along the Nantahala. After the junction for Laurel Creek Trail **(mile 6.0)**, continue on the Bartram until it turns sharply to the right, leaving the road it has been following. At this point **(mile 7.0)** continue straight ahead on the old road, now the Nantahala Trail, for 0.5 mile to Sutherland Gap. The trail is not blazed in this area. At the gap **(mile 7.5)** the trail intersects the London Bald Trail. Turn onto this trail and follow it for 9 miles to its end at Junaluska Gap **(mile 16.5)** and the junction with the Junaluska Trail. The gap is also intersected by Junaluska Road (N.C. 1505). Turn onto the Junaluska Trail and follow it to its end at the Appletree Group Camp **(mile 21.2)**.

For the first 0.6 mile the trail skirts the northern shore of Nantahala Lake and water is readily available. From Nantahala Dam Road to Junaluska Road the trail passes through private property; although the trail has a permanent easement through this area, camping is not allowed.

Water: mile 2.6, stream; mile 3.4, Nantahala River.

Camping: mile 2.7, near Nantahala Lake.

ACCESS POINTS

Nantahala Lake: From Franklin, at the junction of U.S. 441 and U.S. 64, travel west on U.S. 64 for 3.5 miles. Turn right onto N.C. 1442, Old Murphy Road. In a little more than 0.1 mile turn left onto N.C. 1310. Continue on this road for 17 miles, through Wayah Gap, to Nantahala Lake. On the left are two small parking areas next to a large metal Bartram Trail sign.

Appletree Group Camp: From Franklin, follow the directions above to the Nantahala Lake trailhead. From the lake, continue on N.C. 1310 for 0.8 mile to the junction with N.C. 1400. Turn left onto this road, which becomes Junaluska Road (N.C. 1401), and follow it for 2.4 miles. After crossing the Nantahala, the entrance to the camp is immediately to the right. At the entrance, on the right side, is a parking area for public access to the Bartram and other trails. The camp offers four sites for group camping: two for twenty-five people per site; two for fifty people per site. These sites are available from April 1 to October 31, by reservation only. Fee: $30–60 per site. For reservations or more information, contact the USDA Forest Service Cheoah Ranger District, Route 1, Box 16A, Robbinsville, NC 28771; phone: 704-479-6431.

Section 7

Section:	Appletree Group Camp to the Nantahala River
Distance:	11.2 miles
Difficulty:	south to north: moderate; north to south: moderate with difficult climbs
Hazards:	steep drop-offs on the switchbacks descending Rattlesnake Knob
Highlights:	Nantahala River; Piercy Creek; views of Nantahala Gorge
Maps:	Topton; Hewitt (USGS); NCBTS, 6

The trail closely follows the Nantahala River for more than 1.5 miles, offering views of small cascades and rapids, then leaves the river to wind in and out of two large coves, Walnut and Poplar. Climbing out of the latter cove, the footpath crosses over a ridge and descends to Piercy Creek. After fording the stream, the trail intersects Piercy Creek Trail, which leads into the small gorge of the same name. The Bartram Trail then climbs the eastern face of Rattlesnake Knob, affording views of the Nantahala Mountains to the east, and crosses over to the west side of the mountain. This side offers dramatic views of the Snowbird Mountains to the west and Cheoah Bald to the north. The trail descends the steep ridge over a long series of switchbacks. Passing the power company surge tank, the trail follows an access road to N.C. 1310.

The Bartram Trail begins at the small parking area near the entrance to the USDA Forest Service Appletree Group Camp. Walk across the lawn and step over the low wooden post-and-rail fence marked with a Bartram Trail sign. From here, the trail follows the bed of the old Piercy Creek Road, running parallel to the Nantahala River. In 0.25 mile the footpath turns to the right on a gravel road, now closed to vehicles, and runs beside the wooden fence for the group camp. Passing the activity fields for the camp, the path comes to a break in the fence, a passageway leading to Group Sites C and D **(mile 0.4)**. The trail passes by that entrance, continues down the gravel road for 0.2 mile, and then leaves the road, turning sharply to the right. This turn has signs for both the Bartram Trail and the Nantahala Trail **(mile 0.6)**.

For the next mile the Bartram closely parallels the Nantahala River, offering views of small waterfalls and rapids and winding through rhododendron groves interspersed with large stands of white pines and hemlocks. After 0.2 mile **(mile 0.8)** the footpath approaches the very edge of the river, and then in a few hundred feet is completely level with it. This area is alive with wildflowers, including cardinal flower, hawkweed, and bluets, in season, and also a wide variety of ferns, including Christmas ferns and Carolina ferns. Continuing to follow the Nantahala downstream, the path crosses a small, unnamed tributary. After this crossing the floodplain widens, offering flat areas suitable for camping **(mile 1.2)**. From here, the trail enters a grove of hemlocks. To the right is a series of rapids on the Nantahala cascading over three ledges. A short, unmarked spur trail leads to a boulder on the river's edge for a closer view **(mile 1.4)**. Continuing downstream, the path passes through a small boulder field, then descends to another rapid.

From the river's edge, the trail climbs away from the river for less than 0.1 mile, descends to another small stream, levels, and then begins to rise again. After a brief descent the trail joins an old road and begins another ascent, turning to the west (and right) into **Walnut Cove (mile 2.1)**. The footpath par-

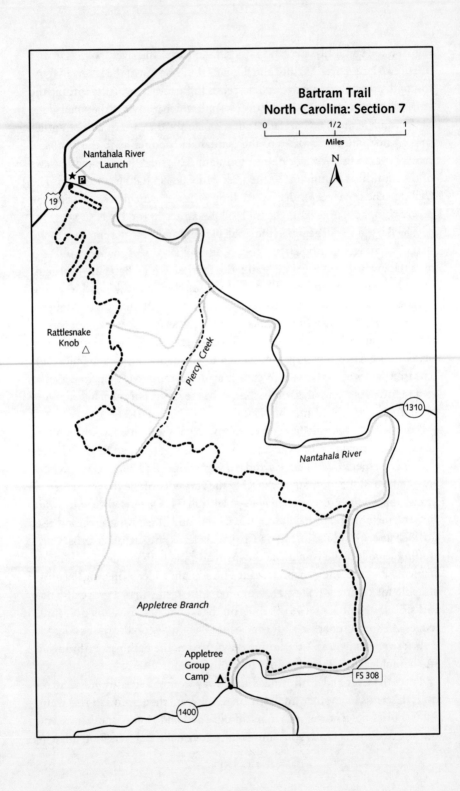

0   1/2   1
Miles

N

Nantahala River
Launch

19

Rattlesnake
Knob

Piercy Creek

1310

Nantahala River

Appletree Branch

Appletree
Group
Camp

FS 308

1400

allels the stream that cuts through the cove, crossing over it in a few hundred feet. The ascent continues after the crossing, at a moderate grade, on the north side of the cove. As the path climbs, it reaches another old jeep road, forming a switchback to the right. The trail and road together exit the cove, level off, and then begin to descend.

After another slight rise of a few hundred feet, the trail descends along an old road into an area where the floor of the forest is carpeted with ferns **(mile 2.4)**. In less than 0.1 mile the footpath leaves the old road and cuts across the east–west ridge. Reaching the ridge's spine in a few hundred feet, it joins an old road and begins to descend into **Poplar Cove**. This descent, at times very steep, returns the Bartram Trail within sight and sound of the river. As the descent continues, the footpath crosses the stream that cuts through Poplar Cove **(mile 2.7)**. Past the crossing, the descent ends in a few hundred feet as the footpath begins running parallel to the Nantahala. Suddenly, it turns sharply to the left and begins a steady climb up the north side of the cove, curling on a wide switchback **(mile 3.0)**. A few hundred feet after the turn, the trail levels, then ascends again at a much gentler pitch. There is a view of a small waterfall in Poplar Cove **(mile 3.4)**. Within a few hundred feet the Bartram Trail again crosses the stream, which is now well below the trail. From here, the ascent continues on another old road, entering a large grove of rhododendrons that form a canopy over the footpath for more than 0.1 mile. Exiting the canopy, the ascent continues and quickly becomes much more pitched **(mile 3.8)** climbing an east–west ridge south of the Nantahala River.

Over the ridge, the path turns right and begins to run down the opposite side of the cove. The trail levels and then begins a gentle climb over the ridge. As the ascent continues, the Bartram joins an old road on the edge of a very steep drop-off to the north, a prelude to the gorge farther to the north **(mile 4.2)**. After leveling, the footpath rolls down and up for 0.1 mile and then descends into a saddle. Crossing the ridge on the opposite side, the path enters Turkey Pen Cove. In the cove the trail enters a wildlife opening **(mile 4.5)**, bearing to the left as it crosses it. Exiting the opening, the trail crosses a small stream and continues to arc to the west and north through this wide cove. Within a few hundred feet there is a junction with an unmarked trail to the left. The Bartram Trail then begins a 0.25-mile descent through large stands of white pines **(mile 5.4)** via a series of wide switchbacks on what were once the hairpin turns of an old road. As the descent ends, the path crosses a tributary of Piercy Creek, then joins the main creek, running parallel to it upstream. Within a few hundred feet it fords **Piercy Creek (mile 5.8)** and then in-

This trail, blazed in blue, follows Piercy Creek to its confluence with the Nantahala River. The trail is 1.5 miles long and descends steadily through the small gorge created by this mountain stream. N.C. 1310 is on the opposite bank of the Nantahala River. The best place to ford the river is approximately 200 feet upstream from Piercy Creek. After heavy rains, the water can be waist-deep or higher.

---

tersects the blue-blazed **Piercy Creek Trail**. In this area are several small flat areas suitable for camping.

From the junction, the Bartram Trail begins to climb again on an old road. In 0.1 mile it intersects the blue-blazed **Laurel Creek Trail (mile 5.9)**. The path continues to ascend into a grove of mountain laurels, which soon form a canopy over the footpath. After crossing a small stream **(mile 6.3)** the trail curls to the left and continues its climb on the old road. As the ascent eases, the Bartram Trail turns sharply to the right, leaving the road **(mile 7.0)**. The trail, now a footpath again, climbs the side of the ridge heading northeast. Curling to the northwest, it climbs one of the tall shoulders of Rattlesnake Knob. Due east are views of Wesser Bald and Cooper Ridge Bald **(mile 7.3)**. At the base of the knob, the footpath begins to wind in and out of a series of nine east-facing coves. As the trail heads in a northerly direction, it generally holds the contour line, rolling gently up and down. In the middle of the second east-facing cove **(mile 7.5)** there is a small stream with water in late May. For the next 0.75 mile the path coils through five additional coves, all offering views of the mountains to the east. The forest is predominantly hardwood interspersed with groves of mountain laurels and rhododendrons. Lining the trail are numerous wildflowers; in late spring, sweet cicely and bluets are in bloom. The inside of the fifth cove offers a small streamlet with water in late May **(mile 8.2)**.

After 0.2 mile the trail passes through a large mountain laurel grove. As it exits the grove the main ridge of the Nantahala Mountains is visible; from south to north: Wayah Bald, Cooper Bald, and Wesser Bald **(mile 8.4)**. In a little more than 0.1 mile the trail curls into the eighth east-facing cove, where it joins with an old jeep road for more than 0.25 mile. Exiting the cove, the trail and road enter the last cove, crossing the last of Rattlesnake's eastern spurs. From the ridge there are views of Cheoah Bald to the north **(mile 8.7)**. As the trail descends, there is a view to the west of a 15-foot waterfall. In a few hundred feet the trail crosses the stream below the waterfall **(mile 8.9)**. The trail gently climbs for a little more than 0.1 mile to a gap on the northern ridge of Rattlesnake Knob **(mile 9.0)**.

From the gap, the trail crosses over to the west side of the ridge and begins a rapid descent of this steep ridge, losing more than 600 feet in less than 0.5 mile. Ten switchbacks moderate the effect of the descent. After the second switchback, the footpath passes a boundary marker for the Nantahala Power and Light Company **(mile 9.2)**. From here there are views of the Snowbird Mountains to the west and Cheoah Bald to the north. After the fifth switchback there is a view of the northern end of the Nantahala Gorge and the overlook on U.S. 129 on the west side of the gorge. After the eighth switchback the path passes through a boulder field. Within a few hundred feet there is the first view of the power company's surge tank **(mile 9.4)**. There is a very small area for camping on the point near the tank. From here the trail continues to descend to the base of the 200-foot tank **(mile 9.5)**.

The Bartram begins a 1.6-mile descent to Nantahala Road, following the power company's gravel access road. Less than 0.25 mile from the tank, on the left, is a spring with water in early June. As the descent continues, the road intersects a road to the right. The trail continues straight ahead. In less than 100 feet there is a second intersection **(mile 10.4)**. The trail takes the road to the right and continues the descent. As it turns to the north there are views of the Nantahala River flowing downstream from right to left **(mile 11.1)**. In less than 0.1 mile the trail turns sharply to the left, leaving the gravel road. A footpath again, the trail continues to descend via a short switchback. The switchback ends at another gravel road, the northern terminus of Section 7, with a small parking area on the side of the road. The road leads to the left, to N.C. 1310 and the parking area for the Nantahala launch site. To continue on to Section 8, turn to the right and follow the road to the right **(mile 11.2)**.

WATER AND CAMPING

Water: miles 0.0–1.5 closely parallel the Nantahala River; mile 2.1, Walnut Cove stream; mile 2.7, Poplar Cove stream; mile 5.8, Piercy Creek; mile 7.5, east cove on Rattlesnake Knob; mile 8.9, stream south of the gap on Rattlesnake Knob.

Camping: mile 1.2, near the Nantahala River; mile 5.8, Piercy Creek just to the north of the trailhead for the Piercy Creek Trail; mile 9.4, small area just north of the surge tank.

ACCESS POINTS

Appletree Group Camp: From Franklin and the junction of U.S. 441 and
U.S. 64, travel west on U.S. 64 for 3.5 miles. Turn right onto N.C. 1442,
Old Murphy Road. In a little more than 0.1 mile, turn left onto N.C.
1310. Continue on this road for 18.0 miles, past both Wayah Bald Road
and Nantahala Lake. Turn left on N.C. 1400 and take this road for 2.5
miles to the Appletree Group Camp.

Nantahala Gorge: At the junction of U.S. 19 and N.C. 1310, turn onto
N.C. 1310, Wayah Road. Take this paved road for 4.1 miles, past the
northern trailhead for Section 7. At the junction with F.S. 308, turn
right onto the gravel road. Take F.S. 308 for 3.2 miles, where it ends at
N.C. 1401. Turn right onto the state highway and cross the bridge over
the Nantahala. The entrance for the group camp is immediately on
the right. There is a small gravel parking lot outside the camp's gate.
Do not park inside the campground.

Nantahala River: At the junction of U.S. 19 and N.C. 1310, turn right on
N.C. 1310. Take this paved road for 0.2 mile, then turn right onto a
gravel road on Nantahala Power and Light Company property. There
is a small parking area just to the right as the road widens.

Section 8

Section: Nantahala River (near the launch site) to Cheoah Bald
Distance: 6.6 miles
Difficulty: difficult (both directions)
Hazards: steep ascents
Highlights: views of Nantahala Gorge; views from Cheoah Bald
Maps: Hewitt (USGS); NCBTS, 7

The last section of the Bartram Trail in North Carolina begins in the Nantahala Gorge. For the first 1.5 miles the trail is level as it follows the course of
the Nantahala River downstream. Crossing the river and U.S. 19, the trail exits the gorge and begins a steady and steep 5-mile climb. The ascending trail
follows the course of Ledbetter Creek upstream. En route are views of the
gorge and Bartram Falls on the creek. The climb ends at the junction with the
Appalachian Trail. Here the Bartram Trail turns east and follows the footpath
of the Appalachian Trail to the summit of Cheoah Bald.

The trailhead for this section is on the south side of N.C. 1310, across from
the parking area. Walk along the highway and across the bridge over the
channel from the power station, turn left, and cut through the parking lot for

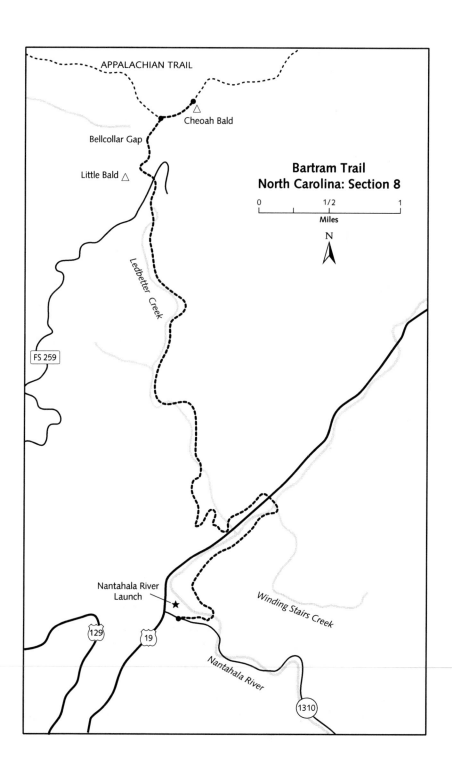

APPALACHIAN TRAIL

Cheoah Bald △

Bellcollar Gap

Little Bald △

**Bartram Trail
North Carolina: Section 8**

0   1/2   1
Miles

N

Ledbetter Creek

FS 259

Nantahala River
Launch ★

Winding Stairs Creek

129   19

Nantahala River

1310

commercial rafting put-ins. In a little more than 200 feet, cross over the channel again on the metal bridge with the **Mountains to the Seas Trail** sign. Follow the path for a few hundred feet to the 150-foot metal bridge over the Nantahala River. The path, now asphalt, follows the river downstream on the east side. For the most part the river is invisible from the trail. The two trails cross over the eastern channel of the Nantahala on **Winding Stairs Bridge (mile 1.4)**, a single-lane highway bridge. In just a few feet the trail crosses the western channel of the river on a second steel highway bridge. The path heads to the west, soon reaching U.S. 19.

Right on the other side of the highway the trail comes to the railroad that parallels U.S. 19. Passing underneath the power lines, the trail begins to climb, heading to the southwest. The footpath descends to cross a small stream **(mile 1.8)**, then quickly ascends on the other side; a few hundred feet after the creek there is a small level area for camping. The path levels out and then curls downward, turning first to the west and then to the north. Soon afterward the trail reaches a trail junction **(mile 1.9)**, a small camping area to the left, and then the first crossing of Ledbetter Creek. For the next 3 miles the Bartram Trail follows the creek's watershed on a steep ascent out of the Nantahala Gorge.

After crossing the creek, the trail begins a steady ascent. In 0.1 mile there is a sharp drop-off to the left with a view of the gorge to the south. As the path approaches the top of the ridge it turns sharply right, forming a long, steep switchback. Climbing the ridge, on the eastern side, the trail turns to the west and then levels for a short distance. The ascent resumes, with sheer drop-offs to the right, ending in a small gap **(mile 2.6)**. From here the trail follows an old roadbed for more than 0.75 mile. After a brief ascent, the footpath descends into the valley created by Ledbetter Creek. En route are small boulder fields and groves of mountain laurels. The trail reaches and then crosses the creek a second time **(mile 3.4)**.

The Bartram Trail follows the creek upstream, curling to the west. The path is level for several hundred feet, then it begins to climb again on an old road, although the pitch is not as steep as before. Climbing on the west side of Ledbetter Creek, the trail crosses over one of the creek's tributaries **(mile 3.8)** on the east side of Nolton Ridge. Continuing to the north the footpath enters a small gorge where the creek winds through a group of room-size boulders. After a few hundred feet the creek shoots through a 100-foot-long sluice, with another sluice immediately upstream. Soon afterward the old road descends to within 15 feet of the creek, then crosses over another side stream, with a second crossing in less than 0.1 mile **(mile 4.3)**. The ascent becomes pitched for less than 0.1 mile. As the path levels, Bartram Falls comes into view to the right **(mile 4.5)**.

From the overlook, the path descends to another side stream, then climbs to near the top of Bartram Falls for a view of the creek cascading downward. The trail continues to climb, at first paralleling the stream and then crossing over it. The path then rises and falls and makes another crossing over Ledbetter Creek **(mile 4.7)**. Another steep ascent begins, interrupted by a descent to a wooden bridge crossing over the creek **(mile 4.9)**. Climbing out of the small gorge, the path begins to roll, with slight descents. The climb resumes, with some sharp ascents, before it intersects an old road. Following the roadbed for a few hundred feet, the Bartram crosses over Ledbetter Creek for the last time **(mile 5.5)**. Immediately beyond the crossing is a small area suitable for camping. In a little more than 0.1 mile the trail intersects F.S. 259.

The trail crosses the road and begins a very sharp climb for more than 0.1 mile (this section would greatly benefit from switchbacks). The climb eases as the Bartram Trail reaches the ridge off the northeast shoulder of Little Bald. On the ridge the ascent continues, although it is not as pitched. The ridge then levels as the trail rolls up and down into Bellcollar Gap **(mile 6.1)**. From the gap, the climb resumes. In less than 0.1 mile there is a level section with views of the mountains to the south and east. The trail curls up the ridge, with two switchbacks, and joins the Appalachian Trail once again **(mile 6.4)**. Just before the junction there is a small camping area. The Bartram Trail continues to the right, following the path of the Appalachian Trail to the summit of **Cheoah Bald**. The climb resumes on the top of a narrow ridge with steep drop-offs to the left and right. In less than 0.1 mile the two trails reach the summit **(mile 6.6)**. Cheoah Bald offers an outstanding view of the Great Smoky Mountains to the north and the Nantahalas to the east.

ACCESS POINTS

Nantahala River (Beechertown): From the junction of U.S. 19 and N.C. 1310, turn right on S.R. 1310. Take this paved road for 0.2 mile, then turn right onto a gravel road that enters Nantahala Power and Light Company property. There is a small parking area just to the right as the road widens. The paved Forest Service lot on the north side of N.C. 1310 is reserved for rafters. Do not park there.

Journey to
the Gulf Coast

Travels to the Creek Nation

After he returned from his journey into Cherokee country, Bartram stayed several weeks at Fort James Dartmouth conducting "little botanical expeditions" into Georgia as far as the head of the Broad River (T375). Regrettably, no account of these expeditions survives. During his stay at the fort he learned that a "company of adventurers" was preparing to set off to West Florida, the newly established British colony spanning the area from Pensacola to the Mississippi. The group was to be led by plantation owner and trader George Whitfield, a nephew of George Whitfield the evangelist, whom Bartram and his father met in 1765 at Bethesda. Bartram joined the company Whitfield had assembled at Fort Charlotte, on the opposite side of the Savannah River. Departing on June 22, the group journeyed down the South Carolina side of the river. Three days later, and without Whitfield (who had been summoned to Charleston by Henry Laurens to profess his loyalty to the Revolutionary cause), they crossed the Savannah River near the location of today's Price Ferry, 5 miles upstream from the mouth of the Little River.[1] In Georgia they followed a road paralleling the Little River that would lead them to Flat Rock and the junction with the "great trading Road from Augusta to the Creek Nation." Flat Rock, a "common rendezvous . . . for traders and Indians" (T376), was located on one of the headwaters of Middle Creek a few miles northwest of today's Camak, Georgia.

Lower Creek Trading Path

At Flat Rock, two more companies of traders from Augusta joined Whitfield's caravan. These traders were also bound for the Creek towns along the Chattahoochee River, south of today's Columbus, Georgia. On June 28 the traders and more than eighty horses set off on the long journey. From Flat Rock they would follow the Lower Creek Trading Path to the southwest, through the sandy fall line at the base of the Piedmont hills. Today, the bed of the Old

1. Cashin, *William Bartram and the American Revolution*, 162.

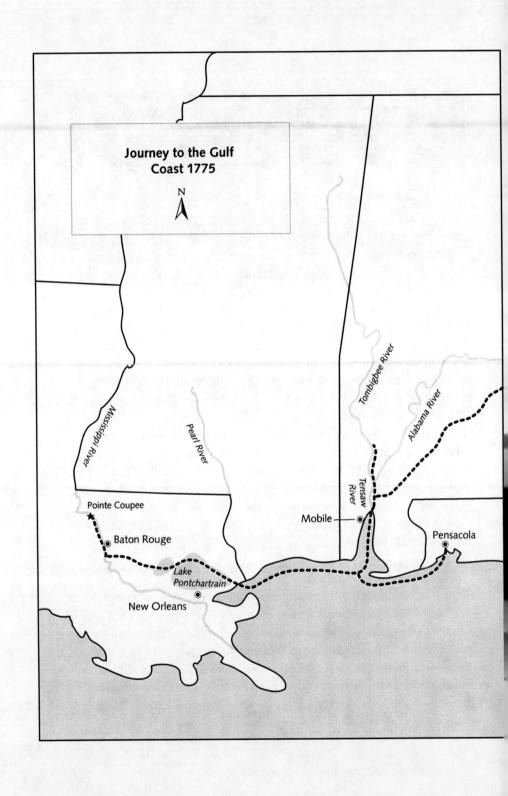

Journey to the Gulf
Coast 1775

N

Mississippi River

Pearl River

Tombigbee River

Alabama River

Tensaw River

Pointe Coupee

Baton Rouge

Lake Pontchartrain

New Orleans

Mobile

Pensacola

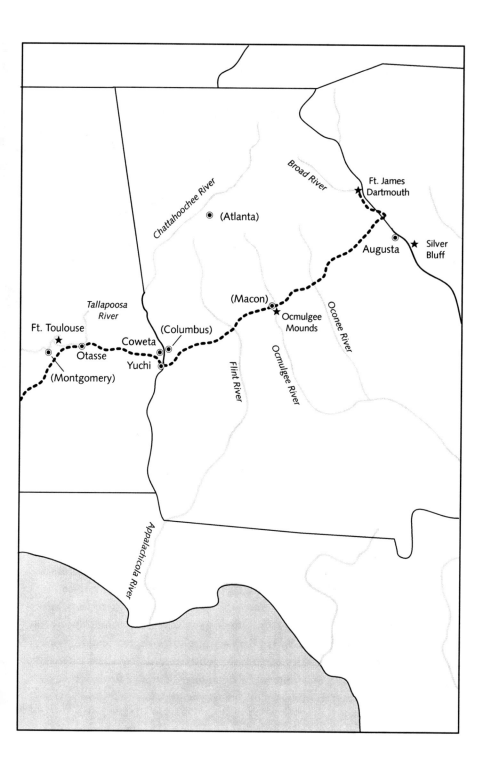

Chattahoochee River

Broad River

Ft. James
Dartmouth

⊙ (Atlanta)

Silver
⊙ Bluff
Augusta

Tallapoosa
River

(Macon)
⊙

Oconee River

Ft. Toulouse
⊙ Otasse

(Columbus)
Coweta
⊙

Ocmulgee
Mounds

(Montgomery)

Yuchi

Flint River

Ocmulgee River

Appalachicola River

Flat Rock, west of Camak, Georgia.

Georgia Railroad best approximates this route from Augusta to Macon (T394). On the evening of July 1, the caravan camped on the banks of the Oconee River at the site of "Old Oconee Town," today's Rock Landing, 5 miles southeast of today's Milledgeville, near Reedy Creek Lake. After the Yamasee War the Oconees had abandoned the town and moved to lands held by the Upper Creeks. (They were not happy with their new home and around 1750 migrated into central Florida, where they became known as Seminoles.) Fording the river, the caravan pressed on to the southwest. As they approached the Ocmulgee River they encountered "the famous Oakmulge fields, where are yet the very wonderful remains of the power and grandeur of the ancients"— the **Ocmulgee Site.**

Creek Nation

Fording the river near the site of today's U.S. 80 bridge in downtown Macon, the caravan rode to the west-southwest. Today's Knoxville Road, from Macon to Knoxville, is built on the bed of the traders' path. The caravan reached the Flint River on July 5. Twenty years later, on the east side of the river on today's Ga. 128, Benjamin Hawkins set up his large plantation, where he acted as the U.S. agent to the Creek Nation.

After fording the river, the caravan continued westward through the site of abandoned Fort Perry. The road continued westward paralleling the Upatoi Creek, the northern boundary of today's Chattahoochee County. Bartram and the traders crossed the Chattahoochee near Kyles Mound, entering the ancient town of **Yuchi** (Bartram's "Uche"), one of the most important towns of the Lower Creeks. The Lower Creeks had been one of the Creek Confederacy's major geopolitical divisions since the seventeenth century, with more than a dozen towns on both sides of the Chattahoochee River from today's West Point, Georgia, to Eufaula, Alabama, as well as towns along the Flint, Ocmulgee, and Oconee Rivers. The other major divisions were the Upper Creeks, who occupied more than thirty-five towns along the Tallapoosa and Alabama Rivers in today's central Alabama, and the Seminoles in Florida. Kathryn Braund notes that although these three divisions "held separate councils, claimed separate territories, and very often pursued different foreign policies" with both other Indians and whites, they considered themselves one people, the Creek Nation.[2]

From Yuchi, Bartram traveled to the south to **Apalachicola**, where he stayed for a week. During that time he visited the ruins of the "antient Apalachicola" and the site of the abandoned Spanish fort.

On July 18 Bartram and the original caravan of traders set out for Mobile.[3] The two groups of traders who had joined them at Flat Rock chose to stay in the Lower Creeks' lands, "betaking themselves to the several towns in the Nation where they were respectively bound" (T395). Bartram's party traveled north for a little more than 10 miles to rejoin the main trading path. At the junction they turned west, passing through present-day Sandfort and Uchee, Alabama. West of Uchee the path turned to the northwest, toward today's Society Hill. The path crossed Opintlocco Creek twice as it worked its way to the

2. Kathryn Braund, *Deerskins and Duffels*, 7.

3. According to Harper (*Travels*, 404), Bartram's use of the date July 13 for the departure from the Lower Creek towns was most likely a slip for July 18.

Tallapoosa River, just west of today's Tuskegee National Forest. After three days Bartram and the traders arrived at Tallassee, the confluence of Euphaupe Creek and the Tallapoosa River (T401). From there they traveled down the left bank of the river, past **Otasse** to Coolome, where they stayed for two days as guests of the town's leading trader, Mr. Germany. **Coolome**, 10 miles northeast of today's Montgomery, was located on a "charming fruitful plain." Bartram was impressed with the Indian town, noting that the "houses are neat, commodious buildings, a wooden frame with plaistered walls, and roofed with Cypress bark or shingles; every habitation consists of four oblong square houses, of the same form and dimensions, and so situated as to form an exact square" (T396–397). The Creeks who lived in these buildings had a purpose for each: cook room, winter house, summerhouse, granary, and warehouse, if engaged in trading.

The Route to Mobile

On July 24 Bartram and the traders set out from Coolome for the weeklong trek to the Tensaw River. They followed the main trading path through modern Mitylene and Pinedale, suburbs of Montgomery. Continuing to the south west, the path passed to the east of modern-day Fort Deposit on its way toward Burnt Corn. In Butler County, Alabama, two highways built on the path have been designated Bartram Trail: a section of Ala. 185 north of Fort Dale, and part of C.R. 54 north of Wolf Creek. South of Butler County, Bartram and the traders followed the ridgeline separating the watersheds of the Alabama and Conecuh Rivers. Today's Old Stage Coach Road on the county line between Monroe and Conecuh Counties follows the route of the trading path. The trading path continued to the southwest, along parts of today's C.R. 47, to a point between today's Stockton and Perdido. Here the main path intersected an east–west trail connecting the main path with the Tensaw River. Bartram and the traders turned west, through today's Gopher Hill, toward the river.

Ocmulgee Site: Ocmulgee National Monument

On the east bank of the Ocmulgee River, just east of downtown Macon, a Mississippian settlement flourished between A.D. 900 and 1000. The Mississippians, who displaced the Woodland Indians, were farmers who raised corn, beans, squash, and tobacco. More than 1,000 people lived in this settlement, most inhabiting thatched huts. Bartram saw, as visitors do today, the seven large earthen mounds that formed the culture's public ceremony sites. The largest, the Great Temple Mound, rises 45 feet from a base of 300 by 270 feet. Little is

Great Temple Mound, Ocmulgee National Monument, Macon, Georgia.

known about the role or function of the mounds. Three of the mounds—Great Temple, Lesser Temple, and Cornfield—were topped by wooden structures. Archaeologists believe that these structures were used for religious ceremonies. The fourth mound, now known as the Funeral Mound, was the burial place for village leaders. Immediately southeast of the Cornfield Mound was the Earth Lodge. This circular building, more than 40 feet in diameter with a wooden roof and clay floor, was not a residence but the council chamber or council house. Lining the walls were permanent "seats," presumably for the council members, with a large seat placed directly opposite the entrance. At the center was a fire pit. The Earth Lodge was reconstructed in 1937 and is open to the public.[4] North of the Great Temple Mound and west

4. Walker, "A Brief History of Ocmulgee Archaeology," 23–24.

Earth Lodge, Ocmulgee National Monument, Macon, Georgia.

of the Funeral Mound is the Trading Post, the site of a migrant Creek settlement. The post was a fortified trading center, two buildings within a stockade. On the perimeter of the stockade was a partially completed ditch, most likely a moat. Surrounding the center were a number of Indian houses, a spur trail to the main trading path, graves, and middens.

The Lower Creeks migrated to the Ocmulgee site in the early 1690s, leaving the Chattahoochee Valley to avoid Spanish aggression and to move closer to their new trading partners in Carolina. Spain's disapproval of the Creeks' new trading relations had been made clear in late 1685, when Spanish soldiers attacked Coweta and destroyed Henry Woodward's half-built trading hut.

Two years later the Spanish built a fortress on the Chattahoochee near the Creek town of Apalachicola. In response, many Creeks left the valley to found new settlements on the Ocmulgee and Oconee Rivers. In the aftermath of the Yamasee War in 1715, the Creeks abandoned Ocmulgee and either returned to the Chattahoochee Valley or moved south into Florida.

The Ocmulgee National Monument offers a trail system connecting all seven of the mounds, including the Earth Lodge, and the site of the Trading Post. Park rangers have laid out four suggested walks—all loop hikes—ranging in distance from 0.6 to 3 miles. All of the trails begin at the visitors' center; three of the trails, hiking clockwise, begin with the monument's Bartram Trail. This short path, 0.3 mile long, descends from the parking lot at the visitors' center, over the railroad tracks, to a small stream. Crossing on a footbridge, the trail rises to its southern terminus at a trail junction near the Southeast Mound. To the right is the Bluff Trail, leading to the Trading Post; to the left is the Opelofa Trail, leading to Walnut Creek and the Great Temple Mound.

The visitors' center houses exhibits on the life and culture of Ocmulgee's earliest inhabitants, from Paleo-Indians (around 9000 B.C.) through the historic period (1690–1715).

The monument is located in Macon, off U.S. 80, east of downtown. Operated by the National Park Service, it is open every day except Christmas and New Year's Day.

LOWER CREEK TOWNS

Chattahoochee Riverwalk

Section:	South Trail: downtown Columbus to National Infantry Museum
Distance:	10.9 miles, all paved
Difficulty:	easy
Hazards:	none
Highlights:	site of Coweta; Uchee Creek

As a part of an effort to revitalize its riverfront, the city of Columbus made plans in 1992 to construct a paved multiuse recreation path along the course of the Chattahoochee. Today this path, the Riverwalk, is 14 miles long in two sections, the North Trail and the South Trail. Both sections begin at the Riverwalk Pavilion, on 9th Street on the river in downtown Columbus. The North

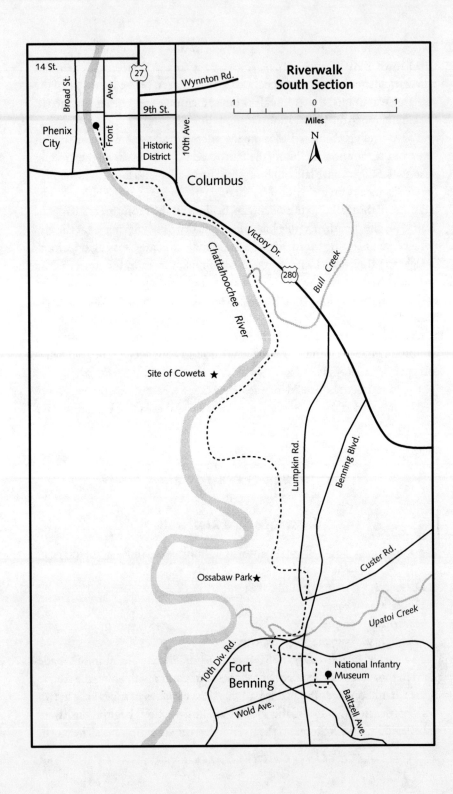

Trail extends upstream to the Eagle and Phenix Dam, built in the early nineteenth century. Below the dam are the rapids described by Benjamin Hawkins as the Chattahoochee Falls, the head of navigation on the river. After a two-block interruption, the trail resumes at 14th Street and continues along the left bank for another 3.5 miles to Municipal Park. When completed, the North Trail will total 7 miles. The 10-mile-long South Trail connects downtown Columbus with Fort Benning. This section, completed in 1996, works downstream, also on the left bank, past Bull Creek and the site of the ancient Creek city of Coweta. After 5 miles the walk leaves the river and meanders around Oxbow Lake, past the Oxbow Environmental Learning Center, then enters Fort Benning, crosses Upatoi Creek, and climbs the bluff to the Main Post.

Riverwalk: South Trail

The trailhead is at the fountain off 9th Street to the west of Bay Street. Continue to the south. In a little more than 0.25 mile there is a steep path to the top of the bluff, near the Coca-Cola Space Science Museum immediately west of Columbus's historic district. Continue south on the paved path under the U.S. 80 bridge **(mile 0.6)**. On the bluff to the left is a sign marking the spot where Bartram forded the river on his return from Manchac in early January 1776. According to the *Travels,* however, he crossed the river near the "point towns" south of today's Fort Mitchell (T457). From the bridge, the Riverwalk enters the South Commons—a large recreation area that is home to Columbus's Civic Center and baseball stadium. As it approaches the southern end of the area, the trail splits **(mile 1.2)**. The trail to the left climbs the bluff, providing access to the Commons, and then returns to the river. The trail to the right remains close to the river, crossing a tributary of the Chattahoochee on a narrow wooden bridge. Just below the point where the two paths merge, the Riverwalk reaches the public boat ramp at Rotary Park. To the left is a large parking area. Between the parking area and the trail is the Bulldog Bait and Tackle Shop, which sells snacks and drinks. To its right are public restrooms. Straight ahead is Rotary Park **(mile 1.9)**. The trail continues to follow the riverbank, moving away from the Chattahoochee to cross Bull Creek **(mile 2.8)**. Near the mouth of the creek was a significant Mississippian site. As the path returns to the riverbank, on the left is the Bull Creek Overlook, a bluff overlooking the river **(mile 3.0)**. A small gazebo surrounded by picnic tables crowns the summit. To the west is a sign for the site of the Creek town of Coweta.

Continue south from the overlook. In a little more than 0.5 mile the River-walk enters Rigdon Park. The first access trail to the park climbs to the left

The ancient city of Coweta sat on the west side of the Chattahoochee River, south of the city limit of today's Phenix City. With a population of approximately 1,000, it was one of the largest Indian towns in the Southeast. The town was nearly 2 miles long. It extended down the right bank of the Chattahoochee from today's Bull Creek Overlook to 0.5 mile north of the mouth of Cochgalchee Creek. In his records Bartram placed the town 12 miles north of Uchee. Coweta was a "bloody town," where wars could be declared and capital punishment carried out, as opposed to a "white," or peace, town.

(mile 3.7). Sitting on a bluff, the park is chiefly a recreation park with athletic fields; it also offers restrooms and parking. The second access trail is a little more than 0.1 mile farther on. Soon the river and path begin to bend to the right and the southwest. After the bend the path crosses a small stream **(mile 4.5)**. In approximately 0.5 mile the Riverwalk veers left and leaves the Chattahoochee. As it nears the Columbus Water Works, there is a large parking area for the trail. The trail crosses the access road to the parking area and then works its way southeast along the banks of Oxbow Lake. In this section there are a number of access points for the trail, each with a small parking area connected to the Columbus Water Works access road. Crossing the access road again **(mile 6.6)** the trail winds between a golf course to the left and Oxbow Park to the right (to the west). The path crosses a small stream over a concrete bridge and approaches a gravel road **(mile 7.9)**. In 0.1 mile the Riverwalk reaches the Oxbow Meadows Environmental Learning Center **(mile 8.0)**.

The path heads directly east, crossing Lumpkin Road **(mile 8.2)**. On the east side of the road the Riverwalk comes into a wooded section as it enters Fort Benning. After it crosses Custer Road, there is a spur trail to the left leading to Fort Benning's information center, with restrooms and adjacent parking. Continue south down the path, which soon angles to the left, joining Benning Road to cross **Upatoi Creek (mile 9.3)**. The path turns to the right and soon crosses, to the left, 10th Division Road **(mile 9.8)**. On the south bank of the creek, parallel to both the road and the Riverwalk, was the trading path that Bartram followed to the Chattahoochee. From the crossing there are two steep climbs, the first to Sigerfoos Road, the second to Lumpkin Road. The climb ends as the Riverwalk reaches the bluff **(mile 10.4)**. The path winds behind houses and then turns south toward Wold Street. Crossing the street, the path becomes a sidewalk to the left of the road. In a few hundred feet the trail ends in front of the **National Infantry Museum (mile 10.9)**.

The city of Columbus established this 1,600-acre park in 1996. The park sits on the city's former landfill and extends north to Oxbow Lake. The land is in the process of being reclaimed as a wetland, as it was before the twentieth century. Southwest of the Riverwalk is the Environmental Learning Center, which has a lecture/presentation room used for educational programs. The center offers a number of exhibits on the flora and fauna of the Chattahoochee Valley. The center is also the trailhead for two short hiking trails: the Riparian Woodlands Loop, around a wetland pond, and the Trail of Measurements. Staff and volunteers offer guided trail walks.

The city of Columbus, the Columbus Water Works, and Columbus State University jointly operate the park, which is an outreach program of Columbus State University.

PARKING AND ACCESS

Riverwalk Pavilion: The pavilion is in downtown Columbus, west of the corner of 9th and Bay Streets. The easiest access is off Dillingham Street just east of the bridge to Phenix City. There is public parking north of the fountain, on Bay Street, and at the Coca-Cola Space Museum.

Columbus Water Works: The Columbus Water Works are located off Lumpkin Drive, south of Victory Drive. Along the plant's access road, Water Drive, are a number of parking areas for Riverwalk users. At the end of the road is a large parking area near the halfway point of the walk.

National Infantry Museum: The museum is on Baltzell Avenue on the Main Post. Signs on I-185 and Benning Road direct visitors to the museum. There is public parking in the drive in front of the museum.

Yuchi Town Bike Tour

Section: National Infantry Museum to Uchee Army Campground
Distance: 11 miles (one-way)
Difficulty: easy
Hazards: none
Highlights: site of Yuchi; Chattahoochee River

This bicycle tour starts at the southern trailhead of the Riverwalk, at the National Infantry Museum. The first 4 miles go through the Main Post of Fort Benning. Gently descending from the bluff, the tour enters the wide flood-

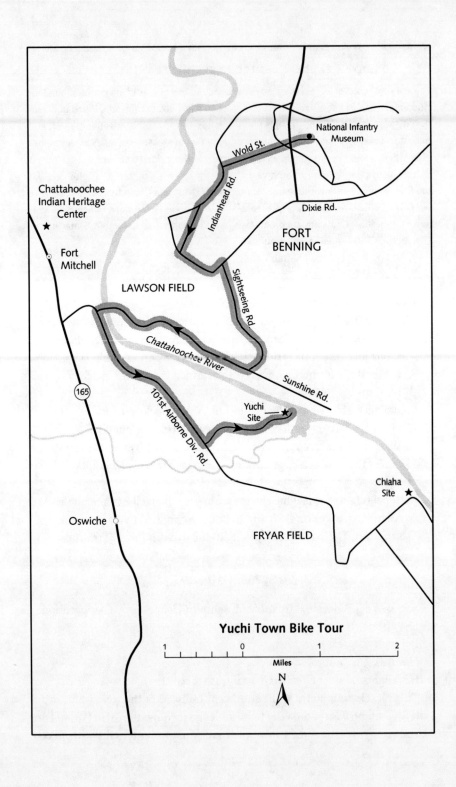

Yuchi Town Bike Tour

Chattahoochee
Indian Heritage
Center ★

Fort
Mitchell ○

National Infantry
Museum ●

Wold St.

Indianhead Rd.

Dixie Rd.

FORT
BENNING

LAWSON FIELD

Sightseeing Rd.

Chattahoochee River

Sunshine Rd.

165

101st Airborne Div. Rd.

Yuchi
Site ★

Chiaha
Site ★

Oswiche ○

FRYAR FIELD

Miles

1   0   1   2

N

plain of the Chattahoochee, the former site of the city of Cusseta, or Kasihta. Crossing the river, the path enters a second-growth forest of mixed pines and hardwoods. The tour ends at the Uchee Army Campground, which has an interpretive display on the Creek towns of Yuchi and old Apalachicola and the Spanish fort nearby. There is a spur trail to the approximate site of Chiaha.

The tour begins on Baltzell Avenue in front of the museum. Follow the road to the right (west). In less than 0.5 mile Baltzell intersects with Lumpkin Road. Continue straight ahead as the street becomes Wold Avenue. A mile past the intersection, turn left onto Anderson Street **(mile 1.5)**. Anderson, after crossing Marchant Street, becomes Indianhead Road. Below the intersection is a fork, with Bradshaw to the right and Indianhead to the left. Continue on Indianhead, which ends at a T intersection with Jacelin Road **(mile 3.0)**. Directly ahead is Lawson Field, an army airfield built on a wide section of the Chattahoochee floodplain. This was the site of Cusseta, one of the most important and largest of the Lower Creek towns. To work around the southeast boundary of the airfield, turn left onto Jacelin. In less than a mile, turn right onto Sightseeing Road **(mile 3.8)**. At the junction with Sunshine Road, turn right. The airfield is on the right side of the road; a pine forest is to the left. Soon the road crosses the Chattahoochee River **(mile 7.2)** and enters Alabama. In 0.5 mile Sunshine Road intersects 101st Airborne Road. Turn left onto this road, which passes through a heavily wooded area used for army training. In less than 2 miles the road reaches Uchee Campground Road **(mile 9.3)**. Turn left and follow the road to the east.

The road continues to work through a wooded section considerably north of Uchee Creek. It passes the Boy Scout camp on the right as it enters the Uchee Creek Army Campground. On the right is the Campground Country Store (open to the public) with water, food, and restrooms. At Barnard Trail Road turn left; in a few hundred feet on the right is the interpretive display for archaeological sites on the base **(mile 11.0)**.

En route from Flat Rock, Bartram and the traders' caravan arrived at the Chattahoochee opposite **Yuchi**. They were ferried across the river on large canoes while the Indians swam their horses across. On the west bank the caravan entered the town, which was just below the mouth of today's Uchee Creek.[5] Bartram described "the Uche town" as "the largest, most compact and best situated Indian town I ever saw; the habitations are large and neatly built; the walls of the houses are constructed of a wooden frame, then lathed

5. Hurt, "The Preliminary Archaeological Survey of the Chattahoochee Valley Area in Alabama," 19.

*The Yuchi Historic Site is on the site of a Yuchi Indian
town on today's Fort Benning (Alabama side).*

From Uche town, Bartram traveled 8 miles south over "a level plain consisting of ancient Indian plantations" to Apalachicola. The town was located on the river 1.5 miles south of the mouth of Ihagee Creek—east of today's Holy Church Monastery and Shrine. Bartram described Apalachicola as the "mother town or capital" of the Lower Creeks. Although the town did not have a large population, it was the leading peace, or "white," town (as opposed to a "bloody town" such as Coweta)—the site where deputies met in conferences to deliberate on subjects of "high importance for the prosperity of the commonwealth" (T399–400). Bartram stayed in Apalachicola for a week while exploring the area. One of his trips was led by the chief trader, who took Bartram to the "ruins and site of the ancient Apalachucla." This town, 1.5 miles downstream from the new town, was the site of the original settlement abandoned

twenty years earlier because of the extensive flooding to which this river bend was subject. Bartram could still make out the old town's key features: "we viewed the mounds or terraces, on which formerly stood their town house or rotunda and square or areopagus" (T390).

Behind the mounds was a "vast artificial terrace or four square mound." This terrace was the foundation for Fort Apalachicola, built by the Spanish on the river in 1689 as part of Spain's attempt to resume trade with the Creeks, which was being diverted to the English in Charleston. Within two years the Spanish had abandoned the fort.

Archaeologists have excavated both sites. Regrettably, the site of the Spanish fort was vandalized and looted, and more recently was damaged by the river. A historical marker on Ala. 165, 5 miles south of Fort Mitchell, commemorates the site of the fort farther to the east.

---

and plaistered inside and out with a reddish well tempered clay or morter, which gives them the appearance of red brick walls" (T388). The town was "populous and thriving" with a population estimated to be close to 1,500 (T388). Although Yuchi was one of the largest of the twenty Creek Lower towns, its people were "conscious of the fact that they were Yuchis, not Muskogees." The Yuchis had their own language, which Bartram mistook for a dialect of Shawnee. They were often at variance with the Creeks, "but wise enough to unite against a common enemy, to support the interest and glory of the general Creek confederacy" (T389). The Yuchis also built villages on the Flint and Chattahoochee Rivers in Georgia and the Coosa and Tallapoosa Rivers in Alabama.

Spur Trail to Chiaha

To visit the site of this Creek town, return to 101st Airborne Road. Turn left at the junction and continue south on the paved road. Soon the road crosses

Uchee Creek. On the right is the turnoff for Fryar Field **(mile 1.6)**. Continue straight ahead on 101st Airborne Road as it bends southeast and passes an airstrip. The road ends at a T intersection **(mile 3.1)**. Turn left and take the road to the east to Bonacre Landing **(mile 4.8)**. The Creek town of Chehaw, or Chiaha, was near here.

Chattahoochee Indian Heritage Center–Fort Mitchell

On a hill south of the road leading to the fort is a monument, a symbolic representation of the square ground of a Creek town and the sacred fire that always burned there. Like a typical Creek town, it is surrounded by four structures—in this case not buildings or homes, but beds or arbors representing the four cardinal directions. Surrounding the monument are plaques with the names of Creek families who inhabited the Chattahoochee River valley. Their names were recorded in a special Indian census of 1832 shortly before they were forced to leave their homes in 1836. The Chattahoochee Indian Heritage Association plans to complete the monument with a bronze and steel flame structure at the heart of the square and with interpretive trails on the hillside. Today there are markers with information on Creek agriculture and the Trail of Tears.

On the plain to the south of the ridge is a reconstructed ball ground at the site where Creeks played "stick ball," a game played with small, lacrosse-like sticks with cupped ends used to catch and advance small deerskin balls covered with squirrel fur. At each end of the field, which might be anywhere from 100 yards to 0.25 mile in length, was a tall pole. The team that carried the ball back to its own pole won the game. Each town had its own team, and towns challenged one another. In preparation for games, towns conducted practice games with teams made up from their own red and white clans. Although the game was a "manly diversion"—the little brother to war—women joined the men in the dances that followed (T509). In 1825 the Marquis de Lafayette witnessed one of the last stickball games played in the Chattahoochee valley.

North and east of the monument is a trace of the old Federal Road, built on the bed of the Creek trading path. Half a mile to the east the road leads to the site of **Fort Mitchell**, built in 1813 during the Creek Civil War. The center plans to reconstruct the fort and a visitors' center, and the Indian Heritage Association also plans to build a visitors' center and to reconstruct the old **Crowell Indian Agency**.

Both the **Chattahoochee Indian Heritage Center** and Fort Mitchell are located 1.3 miles north of 101st Airborne Road on Ala. 165, 3 miles from the intersection of Sunshine Road and 101st Airborne Road, west of the bridge across the river. Ala. 165 is a very busy two-lane highway unsuitable for biking. At the entrance, turn right and take the road up the hill to the parking area.

Columbus Museum

The "Chattahoochee Legacy" gallery offers exhibits on the first European settlers in the region as well as artifacts from Mississippian settlements and Creek towns and villages, from prehistory to the first European encounter. Some of the exhibits include references to Bartram and his descriptions of Yuchi and other Creek towns.

The museum, open Tuesday–Sunday, is at 1251 Wynnton Road, Columbus. Web site: www.columbusmuseum.com

Bartram Recreation Trail
Tuskegee National Forest

Section:	U.S. 29 to Uphapee Creek
Distance:	8.6 miles
Difficulty:	easy to moderate (both directions)
	mountain biking: beginner to intermediate
Hazards:	hiking: none; biking: steep drops and rises
Highlights:	Piedmont coves; Choctafaula Creek

The trail begins on the ridge traversed by U.S. 29. From the ridge, the path descends and climbs again by working in and out of a series of north-facing coves. After crossing F.S. 908 the path follows an east–west ridge to the northwest and then to the west. The trail then descends to the floodplain of an unnamed creek, crosses the creek, and continues west following the contour line of north-facing coves to F.S. 905. From here, it levels—dipping twice to cross small creeks—and passes the ranger station en route to U.S. 80. The second half of the trail differs in being much wetter and more level. Most of this section passes through the floodplain of Choctafaula Creek, working through wetlands and crossing the creek's many tributaries. In the last mile the trail becomes hilly again as it crosses a ridge between Choctafaula and Uphapee Creeks.

The trail begins at the parking area off U.S. 29, east of U.S. 80. The path descends west along the north side of the east–west ridge. Less than 100 feet from the trailhead is the first of several wooden benches along the trail; most are decorated with quotations from the *Travels*. The quotation on the first bench reads: "A stately grove of pine." From the bench, the descent, steep in some sections, continues for 0.2 mile. The trail levels and then reaches the bottom of the ravine, crossing a small stream on a wooden footbridge **(mile 0.3)**. From here it rises and then descends to cross a second bridge. The climb resumes as the trail enters a hardwood forest of red and white oaks. After reaching the top of one of the ridge's shoulders the path descends via a switchback to a wooden footbridge **(mile 0.6)**, traverses a brief level section, then dips again to another footbridge. The trail ascends, levels, and then be-

316

gins the final ascent of a north–south ridge, passing by another bench and through a small stand of sweetgum trees. F.S. 908 is at the top of the ridge. **(mile 1.3).**

The trail crosses the road and gently descends to the northwest, along the spine of the ridge, for 0.25 mile. In this section the forest is predominantly evergreen. As the descent ends **(mile 1.6)**, the trail begins to roll up and down, ending with a short, pitched ascent **(mile 2.0)**. Level again, it rejoins the ridge and then descends to F.S. 906 at the base of a hairpin turn **(mile 2.3)**. The trail crosses the dirt road and continues to the west. In 0.1 mile it crosses a stream on a wooden footbridge. For the next 0.25 mile the trail winds through the floodplain of the unnamed creek. Leaving the plain, it climbs to the top of a shoulder **(mile 2.7)**. From here, it curls around for a little more than 0.1 mile, then descends to another footbridge. After a steep climb the trail reaches the top of the ridge **(mile 2.9)** and turns sharply to the left, into a north-facing cove. Here the forest is predominantly hardwoods, with stands of poplars and hickories mixed with some pines. Holding to the contour line, this section ends at the intersection with F.S. 905 **(mile 3.1)**.

Continuing across the road, the trail levels and then crosses a stream on a wooden footbridge **(mile 3.4)**. Working to the west on a level plateau, the path crosses another stream, also on a wooden footbridge **(mile 3.7)**. From the stream the path climbs to the paved road **(mile 3.9)** leading to the left (south) to the ranger station and straight ahead to the parking area for the trail. The trail continues to the right, past the Bartram Trail sign. To the left, up the access road, is a parking area for day hikers. In the area surrounding the ranger station the forest is predominantly pines. From the road, the trail rises for a short distance and then gradually descends for more than 0.25 mile.

The trail crosses a streamlet on a wooden footbridge **(mile 4.3)** and then begins to climb to F.S. 900. Stately magnolias highlight this section. At the Forest Service road **(mile 4.4)** the trail turns left, onto the road, which intersects U.S. 80 within a few feet.

The trail resumes on the west side of the highway. As the path enters the forest there is a bench with the quotation: "All nature awakens to life and activity." The trail works along the side of a shallow shelf, over the floodplain of Choctafaula Creek. Soon the path enters an extensive wetland **(mile 5.1)**, winding through it via a series of wooden bridges. Some of the bridges are as long as 200 feet. The path approaches within 100 feet of Choctafaula Creek **(mile 5.5)**. To the right is a short spur trail to the bank. On the opposite side of the creek are high, wide sandy banks. The trail continues to parallel the creek downstream, climbing a very short plateau. In this area the trees are

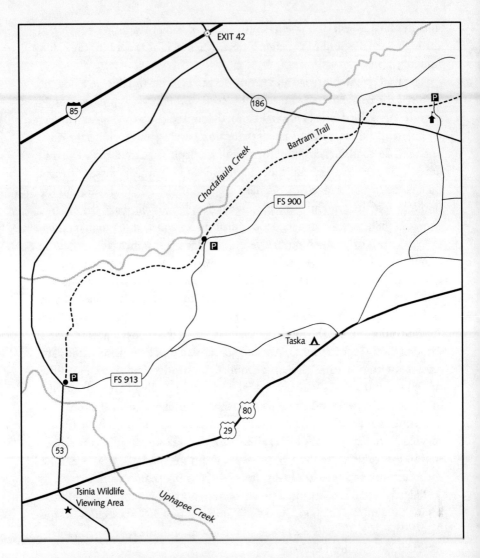

mostly pines mixed with magnolias. The path crosses a small stream on a wooden footbridge **(mile 6.1)** in an area with thick underbrush. To the west it exits onto F.S. 900 **(mile 6.5**) near the trail parking area. The creek can be seen from here.

The trail continues on the west side of the road and intersects a horse trail within a few hundred feet. The footpath works along the northwest face of the ridge. As it turns to the west, it intersects to the left the spur trail **(mile 6.7)** leading to the parking area on F.S. 900. From this point, the trail begins a steady descent paralleling the top of the ridge. As the trail loses elevation, it

JOURNEY TO THE GULF COAST

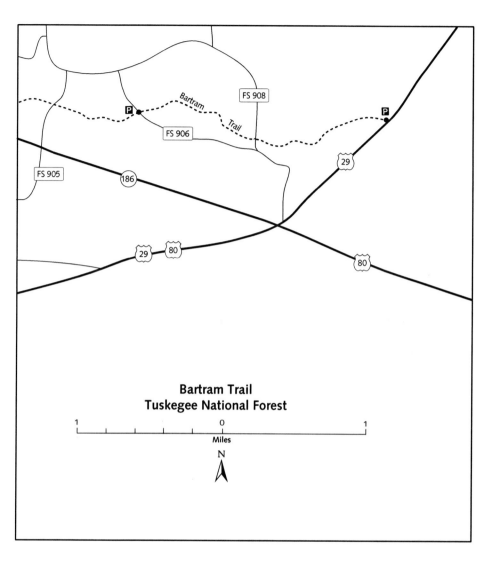

Bartram Trail
Tuskegee National Forest

cuts through a boulder field with a car-size boulder to the right. Soon it returns to the Choctafaula floodplain for a level stretch nearly 0.75 mile long.
As it levels, the path turns right and crosses a long footbridge. Nearby is a
wildlife food plot **(mile 7.0)**. The path remains level as it approaches the creek.
The trail comes within 15 feet of the creek's south bank, then leaves the main
channel and crosses three small tributaries of the Choctafaula on wooden
footbridges. The last footbridge **(mile 7.5)** was in disrepair in the winter of
1999. The trail rejoins the southern bank near a Bartram bench overlooking
the river.

From the shore the trail turns south, leaving Choctafaula Creek behind **(mile 7.65)**. The pathway remains level as it approaches the southern edge of a ridge **(mile 7.9)**. From here the trail begins to climb up the northern face of the ridge. For the most part the climb is gradual, but it is pitched for a few hundred feet as the path approaches the bed of an old jeep road. Once on the road, the ascent eases. In a few hundred feet the Bartram Trail leaves the road, turning to the right as the jeep road continues straight ahead. The footpath continues to rise, reaching the ridge's summit after a climb of a few hundred feet **(mile 8.2)**. The path is level for a brief section, then it begins to descend the southern face of the ridge. On its way down, the trail passes near a well-used campsite. From here the path continues downhill for 0.25 mile, then levels off **(mile 8.5)** and crosses a steep draw over a wooden bridge. In a few hundred feet the trail reaches the parking area off F.S. 913 **(mile 8.6)**.

WATER AND CAMPING

Backpacking is permitted on the trail out of hunting season. Given the length of the trail, however—less than 9 miles—most users are either day hikers or mountain bikers.

Water: Numerous small streamlets, whose source is the ridge to the south of the trail, offer water for camping.

Camping: There are many areas suitable for camping near Choctafaula Creek **(miles 7.0–7.6)** and in the floodplain of the unnamed stream **(miles 2.4–2.6)**.

ACCESS POINTS

U.S. 29 (east trailhead): From the junction of U.S. 29 and U.S. 80, take U.S. 29 North. The parking lot for the trailhead is a mile ahead on the left.

Ranger station: The ranger station is located off Ala. 136, south of I-85. The parking area is less than 0.1 mile past the ranger station, off the paved road.

U.S. 80 (west trailhead): From the junction of U.S. 29/U.S. 80 and C.R. 53, take the county road to the north. In 0.75 mile the road intersects F.S. 913. Turn right on the Forest Service road, which is paved in this section. Less than 0.1 mile on the left is the parking area for the west trailhead.

Alabama

TENSAW TO MOBILE

In late July, Bartram arrived at the banks of the Tensaw River near Halls Creek, 4 miles north of today's Stockton, Alabama. Immediately to the south, 1 mile northeast of today's Bryant Landing, was the plantation of Maj. Robert Farmar. After spending the night as Farmar's guest, Bartram set out early the next day for Mobile more than 30 miles to the south, taking passage on a boat that passed through the wide river delta to Mobile Bay. Later that day he arrived at his destination. Bartram described Mobile "as situated on the easy ascent of a rising bank, extending near half a mile on the level plain above; it has been near a mile in length, though not chiefly in ruins" (T 404). The British gained the city as part of the spoils of the Seven Years' War (1754–63) and incorporated it into the new colony of West Florida. When the British moved in, many of Mobile's French residents left for New Orleans and points west of the Mississippi River, the western boundary of the British colony, leaving their homes and shops vacant. By the 1770s many of these structures were "mouldering to the earth."[1]

The French exodus was not complete, however. In 1764 there were 350 townspeople in Mobile. By the time of Bartram's visit the city's population comprised 330 whites and more than 400 slaves. As Bartram walked through the city streets he observed "a few good buildings inhabited by French gentlemen." The French inhabitants were joined by English, Scotch, and Irish settlers; included in their number were the notable British American traders Swanson and McGillivray (T 404). The British reopened the port, and Mobile continued to function as a trade depot for the Creeks, Chickasaws, and Choctaws as well as gulf coast traders. At the lower end of town, near the bay, stood Fort Conde, a brick fortress built by the French. After the war the British repaired the fort and renamed it Fort Charlotte.

1. A good summary of the history of colonial Mobile is Gregory Waselkov's *Old Mobile Archaeology*.

In Mobile, Bartram sought passage to Manchac and the Mississippi. Unable to find an immediate opportunity, he decided to return to the Farmar plantation and accept the owner's offer of hospitality. On August 5 he set off from Mobile on a trading boat for the one-day trip to Tensaw bluff.

Bartram remained Farmar's guest for most of August. Farmar's plantation, Farm Hall, was on the site of an ancient Indian town called Taensa. With Farm Hall as his base, Bartram explored the surrounding area. His first journey was a brief solo canoe trip. Borrowing one of Farmar's light canoes, he sailed up one of the Tensaw River's east channels to the north, passing both well-cultivated plantations and uncultivated fields. North of Tensaw, Bartram was struck by the appearance of a blooming plant, "gilded with the richest golden yellow," covering the fields—eastern primrose. He canoed 10 miles to the north and camped at a bluff on the river—most likely Pierce Landing. The next day he continued his voyage of discovery past "high forest, and rich swamps, and frequently ruins of ancient French plantations," abandoned when the British took control of the area in 1763 (T407). He camped that night near the junction of the Tombigbee and Alabama Rivers at the head of the Mobile River. From there he canoed 15–20 miles up the Tombigbee. En route he passed the site of an abandoned French fortification that he thought was "perhaps fort louis de la Mobile"—the site of Old Mobile (T410). As in other instances, Bartram was mistaken—Old Mobile was not on the Tombigbee River. Perhaps Bartram saw an ancient Mississippian settlement on the Tombigbee, or perhaps he forgot the location of the Old Mobile site.[2] Bartram continued up the Tombigbee, but as the current grew stronger, he opted to turn around. Paddling with the current, he began his return to Farm Hall. That evening he stayed with a French family at their plantation on the river. By the end of the next day he was back at the bluff on the Tensaw River.

At Farm Hall Bartram succumbed to a fever that plagued him for the remainder of his voyage to Manchac. Learning of "a certain plant of extraordinary medical virtues" that grew 30 miles from the plantation, in the vicinity of Mount Pleasant, Bartram resolved to obtain it. Farmar supplied a horse and guide for the journey (T411), and Bartram was successful in finding the herb, *Collinsonia*. On his return to Farm Hall Bartram learned of "an opportunity for Manchac" and decided to take passage to the Mississippi, although he was still suffering from the fever. In mid-to-late August Bartram de-

2. Waselkov and Braund, *Bartram on the Southeastern Indians*, 95.

Fort Conde in downtown Mobile, Alabama. This structure is a replica of the original French fort.

scended the river to Mobile traveling in the company of Dr. Grant, the surgeon of the Mobile garrison.

Other Sites of Interest

Fort Conde–Mobile

Much of Mobile was in ruins when the British took control of the area after the Seven Years' War, and no building from the colonial period has survived to the present day. As part of the U.S. Bicentennial celebration, the city of Mobile reconstructed a portion of the French fort that overlooked the bay between 1724 and 1735. The modern fort serves as both a visitors' center and a museum on the history of Mobile. The fort is in downtown Mobile, 150 South Royal Street.

Next to the fort is the Conde-Charlotte Museum, 104 Theatre Street, with a furnished English council chamber from the 1770s and a Spanish courtyard from the 1780s, when the Spanish gained Mobile after the Revolutionary War.

Bartram Canoe Trail: Tensaw River

Section: Hubbard Landing to Live Oak Fish Camp
Distance: 20 miles; overnight trip or long day
Difficulty: easy; Tensaw is a tidal river; charts available at any landing
Hazards: snags, motorboats, and many river channels; maps
                required
Highlights: scenic delta; wildlife

This canoe trail, dedicated in 1976 as the Bartram Canoe Trail, is the Alabama Legislature's first officially designated canoe trail. The entire trail is within the wide Mobile-Tensaw Delta, which at 10 miles wide and nearly 50 miles long is one of the largest deltas in the nation. The Upper Delta Wildlife Management Area, managed by the Alabama Department of Conservation and Natural Resources, surrounds most of the route and features the swamps, marshes, and high forests native to this area. The trail is described from north to south. Most of the channels are wide. The chief hazards are submerged logs, motorboat traffic, and taking the wrong channel.

The trail begins at **Hubbard Landing** on Tensaw Lake, one of the many channels crisscrossing the Mobile River delta. From here it is a downstream paddle, although the river is tidal in this section. Immediately to the south, on the left, is Halls Creek, the vicinity of the Farmar plantation. The river winds through Coon Neck Bend, where it is joined by Douglas Lake on the right. From here the trail continues southeast to the mouth of Watson Creek. The river bends again to the west, with the second of four landings, **Upper Bryant Landing**, on the left.

The river continues to the west-northwest and then makes a sharp turn to the south at Dead Lake Island. There is a navigable channel on the far side of the island. The entire west bank of the river, including Dead Lake Island, is part of the Upper Delta Wildlife Management Area. Camping is permitted on the public land wherever there is high ground. The trail curls to the east, and a narrow channel appears to the east. Take the channel, named **Briar Lake**, for more intimate paddling than the main river channel. Continue paddling southeast, with Larry's Island on the right bank. On both banks are small areas suitable for camping. After passing Rice Creek, Briar Lake widens as the trail exits the wildlife area. The lake rejoins the main channel of the Tensaw,

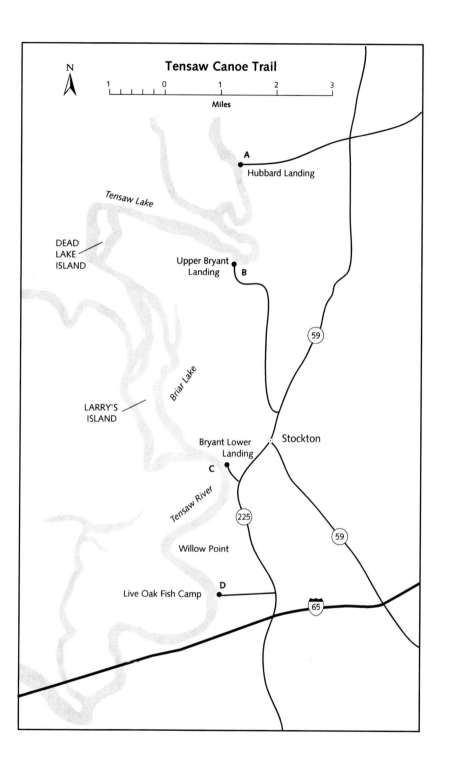

Tensaw Canoe Trail

N

1   0   1   2   3
Miles

A Hubbard Landing

Tensaw Lake

DEAD LAKE ISLAND

Upper Bryant Landing **B**

59

Briar Lake

LARRY'S ISLAND

Bryant Lower Landing   Stockton
C

Tensaw River

225

Willow Point

59

Live Oak Fish Camp **D**

65

Bartram Canoe Trail, Tensaw River.

and soon **Bryant Lower Landing** is on the left. From here the trail doubles back at Willow Point, leading to the final section to the **Live Oak Fish Camp**. On the right bank, the wildlife area returns.

The many channels, marshes, and tributaries make it essential to have the USGS topographic map: Stockton. Launch fees are charged at all landings.

Hubbard Landing: Located at the end of C.R. 96, 2 miles west of S.R. 59, north of Stockton.

Bryant Landing: Located 1.5 miles northwest of Vaughn, off C.R. 21, north of Stockton.

Bryant Lower Landing: Located immediately off Ala. 225, southwest of Stockton.

Live Oak Fish Camp: Less than a mile west of Ala. 225, 0.5 mile north of I-65.

West Florida

MOBILE TO PENSACOLA

After learning that the boat for Manchac would not leave for several days, Bartram "sought opportunities to fill up this time to the best possible advantage." Thus, when he heard about a boat heading to the Perdido River, he went to the captain and requested passage. The captain's objective was to recover a shipwreck at the mouth of the river just west of Pensacola. On September 3, just after sunrise, the salvage party set out on Mobile Bay in "a handsome light sailing-boat" (T413–414). They crossed the bay and stopped at **Mobile Point** for the night. The next day, after doubling around the point, they entered the Gulf of Mexico, sailing to the east along the shore. On the second day they arrived at the wrecked ship and found it "already stripped of her sails." The captain pressed on to **Pensacola**, arriving there that evening.

Pensacola was the capital of the newly established British colony of West Florida, created from Spain's colony La Florida. Spain ceded the land to regain Havana and Manila, both taken by Britain in the Seven Years' War. When the British arrived to occupy Pensacola in August 1763, they found the presidio and town deserted and in ruins. During the next twenty years of British rule, Pensacola emerged as a center of government and commerce. Through the 1760s the city's civilian population grew, overtaking that of Mobile. When Bartram arrived, he found "several hundred habitations" in the city (T416), the most notable being the governor's palace, "a large stone building ornamented with a tower, built by the Spaniards." The palace and the town sat atop a gentle rise overlooking "a spacious harbour, safe and capacious enough to shelter all the navies of Europe" (T415). At the town's center was a "large stockado fortress, the plan of a tetragon with salient angles at each corner, where is a block-house or round tower, one story higher than the curtains." The 500-man infantry battalion stationed at the fortress gave the town a decidedly military character.

According to the *Travels*, Bartram's visit to Pensacola was "accidental and undesigned." Bartram was traveling without papers, testimonials, and letters of introduction, and he did not seek out the governor.[1] Events overtook him, however, when Dr. Lorimer, who knew of Bartram and his avocation and who was himself an expert on the geography of the newly established colony, offered to introduce our traveler to Governor Chester. As Bartram tried to decline the invitation gracefully, the governor's secretary arrived to escort him to Chester's residence on a "farm a few miles from Pensacola." The next morning Bartram met with the governor, who extended an invitation to "continue in West Florida in researches after subjects of natural history." He offered to bear Bartram's expenses as well as provide accommodations with his own family. Bartram declined the generous offer and set out that afternoon to return to Mobile.

Pensacola: Colonial Archaeological Trail

In early 1990 an urban renewal project was under way in the historic district of Pensacola. When the pavement was removed, remnants of the early forts that stood on the site from 1752 to 1821 were uncovered. Archaeologists from the University of West Florida identified the architectural remnants of the main gate of the British fort (1763–81) that Bartram would have seen, as well as the foundations for other buildings in the fort compound. The university and city decided to leave several of these sites exposed to allow for public interpretation. In 1995 the Colonial Archaeological Trail was established to interpret five outdoor sites.

The trail begins on the second floor of the **Wentworth Museum**, where many of the artifacts uncovered from these sites and others are on display. There is also a model of the British fort of the 1770s. Across the street from the

1. In the view of Fred Benton, Bartram's characterization of his meeting with Chester as "accidental" and his visit with Lieutenant Governor Browne at the Rumsey Plantation as "by chance" may have been an effort to conceal his work on behalf of Chester and Browne to establish West Florida as a safe haven for loyalists (*Bartram Heritage*, 188–189). Given Bartram's patriot sympathies and his strong ties with noted revolutionaries such as George Galphin and Lachlan McIntosh, it is highly improbable that he was engaged in such work. Kathryn Braund suggests that Bartram's characterization of his meeting with Chester reflected his desire to avoid the governor and avoid being detained in Pensacola (Kathryn Braund, personal correspondence, March 27, 2000).

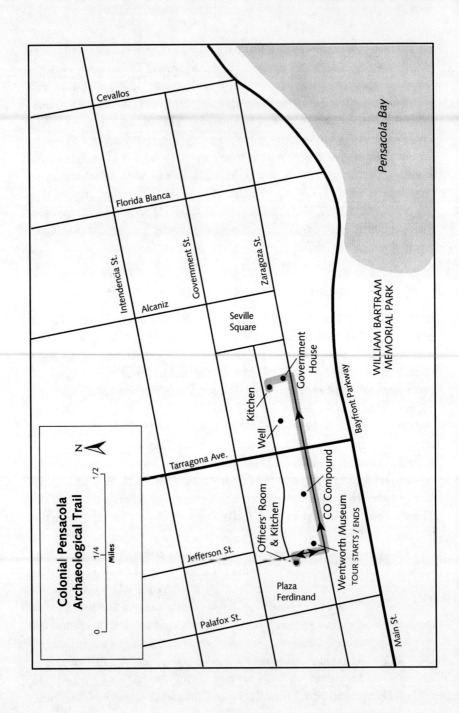

Colonial Pensacola Archaeological Trail

N

Miles

0   1/4   1/2

Palafox St.

Jefferson St.

Plaza
Ferdinand

Officers' Room
& Kitchen

Wentworth Museum

TOUR STARTS / ENDS

Tarragona Ave.

CO Compound

Well

Kitchen

Government
House

Seville
Square

Bayfront Parkway

Alcaniz

Zaragoza St.

Government St.

Intendencia St.

Florida Blanca

Cevallos

Main St.

WILLIAM BARTRAM
MEMORIAL PARK

Pensacola Bay

Foundations of the Officer's Room and Kitchen at the British fort at Pensacola. The fort was constructed after 1775. Colonial Archaeological Trail, Pensacola, Florida.

museum, on Jefferson Street, is part of the foundation of the building known as the **Officers' Room and Kitchen,** constructed shortly after 1775. Less than half a block to the east, on Zaragoza Street, is the site of the **Commanding Officer's Compound,** a structure built in 1775 by the British. *Continue down Zaragoza Street,* past Tarragona. On the left are the three remaining archaeological sites. In the center of the block is the **Garrision Kitchen,** the mess house for the British garrison, constructed about 1771. To the east is **Government House.** The foundation is all that remains of the three-story building. Originally intended to be the governor's residence, it became the site of Pensacola's civil government. The building was destroyed by fire in the 1820s. To the west is the last site, the **well** dug by the British in 1771 to create a reliable water supply within the fort's walls.

Parking for the tour is available on the street. Two blocks to the southeast of the tour, south of the intersection of Florida Blanca and Bayfront Parkway, is **William Bartram Memorial Park** overlooking Pensacola Bay.

Other Areas of Interest

Mobile Point–Bon Secour

Bartram camped on Mobile Point en route to Pensacola. Here he and his companions "collected a quantity of drift wood to keep light and to keep away the musquetoes, and rested well on the clean sandy beach until the cool morning awoke us" (T414). Most of the point is now part of the Bon Secour National Fish and Wildlife Refuge. The northwest section, where Fort Morgan is located, is part of an Alabama state historic site. The Bon Secour Refuge, comprising more than 6,500 acres, is in four units along the gulf coast and Mobile Bay. The refuge offers two hiking trails and two public beach access areas, both accessible by auto. The **Pine Beach Trail**, 4 miles round-trip, is the longest of the two. The trailhead is at a parking lot off Ala. 180. The trail winds through hardwood forest, swamps, and a lake appropriately named Gator Lake. On the lakeshore is a picnic shelter. The trail continues southward to the shore, crossing the secondary and then the primary dunes. Farther to the east on Ala. 180 is the trailhead for the **Jeff Friend Trail**. This 1-mile loop, wheelchair accessible, works down to the northern shore of Little Lagoon. At the western end of the peninsula, at Mobile Point, is a public access area for the beach near where Bartram camped in early September 1775.

Gulf Shores State Park

East of the wildlife refuge, and immediately east of Gulf Shores, this state park features a lodge, restaurant, and large campground that provide a good base for exploring the area. The roads in the park have a bicycle lane, creating a scenic 5.6-mile loop in the middle of the park. There are a variety of short trails in the campground and public beach access on the south side of the campground.

Louisiana

JOURNEY THROUGH THE MISSISSIPPI SOUND

In mid-September 1775 Bartram left Mobile for Manchac. He sailed on a large trading boat that was the property of a French gentleman who was returning to his plantation at the mouth of the Pearl River. They sailed down the west side of the bay, turning to the west through the "channel Oleron"—today's Grant's Pass—separating Dauphin Island from the mainland. There the craft entered the Mississippi Sound, a 90-mile-long channel along the gulf coast from Mobile Bay to the Mississippi Delta. No more than 20 feet deep, the sound continues to provide boating traffic with safe passage and shelter from the gulf waters as it passes behind a series of barrier islands: Dauphin, Horn, Cat, and Ship Islands. Bartram's craft sailed safely through the sound to the Frenchman's plantation just north of Lake Borgne near the mouth of the Pearl River.

On the voyage Bartram fell victim to a serious and debilitating illness: "I was incapable of making any observations, for my eyes could not bear the light . . . by the time I had arrived at the Pearl River, the excruciating pain rendered me almost frantic and stupefied" (T420). Unable to help his ailing guest, the Frenchman directed Bartram to the home of "an English gentleman twelve miles away who had a variety of medicines." Here, at the plantation home of a Mr. Rumsey, Bartram received a "blister plaister," which, placed between his shoulders, provided some relief. Nevertheless, his ailment, which was probably either poison ivy or scarlet fever, caused permanent injury to his left eye (T407). For the next five weeks he stayed on as Rumsey's guest and patient. As he recovered, Bartram explored the flora of the plantation, which was located north of Rigolets and east of Lake Pontchartrain.

On October 17 Bartram resumed his journey to the Mississippi. He entered **Lake Pontchartrain** at Rigolets "in a handsome large boat with three Negroes [Rumsey's slaves] to navigate her." From there to Manchac they followed the main British route through Louisiana, bypassing the sandbars and strong currents of the lower Mississippi River.[1] During the first two days they traveled more than 50 miles along the north shore of the lake, exiting on the west side at Pass Manchac. They navigated 8 miles through the narrow channel, taking the northern channel of the pass through the **Manchac Swamp**. Exiting the pass, they entered **Lake Maurepas**, Lake Pontchartrain's neighbor. They camped the second night on the lakeshore near the pass. The next day they sailed along Maurepas's northern shore for 10 miles to the mouth of the Amite River, where they camped for the night. The next day they began their ascent of the Amite, a narrow river only about 200 feet wide but deep enough to permit small boats. Bartram and the slaves traveled 30 miles upstream and stopped for the night at the plantation of a Scottish gentleman near today's French Settlement. The next day they ascended the river another 20 miles to "the forks," the head of navigation on the Amite.

From the forks the river continued straight ahead to the north; to the left was the Iberville (today's **Bayou Manchac**), an intermittent stream that connected the Amite to the Mississippi. In the spring and at other times of high water, the stream was a navigable waterway to the Mississippi. In times of low water, traders portaged goods via a 9-mile road to the Mississippi River port of Manchac. At the forks was a landing with stores and warehouses where vessels were loaded and unloaded. Bartram spent the night at the landing. The next day, now traveling alone, he took the land route to Manchac through a grand forest of magnolias, tulip poplars, sycamores, and black oaks. That evening, October 21, he arrived at the banks of the Mississippi and "stood for a time as it were fascinated by the magnificence of the great sire of rivers" (T426–427, 408). Today this view is blocked by levees on both sides of the river.

Manchac, a mile south of today's Burtville, Louisiana, was an important trading center in West Florida with stores, warehouses, and a number of permanent residents. At the mouth of the Iberville sat Fort Bute, an abandoned British fortress that was directly opposite a Spanish fortification on the other side of the stream, which formed the boundary between the colony and Spanish Louisiana. At Manchac, Bartram met William Dunbar, the owner of New Richmond, a large plantation to the north near Baton Rouge. Dunbar, also a scientist and later an explorer himself, invited Bartram to join him on a journey upstream, and they set out on the river in a "handsome convenient

1. Dalrymple, *Merchant of Manchac*, 6–7. From Pensacola to Manchac via this route took eight to ten days, in contrast with the seven or eight weeks required for the route through the mouth of the Mississippi (by New Orleans).

boat, rowed by three blacks" (T 429–430). Just north of Manchac they landed briefly at the Indian village of Alabama, near Gardere, before proceeding on to Dunbar's plantation. At New Richmond, Dunbar and his twenty slaves raised rice, tobacco, and cotton, but the plantation's chief produce was small timber products—staves and heads for wooden barrels.

After a visit of a day or two, Bartram and Dunbar decided to make a trip to Pointe Coupee—a French settlement on the western bank of the river. On October 26 Bartram and his host set off on the Mississippi in a "cypress boat with three oars." Traveling upstream, they spent the first night at a plantation near **Browne's White Cliffs**, south of today's Port Hudson. Here Monfort Browne, the former governor of West Florida, sought to lay out a township that would become the seat of government of a new British colony—Mississippi—spanning the territory from Manchac to Natchez.[2] The British government never approved the new colony. Bartram and Dunbar set off on horseback the next day to tour the "White Plains" 8 miles to the northeast, near today's Plains, Louisiana, returning to the plantation that night. The following day they resumed their boat trip upstream, reaching **Pointe Coupee** on the evening of October 28. There a French gentleman, "a wealthy and ancient planter," was their host for the night. The next day Bartram and Dunbar began their return voyage to Baton Rouge.

Mississippi Sound: West Ship Island

As Bartram returned from Baton Rouge to Mobile, he retraced his route through Pass Manchac and Lake Pontchartrain into the Mississippi Sound. Again he traveled on a trader's ship for the week-long journey from Manchac to Mobile. As the craft worked its way eastward through the sound, it passed Cat and Ship Islands. In the eighteenth century, Ship Island was a 14-mile-long barrier island. In 1969 Hurricane Camille cut the island in two by creating an inlet nearly half a mile wide. Today, both islands, as well as Horn Island to the east, are part of the Gulf Islands National Seashore. West Ship Island is open daily to the public from the spring through the fall. An authorized concessionaire offers ferry service from Gulfport to the island—three times a day during the summer. Camping is not permitted on the island, nor are private boats allowed to dock there.

On the western end of the island is Fort Massachusetts. Construction on the fort started in the 1850s, and although it was still unfinished when the

2. Fabel, "An Eighteenth Colony," 658–659, 670–672.

West Ship Island, Gulf Islands National Seashore. Mississippi Sound is to the right.

Civil War broke out, the Confederacy used it as a naval base. When the Confederates abandoned the fort in 1862, the Union army seized it and resumed construction. Park rangers offer tours of the fort. A 4-mile trail from the boat dock to the beach on the gulf side provides views of the channel, the inland marshes, and the Gulf of Mexico. A 0.3-mile boardwalk connects the dock to the beach, which has concessions, a picnic area, and a bathhouse. Although this area is busy during the summer months—the white sand beach is regarded as the best in Mississippi—most of the island is wilderness.

The visitors' center for the Gulf Islands National Seashore, in Ocean Springs, Mississippi, has exhibits on the flora and fauna of the shore and the barrier islands. The park permits wilderness camping on Horn Island, 7 miles offshore, but campers must provide their own transportation.

Canoe Trails: Manchac Swamp

Thousands of acres of wetlands form an hourglass-shaped swamp separating Lake Pontchartrain from Lake Maurepas to the west—Manchac Swamp. The name derives from the French *manche*, for "passageway" or "strait." This swamp occupies more than 20 square miles and, save for two highways (U.S. 51 and I-55), the railroad, and small fishing and trapping communities, is wilderness. Within the swamp are some of the oldest red cypress trees in America, many of them more than 500 years old. There are hundreds of acres of cypress forests, swamp gum, and swamp maple, as well as prairie and marsh. Julia Sims has observed and photographed this area, and her book *Manchac Swamp: Louisiana's Undiscovered Wilderness* captures some of its unique beauty.

At the center of the swamp is Pass Manchac, the main passage between the two lakes, once part of the main route between the Mississippi Sound and the Mississippi River. On the Pontchartrain side of the pass is an abandoned lighthouse now surrounded by water—evidence of the swamp's slow demise as the gulf's water levels rise. Between the two lakes are two Louisiana wildlife management areas. The Joyce Wildlife Management Area, north of the pass, encompasses more than 15,000 acres within its boundaries. The area is chiefly a cypress-tupelo swamp with a small marsh. Off I-55, at Exit 22, there is a short boardwalk trail labeled "The Swamp Walk." Bordering the southern bank of the pass is the Manchac Wildlife Management Area, established by the state in the mid-1970s with more than 8,000 acres. Next to the shore of Lake Pontchartrain is a grassy plain called the Prairie. Both areas, as is true of all the swamp, are home to egrets, herons, ibises, anhingas, and sandhill cranes; deer and bobcats; and, of course, alligators. The Louisiana Department of Wildlife and Fisheries manages both areas. Canoeing in and around the area is not difficult. The waterways do not form a labyrinth, but there are no marked canoe trails.

ACCESS POINTS

There are several public put-ins off U.S. 51. Three are listed below; two are south of Manchac Pass and one is to the north. For more information on the put-ins, consult the *Trail Guide to the Delta Country*, by the New Orleans Chapter of the Sierra Club.

Ruddock: This put-in, 1 mile north of the Ruddock exit on I-55, offers access to the Bayou Desert and the Ruddock Canal—a logging canal that leads to Lake Maurepas. From the put-in one can explore the

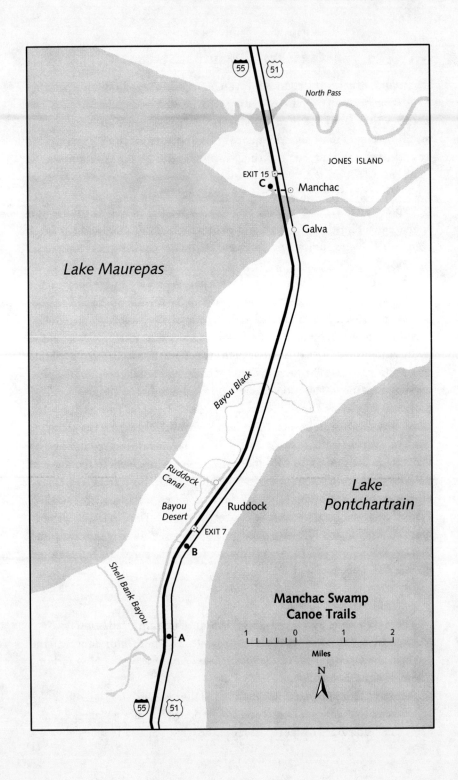

55
51

North Pass

JONES ISLAND

EXIT 15
C ●   ⊙ Manchac

○ Galva

Lake Maurepas

Bayou Black

Ruddock
Canal   ○

*Bayou
Desert*   Ruddock

EXIT 7
B ●

*Lake
Pontchartrain*

Shell Bank Bayou

● A

**Manchac Swamp
Canoe Trails**

1   0   1   2

Miles

N

55
51

marsh and cypress forest around the canal and then head out to the larger lake.

La Place: From this put-in, 2 miles south of the Ruddock exit, one can canoe south into two unnamed lakes, go through another lumber canal, or attempt a passage through Shell Bank Bayou to Lake Maurepas. Most of the time the passage is blocked by water hyacinths.

Jones Island: Immediately below the I-55 bridge over Pass Manchac is a boat ramp on the North Pass. From here, one can canoe into either lake on the north shore of Jones Island. A canal along the interstate leads to the main pass and the mouth of Galvo Canal, ending at the Prairie.

Driving Tour: False River

This 50-mile tour begins west of Baton Rouge and ends north of the city on U.S. 61. The tour works around the western bank of the False River, an oxbow lake that was once the bed of the Mississippi. In the eighteenth century there were a number of plantations that flanked both sides of the river. The tour highlights two that have survived, River Lake and Parlange. Both date to the time of Bartram's journey to Pointe Coupee. The tour travels through New Roads and across the Mississippi at Pointe Coupee on one of the few ferries still in operation on the river. On the east side of the river the tour passes through another historic town, St. Francisville. Nearby is Oakley, an early-nineteenth-century plantation that was briefly the home of John James Audubon. The tour ends at the site of Browne's White Cliffs on the east bank of what was formerly the Mississippi.

The tour begins west of Baton Rouge at the junction of U.S. 190 and La. 1, a little more than 15 miles from the city. *From the junction turn right onto La. 1.* In approximately 4 miles the road intersects La. 416 **(mile 4.2)** at the lake's southern edge. The lake, approximately 20 miles long, is in the form of a C with its northern end east of the town of New Roads. In the eighteenth century, channels connected both ends to the Mississippi River. At times of high water many craft mistook the lake for the main river, thus the name False River. *At the junction, continue to the left on La. 1.*

On the left is a sign for the False River Historical Bike/Hiking Trail. This short trail is now overgrown. The shoulders on La. 1 are wide enough to permit bicycle riding on the road. In a little more than 2 miles the only public boat ramp, Bonaventure, appears on the right. On the left side of the road is the **River Lake Plantation (mile 4.8)**. The house, now privately owned, was

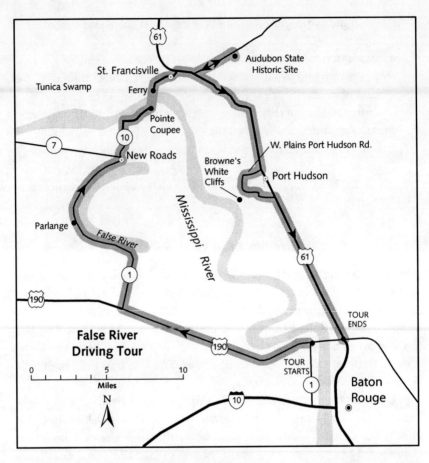

Inside the map:

61

Audubon State
Historic Site

St. Francisville

Tunica Swamp

Ferry

Pointe
Coupee

10

W. Plains Port Hudson Rd.

7

New Roads

Browne's
White
Cliffs

Port Hudson

Mississippi River

Parlange

False River

61

1

190

TOUR
ENDS

190

**False River
Driving Tour**

0   5   10

Miles

N

TOUR
STARTS

1

10

**Baton
Rouge**

built in the early 1760s. Behind the plantation are double row houses that once housed the plantation's slaves. After the Civil War these cabins formed a modern African American community known as Cherie Quarters. One of these homes was the birthplace of the author Earnest Gaines.

The road, with constant views of the lake to the right, bears with the river to the north. The road intersects La. 78 **(mile 8.3)**. A tenth of a mile on the left is the **Parlange Plantation**. This home, five rooms across and two rooms deep, was built in the 1750s and is an example of French-Caribbean colonial architecture. The house is constructed of native materials: hand-made bricks (the molds have been preserved and are on display), cypress, and bousillage (a combination of mud and moss). Several of the live oaks flanking the house are 500 years old. The house is owned by the eighth generation of the Parlange family. Tours are by appointment only.

Parlange Plantation on the False River in Louisiana.

Continue north on La. 1. A tenth of a mile on the right, in one of the former Parlange outbuildings, is the Pointe Coupee Parish Museum, which has exhibits on the area's life and culture. Continuing north, La. 1 enters New Roads, intersecting La. 10 and La. 3131 **(mile 12.5)**. *Continue on La. 1* and in 2 miles, at the junction with West Main Street, the road reaches the center of New Roads **(mile 14.4)**.

Turn left at the junction, continuing on La. 1. In 0.5 mile La. 1 turns to the left. At this intersection, *continue straight ahead on La. 10.* This road is marked for the St. Francisville Ferry. In 5 miles the road intersects La. 981 **(mile 20)**. To the right are views of **Pointe Coupee**, where Bartram crossed the river to meet with a French plantation owner. To reach the ferry, cross the levee and

Pointe Coupee, Louisiana. The French plantation located near this point on the Mississippi River was the furthest point of Bartram's travels.

the railroad tracks. Operated by the Louisiana Department of Transportation, the ferry runs every 30 minutes on the quarter hour, from 4 A.M. to midnight. There is no charge. On the fifteen-minute ferry ride, look back to the southwest for views of Pointe Coupee.

On the west side of the river, continue on La. 10 into St. Francisville. This settlement grew up around a French fort built in 1720. After the area became part of British West Florida in 1763, English settlers soon outnumbered the French and Creole population. None of the colonial buildings survives, but a number of late Federal and Spanish colonial structures have been well preserved. *Turn right off La. 10 onto Royal Street* (**mile 21.0**). On the street are three structures from the early 1800s: Propinquity (no. 523), a Spanish colonial structure from 1809; Market Hall (no. 429), from 1819; and a structure from 1804. In approximately 0.75 mile, Royal Street returns to Ferdinand and La. 10.

Continue on La. 10 through modern St. Francisville. At the junction with Bus. U.S. 61 (mile 22.1), turn right. Follow Bus. U.S. 61 for 1 mile until it ends at U.S. 61. *At the junction, turn right,* taking the main highway to the south. In less than 2 miles the highway intersects La. 965. *Turn left,* and in 3 miles the entrance to the **Audubon State Historic Site** is on the right **(mile 27.5)**.

In this 100-acre forest is the main house for the **Oakley Plantation**, built in 1806. The house's architecture also shows the influence of the West Indies, as, for example, in the shutter details. Some of Oakley's rooms have been restored to the late Federal period (1790–1830). This was the home of Audubon for six months in 1821 while he was the tutor to Miss Eliza Pirrie, the teenage daughter of Mr. and Mrs. James Pirrie. Here he completed or began thirty-two bird paintings. Many first-print editions of the drawings are on display in the home. Tours of the house are available. A picnic area and pavilion and a 1.8-mile nature trail are on the grounds.

Exit the area and *turn left onto La. 965,* returning to U.S. 61 **(mile 30.5)**. *Turn left at the junction and take U.S. 61 South.* After the highway becomes four lanes, it will pass the entrance for the Port Hudson State Historic Site **(mile 39)**. A mile past the entrance, *turn right onto West Port Hudson Plains Road.* In approximately 1.25 miles the road will reach Port Hickey Road. *Turn left* and follow the road to the south. Approximately 0.5 mile to the west is the site of **Browne's White Cliffs**. When Bartram visited this area, the cliffs were more than 100 feet tall and were white as a consequence of the erosion of the loess soil found in this section of Louisiana. The cliffs were named for their former owner Monfort Browne, the lieutenant governor of West Florida and later the governor of the Bahamas. It was here that Browne had hoped to place the capital of the new British colony of Mississippi.

The river has shifted to the west during the last 200 years, and the land is now marsh. Moreover, without the river undercutting the bank, the cliffs have become steps down to the former riverbed. There is no land access to the cliffs because all of the land west of the road is in private hands. The best way to view the cliffs is during the spring, when the river is high and there is sufficient water in the marsh to navigate a canoe or boat. Although Browne's White Cliffs as Bartram saw them no longer exist, one can gain some sense of them from the bluffs just north of Port Hickey, where the river still undercuts the loess bluff. This land is also privately owned, by the Georgia-Pacific Company, but as a private recreation area with access on a permit basis. The entrance to the area, Old Port Hickey Road, is at the sharp turn to the east **(mile 44.2)**.

Browne's White Cliffs on the Mississippi River, near Port Hudson, Louisiana.
Photograph courtesy of Fred Benton, Bartram Trail Conference.

To continue the driving tour, turn left onto La. 2112. Continue east, past the Port Hudson National Cemetery. The road and tour end at U.S. 61 **(mile 47)**, approximately 10 miles north of Baton Rouge.

Other Points of Interest

Colonial Baton Rouge

On Lafayette Street, at numbers 342 and 348 in downtown Baton Rouge, are the Lafayette houses. These two buildings, dating to the 1750s, are the city's only surviving colonial structures.

LSU Rural Life Museum

The museum is on the **Burden Research Plantation** southeast of the Louisiana State University campus. This 450-acre site is divided into three areas. Closest to visitor parking is the **Barn**—an exhibition hall featuring artifacts of Louisiana rural life from prehistoric times to the early twentieth century. Flanking the Barn are seven buildings representing the various cultures of Louisiana; these include the **Pioneer's Cabin, Dogtrot House, Acadian House, and Shotgun House**. To the south, near Windrush Gardens, a nineteenth-century plantation has been reconstructed featuring more than a dozen structures, including an overseer's house, slave cabins, mill, and sugarhouse.

The museum entrance is at 4650 Essen Lane, immediately south of I-10. Admission fee charged. Web site: http://rurallife.lsu.edu.

Return to Philadelphia

Upper Creek Towns

Bartram returned to Baton Rouge after his trip to Pointe Coupee. His plan to conduct further explorations in the area was disrupted by "the sever disorder" in his eyes (T 436–437). On November 10, 1775, he left Baton Rouge to begin the three-month trek to Savannah. He retraced his route to Manchac on a trading boat, spending the night with Messrs. Swanson and Company. The next day he traveled by land to the forks of the Amite, where he boarded one of the trading company's schooners bound for Mobile. The ship sailed down the river to Lake Maurepas, through Pass Manchac, and into Lake Pontchartrain. On the west shore of the lake the craft ran aground on a sandbar and remained stuck throughout the night. The next day, with the ship dislodged by the high tide, Bartram and company exited the lake through Rigolets into the Mississippi Sound. In the Gulf of Mexico they sailed past Cat Island and **Ship Island**. As they approached Mobile Bay they ran aground on a reef of oyster shells and had to spend the night off the shore of Dauphin Island. The next day they were freed by a brisk southerly wind. Later that day, on November 14, they arrived in Mobile. There Bartram entrusted the traders Swanson and McGillivray with his "collections of growing roots, seeds and curious specimens" to be sent to his sponsor, Dr. Fothergill.

Bartram spent two weeks in Mobile preparing for his return to Georgia. His intended route was by horseback through today's Florida panhandle to the Atlantic coast. On hearing of recent Seminole violence against whites at Apalachee Bay, he abandoned that plan in favor of joining a trader's caravan bound for the Creek Nation. On November 27 Bartram set off for Tensaw "in a large boat with the principal trader of the [Swanson] company." They arrived at the landing that evening. Bartram traveled the few miles to the south to the Farmar plantation to recover his horse and visit with his friend for the last time. The next morning he joined the caravan with twenty to thirty horses, two packmen, and the chief trader for the weeklong journey into the Creek Nation along the well-used trading path (T 440). The traders, anxious to reach their destination, traveled in such a "mad manner" that Bartram's horse could not keep pace with them. Our traveler faced the difficult decision of either abandoning his "old slave" or separating himself from the caravan to await his horse's recovery. It is clear from the *Travels* that Bartram considered the first option undesirable and the second dangerous. The traders told him that he "must not be left alone to perish in the wilderness" (T441–442). Happily, a third option presented itself. The next afternoon the caravan encountered another group of traders with a herd of horses for sale. For ten pounds sterling he exchanged his horse for a fresh horse and resumed his travels both "alert and cheerful."

The next morning the caravan crossed Deadman's Creek, a brisk stream named for a white man who had been murdered near it. The fate of a company from Georgia whom the caravan met on the trail further underscored the dangers of traveling in that time and place. The company, "a man, his wife, a young woman, several young children and three stout young men, with about a dozen horses loaded with their property" (T443), were hoping to settle on the Alabama River north of Tensaw. The night after they met up with Bartram's group the Georgians were attacked and robbed by a group of Choctaws.

As the caravan neared the Upper Creek towns, the chief trader and one of the packmen set off to give notice of their approach. Bartram and the other packman, a young Mustee Creek, were charged with bringing in the packhorses and merchandise. At Catoma Creek, southwest of today's Montgomery, the two men faced a flooded river too dangerous to ford. They ferried the goods across the river on a makeshift raft made of cane and logs. A grapevine tied to one end of the raft allowed the young Creek, standing on the opposite bank, to pull the loaded raft across the river. Bartram, holding a vine tied to the other end, would retrieve the raft to be loaded for another trip. Afterward Bartram drove the horses into the creek to swim across and followed them in, nearly naked in the cold water. That evening, most likely December 5, Bartram and the Creek reached their destination on the banks of the Tallapoosa River. There, opposite the town of Savannuca, they camped "under shelter of some Indian cabins" (T446). At the campfire, a guest joined them—a young man who was the sole escapee from the Choctaw raid on the Georgia company.

Bartram spent the next day at Muccolossus (Mucclasse), a mile downstream from Savannuca, where he was the guest of honor at the ceremony celebrating the marriage of a young Mustee Creek and a local Creek girl. The next morning the chief trader escorted Bartram farther downstream to a town of Alabama Indians, who formed one of the three main tribes of the Upper Creeks (the Tallapoosas and the Abeikas were the others).[1] Near the town Bartram saw traces of Fort Toulouse, an abandoned French fortress. The chief trader and his guest spent that night in a "grand entertainment at the public square." The next day they returned to Muccolossus, where Bartram learned that another trader's caravan would leave from Tuckabatchee for Augusta, providing safe passage for him to Georgia. Tuckabatchee, 15 miles upstream on the Tallapoosa River opposite the mouth of Uphapee Creek, was the mother town of the Tallapoosas and one of the largest Upper Creek towns, with a population exceeding 3,000. Bartram reached the town the next day only to discover that the caravan had already departed. On learning that another caravan would depart from Otasse in two to three weeks, he returned to Muccolossus to wait.

On his arrival, Bartram discovered that his host, the chief trader, was in serious trouble. The trader's stores were closed and he was in hiding after being caught in an affair with the wife of one of the town's young chiefs. The Creeks' penalty for adultery was "cropping"—cutting off both ears close to the head—and the elders had ruled that "he must loose his ears, or forfeit all his goods . . . and even that forfeiture would not save his ears, unless Mr. Golphin interposed in his behalf" (т449). The trader pleaded with Bartram to inform Galphin of his dangerous situation and solicit "that gentleman's most speedy and effectual interference." Bartram agreed to carry the appeal to Silver Bluff and left Muccolossus the next morning for Otasse 5 miles upstream. En route he stopped again at Coolome and visited with the chief trader, Mr. Germany, then continued upstream. He arrived at his destination that evening; it was sometime before Christmas 1775.

JOURNEY TO SAVANNAH

Bartram left Otasse on January 2, 1776, in a trader's caravan with four men and about thirty horses bound for Augusta. After three days on the trading path they arrived at the Chattahoochee River. They forded the river near today's U.S. 80 bridge, a mile south of Columbus, Georgia. In Georgia, they followed the familiar route of the trading path to the Ocmulgee River. The winter rains that year were heavy, and the rivers were swollen and dangerous. After waiting two nights on the west bank they decided to ferry their goods across on an 8-foot portable leather boat. Several trips were required to se-

---

1. Braund, personal correspondence, March 27, 2000.

cure all the goods on the east bank. Afterward they drove the horses across, then pressed on to the east to the Oconee River, which they crossed in the same manner. Farther to the east, on one of the headwaters of the Ogeechee, the traders did attempt a ford. Bartram fell into the river, but he and his horse recovered and gained the far shore. After two more days of hard traveling they reached their destination.

Bartram stayed in Augusta only two to three days, as the guest of his friend Humphrey Wells, while he refitted himself and bought a new horse. Newly clothed and with a "tolerable Indian pony," he headed for Savannah (T460). Traveling alone again, he made the familiar detour to Silver Bluff, South Carolina, where he visited with his friend and benefactor George Galphin and informed him of the predicament of the chief trader of Muccolossus. From Carolina he crossed over into Georgia and picked up the road to Savannah. He was joined for this part of the journey by an Irish gentleman who was scouting for a plantation. The two men camped at Blue Springs—an "amazing fountain of transparent cool water" on Beaver Dam Creek near today's Hilltonia—and from there rode together to Georgia's troubled capital city.

Fort Toulouse and the Alabama Indian Town

The Alabama town Bartram visited in the winter of 1775 was built on the wide, flat plain between the Tallapoosa and Coosa Rivers. He described it as "one of the most eligible situations for a city in the world, a level plain between the conflux of two majestic rivers."

Fort Toulouse was one of a series of forts constructed by the French from Canada to the Gulf of Mexico in the first half of the eighteenth century. Although built to check the westward expansion of British colonists, these forts also served as trading centers with the surrounding Indian populations. The French built the wooden stockade named Fort Toulouse at the head of the Alabama River in 1717. By the 1740s, after thirty years of southern weather and insects, the fort was in a state of serious disrepair. In 1748 the French rebuilt the fortress approximately 100 feet south of the original fort but abandoned it in 1763 at the end of the Seven Years' War. Afterward the French, soldiers and civilians alike, as well as many Alabamas, left for Spanish Louisiana.

By the time of Bartram's visit a few half-buried cannonballs, cannons, and remnants of an apple orchard planted by the French were all that remained of the settlement. Archaeologists have uncovered the foundations and remains of both forts, as well as the foundation of Fort Jackson, built by Andrew Jackson during the Creek War on top of the remains of the two French

Fort Toulouse at Fort Toulouse–Fort Jackson Park, Wetumpka, Alabama. This structure is a replica of the original French fort.

forts. Located near the entrance to today's park is a replica of the second French fort. Every month **Fort Toulouse–Fort Jackson Park** sponsors historical reenactments of French civilian and military life at the fort and Alabama Indian life at a reconstructed village adjacent to the fort. On the first weekend in November, the park hosts Frontier Days, with historical reenactments that include one actor portraying Bartram.

William Bartram Arboretum

Between the two rivers are two loop trails, each taking the hiker through distinct types of forests. Near the visitors' center is the Upland Forest Area with a loop trail a little more than 0.1 mile long. The trail, well graded with gravel, takes the hiker through hardwood forests. The forest's upper canopy is chiefly sweetgum, laurel oak, and white ash; the lower canopy includes holly and black cherry. Small signs identify many of the trees. Along the path

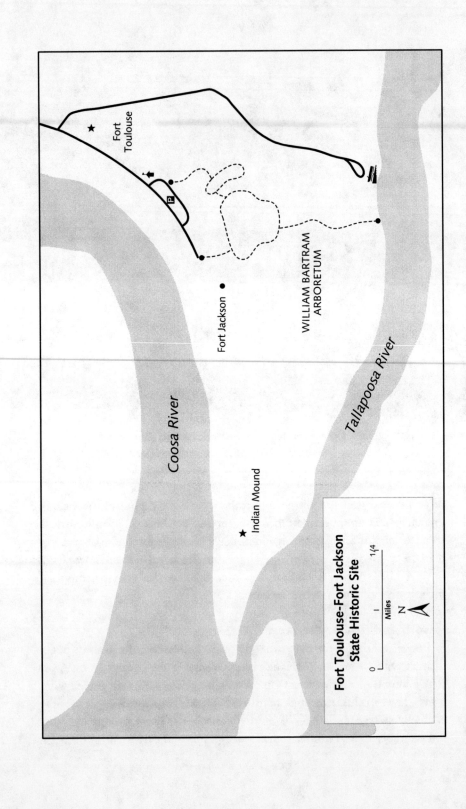

Fort Toulouse

Coosa River

Fort Jackson

WILLIAM BARTRAM
ARBORETUM

Indian Mound

Tallapoosa River

**Fort Toulouse–Fort Jackson
State Historic Site**

N

0   Miles   1/4

are signs interpreting the area's natural history as well as the life and culture of the Alabamas and the Creeks. There are also signs interpreting Bartram's visit to the area in the winter of 1775. At the southern end of the loop is a trail that connects to the next loop via a footbridge crossing a ravine.

The triangular **Lowland Forest Loop** is approximately 0.75 mile long, and begins and ends at an overlook platform built around a large willow. Taking the loop counterclockwise, the hiker descends the steps to the right and then follows a ridge through stands of eastern redbud and sassafras. In about 0.2 mile the trail comes to the trailhead near Fort Jackson. To the right a spur trail leads to the remnants of the fort. Parts of the wall and the moat are still visible. From the fort trailhead, continue on the arboretum trail to the left, entering the floodplain of the Tallapoosa River. Soon the trail reaches a junction with a 0.25-mile spur trail that leads to an overlook of the river. To continue on the main trail, stay to the left. This last leg of the loop, a little more than 0.25 mile, returns to the platform surrounding the willow.

Fort Toulouse–Fort Jackson Park offers picnic areas, a boat ramp, and a developed campground. The visitors' center has exhibits on the area's history. Located 5 miles south of Wetumpka, Alabama, off U.S. 231, the park is open daily, sunrise to sunset; closed on major holidays.

Return to Carolina

CAPE FEAR

We now come to a ten-month gap in the *Travels*. All Bartram had to say about the period from February to October 1776 is: "After my return from the Creek nation, I employed myself during the spring and fore part of summer, in re-visiting the several districts of Florida." On this eventful period for the new nation the *Travels* is thus largely silent. Bartram's later manuscript entitled "Some Hints and Observations concerning the civilization of the Indians . . ." notes that he passed through the Creek Confederacy "at the most critical period of the contest; that was, when a declaration of Independence was made" (SH0194), suggesting that he was in Creek country in July 1776. The same manuscript recounts an attempted British invasion of Georgia from Florida: "When I was at Gen'l McIntoshes on the Alatamaha, the English attempted to invade Georgia."[1] Ed Cashin speculates on the basis of that account that Bartram accompanied William McIntosh in July 1776 on a military campaign to check the long-awaited British invasion from Florida. The Georgians met the invading force at the St. Marys River while the British were still on the Florida side. Fighting with the British were Seminoles, perhaps led by Bartram's friend Cowkeeper. After exchanging gunfire across the river for most of the day, the "Chief of Indians" threw down his gun and declared to the Georgians "they were Brother's and friends and that he knew not any cause why they should spill each others blood." The conflict ended and Bartram returned to the Altamaha. Francis Harper offers a third alternative for Bartram's whereabouts during the ten-month silence, based on Bartram's observation of a lunar eclipse during his canoe trip up the Altamaha River, which, Harper suggests, took place in 1776.

The *Travels'* brief section on coastal Georgia in 1776 concludes with Bartram's description of *Franklinia altamaha*, the rare flowering tree he had first seen eleven years earlier near Fort Barrington while traveling with his father.

1. Cashin, *William Bartram and the American Revolution*, 223.

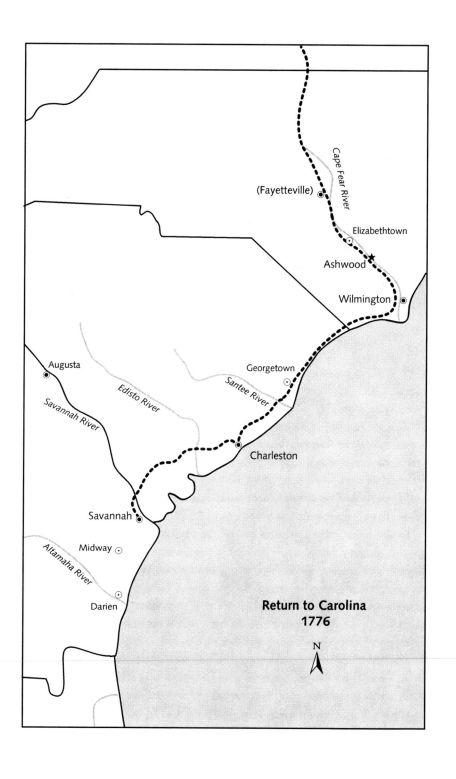

(Fayetteville)

Cape Fear River

Elizabethtown

Ashwood

Wilmington

Augusta

Edisto River

Georgetown

Santee River

Savannah River

Charleston

Savannah

Midway

Altamaha River

Darien

**Return to Carolina
1776**

N

Alligator near the Laurel Hill Wildlife Drive in the Savannah National Wildlife Refuge. Jonathan Bryan's plantation, Brampton, was located across the Savannah River just below the mouth of Pipemaker's Creek.

If Bartram did make his trip up the Altamaha in the summer of 1776, he would have had the opportunity to witness the tree in bloom for the first time (the earlier trip with his father was made in late autumn). And indeed, Bartram noted that *Franklinia* "is a flowering tree, of the first order for beauty and fragrance of blossoms" (T467). Bartram never saw the tree in any other place "from Pennsylvania to Point Coupe."

In the fall of 1776 Bartram started the final leg of his travels. His two-month journey home to Philadelphia began when he accepted Jonathan Bryan's offer to stay at his plantation, Brampton, on the Savannah River 3 miles upstream from Savannah. Bryan, one of Georgia's wealthiest plantation owners, operated several plantations in the vicinity of the capital. After spending the night at Brampton, Bartram set off for Zubley's Ferry, 17 more miles upstream, where he crossed over into South Carolina. Three days later he reached Charleston on the road through present-day Jacksonsboro.

At Charleston he was again the guest of Mary Lamboll and her two girls. After a stay that lasted less than three days, he left the city on a road to the northeast, following the right bank of the Cooper River. Nine miles north of the city, he took the public ferry across to Thomas Island at the site of today's

On the right bank of the Santee River north of the Old Georgetown Road was the site of one of South Carolina's most prosperous rice plantations. Elias Horry and his family established the plantation in the early 1700s. By 1765, when William Bartram made his first visit to South Carolina, it comprised 5,000 acres. Horry's slaves cleared the swamplands between Wambaw Creek and the Santee and constructed a rice field, a grid of dikes and canals to control the water level so that the rice would be flooded after planting and drained before harvest. Indigo was grown on the plantation as well.

The Horrys built the first plantation house before 1760. It is the center section of today's mansion. After the Revolution the family made major additions to the original structure: the ballroom, additional rooms at each side of the house, and the front portico. Sections of the interior walls are exposed to show the construction details for these additions. In the early nineteenth century the plantation passed by marriage to the Rutledges, one of South Carolina's most influential families. At the end of the Civil War, the rice plantation was abandoned. In the twentieth century Hampton was the home of Archibald Rutledge, the poet laureate of South Carolina, who sold the house and land to the state of South Carolina.

The park is open Thursday–Monday, 9 A.M.–6 P.M. The mansion is open for tours the same days, 1–4 P.M. Located at 1950 Rutledge Road, McClellansville, South Carolina, 15 miles south of Georgetown, South Carolina, off U.S. 17. Admission fee for the mansion.

---

navy base. From here he followed an old road, approximated by today's S.C. 33, paralleling the Wando River upstream. Past the river's headwaters he took a connecting path to Awendaw, where he picked up the Old Georgetown Road, the main road from Charleston to Georgetown, southwest of today's Myrtle Beach, South Carolina. Portions of this road can still be traveled by taking county roads 913 and 1135 from the Buck Hall Recreation Area to the South Santee.

Continuing northeast, he crossed the Santee River at Cochran's Ferry, just south of **Hampton Plantation**. Instead of taking the road into **Georgetown**, he took an alternate route, crossing Winyah Bay below the city. On Waccamaw Neck, four days from Charleston, he took an old road that followed the highest ground of the neck. Near Murrells Inlet the road joined the northern section of the Old Georgetown Road, going from Georgetown to the Cape Fear River. Here he spent the night at an indigo plantation. The next day Bartram pressed ahead on the main road, which approached within a few miles of the Atlantic beach. For the next 15 miles the road continued northeast on the

Hampton Plantation, c. 1736, Hampton Plantation State Park, South Carolina.

hard sands of the Grand Strand, past **Hurl Rock**. On the beach Bartram encountered what he thought might have been a "predatory band of Negroes" traveling in the opposite direction. He had heard accounts of such a band in this area that attacked, robbed, and even murdered people. But the group, armed with clubs, axes, and hoes, let Bartram pass without challenge (T472). Past Lewis Swash, northeast of today's Myrtle Beach, the road left the shore and paralleled the coast several miles inland.

The next day Bartram crossed the Little River and entered North Carolina. He continued on the Old Georgetown Road, passing through present-day Calabash, Shallotte, and Supply. He rode through ample savannas and ascended the sandhills to open pine forests (T473). Today's traveler can view an

Old Georgetown Road connected Charleston with Georgetown to the north. This photograph was taken south of the Santee River in South Carolina.

excellent example of a longleaf pine savanna in the area between Boiling Springs Lakes and N.C. 87, just west of Brunswick Town.[2] That evening Bartram reached the **Cape Fear River** at the Old Town near Brunswick, where he lodged for the night.

From Brunswick Town, Bartram took the main road north, on the right bank of the Cape Fear River. Near the forks of the Cape Fear was the ferry across both rivers to Wilmington. Bartram did not visit the city, but continued to the northwest, taking the road parallel to the West Fork. Crossing Livingston Creek into today's Bladen County, he arrived at the plantation of F. Lucas, where he spent two to three days. From there, it was less than a day's journey to his second family home—**Ashwood**, the home of "Uncle Billy" Bartram, where he stopped for a visit.

The *Travels* describes the trees and shrubs Bartram saw on this visit to Ashwood and includes a brief account of the fossils he found near the river. Though he visited the plantation in late fall, he described the flowers of

2. Frankenberg, *The Nature of North Carolina's Southern Coast*, 202.

Hurl Rock, 1 mile southwest of downtown Myrtle Beach, South Carolina.

plants, such as red buckeye and silky camellia, that bloom in the spring or summer. Clearly this account in the *Travels* is based on Bartram's earlier visits to the Cape Fear River.

From Ashwood, Bartram continued on the road parallel to the river, through today's Elizabethtown. Today's N.C. 87 closely follows this route. At the head of navigation on the river he arrived at Cambelton, since renamed Fayetteville in honor of the French general. From there he took the road that passes through modern Sprout Springs, Sanford, and Pittsboro. At Hillsborough, northeast of today's Durham, he traveled northeast through today's Oxford to the Roanoke River. Crossing the river, he entered Virginia. At this point Bartram stopped recording his botanical observations because the cultivated regions of Virginia and Maryland had been described by "very able

Founded in 1729, Georgetown quickly became an important rice and indigo port. By the 1840s almost half the rice consumed in the United States was grown in the plantations surrounding the city. The history of the rice trade from the early 1700s to the late nineteenth century is captured in the city's **Rice Museum**. Located on Front Street, the museum features a diorama depicting rice and indigo production. Open Monday–Saturday, 9:30 A.M.–4:30 P.M. Admission charged.

Georgetown is now a manufacturing town with a large steel mill adjacent to downtown and the largest Kraft paper mill in the world. The center of the town, from Front Street to Church Street, is a historic district with more than twenty structures built before the Revolution. Many of the buildings have been fully restored, including the **Charles Fyffe House** (c. 1765), the **Mary Gilbert House** (c. 1737), the **Francis Withers House** (c. 1760), and the **Kaminski House Museum** (c. 1769) on Front Street. Front Street faces the Sampit River, directly across from Goat Island. Along the left bank of the river is the **Harborwalk**, a boardwalk and park that spans the downtown riverfront.

men in every branch of natural history." He arrived at Alexandria on the day after Christmas 1776. He crossed the Potomac and rode through Georgetown in a snowstorm. Despite the awful weather, he avoided the most direct route to Philadelphia, which would have taken him through Baltimore and Wilmington, Delaware, and instead rode directly north into east-central Pennsylvania, reaching the Susquehanna River at Wrights Ferry. The river appeared to be frozen, but Bartram decided to err on the side of caution and traveled 5 miles farther north to Anderson's Ferry, west of Lancaster. There he and a group of group of traders made a careful crossing of the river, keeping a good distance between each other. On the east bank of the river he rode into Lancaster, where he spent the evening. The next day the party headed east to Philadelphia. Two days later, in early January 1777, he arrived at his father's "house on the banks of the river Schuylkill" (T480).

Other Sites of Interest

Brunswick Town

Brunswick Town was situated 15 miles south of Wilmington on the west shore of the Cape Fear River. After its founding in 1725 the coastal town quickly became one of North Carolina's leading ports for exporting tar, turpentine, and pitch. During the 1750s and 1760s it was the political center of North Carolina as well, being the home of two successive royal governors: Arthur Dobbs, who built Russelborough; and his successor, William Tryon, who continued to live and conduct business in Brunswick until the Revolution made life there too uncomfortable. Both convened the colony's assembly in the courthouse near the governor's home.

Brunswick eventually declined in importance. The founding of the new port city of Wilmington some 15 miles upstream inhibited its growth, and its proximity to the ocean made it vulnerable to hurricanes and other storms. Its decline also coincided with the revolutionary fervor of the townspeople. In 1765 residents took to the streets supporting the Sons of Liberty in their armed resistance to the Stamp Act. In 1770 the royal governor left the town for New Bern. In the spring of 1776 the British punished the town by burning it to the ground. Brunswick Town never recovered its prominence after the Revolutionary War. By the middle of the nineteenth century it had been completely abandoned.

In 1955 the state of North Carolina protected the ruins of the former capital by dedicating the Brunswick Town State Historic Site. Today, visitors can see the walls of St. Philip's Church, dating to 1754, and the foundations of Russelborough (ca. 1760), the home of two royal governors. Near the church is the cemetery, which includes the tombstone for Arthur Dobbs. A walking tour passes the excavated ruins of sixty other structures from the colonial period. Most of these are foundations excavated by archaeologists who continue active research at the site. There is a short nature trail leading from the town to nearby Brunswick Pond.

The site offers a visitors' center and a museum with exhibits on the colonial period and the Revolutionary War in Carolina. Open daily. Admission free. Web site: http://www.ah.dcr.state.nc.us/sections/hs/brunswic/brunswic.htm

Ashwood

Ashwood was the "ancient seat of Colonel William Bartram," the half-brother to John Bartram. "Uncle Billy," as he was affectionately called, spent his early years in Pennsylvania and North Carolina. After the murder of his father by White Oak Indians, he moved back to Pennsylvania. He returned to North Carolina in 1726 and acquired a tract of land on the Cape Fear River near the mouth of Donoho Creek from the Ashe family. There he established a plantation, Ashwood. The colonel took his title from his service in the colony's militia; he also held a seat in the colony's assembly.

Situated on the "high banks of river, near seventy feet in height," Ashwood

Oakland Plantation, built in the late eighteenth century, stands on a bluff overlooking the Cape Fear River near the site of Uncle Billy's trading store.

was a familiar and a special place to the son of John Bartram. William lived here from 1761 to 1765, and then again from 1769 to 1772. During his second stay, in 1770, Uncle Billy died. After the deaths of Uncle Billy and, two years later, his wife, Ashwood and its land passed to their daughter, Sarah, who married Thomas Brown, the Revolutionary War general.

Thomas and Sarah Brown built a new plantation house nearby with piazzas on the front and back, and named it **Oakland**. That house is still standing. Although the land stayed in the Bartram family until the twentieth century, Ashwood was apparently destroyed after the Civil War. By the 1940s all that survived was a cellar excavation an a few chimney bricks.

Lake Waccamaw State Park

Lake Waccamaw is 25 miles southwest of Ashwood. This shallow lake, no more than 20 feet deep, is one of hundreds of "Carolina bays" in the Carolinas. Geologists still speculate as to what caused these depressions; the theories range from underground springs to the impact of meteors. Typically, the bays are small, with an average size of 500 acres. Most do not have any inlet or outlet, making their water levels dependent on rainwater. Many bays contain characteristic trees such as black gum, sweetgum, bald cypress, and maple; and shrubs such as sumac, buttonbush, and red bay. Some, like Waccamaw, are clear. Lake Waccamaw, at 9,000 acres, is larger than average. It is also the headwaters for the Waccamaw River. The *Travels* describes "beautiful lake Wakamaw, which is the source of a fine river of that name, and runs a South course seventy or eighty miles, delivering its waters into Winyaw bay at George-town" (T473). William visited the lake in the company of his father in 1765. Before that, while he was living with his Uncle Billy between 1761 and 1765, he would have had many occasions to visit Lake Waccamaw.

Lake Waccamaw State Park is 12 miles east of Whiteville and 38 miles west of Wilmington. The park offers primitive camping, hiking trails, and canoe rentals for exploring the lake.

Kingsessing

William arrived home in January 1777 and was welcomed by his father and mother, his brother John Jr., and John's family. John Jr. was still managing the family botanical garden and business at Kingsessing, as he had since 1771, although the Revolution had sharply curtailed business.

During the spring and summer of 1777 father and son doubtless discussed William's "wonderful new experiences and discoveries in the Southland." The nature of these discussions has been the subject of a great deal of recent speculation (T422). According to Francis Harper, John Bartram "realized that his truly talented son had now attained full stature." In the view of Thomas Slaughter, however, John Bartram continued to see his son as a failure, "and surely they knew that without any words passing between them."[1] There is no contemporary account of William's homecoming; no correspondence, diary, or source records the thoughts of father or son. The silence of these two "rare spirits" may have been the result of the apprehension then afflicting Philadelphia—the fear of a British invasion.

John Bartram did not live to see that happen. He died on September 22, 1777, as the British advanced toward Philadelphia. He left the garden and house to his younger son, John Jr. Given William's string of business failures, it is not surprising that his father left him 200 pounds sterling rather than the family business.

Bartram Gardens: Seed and Plant Trade

The British occupation of Philadelphia was orderly, and the Bartrams were able to continue living at Kingsessing. The Revolution had put an end to the profitable trade with practical botanists in England, however. The family business suffered, and the gardens were neglected. The British withdrew from the city in 1778, and soon afterward John Jr. and William began the work of reestablishing the garden for the seed and plant trade. They had lost Britain as a trading partner, but they took advantage of the nation's new ally and de-

---

1. Slaughter, *Natures*, 223.

Bartram House, Philadelphia. View of the front of the house facing the garden and the Schuylkill River.

veloped a market for American plants and seeds in France. In 1783 John Jr., with William's assistance, issued the first plant catalog to be published in North America. Its focus was on southern plants, and the list included more than 200 trees, shrubs, and flowers—many of which William had discovered on his travels. The featured plant was *Franklinia altamaha*.

The next catalog, published in 1807, listed more than 900 plants. After John died in 1812, the business was turned over to his daughter Ann, who had been born and raised at the garden and learned natural history from her Uncle Billy. She managed the garden with her husband, Robert Carr, and then passed it on to their son, John Bartram Carr (d. 1839). With his early death, the family gardening tradition ended.

Publication of the *Travels*

In the early 1780s William began preparations to publish his notes on his southeastern journeys. He completed illustrations of the plants he regarded as his most important discoveries to be included in the forthcoming book. In 1783 Johann David Schoepf mentioned in his correspondence that he saw at

Kingsessing a manuscript on the "nations and products of Florida."[2] Three years later the Philadelphia publisher Enoch Story issued a broadside giving notice that Bartram's book would soon be coming out, but the book was not published at that time. Gregory Waselkov and Kathryn Braund suggest that the interference of Benjamin Smith Barton, a young and ambitious Philadelphia botanist who had befriended Bartram, played a key role in preventing the publication. Indeed, Enoch Story accused Barton of plotting to have Bartram's manuscript published in Britain. Barton replied to the accusation with a letter castigating the American press, and he encouraged Bartram to publish the book with one of the more established London printing houses. The work Barton envisioned would be a collaboration, with Barton and Bartram as coauthors. Bartram declined the offer.

A year later, Bartram seemed tentative about publishing the work at all. He told Barton in a 1787 letter that he was uncertain about the value of his "improper Embryo." He also wanted to return to the South to retrace his route, but his slow recuperation from a broken leg suffered in a fall from a tree prevented him from doing so. In 1786 Bartram acquired an important source of information for his travelogue when Mary Lamboll Thomas of Charleston forwarded the trunk that he had left with her in 1776. Inside it were botanical specimens, books, and papers from his southern journeys. During the next four years Bartram completed the manuscript to his satisfaction, and in 1791 the Philadelphia publishing house of James and Johnson published *The Travels of William Bartram*.

Although the book's scientific value was recognized in both the United States and Europe, its reception in the former was tepid. The reviews of several American magazines, including *The Universal Asylum and Columbian Magazine,* the leading journal of the day, criticized Bartram for his "unusual literary style" and "rapturous effusions." Sales of the *Travels* were poor in the United States, although in truth, few American imprints save the Bible sold well. The first American reprinting did not occur until 1928. In Britain and Europe, however, the book was a critical and financial success. Within three years the book was published in England, Ireland, France, and Germany.

"Botanist, Traveller, and Philosopher"

The fourteen-year delay in publishing the *Travels* cost William dearly in terms of getting credit for his botanical discoveries. Other naturalists had de-

2. Peck, *William Bartram and His Travels*, 41.

scribed many of his finds, often from Bartram's accounts. Nonetheless, he was responsible for identifying and describing more than 200 new birds and plants, and his discoveries earned him an important place in Philadelphia's intellectual community. In 1782 the trustees of the University of the State of Pennsylvania elected him a professor of botany, although he never gave a lecture. In 1787 Bartram hosted a delegation from the Constitutional Convention—including Alexander Hamilton, James Madison, and James Mason—at the garden.[3] George Washington visited Kingsessing twice. Thomas Jefferson lived at Grey's Landing, on the opposite bank of the Schuylkill, when the U.S. government seat was at Philadelphia. Bartram and Jefferson met to talk about natural history and horticulture; they no doubt also talked about the Indians of the Southeast.

Bartram and Barton remained good friends from their first correspondence in the late 1780s until Barton died in 1815. In 1787 Barton left Philadelphia for Europe to pursue studies in medicine and natural history. From Amsterdam, he wrote to Bartram in December 1788 posing a series of questions on the history and culture of the Creeks and Cherokees. Bartram replied a year later with responses to the sixteen queries that included illustrations. Neither Barton nor Bartram published the work, but the manuscript, "Observations on the Creek and Cherokee Indians," survives today as an important source on the history and culture of southeastern Indians. As long as Barton taught his botany course, he took his students to study specimens at the Bartram family's gardens. In 1803 Barton published the first American textbook on botany, *Elements of Botany* (1803), illustrated by Bartram.

Bartram and the family gardens achieved an important place in American natural history. Barton arranged for Thomas Nuttall, the distinguished British botanist and ornithologist, to be introduced to Bartram. Soon Nuttall was living at Kingsessing while he completed work on his *Genera of North American Plants* (1818). Bartram was honored again by Philadelphia's scientific community with his election to the Academy of Natural Science of Philadelphia in 1812.

The French botanist André Michaux visited Kingsessing in 1786, and returned again and again. Alexander Wilson, the father of American ornithology, was the schoolmaster of an academy less than a mile from Kingsessing. Wilson and Bartram corresponded, but more often Wilson visited Bartram at the gardens. Bartram encouraged Wilson in his publication of *American Ornithology* (1808), contributing notes on the plates. Six more volumes were

3. Fry, "International Catalogue," 3.

published, several of them written when Wilson lived at Kingsessing from 1811 to 1813.

Thomas Say, one of Uncle Billy's great-nephews, also lived at the Bartram house before attending the Quaker academy at Westside. Uncle Billy had encouraged Say to collect beetles and butterflies, and he made a career of it. *American Entomology*, published in 1824, established Say's reputation as the father of American entomology.

Travels Contemplated

Thomas Jefferson visited Bartram frequently in 1793. In 1803 President Jefferson invited Bartram to join the expedition up the Red River, but he declined the offer. Years earlier, in 1796, in a letter to his dear friend Lachlan McIntosh, Bartram mentioned that he had considered another trip to the Southeast. Having reached the advanced age of fifty-six, however, he decided against it. He told McIntosh, "I however still enjoy some degree of comfort and pleasure when I recollect the various scenes and occurrences of my long pilgrimage through your southern Territories and the Floridas the Traveling over again in Idea." His only recorded trip outside Philadelphia during his later years was with André Michaux. Together they traveled south to Wilmington, Delaware, as Michaux was heading to the Southeast. Bartram died on July 23, 1823, while on a morning stroll through the garden.

Bartram House and Garden: Yesterday and Today

John Bartram purchased the two-story stone Swedish farmhouse and surrounding land near Philadelphia for forty pounds in 1728. He soon enlarged the house, between 1731 and 1760 adding four rooms made of stone quarried at Kingsessing. He also added a classical façade with three columns supporting a second-story porch. Below the library John Bartram placed a stone with the inscription: "It is God Alone Almyty Lord the Holy One by men Adord, 1770 John Bartram." The interior of the house has been restored with furnishings that are typical of eighteenth-century Philadelphia. The house is open to the public.

Historic Bartram's Garden, America's oldest surviving botanical garden,[4] is located in southeast Philadelphia on the left bank of the Schuylkill River, 5 miles from today's Center City. At its height in the early nineteenth century, the Bartram family garden comprised 102 acres and spanned the grounds from the house to the river. With the death of John Bartram Carr in 1839, the

4. Klein, *Gardens of Philadelphia and the Delaware Valley,* 71.

garden ceased to be a family business. As early as 1850 the Philadelphia industrialist Andrew Eastwick sought to preserve the garden. Toward the end of the nineteenth century he purchased the house and garden to save them from industrial sprawl. The garden became part of the city's park system in 1891. Two years later, descendants of John Bartram formed the John Bartram Association to aid the city in the preservation of the site.

The gardens now occupy 44 acres and are divided into the Upper Garden and Lower Garden. The Upper Garden, close to the house, comprises three large sections. From south to north, the first section, shaped as a square, is the New Flower Garden—the nursery where new cuttings and seeds were planted. The middle section or square is the Common Flower Garden, where herbaceous plants and bulbs were grown for exchange with other collectors. In this square the Historic Garden has reestablished beds of plants listed in the garden's catalogs. The northern section was the Upper Kitchen Garden, extending from the north end of the house to the barn. It was largely the domain of Ann Bartram, John's wife, where she raised vegetables and herbs used for cooking and medicinal purposes. Today the Historic Garden has restored six beds with more than thirty plants such as chamomile, horseradish, thyme, and sweet violet.

Immediately below the Upper Garden is the Lower Garden. Toward the south end of the house are two long tree-lined walks, about 100 feet apart, that descend to the river. Each is about 150 yards long. On the right path, going away from the house, is a small grove of *Franklinia altamaha*. At the river's edge is a cider mill. A river trail that begins here winds through the floodplain. Off the northern Long Walk is a fishpond. Near the pond and the northern walk is an 8,000-square-foot section featuring more than 1,000 herbaceous and 500 woody plants, including all of the plants listed in the 1783 catalog.

South of the Lower Garden, along the river, is a restored wetland. A trail circles the 1.5-acre freshwater marsh, which contains pickerelweed, jewelweed, and buttonbush. North of the Lower Garden is a 15-acre meadow created from a former industrial site. The Historic Gardens planted meadow grasses and wildflowers here.

Historic Bartram's Garden is located at 54th Street and Lindbergh Boulevard, Philadelphia. Web site: www.libertynet.com/~bartram

BIBLIOGRAPHY

Bailyn, Bernard. *Voyages to the West: A Passage in the Peopling of America on the Eve of the Revolution*. New York: Knopf, 1986.

Bartram, John. *The Correspondence of John Bartram, 1734–1777*. Edited by Edmund Berkeley and Dorothy Smith Berkeley. Gainesville: University Press of Florida, 1992.

———. "Diary of a Journey through the Carolinas, Georgia, and Florida from July 1, 1765 to April 10, 1766." *Transactions of the American Philosophical Society*, new series, vol. 33, pt. 1. Philadelphia: American Philosophical Society, 1942.

Bartram, William. *Botanical and Zoological Drawings, 1756–1788; Reproduced from the Fothergill Album in the British Museum (Natural History)*. Edited with an introduction and commentary by Joseph Ewan. Philadelphia: American Philosophical Society, 1968.

———. *Travels and Other Writings*. Edited by Thomas P. Slaughter. New York: Library of America, 1996.

———. "Travels in Georgia and Florida, 1773–1774: A Report to Dr. John Fothergill." Annotated by Francis Harper. *Transactions of the American Philosophical Society*, new series, vol. 33, pt. 2. Philadelphia: American Philosophical Society, 1942.

———. *The Travels of William Bartram*. Naturalist edition. Edited with commentary and an annotated index by Francis Harper. New Haven: Yale University Press, 1958. Reprint, Athens: University of Georgia Press, 1998.

Bartram Trail Conference. *Bartram Heritage: A Study of the Life of William Bartram*. Montgomery, Ala.: The Conference, 1979.

———. *The Bartram Trail Conference and Symposium. Proceedings of the Symposium "Celebration of Travels, 1791."* Savannah: The Conference, 1991.

Berger, Karen. *Hiking and Backpacking: A Complete Guide*. A Trailside Series Guide. New York: Norton, 1995.

Berkeley, Edmund, and Dorothy Smith Berkeley. *Dr. Alexander Garden of Charleston*. Chapel Hill: University of North Carolina Press, 1969.

———. *The Life and Travels of John Bartram from Lake Ontario to the River St. John*. Tallahassee: University Presses of Florida, 1982.

Bishir, Catherine W., and Michael T. Southern. *A Guide to the Historic Architecture of Eastern North Carolina*. Chapel Hill: University of North Carolina Press, 1996.

Black, Mrs. Claude A. "The Botanical Heritage of LeConte-Woodmanston." In *An Introduction to LeConte-Woodmanston*, 24–33. N.p., n.p., 1978.

Bonner, James C. *A History of Georgia Agriculture, 1732–1860*. Athens: University of Georgia Press, 1964.

Braund, Kathryn E. Holland. *Deerskins and Duffels: The Creek Indian Trade with Anglo-America, 1685–1815*. Lincoln: University of Nebraska Press, 1993.

Briggs, Loutrel W. *Charleston Gardens*. Photographs by R. Adamson Brown and others. Columbia: University of South Carolina Press, 1951.

Brown, Randall B., Earl L. Stone, and Victor W. Carlisle. "Soils." In *Ecosystems of Florida*, ed. Roland L. Myers and John J. Ewell. Orlando: University of Central Florida Press, 1990.

Bullard, Mary Ricketson. *An Abandoned Black Settlement on Cumberland Island, Georgia*. De Leon Springs, Fla.: E. O. Painter Printing, 1982.

———. *Robert Stafford of Cumberland Island: Growth of a Planter*. De Leon Springs, Fla.: E. O. Painter Printing, 1986.

———. "In Search of Cumberland Island's Dungeness: Its Origins and English Antecedents." *Georgia Historical Quarterly* 86 (1992): 67–86.

Burger, Suzanne, ed. *Georgia Wildlands: A Guide to Lands Protected by the Nature Conservancy of Georgia*. Atlanta: The Nature Conservancy of Georgia, 1996.

Cashin, Edward J. *The King's Ranger: Thomas Brown and the American Revolution on the Southern Frontier*. New York: Fordham University Press, 1999.

———. *Lachlan McGillivray, Indian Trader: The Shaping of the Southern Colonial Frontier*. Athens: University of Georgia Press, 1992.

———. *Old Springfield: Race and Religion in Augusta, Georgia*. Augusta, Ga.: Springfield Village Park Association, 1995.

———. *The Story of Augusta*. Augusta, Ga.: Richmond County Board of Education, 1980.

———. *William Bartram and the American Revolution on the Southern Frontier*. Columbia: University of South Carolina Press, 2000.

Cohen, A. D., ed. *The Okefenokee Swamp: Its Natural History, Geology, and Geochemistry*. Los Alamos, N.M.: Wetland Surveys, 1984.

Coker, William S., and Thomas D. Watson. *Indian Traders of the Southeastern Spanish Borderlands: Panton, Leslie and Company and John Forbes and Company, 1783–1847*. Gainesville: University Presses of Florida, 1985.

Coleman, Kenneth. *Colonial Georgia: A History*. Athens: University of Georgia Press, 1976.

Coleman, Kenneth, and Stephen Gurr, eds. *Dictionary of Georgia Biography*. 2 vols. Athens: University of Georgia Press, 1983.

Corkran, David H. *The Carolina Indian Frontier*. Columbia: University of South Carolina Press, 1970.

———. *The Cherokee Frontier: Conflict and Survival, 1740–1762*. Norman: University of Oklahoma Press, 1962.

———. *The Creek Frontier, 1540–1783*. Norman: University of Oklahoma Press, 1967.

Cothran, James R. *Gardens of Historic Charleston*. Columbia: University of South Carolina Press, 1995.

Coulter, E. Merton. "Nancy Hart, Georgia Heroine of the Revolution: The Story of the Growth of a Tradition." *Georgia Historical Quarterly* 39 (1955): 118–151.

———. "The Okefenokee Swamp, Its History and Legends." *Georgia Historical Quarterly* 48 (1964): 166–192, 219–312.

———. *Old Petersburg and the Broad River Valley of Georgia: Their Rise and Decline.* Athens: University of Georgia Press, 1965.

———. *Thomas Spalding of Sapelo.* Baton Rouge: Louisiana State University Press, 1940.

Covington, James W. *The Seminoles of Florida.* Gainesville: University Press of Florida, 1993.

Cumberland Island National Seashore, Georgia: Official Map and Guide. Washington, D.C.: National Park Service, 1988.

Cumming, William P. *The Southeast in Early Maps.* Third edition, revised and enlarged by Louis De Vorsey Jr. Chapel Hill: University of North Carolina Press, 1998.

———. *North Carolina in Maps.* Raleigh: North Carolina Department of Archives and History, 1966. [Fifteen facsimile maps dated from 1585 to 1896.]

Darlington, William. *Memorials of John Bartram and Humphry Marshall. With Notices of Their Botanical Contemporaries.* Philadelphia: Lindsay and Blakiston, 1849.

Davis, Edwin Adams. *Louisiana: The Pelican State.* Baton Rouge: Louisiana State University Press, 1959.

Davis, Harold E. *The Fledgling Province: Social and Cultural Life in Colonial Georgia 1733–1776.* Chapel Hill: University of North Carolina Press, 1976.

De Vorsey, Louis Jr. "Bartram's Buffalo Lick." *Athens Historian* 4 (1999): 4–13.

———. *The Indian Boundary in the Southern Colonies, 1763–1775.* Chapel Hill: University of North Carolina Press, 1966.

Derr, Mark. *Some Kind of Paradise: A Chronicle of Man and the Land in Florida.* Gainesville: University Press of Florida, 1998.

Dickens, Roy S. "The Route of Rutherford's Expedition against the North Carolina Cherokees." *Southern Indian Studies* 19 (1967): 3–24.

Drayton, John. *Memoirs of the American Revolution.* 2 vols. Charleston, S.C., 1812.

Edwards, Elliott O. "Sketch of William Bartram Trail in Georgia." *Tipularia* 11 (1996): 16–25.

Ehrenhard, John E. *Cumberland Island National Seashore: Assessment of Archaeological and Historical Resources.* Tallahassee: Southeast Archaeological Center, 1976.

Fabel, Robin F. A. *The Economy of British West Florida, 1763–1783.* Tuscaloosa: University of Alabama Press, 1988.

———. "An Eighteenth Colony: Dreams for Mississippi on the Eve of the Revolution." *Journal of Southern History* 59 (1993): 658–659, 670–672.

Faden, William. "A Map of South Carolina and a part of Georgia." Longon, 1780. Reprint. Washington, D.C.: U.S. Geological Survey, 1937.

Fitzpatrick, John. *The Merchant of Manchac: The Letterbooks of John Fitzpatrick, 1768–1790.* Edited with an introduction by Margaret Fisher Dalrymple. Baton Rouge: Louisiana State University Press, 1978.

Fothergill, John. *Chain of Friendship: Selected Letters of Dr. John Fothergill of London, 1735–1780*. With introduction and notes by Betsy C. Corner and Christopher C. Booth. Cambridge: Belknap Press of Harvard University, 1971.

Frankenberg, Dirk. *The Nature of North Carolina's Southern Coast: Barrier Islands, Coastal Waters, and Wetlands*. Chapel Hill: University of North Carolina Press, 1997.

Fraser, Walter J. *Charleston! Charleston! The History of a Southern City*. Columbia: University of South Carolina Press, 1989.

Frome, Michael. *Strangers in High Places: The Story of the Great Smoky Mountains*. Expanded edition. Knoxville: University of Tennessee Press, 1994.

Fry, Joel T. *Bartram's Garden Catalogue of North American Plants, 1783*. London: Taylor and Francis, 1996.

Godfrey, Robert K. *Trees, Shrubs, and Woody Vines of Northern Florida and Adjacent Georgia and Alabama*. Athens: University of Georgia Press, 1988.

Grant, Gordon. *Canoeing: A Trailside Guide*. A Trailside Series Guide. New York: Norton, 1997.

Hally, David J., ed. *Ocmulgee Archaeology, 1936–1986*. Athens: University of Georgia Press, 1994.

Hamer, Friedrich P. "Indian Traders, Land and Power: A Comparative Study of George Galphin on the Southern Frontier and Three Northern Traders." Master's thesis, University of South Carolina, 1982.

Hamilton, Virginia Van der Veer, and Jacqueline Matte. *Seeing Historic Alabama: Fifteen Guided Tours*. New edition. Tuscaloosa: University of Alabama Press, 1996.

Hann, John H. *Apalachee: The Land between the Rivers*. Gainesville: University Presses of Florida, 1988.

———. *A History of the Timucua Indians and Missions*. Gainesville: University Press of Florida, 1996.

Harris, W. Stuart. *Dead Towns of Alabama*. Tuscaloosa: University of Alabama Press, 1977.

Hatley, M. Thomas. *The Dividing Paths: Cherokees and South Carolinians through the Era of Revolution*. New York: Oxford University Press, 1993.

———. "The Three Lives of Keowee: Loss and Recovery in Eighteenth-Century Cherokee Villages." In *Powhatan's Mantle: Indians of the Colonial Southeast*, ed. Peter H. Wood, Gregory A. Waselkov, and M. Thomas Hatley, 223–248. Lincoln: University of Nebraska Press, 1989.

Hitz, Alex H. "The Wrightsborough Quaker Town and Township in Georgia." *Quaker History* 46 (1957): 10–11, 16–17.

Hudson, Charles M. *Knights of Spain, Warriors of the Sun: Hernando de Soto and the South's Ancient Chiefdoms*. Athens: University of Georgia Press, 1997.

———. *The Southeastern Indians*. Knoxville: University of Tennessee Press, 1976.

Hurt, Wesley R. "The Preliminary Archaeological Survey of the Chattahoochee Valley Area in Alabama." In *Archaeological Salvage in the Walter F. George Basin of the Chattahoochee River in Alabama,* ed. David L. DeJarnette. Tuscaloosa: University of Alabama Press, 1975.

Ivers, Larry E. *Colonial Forts of South Carolina, 1670–1775.* Columbia: University of South Carolina Press, 1970.

———. "Rangers, Scouts, and Tythingmen." In *Forty Years of Diversity: Essays on Colonial Georgia.* Athens: University of Georgia Press, 1984.

Jackson, Harvey H. *Lachlan McIntosh and the Politics of Revolutionary Georgia.* Athens: University of Georgia Press, 1979.

Kelso, William M. *Captain Jones' Wormslow: A Historical, Archaeological, and Architectural Study of an Eighteenth Century Plantation Site near Savannah.* Athens: University of Georgia Press, 1979.

King, Duane H., ed. *The Cherokee Indian Nation: A Troubled History.* Knoxville: University of Tennessee Press, 1979.

Klein, William M. *Gardens of Philadelphia and the Delaware Valley.* Philadelphia: Temple University Press, 1989.

Kniffen, Fred B., Hiram F. Gregory, and George A. Stokes. *The Historic Indian Tribes of Louisiana: From 1542 to the Present.* Baton Rouge: Louisiana State University Press, 1987.

Krauzer, Steven M. *Kayaking: Whitewater and Touring Basics.* A Trailside Series Guide. New York: Norton, 1995.

Kurz, Herman, and Robert K. Godfrey. *Trees of Northern Florida.* Gainesville: University Press of Florida, 1993.

Kushlan, James A. "Freshwater Marshes." In *Ecosystems of Florida,* ed. Roland L. Myers and John J. Ewell. Orlando: University of Central Florida Press, 1990.

Larson, Ron. *Swamp Song: A Natural History of Florida's Swamps.* Gainesville: University Press of Florida, 1995.

Laurens, Henry. *The Papers of Henry Laurens.* Vol. 9. Ed. George C. Rogers and others. Columbia: University of South Carolina Press, 1981.

Leigh, Jack. *The Ogeechee: A River and Its People.* Athens: University of Georgia Press, 1986.

Linley, John. *Georgia Catalog, Historic American Buildings Survey: A Guide to the Architecture of the State.* Athens: University of Georgia Press, 1982.

Mails, Thomas E. *The Cherokee People: The Story of the Cherokees from Earliest Origins to Contemporary Times.* Tulsa, Okla.: Council Oak Books, 1992.

Malone, Henry T. *Cherokees of the Old South: A People in Transition.* Athens: University of Georgia Press, 1956.

Marshall, Ian. *Story Line: Exploring the Literature of the Appalachian Trail.* Charlottesville: University of Virginia Press, 1998.

Meyers, Amy R. W., and Margaret Beck Pritchard, eds. *Empire's Nature: Mark Catesby's New World Vision.* Chapel Hill: University of North Carolina Press, 1998.

Milanich, Jerald T. *Florida Indians and the Invasion from Europe.* Gainesville: University Press of Florida, 1995.

————. *The Timucua.* Cambridge, Mass.: Blackwell Publishers, 1996.

Miller, James J. *An Environmental History of Northeast Florida.* Gainesville: University Press of Florida, 1998.

Mooney, James. *Myths of the Cherokee.* Washington, D.C.: Government Printing Office, 1902.

Morrison, Mary L., ed. *Historic Savannah: Survey of Significant Buildings in the Historic and Victorian Districts of Savannah, Georgia.* Second edition. Savannah: Historic Savannah Commission, 1979.

National Water Summary on Wetland Resources. Washington, D.C.: U.S. Geological Survey, 1996.

The New Georgia Guide. Athens: University of Georgia Press, 1996.

North Carolina: The WPA Guide to the Old North State. Compiled and written by the Federal Writers' Project of the Federal Works Agency, Work Projects Administration, for the state of North Carolina. Sponsored by the North Carolina Department of Conservation and Development; with a new introduction by William S. Powell. Columbia: University of South Carolina Press, 1988.

Oliver, Peter. *Bicycling: Touring and Mountain Bike Basics.* New York: Norton, 2002.

Peck, Robert M. "William Bartram and His Travels." In *Contributions to the History of North American Natural History,* 35–50. London: Society for the Bibliography of Natural History, 1983.

Perdue, Theda. *Cherokee Women: Gender and Cultural Change, 1700–1835.* Lincoln: University of Nebraska Press, 1998.

Porter, Charlotte M. "Philadelphia Story: Florida Gives William Bartram a Second Chance." *Florida Historical Quarterly* 71 (1993): 310–323.

————. *William Bartram's Florida: A Naturalist's Vision.* Teachers' Manual. Gainesville: Florida State Museum, 1986.

————. "William Bartram's Travels in the Indian Nations." *Florida Historical Quarterly* 70 (1992): 434–450.

Poston, Jonathan H. *The Buildings of Charleston: A Guide to the City's Architecture.* Columbia: University of South Carolina Press, 1997.

Rea, Robert R. *Major Robert Farmar of Mobile.* Tuscaloosa: University of Alabama Press, 1990.

Regis, Pamela. *Describing Early America: Bartram, Jefferson, Crevecoeur, and the Influence of Natural History.* Philadelphia: University of Pennsylvania Press, 1999.

Ritchie, Andrew J. *Sketches of Rabun County History.* Clayton, Ga., 1948.

Robertson, Heard, and Thomas H. Robertson. "The Town and Fort of Augusta." In *Colonial Augusta,* ed. Edward Cashin. Macon: Mercer University Press, 1986.

Romans, Bernard. *A Concise Natural History of East and West Florida.* Edited by Kathryn E. Braund. Tuscaloosa: University of Alabama Press, 1999.

Sanders, Albert E., and William D. Anderson Jr. *Natural History Investigations in*

South Carolina from Colonial Times to the Present. Columbia: University of South Carolina Press, 1999.

Schafer, Daniel. "The Forlorn State of Poor Billy Bartram." *El Escribano* 32 (1995): 1–11.

Simpkins, Daniel L., and Alan E. McMichael. "Sapelo Island: A Preliminary Report." *Southeastern Archaeological Conference Bulletin* 19 (1976): 95–99.

Slaughter, Thomas P. *The Natures of John and William Bartram*. New York: Vintage Books, 1997.

Smith, Betty Anderson. "Distribution of Eighteenth-Century Cherokee Settlements." In *The Cherokee Indian Nation: A Troubled History*, ed. Duane H. King. Knoxville: University of Tennessee Press, 1979.

Snapp, J. Russell. *John Stuart and the Struggle for Empire on the Southern Frontier*. Baton Rouge: Louisiana State University Press, 1996.

South Carolina. A Guide to the Palmetto State. Compiled by workers of the Writers' Program of the Work Projects Administration in the state of South Carolina. New York: Oxford University Press, 1941.

Toledano, Roulhac. *The National Trust Guide to Savannah*. New York: John Wiley and Sons, 1997.

Walker, John A. "A Brief History of Ocmulgee Archaeology." In *Ocmulgee Archaeology 1936–1986*, ed. David J. Hally. Athens: University of Georgia Press, 1994.

Waselkov, Gregory. *Old Mobile Archaeology*. Mobile: University of South Alabama, 1999.

Waselkov, Gregory A., and Kathryn E. Holland Braund. *William Bartram on the Southeastern Indians*. Lincoln: University of Nebraska Press, 1995.

Weir, Robert M. *Colonial South Carolina: A History*. Columbia: University of South Carolina Press, 1997.

Weisman, Brent Richards. *Unconquered People: Florida's Seminole and Miccosukee Indians*. Gainesville: University Press of Florida, 1999.

Wharton, Charles H. *The Natural Environments of Georgia*. Atlanta: Georgia Department of Natural Resources, 1977.

Willoughby, Lynn. *Flowing through Time: A History of the Lower Chattahoochee*. Tuscaloosa: University of Alabama Press, 1999.

Wood, Peter H., Gregory A. Waselkov, and M. Thomas Hatley, eds. *Powhatan's Mantle: Indians in the Colonial Southeast*. Lincoln: University of Nebraska Press, 1989.

APPENDIX
Selected Flora from the Travels

On his travels throughout the Southeast, William Bartram identified 358 species of plants, of which 158 were new to science at that time. Bartram usually referred to plants by the binomial scientific name in use at the time, although he sometimes used common names and sometimes referred to plants by their genus or species name alone. He often misspelled names and sometimes wrongly identified plants.

Francis Harper, in his comprehensive Annotated Index to Bartram's *Travels*, interpreted and corrected Bartram's plant identifications and provided common names, scientific names, and locales for each plant. We have selected ten important and representative Bartram "sites" and listed the plants noted by Bartram as interpreted by Harper. Several changes in Harper's nomenclature suggested by Prof. J. Dan Pattillo of Western Carolina University and Prof. Ed Bostic of Kennesaw State University have been incorporated into our Bartram plant lists. In instances where Harper questioned the accuracy of Bartram's plant identification, we have noted these plants with a question mark. We hope modern visitors to these locations will be able to see many of these plants and thus enhance their Bartram experience.

ALTAMAHA RIVER, GEORGIA

COMMON NAME	SCIENTIFIC NAME
Bald, river, or pond cypress	*Taxodium distichum* or *T. ascendens*
Bog spicebush?	*Lindera subcoriacea*
Carolina buckthorn (Indian cherry)	*Rhamnus carolinianus* (*Frangula caroliniana*)
Carolina laurel cherry	*Prunus caroliniana*
Chickasaw plum	*Prunus angustifolia*
Dwarf pawpaw	*Asimina pigmea*
Flag or woolly pawpaw or polecat bush	*Asimina incana*
Live oak	*Quercus virginiana*
Longleaf pine	*Pinus palustris*
Oak (laurel or water oak?)	*Quercus* sp.
Pinckneya (fevertree)	*Pinckneya bracteata*
Pines	*Pinus* spp.
Pink sandhill lupine	*Lupinus villosus*
Purple anise	*Illicium floridanum*
Red bay or sweet bay?	*Persea borbonia* or *P. pubescens*
Rice	*Oryza sativa*
Small cane or giant cane	*Arundinaria tecta* or *A. gigantea*
Southern bayberry	*Cerothamnus ceviferus*

COMMON NAME	SCIENTIFIC NAME
Southern magnolia	*Magnolia grandiflora*
Sweetgum	*Liquidambar styraciflua*
Switch cane or giant cane	*Arundinaria tecta* or *A. gigantea*

CAPE FEAR RIVER, NORTH CAROLINA

COMMON NAME	SCIENTIFIC NAME
Basswood	*Tilia* sp.
Bitternut hickory?	*Carya cordiformis*
Black gum	*Nyssa sylvatica*
Black oak	*Quercus velutina*
Black walnut	*Juglans nigra*
Blue beech?	*Carpinus caroliniana*
Buckthorn	*Bumelia* sp. (*Sideroxylon lycioides* L.)
Carolina buckeye (dwarf buckeye)	*Aesculus sylvatica*
Cotton	*Ossypium* sp.
Dahoon holly or cassena	*Ilex cassine*
Darlington oak	*Quercus hemisphaerica*
Devilwood (wild olive)	*Osmanthus americanus*
Elm	*Ulmus* sp.
Flax	*Linum* sp.
French mulberry (beautyberry)	*Callicarpa americana*
Hemp	*Cannabis sativa*
Hickory	*Carya* sp.
Honey locust	*Gleditsia triacanthos*
Horse sugar (sweet leaf)	*Symplocos tinctoria*
Indian corn (maize)	*Zea mays*
Lead plant	*Amorpha* sp.
Mountain laurel?	*Kalmia latifolia*
Pines	*Pinus* spp.
Red buckeye	*Aesculus pavia*
Red mulberry	*Morus rubra*
River or pond cypress	*Taxodium distichum* or *T. ascendens*
Silky camellia	*Stewartia malachodendron*
Small cane or giant cane	*Arundinaria* sp.
Storaxes	*Halesia* spp. or *Styrax* spp.
Sweetgum	*Liquidambar styraciflua*
Sycamore	*Platanus occidentalis*
Titi (leatherwood)	*Cyrilla racemiflora* (*Dirca palustris*)
Tulip tree	*Liriodendron tulipifera*
Water ash	*Ptelea trifoliata*
Water chinquapin (lotus lily)	*Nelumbo lutea*
Wax myrtle	*Myrica cerifera*

COMMON NAME	SCIENTIFIC NAME
Wheat	*Triticum* sp.
White ash	*Fraxinus americana*
White oak	*Quercus alba*
Willow oak	*Quercus phellos*
Witch-alders	*Fothergilla gardenii* L.? (*F. major* not here)
Yaupon	*Ilex vomitoria*

COLONELS ISLAND, GEORGIA (BARTRAM'S ST. CATHERINES ISLAND)

COMMON NAME	SCIENTIFIC NAME
American holly	*Ilex opaca*
Blue beech	*Carpinus caroliniana*
Blueberry	*Vaccinium* sp.
Buckthorn (Indian cherry)	*Rhamnus carolinianus*
Buttonbush	*Cephalanthus occidentalis*
Cabbage palmetto	*Sabal palmetto*
Coastal witch-alder	*Fothergilla gardenii*
Corn	*Zea mays*
Darlington or black oak	*Quercus hemisphaerica* or *Q. nigra*
Devilwood (wild olive)	*Osmanthus americanus*
Florida soapberry	*Sapindus marginatus*
Flowering dogwood	*Cornus florida*
French mulberry (beautyberry)	*Callicarpa americana*
Gallberry?	*Ilex coriacea* or *I. glabra*
Hairy laurel	*Kalmia hirsuta*
Hop hornbeam (ironwood)	*Ostrya virginiana*
Indian reed (sweetspire)	*Itea virginica*
Indigo	*Indigofera* sp.
Latherbush	*Clethra alnifolia*
Laurel cherry	*Prunus caroliniana*
Live oak	*Quercus virginiana*
Loblolly pine	*Pinus taeda*
Longleaf pine	*Pinus palustris*
Marsh elder	*Iva* sp.
Oak runner	*Quercus pumila*
Old man's beard (fringe-tree)	*Chionanthus virginicus*
Red bay	*Persea borbonia*
Red bay or sweet bay?	*Persea borbonia* or *P. pubescens*
Red buckeye	*Aesculus pavia*
Red maple	*Acer rubrum*
Red mulberry	*Morus rubra*
Red or southern red cedar	*Juniperus virginiana* or *J. siliciola*

COMMON NAME	SCIENTIFIC NAME
Redbud	*Cercis canadensis*
Saw palmetto	*Serenoa repens*
Shortleaf pine	*Pinus echinata*
Silky dogwood	*Cornus amomum*
Slash pine	*Pinus elliottii*
Southern arrow-wood	*Viburnum dentatum*
Southern black haw	*Viburnum rufidulum*
Southern magnolia	*Magnolia grandiflora*
Southern swamp dogwood	*Cornus stricta*
Sweet potato	*Ipomoea batatas*
Sweetgum	*Liquidambar styraciflua*
Two-wing silverbell tree	*Halesia diptera*
Tyty (titi, leatherwood, Carolina ash)	*Cyrilla racemiflora*
Water ash	*Fraxinus caroliniana*
Water oak	*Quercus nigra*
Wax myrtle	*Myrica cerifera*
White ash	*Fraxinus americana*
White bay	*Magnolia glauca*
Willow oak	*Quercus phellos*
Witch-alder	*Fothergilla gardenii* L.
Yaupon	*Ilex vomitoria*

LAKE GEORGE, FLORIDA

COMMON NAME	SCIENTIFIC NAME
Bitter-sweet or sweet orange	*Citrus aurantium* or *C. siensis*
Buckthorn	*Bumelia* sp. (*Sideroxylon lycioides*)
Cabbage palmetto	*Sabal palmetto*
Carolina buckthorn (Indian cherry)	*Rhamnus carolinianus* (*Frangula caroliniana*)
Devilwood (wild olive)	*Osmanthus americanus*
French mulberry (beautyberry)	*Callicarpa americana*
Indigo	*Indigofera* sp.
Live oak	*Quercus virginiana*
Moon flower?	*Calonyction aculeatum* (*Ipomoea aculeatum*)
Morning-glories	*Ipomoea* spp.
Oaks	*Quercus* spp.
Red mulberry	*Morus rubra*
Sea Island cotton	*Gossypium barbadense*
Silverbell trees	*Halesia* spp.
Southern magnolia	*Magnolia grandiflora*
Spanish bayonet (Spanish dagger)	*Yucca gloriosa*

COMMON NAME	SCIENTIFIC NAME
Swamp lily	*Crinum americanum*
Toothache tree	*Zanthoxylum americanum*
Wafer ash	*Ptelea trifoliata*
Water chinquapin (lotus lily)	*Nelumbo lutea*
Water lettuce	*Pistia stratiotes*
Wax myrtle	*Myrica cerifera*

MARTIN CREEK, GEORGIA (BARTRAM'S FALLING CREEK)

COMMON NAME	SCIENTIFIC NAME
Bellwort	*Uvularia perfoliata* or *U. grandiflora*
Bloodroot	*Sanguinaria canadensis*
Blue cohosh	*Caulophyllum thalictroides*
Coral honeysuckle	*Lonicera sempervirens*
Flame azalea	*Rhododendron calendulaceum* (*Azalea flamula*)
Hepatica	*Hepatica* sp. or *H. americana*
Ladies'-tresses	*Spiranthes* sp.
Lady's slipper	*Cypripedium acaule, C. pubesens, C. parviform*
Lesser rose-bay (Piedmont rhododendron)	*Rhododendron minus*
Little sweet betsy (whippoorwill flower)	*Trillium cuneatum*
Locust	*Robinia pseudoacacia* (most common)
Mountain camellia	*Stewartia ovata*
Mountain laurel	*Kalmia latifolia*
Mountain magnolia (Fraser magnolia)	*Magnolia fraseri*
Nodding wake-robin (white nodding trillium)	*Trillium rugelei*
Partridge berry	*Mitchella repens*
Rue anemone	*Anemonella thalictroides* (*Thalictrum thalictrode*)
Silverbell trees	*Halesia tetraptera* (most likely here)
Small's twayblade	*Listera smallii*
Spreading pogonia?	*Cleistes divaricata*
Storaxes	*Styrax grandifolia* (most likely)
Sweetshrub	*Calycanthus floridus*
Syringa (lilac)	*Syringa vulgaris*
Trailing arbutus	*Epigaea repens*
Violets	*Viola* spp.
Wild rose (pasture rose)	*Rosa carolina*

PAYNES PRAIRIE, FLORIDA (BARTRAM'S ALACHUA SAVANNA)

COMMON NAME	SCIENTIFIC NAME
American beech	*Fagus grandifolia*
Basswood	*Tilia americana* var. *caroliniana*
Bitternut hickory	*Carya cordiformis*
Bitter-sweet or sweet orange	*Citrus aurantium* or *C. siensis*
Black jack oak	*Quercus marilandica*
Buckthorn	*Bumelia* sp. (*Sideroxylon lycioides*)
Bush pumpkin or squash	*Cucurbita pepo* var.
Cabbage palmetto	*Sabal palmetto*
Corn	*Zea mays*
Cowpea	*Vigna unquiculata*
Cymling (summer squash)	*Cucurbita pepo* var.
Devilwood (wild olive)	*Osmanthus americanus*
Dwarf wax myrtle?	*Myrica pusilla*
Field pumpkin	*Cucurbita pepo* var.
Florida elm	*Ulmus americana* var. *floridana*
Flowering dogwood	*Cornus florida*
Four-wing silverbell tree	*Halesia tetraptera*
French mulberry (beautyberry)	*Callicarpa americana*
Gallberry (inkberry holly)	*Ilex glabra*
Gourd	*Cucurbita lagenaria*
Horse sugar (sweet leaf)	*Symplocos tinctoria*
Indian corn	*Zea mays*
Laurel cherry	*Prunus caroliniana*
Live oak	*Quercus virginiana*
Longleaf pine	*Pinus palustris*
Maidencane?	*Panicum hemitomon*
Pepper vine	*Ampelopsis arborea*
Pines	*Pinus* spp.
Pitch pine	*Pinus rigida*
Red bay	*Persea borbonia*
Red buckeye	*Aesculus pavia*
Red maple	*Acer rubrum*
Red mulberry	*Morus rubra*
Redbud	*Cercis canadensis*
Redshank grape?	*Vitis rufotomentosa* (*V. aestivalis*)
Rushes	*Juncus* sp.?
Small cane, giant cane, or river cane?	*Arundinaria teca* or *A. gigantea*?
Sourwood	*Oxydendrum arboreum*
Southern magnolia	*Magnolia grandiflora*
Southern red oak	*Quercus rubra*

COMMON NAME	SCIENTIFIC NAME
Sweet potato	*Ipomoea batatas*
Sweetgum	*Liquidambar styraciflua*
Toothache tree	*Zanthoxylum americanum*
Two-wing silverbell tree	*Halesia diptera*
Virginia creeper	*Parthenocissus quinquefolia*
Watermelon	*Citrullus vulgaris* (*C. lanatus*)
White ash	*Fraxinus americana*
Wild or black cherry	*Prunus serotina*
Yaupon	*Ilex vomitoria*

RIGOLETS, LOUISIANA

COMMON NAME	SCIENTIFIC NAME
Basswood or wafer ash?	*Tilia* sp. or *Ptelea trifoliata*?
Buckthorn (Indian cherry)	*Rhamnus carolinianus* (*Frangula caroliniana*)
Buckthorn	*Bumelia* sp. (*Sideroxylon lycioides*)
Christmas berry	*Lycium carolinianum*
Corn	*Zea mays*
Cotton	*Gossypium* sp.
Cowpeas or English peas?	*Vigna unquiculata* or *Pisum sativum*
Devilwood (wild olive)	*Osmanthus americanus*
Fig tree	*Ficus carica*
French mulberry (beautyberry)	*Callicarpa americana*
Grapes	*Vitis* spp.
Honey or water locust?	*Gleditsia triancanthos* or *G. aquatica*
Indigo	*Indigofera* sp.
Live oak	*Quercus virginiana*
Peach trees	*Prunus persica*
Pear trees	*Carica papaya*
Plums	*Prunus domestica*?
Prairie bundleflower?	*Desmanthus illinoensis*?
Red bay or sweet bay?	*Persea borbonia* or *P. pubescens*
Red mulberry	*Morus rubra*
Red or southern red cedar?	*Juniperus virginiana* or *J. siliciola*
Sassafras	*Sassafras albidum*
Silverbell trees	*Halesia* spp.
Southern magnolia	*Magnolia grandiflora*
Sweet potato	*Ipomoea batatas*
Sweetgum	*Liquidambar styraciflua*
Toothache tree	*Zanthoxylum americanum*
Wax myrtle	*Myrica cerifera*

STATION MOUNTAIN, SOUTH CAROLINA (BARTRAM'S OCONEE MOUNTAIN)

COMMON NAME	SCIENTIFIC NAME
Black birch?	*Betula lenta*
Bladdernut	*Staphylea trifolia*
Canada hemlock	*Tsuga canadensis*
Carolina rhododendron	*Rhododendron carolinianum*
Clammy locust	*Robinia viscosa*
Dutchman's pipe?	*Aristolochia macrophylla*
Eastern cottonwood	*Populus deltoides*
Flame azalea	*Rhododendron calendulaceum*
Four-wing silverbell tree	*Halesia tetraptera*
Lilac	*Syringa vulgaris*
Mountain camellia	*Stewartia ovata*
Mountain laurel	*Kalmia latifolia*
Red buckeye	*Aesculus pavia*
Storax	*Styrax americana*
Strawberry	*Fragaria virginiana*
Strawberry bush	*Euonymus americanus*
Sugar maple	*Acer saccharum*
Sweetshrub	*Calycanthus floridus*
Wafer ash	*Ptelea trifoliata*
White hickory	*Carya alba*
White pine	*Pinus strobus*
Witch hazel	*Hamamelis virginiana*

TENSAW RIVER, ALABAMA

COMMON NAME	SCIENTIFIC NAME
Buckthorn (Indian cherry)	*Rhamnus carolinianus* (*Frangula caroliniana*)
Buckthorn	*Bumelia* sp. (*Sideroxylon lycioides*)
Coral honeysuckle	*Lonicera sempervirens*
Fig tree	*Ficus carica*
Giant cane	*Arundinaria gigantea*
Large-leaved magnolia (bigleaf magnolia)	*Magnolia macrophylla*
Oak-leaved hydrangea	*Hydrangea quercifolia*
Odorless bayberry	*Myrica inodora* (*Cerothamnus odorus*)
Peach trees	*Prunus persica*
Purple anise	*Illicium floridanum*
Red buckeye	*Aesculus pavia*
River or pond cypress	*Taxodium distichum* or *T. ascendens*
Silverbell trees	*Halesia diptera*
Small cane or giant cane	*Arundinaria* sp.

COMMON NAME	SCIENTIFIC NAME
Southern magnolia	*Magnolia grandiflora*
Wax myrtle	*Myrica cerifera* (*Cerothamnus ceriferus*)
White buckeye	*Aesculus parviflora*
Yaupon	*Ilex vomitoria*

WAYAH GAP, NORTH CAROLINA

COMMON NAME	SCIENTIFIC NAME
Basswood	*Tilia* sp.
Black birch	*Betula lenta*
Black oak	*Quercus velutina*
Cucumber tree	*Magnolia acuminata*
Dutchman's pipe	*Aristolochia macrophylla*
Flowering dogwood?	*Cornus florida* (at lower elevations)
Ginseng	*Panax quinquefolius*
Hickory	*Carya* sp.
Mountain maple	*Acer spicatum*
Northern red oak	*Quercus rubra* var. *borealis*
Red maple	*Acer rubrum*
Rock chestnut oak	*Quercus prinus* (*Q. montana*)
Silverbell trees?	*Halesia tetraptera* (at lower elevations)
Strawberry bush	*Euonymus americanus?* (lower elevations)
White ash	*Fraxinus americana*
White hickory?	*Carya tomentosa* (lower elevations)
White oak	*Quercus alba*

INDEX

Italicized page numbers refer to appearances in pictures and on maps.

Bartram Falls, 290, 293
Bartram Heritage Program, xiii
Bartram House, *368*, 371
Bartram, John, 364; and Charleston, 3,
5, 11; house of, 371, 372; relationship
with William, 132, 367; travels with
William, xvii, 25, 125
Bartram Recreation Trail, xiv, 104, 211,
229, 316
Bartram Trail, xiii, xxi; and the Augusta
Canal Trail, 89, 91; historical markers,
88, 99, 144, 145; J. Strom Thurmond
Lake, 104; in the Nantahala National
Forest, 259
Bartram Trail Conference, xiii, 104
Bartram Trail Regional Library, 103
Bartram, William, 25, 112, 117, 157–158,
162–168, 201, 206–207, 211, 213–219
passim, 297, 311, 313; early life, xvii–
xviii; trips with father, xvii–xviii; at
Ashwood (1761–65), 364–365; plantation on the St. Johns River at Florence Cove, xviii, 131–132; in St. Augustine (1766), 133, 135; returns to
Philadelphia, xviii; returns to the
Cape Fear River (1769–72), 365; proposal to Fothergill, xviii; travels to
Charleston, 3–5, 10; on Georgia coast,
17–19, 27–29, 31–35, 41–43, 45, 27, 49,
71–72; description of the Okefenokee
swamp, 62; travels to Augusta, 79, 81–
82, 91; at Silver Bluff, 93–95; on the
Ceded Lands Survey, 98–103; to
Spalding's Lower Store, 125, 127–133;
travels to the Alachua Savanna, 139–
140, 143–150; joins traders party to
Talahasochte, 139–140; returns to
Charleston, 183; travels into Cherokee Country, 179, 181–186; meeting
with Attakullakulla, 186; joins caravan for Mobile, 297; at Lower Creek
Towns, 301–302; description of "Uche
town," 311, 313; at Apalachicola, 313; at

Mobile, 321–322; exploration of the
Tensaw and Tombigbee Rivers, 322;
visits Pensacola, 328–329, 332; journey to Manchac, 333–335; explorations along the Mississippi, 335, 339,
341; at Browne's White Cliffs, 343;
return to Mobile, 335; through the
Creek Nation, 307, 349–353, 355; returns to the Georgia coast, 356, 358;
departs Georgia, 358–361; revisits
Ashwood, 361–362; route to Philadelphia (1776–77), 362–363; at Kingsessing, 367–371; publication of the *Travels*, 368–369; death, xix. Works:
*Observations on the Creek and Chero-
kee Indians*, 370; *Travels* (see *Bartram's Travels*)
Bartram, William "Billy" (uncle), 361,
364–366, 368, 371
Bartram's Travels, xvii, xix–xxi, 33, 82,
179, 181, 185, 350; Alachua Savanna in,
143, 146, 147, 150; Altamaha River in,
17, 19, 35; Ashwood in, 361–362; Bartram Recreation Trail in, 316; Cumberland Island in, 62; descriptions in,
versus contemporary landscape of
Florida, 135; Lake Waccamaw in, 366;
Okefenokee Swamp in, 54; Pensacola
in, 328; publication of, 368–369; reception of, xix; St. Johns River in, 125,
127, 128, 132, 162; ten-year gap in, 356;
in work of Coleridge, 165–166
Baton Rouge, La., 334, 335, 339, 344, 349
Battle Lagoon, St. Johns River, 127, 162,
164, 171, 172
Battle of Bloody Marsh, 52
Bayou Desert, 337
Bayou Manchac, 334
Beard's Bluff, 71
Beaverdam Creek, xiv, 79
Beck Ridge, 179, 185, 201, 241
Becky Branch, 195, 234, 247, 251
Becky Branch Falls, 195, 234, 247

Gardens: Charleston, 3, 5–11; Fatio Plantation, 130; Kanapaha Botanical Gardens, 145–146; Kingsessing, 367–372; Middleton Place, 13; State Botanical Garden of Georgia, 101, *102;* Windrush Gardens, 345; Woodmanston Plantation, 33–34
Generals Island, 41, 45, 71
George, David, 86
Georgetown, S.C., 363
Georgia Bartram Trail Society, 82, 89, 100, 103, 104, 234
Germany, James, 302, 351, 369
Gold Mine Branch, *235*
Gonzalez-Alvarez House ("The Oldest House"), 136, *136*
Government House, St. Augustine, 136, 331
Grand Strand, 360
Gray, Edmund, 65–66
Great Buffalo Lick, 100
Great Smoky Mountains, 182, 185, 209, 213, 221, 256, 266, 274, 293; national park at, 209, 256
Great Temple Mound, Ocmulgee National Monument, 302–303, *303*, 305
Green Gap, 245
Green Trail, Okefenokee Swamp, 58–60
Greene, Nathaniel, 22, 25, 66
Greene Square, Savannah, 22
Guale Indians, 38, 42
Gulf Coast, *298–299*
Gulf Islands National Seashore, 335, 336
Gulf Shores State Park, 332
Gulfport, Miss., 335

Habersham House ("The Pink House"), 21, 22
Hale Ridge Road, 234, 253, 256, 257–260, 264
Hampton Lillibridge House, *20,* 25
Hampton Plantation, 359, *360*
Hanahan, S.C., 16

Hannover Square, 50
Harper, Francis, xxi, 56, 99, 145, 213, 356, 367; observation of the Alachua Sink, 149; observation of wildlife on Paynes Prairie, 150
Harper, Jean, 56
Harrison Gap, 211, 272, 275
Haw Knob Slopes, 225
Hawkins, Benjamin, 301, 307
Hawkinsville, 162, 164
Hawthorne, Fla., 143
Hemlocks, 201, 222, 231–232, 237–238, 249, 263, 285
Herb House, 22
Heyward-Washington House, 5; garden, *8*
Hickory Gap, 260, 263
Hickory Gap Road, 263
Hickory Mountain, 232
High Water Trail, 282
Highlands, N.C., 198
Hillsborough, 362
Historic Bartram's Garden, 371–372
Hofwyl-Broadfield Plantation, 46
Hog Hammock, 35, 37, 39
Hogback Mountain, 250
Holden Branch, 236
Hontoon Island Canoe Trail, *175*
Hontoon Island State Park, 175
Hooper Bald Trailhead, 225
Hooper Cove, 223
Horseshoe Landing, 170
Horton, William, 52; house of, *40,* 52
Hubbard Landing, Tensaw River, 324, *325,* 327
Huckleberry Knob Trail, 223
Hurl Rock, 360, *362*
Hurrah Ridge Trail, *260,* 262
Hush Your Mouth Island, 64

Ice House Museum, 69
Idlewilde Dock (St. Johns River), 162
Idlewilde Point (St. Johns River), 172

CPSIA information can be obtained at www.ICGtesting.com
Printed in the USA
239343LV00001B/31/P